O9-ABH-073

Europe and the Making of Modernity, 1815–1914

Other Volumes Available from Oxford University Press

The Ancient Mediterranean World: From the Stone Age to A.D. 600
Robin W. Winks and Susan P. Mattern-Parkes

Medieval Europe and the World: From Late Antiquity to Modernity, 400–1500
Robin W. Winks and Teofilo Ruiz

Europe in a Wider World, 1350–1650
Robin W. Winks and Lee Palmer Wandel

Europe, 1648–1815: From the Old Regime to the Age of Revolution
Robin W. Winks and Thomas Kaiser

Europe, 1890–1945: Crisis and Conflict
Robin W. Winks and R. J. Q. Adams

Europe, 1945 to the Present
Robin W. Winks and John E. Talbott

Europe and the Making of Modernity

1815–1914

Robin W. Winks
Late of Yale University

Joan Neuberger
University of Texas at Austin

New York Oxford
OXFORD UNIVERSITY PRESS
2005

Oxford University Press

Oxford New York
Auckland Bangkok Buenos Aires Cape Town Chennai
Dar es Salaam Delhi Hong Kong Istanbul Karachi Kolkata
Kuala Lumpur Madrid Melbourne Mexico City Mumbai
Nairobi São Paulo Shanghai Taipei Tokyo Toronto

Copyright © 2005 by Oxford University Press, Inc.

Published by Oxford University Press, Inc.
198 Madison Avenue, New York, New York, 10016
http://www.oup.com

Oxford is a registered trademark of Oxford University Press

All rights reserved. No part of this publication may be reproduced,
stored in a retrieval system, or transmitted, in any form or by any means,
electronic, mechanical, photocopying, recording, or otherwise,
without the prior permission of Oxford University Press.

Library of Congress Cataloging-in-Publication Data
Winks, Robin W.
Europe and the making of modernity, 1815–1914 / by Robin W. Winks and Joan Neuberger.
p. cm.
Includes bibliographical references and index.
ISBN-13: 978-0-19-515621-8
ISBN-13: 978-0-19-515622-5 (pbk.)
1. History, Modern—19th century. I. Neuberger, Joan, 1953– II. Title.

D358.W683 2005
940.2'8—dc22 2004058129

Printed in the United States of America
on acid-free paper

Contents

Maps and Boxes

Maps

Boxes

Preface

The Value of History

History is a series of arguments to be debated, not a body of data to be recorded or a set of facts to be memorized. Thus controversy in historical interpretation—over what an event actually means, over what really happened at an occurrence called "an event," over how best to generalize about the event—is at the heart of its value. Of course history teaches us about ourselves. Of course it teaches us to understand and to entertain a proper respect for our collective past. Of course it transmits to us specific skills—how to ask questions, how to seek out answers, how to think logically, cogently, lucidly, purposefully. Of course it is, or ought to be, a pleasure. But we also discover something fundamental about a people in what they choose to argue over in their past. When a society suppresses portions of its past record, that society (or its leadership) tells us something about itself. When a society seeks to alter how the record is presented, well-proven facts notwithstanding, we learn how history can be distorted to political ends.

Who controls history, and how it is written, controls the past, and who controls the past controls the present. Those who would close off historical controversy with the argument either that we know all that we need to know about a subject, or that what we know is so irrefutably correct that anyone who attacks the conventional wisdom about the subject must have destructive purposes in mind, are in the end intent upon destroying the very value of history itself—that value being that history teaches us to argue productively with each other.

Obviously, then, history is a social necessity. It gives us our identity. It helps us to find our bearings in an ever more complex present, providing us with a navigator's chart by which we may to some degree orient ourselves. When we ask who we are, and how it is that we are so, we learn skepticism and acquire the beginnings of critical judgment. Along with a sense of narrative, history also provides us with tools for explanation and analysis. It helps us to find the particular example, to see the uniqueness in a past age or past event, while also helping us to see how the particular and the unique contribute to the general. History thus shows us humanity at work and play, in society, changing through time. By letting us experience other lifestyles, history shows us the values of both subjectivity and objectivity—those twin conditions of our individual view of the world in which we live, conditions between which we constantly, and usually almost without knowing it, move. Thus, history is both a form of truth and a matter of opinion, and the close study of history should help us to distinguish between the two. It is important to make such distinctions, for as Sir Walter Raleigh wrote, "It is not truth but opinion that can travel the world without a passport." Far too often what we read, see, and hear and believe to be the truth—in our newspapers, on our television sets, from our friends—is opinion, not fact.

History is an activity. That activity asks specific questions as a means of arriving at general questions. A textbook such as this is concerned overwhelmingly with general questions, even though at times it must ask specific questions or present specific facts as a means of stalking the general. The great philosopher Karl Jaspers once remarked, "Who I am and where I belong, I first learned to know from the mirror of history." It is this mirror that any honest book must reflect.

To speak of "civilization" (of which this book is a history) is at once to plunge into controversy, so that our very first words illustrate why some people are so fearful of the study of history. To speak of "Western civilization" is even more restrictive, too limited in the eyes of some historians. Yet if we are to understand history as a process, we must approach it through a sense of place: our continuity, our standards, our process. Still, we must recognize an inherent bias in such a term as "Western civilization," indeed two inherent biases: first, that we know what it means to be "civilized"and have attained that stature; and second, that the West as a whole is a single unitary civilization. This second bias is made plain when we recognize that most scholars and virtually all college courses refer not to "Eastern civilization" but to "the civilizations of the East"—a terminology that suggests that while the West is a unity, the East is not. These are conventional phrases, buried in Western perception of reality, just as our common geographical references show a Western bias. The Near East or the Far East are, after all, "near" or "far" only in reference to a geographical location focused on western Europe. The Japanese do not refer to London as being in the far West, or Los Angeles as being in the far East, although both references would be correct if they saw the world as though they stood at its center. Although this text will accept these conventional phrases, precisely because they are traditionally embedded in our Western languages, one of the uses of history—and of the writing of a book such as this one—is to alert us to the biases buried in our language, even when necessity requires that we continue to use its conventional forms of shorthand.

But if we are to speak of civilization, we must have, at the outset, some definition of what we mean by "being civilized." Hundreds of books have been written on this subject. The average person often means only that others, the "noncivilized," speak a different language and practice alien customs. The Chinese customarily referred to all foreigners as barbarians, and the ancient Greeks spoke of those who could not communicate in Greek as *bar-bar*—those who do not speak our tongue. Yet today the ability to communicate in more than one language is one hallmark of a "civilized" person. Thus definitions of civilization, at least as used by those who think little about the meaning of their words, obviously change.

For our purposes, however, we must have a somewhat more exacting definition of the term, since it guides and shapes any book that attempts to cover the entire sweep of Western history. Anthropologists, sociologists, historians, and others may reasonably differ as to whether, for example, there is a separate American civilization that stands apart from, say, a British or Italian civilization, or whether these civilizations are simply particular variants on one larger entity, with only that larger entity—the West—entitled to be called "a civilization." Such an argument is of no major importance here, although it is instructive that it should occur. Rather, what is needed is a definition sufficiently clear to be used throughout the narrative and analysis to follow. This working definition, therefore, will hold that "civilization" involves the presence of several (although not necessarily all) of the following conditions within a society or group of interdependent societies:

1. There will be some form of government by which people administer to their political needs and responsibilities.
2. There will be some development of urban society, that is, of city life, so that the culture is not nomadic, dispersed, and thus unable to leave significant and surviving physical remnants of its presence.
3. Human beings will have become toolmakers, able through the use of metals to transform, however modestly, their physical environment, and thus their social and economic environment as well.
4. Some degree of specialization of function will have begun, usually at the workplace, so that pride, place, and purpose work together as cohesive elements in the society.
5. Social classes will have emerged, whether antagonistic to or sustaining of one another.
6. A form of literacy will have developed, so that group may communicate with group and, more important, generation with generation in writing.
7. There will be a concept of leisure time—that life is not solely for the workplace, or for the assigned class function or specialization—so that, for example, art may develop beyond (although not excluding) mere decoration and sports beyond mere competition.
8. There will be a concept of a higher being, although not necessarily through organized religion, by which a people may take themselves outside themselves to explain events and find purpose.
9. There will be a concept of time, by which the society links itself to a past and to the presumption of a future.
10. There will have developed a faculty for criticism. This faculty need not be the rationalism of the West, or intuition, or any specific religious or political mechanism, but it must exist, so that the society may contemplate change from within, rather than awaiting attack (and possible destruction) from without.

A common Western bias is to measure "progress" through technological change and to suggest that societies that show (at least until quite recently in historical time) little dramatic technological change are not civilized. In truth, neither a written record nor dramatic technological changes are essential to being civilized, although both are no doubt present in societies we would call civilized. Perhaps, as we study history, we ought to remember all three of the elements inherent in historical action as recorded by the English critic John Ruskin: "Great nations write their autobiographies in three manuscripts, the book of their deeds, the book of their words, and the book of their art."

The issue here is not whether we "learn from the past." Most often we do not, at least at the simple-minded level; we do not, as a nation, decide upon a course of action in diplomacy, for example, simply because a somewhat similar course in the past worked. We are wise enough to know that circumstances alter cases and that new knowledge brings new duties. Of course individuals "learn from the past"; the victim of a mugging takes precautions in the future. To dignify such an experience as "a lesson of history," however, is to turn mere individual growth from child into adult into history when, at most, such growth is a personal experience in biography.

We also sometimes learn the "wrong lessons" from history. Virtually anyone who wishes to argue passionately for a specific course of future action can find a lesson from the past that will convince the gullible that history repeats itself and therefore that the past is a map to the future. No serious historian argues this, however. General patterns may, and sometimes do, repeat themselves, but specific chains of events do not. Unlike those subjects that operate at the very highest level of generalization (political science, theology, science), history simply does not believe in ironclad laws. But history is not solely a series of unrelated events. There are general patterns, clusters of causes, intermediate levels of generalization that prove true. Thus, history works at a level uncomfortable to many: above the specific, below the absolute.

If complex problems never present themselves twice in the same or even in recognizably similar form—if, to borrow a frequent image from the military world, generals always prepare for the last war instead of the next one—then does the study of history offer society any help in solving its problems? The answer surely is yes—but only in a limited way. History offers a rich collection of clinical reports on human behavior in various situations—individual and collective, political, economic, military, social, cultural—that tell us in detail how the human race has conducted its affairs and that suggest ways of handling similar problems in the present. President Harry S. Truman's secretary of state, a former chief of staff, General George Marshall, once remarked that nobody could think about the problems of the 1950s who had not reflected upon the fall of Athens in the fifth century B.C. He was referring to the extraordinary history of the war between Athens and Sparta written just after it was over by Thucydides, an Athenian who fought in the war. There were no nuclear weapons, no telecommunications, no guns or gunpowder in the fifth century B.C., and the logistics of war were altogether primitive, yet twenty-three hundred years later one of the most distinguished leaders of

American military and political affairs found Thucydides indispensable to his thinking.

History, then, can only approximate the range of human behavior, with some indication of its extremes and averages. It can, although not perfectly, show how and within what limits human behavior changes. This last point is especially important for the social scientist, the economist, the sociologist, the executive, the journalist, or the diplomat. History provides materials that even an inspiring leader—a prophet, a reformer, a politician—would do well to master before seeking to lead us into new ways. For it can tell us something about what human material can and cannot stand, just as science and technology can tell engineers what stresses metals can tolerate. History can provide an awareness of the depth of time and space that should check the optimism and the overconfidence of the reformer. For example, we may wish to protect the environment in which we live—to eliminate acid rain, to cleanse our rivers, to protect our wildlife, to preserve our majestic natural scenery. History may show us that most peoples have failed to do so and may provide us with some guidance on how to avoid the mistakes of the past. But history will also show that there are substantial differences of public and private opinion over how best to protect our environment, that there are many people who do not believe such protection is necessary, or that there are people who accept the need for protection but are equally convinced that lower levels of protection must be traded off for higher levels of productivity from our natural resources. History can provide the setting by which we may understand differing opinions, but recourse to history will not get the legislation passed, make the angry happy, or make the future clean and safe. History will not define river pollution, although it can provide us with statistics from the past for comparative measurement. The definition will arise from the politics of today and our judgments about tomorrow. History is for the long and at times for the intermediate run, but seldom for the short run.

So if we are willing to accept a "relevance" that is more difficult to see at first than the immediate applicability of science and more remote than direct action, we will have to admit that history is "relevant." It may not actually build the highway or clear the slum, but it can give enormous help to those who wish to do so. And failure to take it into account may lead to failure in the sphere of action.

But history is also fun, at least for those who enjoy giving their curiosity free reign. Whether it is historical gossip we prefer (how many lovers did Catherine the Great of Russia actually take in a given year, and how much political influence did their activity in the imperial bedroom give them?), the details of historical investigation (how does it happen that the actual treasures found in a buried Viking ship correspond to those described in an Anglo-Saxon poetic account of a ship-burial?), more complex questions of cause-and-effect (how influential have the writings of revolutionary intellectuals been upon the course of actual revolutions?), the relationships between politics and economics (how far does the rise and decline of Spanish power in modern times depend upon the supply of gold and silver from New World colonies?), or cultural problems (why did western Europe choose to revive classical Greek and Roman art and literature instead of turning to some altogether new experiment?), those who enjoy history will read almost greedily to discover what they want to know. Having discovered it, they may want to know how we know what we have learned and may want to turn to those sources closest in time to the persons and questions concerned—to the original words of the participants. To read about Socrates, Columbus, or Churchill is fun; to read their own words, to visit with them as it were, is even more so. To see them in context is important; to see how we have taken their thoughts and woven them to purposes of our own is at least equally important. Readers will find the path across the mine-studded fields of history helped just a little by extracts from these voices—voices of the past but also of the present. They can also be helped by chronologies, bibliographies, pictures, maps—devices through which historians share their sense of fun and immediacy with a reader.

In the end, to know the past is to know ourselves—not entirely, not enough, but a little better. History can help us to achieve some grace and elegance of action, some cogency and completion of thought, some harmony and tolerance in human relationships. Most of all, history can give us a sense of excitement, a personal zest for watching and perhaps participating in the events around us that will, one day, be history too.

History is a narrative, a story; history is concerned foremost with major themes, even as it recognizes the significance of many fascinating digressions. Because history is largely about how and why people behave as they do, it is also about patterns of thought and belief. Ultimately, history is about what people believe to be true. To this extent, virtually all history is intellectual history, for the perceived meaning of a specific treaty, battle, or scientific discovery lies in what those involved in it and those who came after thought was most significant about it. History makes it clear that we may die, as we may live, as a result of what someone believed to be quite true in the relatively remote past.

We cannot each be our own historian. In everyday life we may reconstruct our personal past, acting as detectives for our motivations and attitudes. But formal history is a much more rigorous study. History may give us some very small capacity to predict the future. More certainly, it should help us arrange the causes for given events into meaningful patterns. History also should help us to be tolerant of the historical views of others, even as it helps to shape our own convictions. History must help us sort out the important from the less important, the relevant from the irrelevant, so that we do not fall prey to those who propose simple-minded solutions to vastly complex human problems. We must not yield to the temptation to blame one group or individual for our problems, and yet we must not fail to defend our convictions with vigor.

To recognize, indeed to celebrate, the value of all civilizations is essential to the civilized life itself. To understand that we see all civilizations through the prism of our specific historical past—for which we feel affection, in which we may feel comfortable and secure, and by which we interpret all else that we encounter—is simply to recognize that we too are the products of history. That is why we must study history and ask our own questions in our own way. For if we ask no questions of our past, there may be no questions to ask of our future.

Robin W. Winks

Introduction

The French writer Alexis de Tocqueville claimed that his generation in the 1820s and 1830s did not "resemble their fathers; nay they perpetually differ from themselves, for they live in a state of incessant change." In the nineteenth century, Europeans of every class saw changes in every arena of public and private life. Change was rapid, unprecedented, thrilling, terrifying, and unpredictable. For pessimists and those who stood to lose the most, change was not welcome. The historian Thomas Carlyle wrote: "The time is sick and out of joint." At the other end of the spectrum, optimists thought that change brought unity, comfort, and progress. "Commerce may go freely forth," said Britain's Lord Palmerston, "leading civilization with one hand, and peace with the other, to render mankind happier, wiser, better . . . this is the dispensation of Providence." Dramatic change and the conflicts it produced were the first hallmarks of what we call modernity.

The Making of Modernity

Until the nineteenth century, the word *modern* had negative connotations, conveying the loss of qualities associated with the Renaissance and ancient times. The positive values many people began to associate with change in the nineteenth century gave the word *modern* new meanings. Today, modernity is most often associated with some combination of:

- rapid social, economic, and technological change
- industrial, mechanized production and the growth of cities
- individualism as a basic source of cultural expression, political rights, and public and private identities
- struggles over popular sovereignty
- the power of states organized as nations and based on mass mobilization
- bureaucratic routinization and governmental interference in life
- tension between a worldview based on reason and science, and one based on feeling and religion
- nationalism as the primary source of public loyalty and cohesion

Nineteenth-century advocates of modernity often saw these developments as the inevitable results of human progress, as evidence of Europe's superiority, or as justification for European imperialism. This was a powerful perspective that continues to influence the way people think about modernity today. But it distorts the history of the nineteenth century by making modernity seem both preordained and uniform. It suggests that when modernity came, everything else immediately fled.

Recently the concept of modernity has been questioned by historians of European imperialism because it has been used to detract from the experience of non-European countries. These historians argue that when modernity is used as a yardstick with which to measure progress toward some Eurocentric standards of civilization (which Europeans themselves often failed to meet), we miss the unique experiences of those countries and tend to ignore the ways in which Europeans sought to impose modernity on their colonies. This is a useful critique because we have the same problem within Europe itself if we see modernity as a finish line toward which all peoples were inevitably racing. Historians of Germany and Russia, using modernity in this way, once argued that these countries followed a "separate path," different from "western" Europe, in order to explain the rise of twentieth-century dictatorships there. But in fact, even in the "west" there was not a single country where the practices of modernity appeared in a pure, ideal form.

Two points need to be stressed here. First, there was no single, model "western" path from which some countries deviated to create "alternate" modernities. Second, wherever and whenever elements of modernity appeared, they conflicted with nonmodern or traditional ways of life. Every element of modernity was contested when it appeared and for years afterward among people in different sectors of society, in every society. Everywhere, even in England, which is often seen as the model of western development, some elements of modernity were chosen and embraced, others were imposed by force, and others appeared by accident or as unintended consequences. Continual conflict over modernity as a process is the one common feature shared by all peoples who encountered it in any form in the nineteenth century, whether in England, Russia, Bosnia, or Hungary, or China, Egypt, South Africa, Brazil, or Kazakhstan. Modernity is defined by the conflicts it introduced between the old and the new, between the powerful and the powerless, between the privileged and the downtrodden, whether those pockets of modernity within a single country were sizable or small. Even in England where industrial capitalism and popular sovereignty appeared first, the beneficiaries of modernity lived across the street from bastions of tradition, and elements of premodern society coexisted with modernity well into the twentieth century.

The challenge for students of modern history is to account for differences in historical development without resorting to a fictional west European concept of modernity as a measure for other cultures, whether east-, central-, or non-European. In this book we will identify modernity as a set of practices and attitudes that were imposed by some and embraced by others. We will explore the specific geographic and historical conditions that determined which features of modernity succeeded in any given environment, how those features were contested, and by whom. And we will examine how diverse Europeans used ideologies of modernity to extend their power over peoples of their own countries and into the non-European world, how conflicts over modernity in European colonies matched and differed from similar conflicts in Europe, as well as how those conflicts continually redefined European practices of modernity at home.

To a large extent this definition of modernity differs from the way modernity was viewed by nineteenth-century Europeans. Proponents and admirers of change like Lord Palmerston would speak of modernity as "progress," conceiving of modernity as the capstone of human history. But even for its adherents, the positive values associated with modernity in Europe would always be shadowed by modernity's woes: mass poverty, the intrusion of noise and squalor in the modern city, the conflicts over democracy, the instability of gender roles, the dark side of imperial conquest and nationalism, the intrusion of the state in individual life through bureaucratization and routinization. Prosperity and mass political mobilization created the new opportunities for self-expression and self-determination and a dynamic society, in which all changes seemed possible. But in the absence or waning of the absolute power of kings, new modern forms of power emerged, which idealized self-discipline and constraint, bureaucratic controls, and the power of new professional and intellectual elites to categorize and restrict public behavior and private values. These more diffuse forms of power had significant influence on everyday life in Europe by the end of the nineteenth century. Throughout the century, and in ways that were increasingly apparent by the turn of the century and on the eve of the First World War, modernity meant stability *and* conflict, progress *and* poverty, civilization *and* savagery, self-expression *and* self-discipline.

The Eighteenth-century Background

The rapid changes in European life in the nineteenth century were initiated by three interrelated sets of events that had occurred or begun earlier: the intellectual movements known as the Enlightenment and early Romanticism, the political turbulence of the French Revolution, and the economic transformation begun in Great Britain known as the Industrial Revolution. Romanticism and industrial revolution continued well into the nineteenth century and will be treated extensively in separate chapters that follow. But the Enlightenment and the French Revolution, which had such a profound influence on nineteenth-century culture and events, require an introduction here.

The Enlightenment

The intellectual movements of the eighteenth century that have come to be called the Enlightenment were founded first and foremost on the optimistic celebration of human reason. As reasoning individuals, scientists had solved scientific problems and discovered laws of nature. Philosophers who studied society and human nature came to believe that reason would allow them to establish a parallel set of laws of society that could solve existing social problems. These ideas about the power of reason also brought about a new emphasis on individualism. Enlightenment thinkers believed that people were endowed with "natural" rights by virtue of being human. These were empowering ideas. In countries with repressive institutions and laws restricting opportunities and free expression, the intellectuals' faith in human reason, rights, and agency led many eighteenth-century thinkers to reject received authorities—political and religious. In an article entitled "What Is Enlightenment?" the philosopher Immanuel Kant (1724–1804) wrote:

> All that is required for this enlightenment is *freedom;* . . . the freedom for man to make *public use* of his reason in all matters. But. . . . The officer says: Don't argue, drill! The pastor: Don't argue, believe! . . . Here we have restrictions on freedom everywhere. Which restriction is hampering enlightenment, and which . . . promotes it? I answer: The *public use* of a man's reason must be free at all times, and this alone can bring enlightenment among men.

The principal concern of nineteenth-century philosophers, historians, artists, and other social observers would be the need to respond to the Enlightenment's image of human nature as essentially and transparently rational. In the nineteenth century, the Enlightenment's emphasis on individual abilities as opposed to institutional authorities, and on natural rights and reason in place of divinely imposed duties, would provide the foundation for great political, scientific, and technological advances, as well as for the critique of the Enlightenment rationality: two interacting and mutually dependent strands in nineteenth-century culture. In support of Enlightenment optimism, the empirical sciences made great strides during the nineteenth century and played a major role in reinforcing European cultural identities as self-confident, even arrogant. At the same time, the greatest cultural achievements of the nineteenth century would challenge the Enlightenment view of human nature, probing the unconscious, emotional, and irrational, while incorporating the individualism and the technical and commercial advances that derived from the Enlightenment. On the one hand, Europeans possessed great certainty about reason, scientific and other kinds of progress, secularization, and the spread of knowledge. These rational, progressive, and secular movements were continually challenged by explorations of feeling and religion revivals, however, with critics emphasizing the value of the past and the importance of the irrational in human nature. The nineteenth century was the great age of science and empiricism as well as the crucible of romanticism and modernism.

The French Revolution

The French Revolution was a twenty-year-long experiment in politics that inspired and terrified Europeans, and left an enduring imprint on the nineteenth century. One can divide the French Revolution into three phases, each with its own legacy: a liberal phase, a radical republican phase, and a Napoleonic phase.

From 1789 to 1792, the first phase of the revolution saw the establishment of a constitutional monarchy, in which an elected National Assembly was to rule alongside the king. *The Declaration of the Rights of Man and Citizen* issued by the National Assembly in 1789 was an Enlightenment document that established the individual right to liberty, equality of all before the law, freedom of speech, and the abolition of serfdom, feudalism, and aristocratic privileges. These rights were summarized and advertised under the slogan, "Liberty, Equality, and Fraternity." The revolutionary authors of the *Declaration* also invested political sovereignty in "the nation," rather than in an ancient, divinely sanctioned monarchy. Revolutionary political sovereignty did not include rights for women or any provisions for economic equality or security for the poor. At the same time, one should not underestimate the radicalism of revolutionary change. This first phase of the revolution defied the entire absolutist order of European power by attacking the king's claim to rule alone. The first years of revolution showed Europeans that ancient, time-honored institutions could be transformed, that radical change was possible, and that a government could (and should) represent the nation.

Historians debate about why the liberal, constitutional monarchy did not last. The revolutionary electoral system of the first phase favored property-owning elites, which meant that poor urban artisans and rural peasants believed that the political revolution in Paris would neither represent their interests nor feed their families. The international situation deteriorated as the French radical government, fearing invasion and counterrevolution, declared war on Prussia and Austria, which had signed an agreement to restore the king of France to his full powers. The king, himself, could never entirely accept constitutional rule. Military defeats coupled with foreign threats to destroy Paris if the king were harmed in any way increased popular discontent and radical resolve. On August 10, 1792, a radical republican committee overthrew the king, placed him and his family under arrest, declared France to be a republic, and initiated a new radical revolutionary phase.

The second phase of the French Revolution was the shortest and the most tumultuous. It also displayed what would become one of the most common features of modern revolutions: their development of a momentum of their own, devolving from unity and relatively orderly change into anarchy and violence. After the French radicals declared their government to be a republic, elections were held for the new ruling body, the National Convention. In January 1793, the National Convention voted to have Louis XVI put to death. He was executed by guillotine on January 21. A new calendar was introduced, renaming all the months and establishing 1793 as the Year One, to symbolize the revolutionaries' belief that they were creating an entirely new kind of society. Ordinary people gained unprecedented political power in French towns and villages, and radical economic and educational legislation was passed in an attempt to provide advancement for the poor.

During this entire phase the French were at war with Prussia and Austria. In 1793–1794, France was forced to confront foreign invasion, and hundreds of thousands of men were mobilized for the war effort. A militant minority of radical artisans, the *sans culottes,* demanded repression of all enemies of the republic, and the revolutionary government began to execute its opponents to provide security for itself. Maximilien Robespierre, leader of the republican government, maintained that to protect French democracy, "false" revolutionaries had to be destroyed, with the guillotine as the "scythe of equality." The result was an accelerating spiral of political arrests and executions, known as the Reign of Terror. Approximately fourteen thousand people, including many in the first generation of revolutionaries, lost their heads to the guillotines of the Terror. Aristocrats and priests were only the most prominent victims; the majority of those executed were ordinary peasants and artisans identified as "enemies" by special surveillance agents and tried by special tribunals. In 1794 Robespierre's former comrades decided that Robespierre himself was a false revolutionary and marched him to the guillotine.

This second phase of revolution was the most radical in its political and cultural innovations, and it was the most ruthless and anarchic in its assault on perceived enemies. It showed the possibilities and the dangers of popular political power, dramatically illustrating the unintended consequences of political change. Many in the nineteenth century would associate all democratic change with the most radical phase of the French Revolution.

The third phase of the revolution, the Napoleonic phase, arose from the domestic chaos following the Terror and the international conflict that had been the backdrop to the revolution since 1792. A collective administration called the Executive Directory of the Republican Convention came to power in 1794 with a mandate to end the Reign of Terror and reestablish order. Protests from the left were suppressed with force.

The European friends of the French monarchy, and of monarchy as a principle, could not sit idly by and watch revolutionaries in France destroy a centuries-old form of government. Since 1792 the armies of Austria and Prussia had tried to put a stop to the revolution by attacking it from without. But the French had two new weapons that the European leaders failed to anticipate: nationalism and Napoleon. After initial defeats, a surprisingly disciplined, ragtag army of ordinary men fighting for a country they had themselves made was able to prevent foreign invasion and then export the revolution. In part this was due to the pride in popular sovereignty that France had achieved, and in part to the military genius of Napoleon Bonaparte, a middle-class cadet from Corsica who rose through the ranks on sheer merit (mostly) to reach the heights of power and bring glory to his people and his nation.

After military victories brought Napoleon to prominence and made him a hero, and when the central government again appeared to be on the brink of collapse in the late 1790s, Napoleon acquired political leadership as well. He seized power in 1799 and ruled in the name of the republic, but he ruled with the extraordinary powers of a military dictator. In 1804 all pretense of a republic was eliminated when he was named Consul for Life and crowned himself emperor.

Napoleon consolidated some of the gains of the revolution and overturned others. He reaffirmed the end of feudalism and aristocratic privilege. The ruler himself was a model of the "career open to talent." He established unified national institutions to administer France, as well as a civil law code, the Napoleonic Code, to make administration uniform. He came to an agreement with the church, that left the state in control of many aspects of religious life, while protecting the church from further violent attacks. Civil rights were guaranteed for all. Property was declared inviolable. The concept of national citizenship was established on the basis of what the Abbé Sièyes called "unmediated, undifferentiated, individual membership of the state." But revolutionary France under Napoleon mixed legal equality with dictatorship: Napoleon consolidated his powers by minimizing the authority of the legislature and appealing directly to the people through plebiscites, in which he was the only candidate. He extended his reach into France through an extensive network of national administrative institutions and through the victorious conquest of most of the European continent, which won him widespread popular acclaim at home for bringing glory to the revolution and France.

Napoleonic rule brought sweeping changes in occupied Europe as well, welcomed by those who benefited from them and despised by those who did not. Serfdom was abolished in many German and Italian states and in Poland, and legal systems were standardized under the Napoleonic Code. Governments became more efficient and invasive. Public administration and educational systems (still rather limited in scope by twentieth-century standards) were secularized. Even where people benefited from these reforms, their association with foreign occupation and rule discredited them. In western Germany, Belgium, and the Netherlands, French religious policy was widely detested; political reforms in Italy, Switzerland, and the Netherlands were popular only with the members of the middle classes hired to run the new administrations. In Poland, Napoleon was greeted as a liberator who freed the serfs from their masters and the Polish people from Russian, Austrian, and Prussian occupation. In Russia, Napoleon was viewed literally as the Antichrist.

Ultimately Napoleon overreached his grasp. Invading Russia late in the summer of 1812, his army was caught far from home, short of supplies, outfoxed by Tsar Alexander I, and facing the approach of winter. Napoleon's devastating retreat from Moscow at the end of 1812 became a symbol of the disastrous consequences of military arrogance for the entire century that followed. By the time the French army reached Russia's border, at least three-quarters of the troops had died of disease, starvation, and cold. Then Alexander and a growing coalition of forces chased Napoleon back to Paris and defeat.

Over the course of the French Revolution, the entire social, legal, and political structure of France was destroyed and recreated based on greater recognition of individual rights, representative government, and new ideas about national unity. Old elites would retain their wealth and privileges through the nineteenth century, but the French Revolution established the principle of reward and accomplishment based on individual achievement. Those who could take most advantage of the new opportunities were the educated and propertied: the new middle class. The nineteenth century has sometimes been called the Age of the Bourgeoisie, after the French word for middle class.

Every country in Europe was affected by the French Revolution, but not all experiments in social and political change would outlast the revolutionary era, and actual accomplishments were not as great as they had seemed at the time. France changed most, gaining a central, relatively efficient governing administration, an enduring legal code, and an end to legal privileges of aristocracy. The state gained in competence and power, and was increasingly involved in everyday economic and social life. Twenty years of warfare, however, took the lives of approximately 1.4 million soldiers fighting for France and another half-million European troops of other nationalities killed in battle or by disease and starvation. In economic terms the revolution probably delayed development and industrialization in France.

Some of the social changes instituted by revolution remained, but often with mixed results. The French aristocracy lost its monopoly on commanding military and government positions but remained the dominant social and political force in France (and in the rest of Europe) for the next century. Women gained nothing at all in legal terms, and in social and cultural life they found the public sphere increasingly defined as a male preserve.

The French Revolution was an unprecedented effort on the part of people from different walks of life to make a decisive break with the past. As such, it had a profound impact on European attitudes toward change itself. By attacking and replacing ancient institutions, the French Revolution made change seem possible and desirable. But the chaos and violence associated with revolutionary change would earn stability and security many defenders. During the nineteenth century, peoples and nations would debate and contest the pace of change; some would attempt to turn the clock back, others to accelerate, while yet others would try to find a balance between change and stability.

The most important and long-lasting effects of the French Revolution occurred in the arena of political culture. Revolutionary France provided a living example of a state and society in which citizens with equal rights before the law experimented with the creation of a new political order based on ideas of popular sovereignty. Although this experiment failed to bring true equality to men and women of all classes and was in many places entirely rejected after Napoleon's defeat, and although the revolution brought terror, warfare, and foreign occupation, it publicized the concept of popular sovereignty and displayed the power inherent in a nation organized on the basis of mass mobilization. The belief that the highest political authority resided in "the people" was a genie that once released could not be returned to its bottle. In the nineteenth century, people in Europe and elsewhere would be inspired by the model of revolution in France to press for popular sovereignty, national unity and independence, and an expansion of democratic political rights.

The French Revolution posed a profound challenge to the rest of Europe. As Europeans struggled to articulate their responses to the events in France, the modern age of political ideology came into being. Governments and individuals alike had to decide where they stood in relation to individual rights, meritocracy, democracy, religion, the role of the state, and the rise of the middle classes. The answers to these questions coalesced around the ideologies that would form the great political parties of the nineteenth century. For all its sensational changes, though, the French Revolution did not immediately terminate old ways of life. Democracy did not entirely replace monarchies or enfranchise all of Europe's people, and industrial workers remained far smaller portions of the population than peasants. Science and rational secularism changed the way many people practiced religion, but practice it they did. And although many Europeans believed that they were on the brink of abolishing the need for international warfare, the advances in military technology during the nineteenth century created a new imperative to go to war.

ONE

Restoration and Revolution, 1815–1840

When Napoleon was defeated in 1814–1815, the victors had to reestablish an international political order in Europe and reckon with the effects of more than two decades of revolutionary turmoil and war. The first years after 1815 saw three conflicting but interrelated developments: the restoration of prerevolutionary borders and ruling monarchies, the continuation and spread of revolutionary activity, and the appearance of a new politics and culture of nationalism. All three were connected in some way with the broad cultural movement known as Romanticism, which is to be discussed in Chapter Two.

This was a period of "reaction" in two senses of the word. First, the most conservative political forces sought to turn back the clock to the social and political order that existed before the French Revolution and before the Enlightenment. This set of ideas and policies came to be called the Restoration. The political reaction came of age at the Congress of Vienna in 1814–1815, where the leaders of the last coalition against Napoleon reestablished the European balance of power, repudiated revolutionary principles, and restored some of the old regimes while creating much that was new. Second, this was a period of reaction because rulers, politicians, diplomats, and ordinary people were reacting to revolutionary democratic promise as well as to the threat of revolutionary terror. They reacted to ideas of science, reason, early industrialization, and urbanization by developing new ideas, and new cultural and political movements. By 1815 Europe was reacting strongly against the French Revolution, which had made Napoleon possible, and against the Enlightenment, which was believed to have made the Revolution possible. At first the forces of reaction and restoration seemed to hold sway, but the revolutionary spirit of 1789 did not die in 1815. It inspired new and progressively more intense outbreaks of revolution in the 1820s, in 1830, and in 1848.

The Congress of Vienna, 1814–1815

The treaties that accounted for the reconstruction of Europe at the Congress of Vienna were among the most important international agreements in

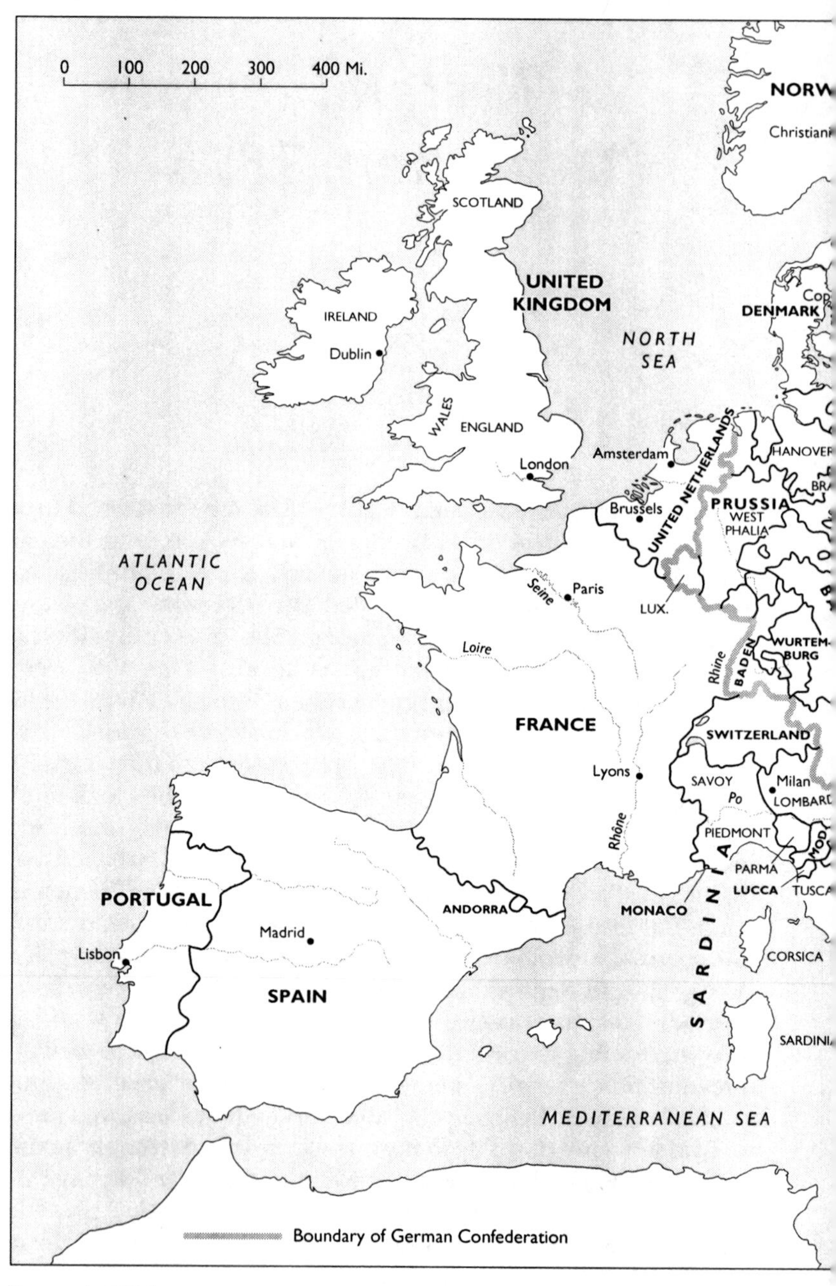

Europe in 1815

Helsinki
St. Petersburg
Stockholm
Moscow
Riga
Dvina
BALTIC SEA
Vilnius
Danzig
EAST PRUSSIA
RUSSIAN EMPIRE
Don
POLAND
Vistula
Warsaw
K. OF SAXONY
REP. OF KRAKOW
Oder
Dnepr
Krakow
Dnestr
AUSTRIAN EMPIRE
Buda
Pest
MOLDAVIA
Odessa
CRIMEA
HUNGARY
WALLACHIA
Belgrade
Bucharest
BLACK SEA
Danube
BOSNIA
SERBIA
BULGARIA
OTTOMAN EMPIRE
MONTENEGRO
Sofia
Istanbul
(Constantinople)
ALBANIA
AEGEAN SEA
CHIOS
GREECE
Athens
MOREA
RHODES
KINGDOM OF THE TWO SICILIES
CRETE
CYPRUS

European history. They were preceded by almost a year of complex negotiations among the four powers that had defeated Napoleon—Russia, Prussia, Great Britain, and Austria. The diplomatic dexterity of the French foreign minister, Maurice de Talleyrand (1754–1838), along with the leniency of the allies, gave France both a role in the negotiations and chance at postwar stability. The "so-called Congress System" that emerged from these negotiations was a repudiation of previous centuries' diplomatic practice and was based on an entirely new set of rules and goals that would prevail more or less unchanged until the end of the nineteenth century. The goal of the Congress of Vienna was to construct a system that would promote peace and stability through the *balance of powers.* International agreements were forged to prevent any one country, such as France or Russia, from acquiring so much power that it could threaten the rest of Europe. In 1815 the main European rulers were persuaded that stability and peace would provide greater benefits than territorial gain and competitive advantage within Europe. According to historian Paul Schroeder, this transformation in diplomatic goals and practices amounted to a "revolution" as important as the political and economic revolutions that shaped the nineteenth century.

Negotiations at the Congress of Vienna were carried out behind closed doors in a series of informal meetings over the course of several months. At the end of the Napoleonic wars, the most powerful countries in Europe were Russia and Great Britain. Russia was represented at the Congress by its monarch, Tsar Alexander I (ruled 1801–1825), whose military skill and determination forced the European powers to battle until Napoleon was defeated rather than sign a truce with him. Great Britain sent its foreign secretary Viscount Robert Castlereagh (1769–1822). Prussia, represented by its state chancellor, Prince Karl August von Hardenberg (1750–1822), played a weaker role owing to its dependence on Alexander. The political character of the settlement of postwar Europe is primarily associated with the Austrian foreign minister, Prince Klemens von Metternich (1773–1859), who came to dominate the negotiations and pressed for its decisions to be upheld in the decades that followed.

The first order of business was defeated France. Some boundary and political issues had been settled earlier, in March and May 1814. France was restored to its 1792 borders; independent Switzerland and Holland (united with Belgium) were formed; the independence of Italian and German principalities were reestablished and prerevolutionary Bourbon monarchies were restored in Spain and France. Tsar Alexander had opposed the restoration of Louis the XVIII in France, because he feared the dynasty's unpopularity with the French people, but he was able to limit the king's authority by insisting on a constitutional charter (with powers Alexander would never permit at home in Russia) that included guarantees of civil and religious liberties and a two-chamber government of appointed and elected representatives.

The settlement of central Europe and the broader character of post-Napoleonic international relations were decided at the actual Congress of Vienna, which met from November 1814 through June 1815. It was a huge

Prince Klemens von Metternich, architect of the Congress of Vienna and resolute defender of absolutism. (*Bundeskanzlerant, Vienna*)

event, marked by the return of glamorous aristocratic balls, lavish entertainments, concerts, and hunting parties. Ruling houses and aristocrats from all over Europe were invited to Vienna, but a secret agreement made in Paris the previous spring specified that decisions on all major issues would be determined by the Great Powers of the Quadruple Alliance. Behind the scenes, the major negotiators met almost daily in Metternich's residence, while the Austrian king Franz I entertained the monarchs and titled nobility of the smaller and less powerful states in an extravagant display of restored aristocratic luxury and privilege.

The first major problem to arise was a disagreement over postwar Poland, whose unhappy location between Russia, Prussia, and Austria made it a crossroads of contentious international policy from the seventeenth century through the twentieth. Poles had welcomed Napoleon as a liberator, so after the war Russia wanted Poland punished. To make things more complicated, Alexander I made contradictory promises about Poland's future to various players, promising both autonomy and a constitution to some and Russia's hegemony in Poland to others. At the Congress itself Alexander proposed restoration of eighteenth-century Poland, with the Russian tsar as its king. Austria and Prussia would lose their Polish territories, but Prussia was won over with promises to recognize its annexation of Saxony. Austria and Britain remained opposed to the prospect of a large, Russian-dominated Poland.

Talleyrand joined Metternich and Castlereagh in threatening both Prussia and Russia with war unless they moderated their demands. The threat produced an immediate settlement. Alexander obtained Poland but agreed to reduce its size and to allow Prussia and Austria to keep part of their gains from the partitions. Prussia took about half of Saxony, while the king of Saxony was allowed to keep the rest. The Polish constitution called for an elected, consultative assembly (the *Sejm*) and significant civil and political rights. More people had the right to vote in Poland than in France, but the king in this constitutional monarchy was the Russian tsar, who appointed a powerful viceroy as his representative in Poland. The Poles would never be reconciled to Russian domination and the nineteenth century would see two major uprisings in Poland. This limited constitution, however, was the envy of Russian liberals, bitterly disappointed that Alexander would favor such rights for Spain and Poland but not for his own countrymen.

The negotiations over Poland are instructive for understanding the new goals and practices emerging as the Concert of Europe. The western powers were wary of excessive Russian power in eastern Europe and were unsure of Russian ambitions in light of the growing weakness of the Ottoman Empire in southeastern Europe. If European stability were to be preserved, the balance of powers in eastern Europe between Russia and the Ottoman Empire would have to be watched carefully. But Russia shared the desire for stability, and Alexander showed restraint at a juncture when Russia had the power to insist on its own prerogatives.

Once the Saxon–Polish question was out of the way, the Congress was able to turn to other important dynastic and territorial questions. According to what Talleyrand christened "the sacred principle of legitimacy," thrones and frontiers were to be reestablished as they had existed in 1789. In practice, however, legitimacy was ignored almost as often as it was applied, since the diplomats realized that they could not undo all the changes brought about by the revolution and Napoleon. Although they sanctioned the return of the Bourbons to the thrones of France, Spain, and Naples in the name of legitimacy, they did not attempt to resurrect the republic of Venice or to revive all the hundreds of German states that had vanished since 1789. In Germany the Congress provided for thirty-nine states grouped in a weak German Confederation. The Diet, the chief assembly of the confederation, was to be a council of diplomats from sovereign states rather than a representative national assembly. Its most important members were to be Prussia and Austria, for the German-speaking provinces of the Habsburg realm were considered part of Germany. Thus Austria played an ambiguous role that would cause serious conflicts during the century to come: it was both a German province and member of the German Confederation, but it was also the dominant province of the separate Austrian empire ruled by the Habsburg dynasty.

Each of the states of the Quadruple Alliance received new territories. France at first was given its boundaries of 1792, which included minor territorial acquisitions made during the early days of the revolution. Then came Napoleon's escape from exile in March 1815, and his attempt to reassert power, known as the Hundred Days, followed by his defeat at Waterloo in June. France was punished by the return of its borders to those of 1790 and by the imposition of financial reparations.

The Congress of Vienna resulted in two major international treaties, one based on conventional pragmatism, the other based on principles, a diplomatic innovation. First, the four allies signed an agreement to continue the Quadruple Alliance, with its commitment to use force if necessary to preserve the Vienna settlement. Second, Alexander, who had undergone a religious experience during Napoleon's invasion of Russia, proposed that the alliance become a Holy Alliance, to be based upon "the immutable principles of the Christian religion," as the "only foundation of the political order and of the social order with which sovereigns, making common cause, will refine their principles of state." In September 1815 Franz I of Austria and Friedrich Wilhelm III of Prussia signed the Holy Alliance, which asserted that the signatories were part of a single Christian nation, and would be guided by "principles of justice, Christian charity and peace" in ruling their own peoples and in international dealings. Pragmatic Castlereagh dismissed the Holy Alliance as a "piece of sublime mysticism," and the British prince regent avoided signing it. Metternich found it equally a "noisy nothing" but recognized its usefulness for his purposes of combatting revolution and liberalism and maintaining traditional forms of rule in Austria and the rest of Europe.

Neither alliance entirely fulfilled the expectations of its architects. Russia was too powerful to ignore in 1815, so the Holy Alliance was signed, but its principles were rarely observed, even in Russia, where Alexander broke all his earlier promises to alleviate the dual injustices of serfdom and absolute autocracy. At the first meeting of the Quadruple Alliance, in 1818, the allies agreed to withdraw their occupation forces from France, which had paid its indemnity, whereupon the network became a quintuple alliance as France took its place as one of the Great Powers. Two years later, however, at the next meeting of the allies, Metternich and Castlereagh would find themselves ranged on opposite sides on the issue of putting down revolutions under international auspices.

Yet, the Congress of Vienna produced the general agreement known as the Concert of Europe, which was largely responsible for the unprecedented international stability of the nineteenth century. Most of the national borders determined in 1815 were still in place in 1914. War among the Great Powers was rare, and limited in scope and duration. The reasons for such an unusually protracted period of peace can be found in the Congress of Vienna's network of treaties and its reasonable determination of national boundaries, together with the lessons learned from the revolutionary and Napoleonic upheaval. During the nineteenth century, peace was maintained because rulers and governments agreed that peace was worth preserving, that war and aggression undermined the rulers' own stability. Difficult international agreements were repeatedly made, in the belief that everyone would benefit from playing by the rules. In addition, the states with the greatest power, Russia and Britain, both restrained themselves and were restrained by others. The most remarkable aspect of this period of stability and consensus is that it continued despite the rapid and profound changes occurring in politics, economics, and society in the nineteenth century. Just as important, it transcended the deep political differences that would come to the fore beginning around 1820.

It is important to understand the difference between the Congress System that governed international affairs after 1815 and what has been called the Metternich System, which attempted to contain revolutionary, liberal, and nationalist movements. Both derived from negotiations at the Congress of Vienna and both sought to maintain international peace and stability, but the two systems had separate strategies and different fates.

From 1815 to 1848 Metternich led an international campaign to protect absolutist monarchies in Europe and to preserve the multinational Austrian empire. This period is often identified with Metternich personally. But, as so often occurs in history, extreme efforts to repress movements for democratic reform only inflamed the passions of those fighting for change. In another irony, it was the *failure* of one of the fundamental agreements of the Quadruple Alliance that helped preserve general peace in Europe during this period. Metternich's repressive policies did not halt revolutionary uprisings. When they did break out, however, two factors prevented general warfare among the Great Powers: the refusal by England (and France) to join others in suppressing the uprisings and Metternich's fears of Russia's enthusiastic drive to become the "policeman of Europe."

The Persistence of Revolution, 1820–1823

The revolutionary leaders of the post-Napoleonic generation remained firm in their support for liberty, equality, and fraternity. The first two parts of the French revolutionary motto continued to signify the abolition of noble and clerical privileges in society and, with few exceptions, the retention of laissez-faire economics. The goals of these movements also involved broadening civil rights, instituting representative assemblies, establishing or expanding the right to vote, and granting constitutions, which would limit the power of monarchs. The most radical movements called for the abolition of monarchy altogether and the establishment of a republic with universal male suffrage.

Fraternity, intensified by the romantic cult of the nation, continued to evolve into the formidable doctrine of nationalism. The nationalists of the post-1815 generation dreamed of a world in which each nation would be free of domination by any other, and all nations would live together harmoniously. In practical terms, this signified movements toward national unity and national independence. It meant growing pressure for the unification of Germany and Italy. And it inspired demands for freedom by peoples living under the con-

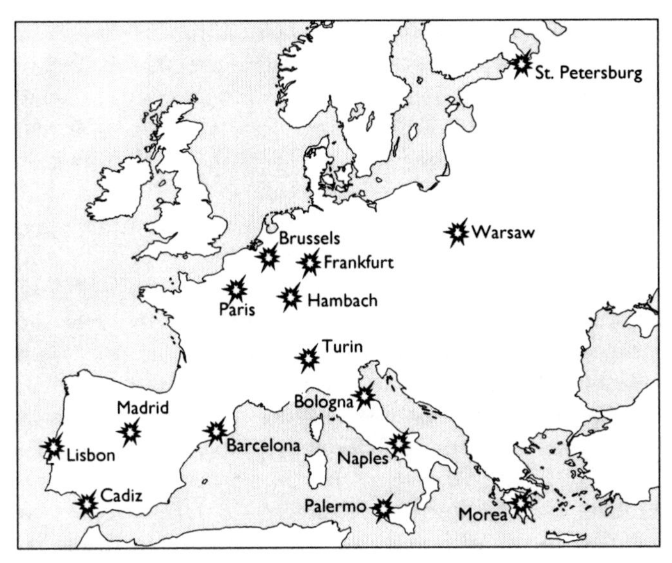

Centers of Revolutionary Activity, 1820–1830

trol of a foreign power—by Belgians against their Dutch rulers, by Poles against Russians, by Greeks and Serbs against Ottoman Turks, and by Italians, Hungarians, and Czechs against the Habsburgs of the Austrian empire.

In the early 1820s a series of revolts pitted revolutionary movements based on the conceptions of liberty, equality, and fraternity against rulers who were determined to prevent political change. The first revolutionary outbreaks after 1815 took place in Spain, Portugal, and Piedmont-Sardinia in northern Italy, and in the Kingdom of the Two Sicilies in the south.

During the war against Napoleon, representatives of the Spanish liberal middle class in Cadiz and other commercial towns had framed the Constitution of 1812. Based on the French constitution of 1791, this document greatly limited the power of the monarchy, gave wide authority to the Cortes—a representative assembly elected by a broad suffrage—and deprived the Spanish church of some of its lands and privileges. When the Bourbon Ferdinand VII (r. 1814–1833) was restored to power, he suspended the constitution, resurrected the social inequalities of the prerevolutionary regime, reestablished the Inquisition, and restored the Jesuits to their former position of influence. These measures were unpopular with the small class of Enlightenment intellectuals, but Ferdinand also had supporters.

It was Ferdinand's attempt to subdue Spain's rebellious colonies across the Atlantic that triggered revolution at home. The independence movement in Spanish America arose out of the colonial population's refusal to accept Napoleon's brother Joseph as their king in 1808 or the closer ties between colonies and metropole implicit in the Constitution of 1812. Behind the movement lay several other factors: the powerful examples of the American and French revolutions, the sympathetic interest of Great Britain, and the resentment of colonial peoples, accumulated over centuries of indifferent rule by Spanish governors. Napoleon's placement of his brother on the Spanish throne in 1808 had provoked many people in Spanish American colonies to seek liberation from Spanish rule, with its heavy taxes, disastrous market manipulation, and heavy-handed administration. The colonial rebels had won their initial success at Buenos Aires in 1810, and their movement spread rapidly to Spain's other American possessions.

The Creoles—people of Spanish descent who were born in America—led the way, for they had held many important positions from which a nervous Spain had been removing them for years. With the loss of their king, they argued that sovereignty had moved from the monarchy to the people, by which they meant themselves. They intended no reconstruction of society, for they controlled wealth and education and considered themselves to be superior to the indigenous peoples and to those of mixed race. They wished to govern the colonies without interference from Spain. Their leader, Simón Bolívar (1783–1830), "the Liberator," led Spanish American armies to victory over the royalists. In 1819 Bolívar became president of Greater Colombia, and in 1826 he called for a conference of South American republics to meet in Panama. He organized the government of Bolivia, was head of state in Peru, and inspired followers throughout Latin America. Competing interest groups, regional differences, and unstable economies split Greater Colombia, however, and Bolívar went into exile, declaring America to be ungovernable. Nonetheless, by 1825 all of Latin America had broken away from Spain.

King Ferdinand had been determined to crush the colonial rebellion by force but was unable to do so because he faced rebellion at home as well. In 1820 a mutiny broke out at Cadiz and liberals (with military support) seized power in Madrid, Barcelona, and other Spanish cities. Ferdinand, virtually a prisoner, was forced to restore the Constitution of 1812.

Liberal minorities in Portugal and Naples followed the Spanish lead. An army faction seized control of the Portuguese government in 1820, abolished the Inquisition, and set up a constitution. Brazil declared its independence, with a prince of the Portuguese royal house as its emperor.

In the Italian states, the post-Napoleonic Restoration had repudiated liberal Enlightenment ideas and institutions, reinstituted censorship, and done nothing to alleviate mass poverty. The liberal middle class was small in number, as in Spain, but active, especially in secret societies. In Naples the revolution was the work of the Carbonari, a secret society, with a membership exceeding fifty thousand army officers, professionals, artisans, and poorer clergymen. The Carbonari had been opposed to the French and their reforms in the days of Napoleon, but now sponsored a vaguely liberal program inspired by the French Revolution and the 1812 Spanish constitution. Ferdinand I (r. 1816–1825) of the kingdom of the Two Sicilies gave in at the first sign of opposition in 1820 and accepted a constitution. But divisions within the movement made it impossible to withstand the forces of the Austrian army, which arrived in 1821 to crush the rebellion, abolish the constitution, and restore the king's absolute powers. Austrian troops easily suppressed a similar revolt in Piedmont in the north.

Somewhat milder forms of resistance appeared in some German states, and there Metternich saw to it that they were suppressed with all due force. As in Italy, German liberals abhorred French domination but appreciated many of the reforms—and the spirit of reformism—that came with Napoleonic rule. In Prussia, a reformist government came into power under Napoleon that sought to introduce representative institutions, free trade, equality of all before the law, and the abolition of certain privileges of the elite. These reforms were justified in part as unifying and mobilizing the nation to fight France. After the expulsion of the French and the Congress of Vienna, the Prussian government felt less need for reform, and Metternich actively opposed the idea of a united Germany and a politically active nation. Even government reformers like Hardenberg, a persistent advocate of constitutional rule, began to fear the potentially destabilizing effects of a politically mobilized nation and came to favor reinstating censorship. After 1815, liberalism and nationalism became oppositional ideologies whose main adherents were students and middle-class intellectuals.

German university students formed societies called the *Burschenschaft* (Students' union). In October 1817 students at the University of Jena held a rally during which the Burschenschaft burned books by reactionary writers. In May 1819 one of these writers, August von Kotzebue (1761–1819), a reactionary publicist as well as a Russian agent, was assassinated by a student, Karl Ludwig Sand, as "a traitor to the fatherland." This occurred at a particularly sensitive moment, when King Friedrich Wilhelm III of Prussia was vacillating between issuing a constitution and cracking down on free speech and civil liberties. As Austrian chancellor, Metternich exercised considerable power through the German Confederation, but he could not express his opposition to constitution openly. He used the assassination, however, to persuade the Diet of the German Confederation to approve the repressive Karlsbad Decrees in September 1819. The Karlsbad Decrees crushed the nascent liberal nationalist movement by instituting harsh controls on speech and authorizing surveillance, interrogation, and imprisonment of any suspected political opponents. The new laws dissolved the Burschenschaft societies and curtailed academic freedom. Metternich described the threat of revolution in Germany as a malignant cancer, and even Hardenberg favored the harsh suppression of political opposition. Government officials who opposed the Karlsbad Decrees were forced out of government. Less than a year later, the uprisings in Spain and Italy convinced rulers in Vienna and Berlin that they had been right to back away from political reform.

The revolts in southern and central Europe so alarmed the conservative leaders of the Great Powers elsewhere in Europe that they sponsored counterrevolutions, which tested both the stability of the Concert of Europe and the solidarity of the Quadruple Alliance. Though legitimacy was restored in Spain and Italy, the Quadruple Alliance was split over how to respond. While the allies increasingly favored armed intervention to suppress revolution, Britain inclined toward nonintervention. The split became evident at the meeting of the Quadruple Alliance at Troppau in Silesia late in 1820. Castlereagh was

The Written Record

THE KARLSBAD DECREES

A special representative of the ruler of each state shall be appointed for each university. . . . The function of this agent shall be to see to the strictest enforcement of existing laws and disciplinary regulations; to observe carefully the spirit which is shown by the instructors in the university in their public lectures and regular courses, . . .

The confederated government mutually pledge themselves to remove from the universities or other public educational institutions all teachers who, by obvious deviation from their duty, or by exceeding the limits of their functions, or by the abuse of their legitimate influence over the youthful minds, or by propagating harmful doctrines hostile to public order or subversive of existing governmental institutions, shall have unmistakably proved their unfitness for the important office entrusted to them. . . .

Those laws which have for a long period been directed against secret and unauthorized societies in the universities shall be strictly enforced. These laws apply especially to that association established some years since under the name Universal Students' Union (*Allgemeine Burschenschaft*), since the very conception of the society implies the utterly unallowable plan of permanent fellowship and constant communication between the various universities. . . .

Readings in European History, trans. James Harvey Robinson, ed. James Harvey Robinson, vol. 2 (Boston: 1906), pp. 547–48.

willing to see Austria intervene in Naples, but without the backing of the Alliance. The Alliance, Castlereagh declared, was never designed "for the superintendence of the internal affairs of other states," and Britain refused to participate formally in the Troppau meeting. Metternich, supported by Alexander, pressed for a blanket commitment from the Alliance, and the result was the Troppau Protocol, signed by Austria, Prussia, and Russia. It declared war on all revolutionary governments that threatened European stability. It was under the terms of the Troppau Protocol that the Austrian army toppled the revolutionary governments of Naples and Piedmont in 1821. Spanish absolutism, however, was not so easily restored.

In 1822 Castlereagh committed suicide and Great Britain removed itself further from interventionist forces, opening the door to a major show of foreign military intervention. By now, Tsar Alexander was coming to regret his support for the Spanish constitution in 1812 and moved much closer to Metternich in supporting the intervention. In 1823 a French force of two hundred thousand soldiers with the backing of Russia, Prussia, and Austria entered Spain to suppress the revolutionary government and restore Ferdinand VII to the throne. The revolution itself had been weakened when the hasty introduction of reforms by inexperienced liberal leaders alienated much of the population. The Spanish revolutionaries were further weakened by a split between the *moderados*, or moderates, and the *exaltados*, who favored a radically anticlerical republic. Once restored to power, Ferdinand promptly revoked the constitution (again) and treated the revolutionaries to arrest, torture, and execution. Only in Portugal did the revolutionary regime survive, and only because there it had British protection.

French intervention in Spain provoked the strong opposition of Great Britain and ended the Quadruple Alliance. George Canning (1770–1827), who became British foreign minister in 1822, suspected that the Continental powers might now help Spain recover its former American colonies; so did the United States, which had recognized the independence of the new Latin American republics. A message to the U.S. Congress in December 1823 by President James Monroe (1758–1831) included a statement opposing European intervention in the Americas. What later became known as the Monroe Doctrine marked an important assertion of policy by the youthful American republic. It had little immediate international significance because European powers were not fully committed to restoring Spain's American empire in any event, but it established one of the foundations of modern U.S. foreign policy.

Serbian and Greek Independence, 1804–1829

The Greek movement for independence from the Ottoman Empire became a decades-long war of liberation and a popular cause all over Europe. During the last quarter of the eighteenth century many peoples of the Balkan peninsula were awakening to a sense of national identity under the impact of French revolutionary and Romantic ideas. They examined their national past with new interest and put particular stress on their native languages and on their Christian religion, which distinguished them from the Ottoman Muslims. At the same time, Ottoman power declined in the Balkans during the eighteenth century through both internal corruption and assaults by the rising Russian empire. These developments, more than any others during the first half of the nineteenth century, threatened to disturb the balance of power in Europe. As Ottoman power waned, Russia and Austria would come to conflict over former Ottoman territories. The western powers, Great Britain in particular, were suspicious of Russian motives in the region and wary of the growing power of the Russian empire throughout the previous century. Much of the tension associated with Great Power conflict in the region centered on the Black Sea and access to the Mediterranean through the straits of the Dardanelles and the Bosporus. Though Russia would repeatedly show restraint and a commitment to the balance of power and European stability, any political change in eastern Europe was of interest to the whole Concert of Europe.

The first outbreak against the Ottoman authorities came in 1804 among the Serbs. Ably led by Karadjordje Petrovic (c. 1752–1817), the early Serbian nationalists knew they would need outside help to win their independence. Some turned to Austria, which was nearby and ruled over their fellow south

Slavs, the Croats and Slovenes. Other Serbs looked to Russia, which though more distant, shared the Serbs' Slavic language and Orthodox Christianity (the other south Slavs were Roman Catholic). Russia was conflicted over support for the Serbs and the consequent weakening of Ottoman power in the Balkans on the one hand and support for the Ottoman sultan as the legitimate ruler of the region on the other. Inconsistency of Russian support undermined Karadjordje in 1812, and he fled to Austria. Leadership of Serb nationalism passed to his rival, Miloš Obrenovich (1780–1860), who won Russian support and succeeded by 1830 in becoming prince of an autonomous Serbia. Although Miloš still paid tribute to the Ottoman emperor and a Turkish garrison remained in the Serb capital of Belgrade, a major step toward independence had been completed.

These events were carefully watched in Greece, where nationalism was even more developed than in Serbia. The Greek wars for independence were monitored in the rest of Europe, as well, because of the country's strategic importance and because since the Enlightenment it had been widely viewed as the birthplace of European democracy and culture. Famous writers and artists would embrace the struggle and pressure their governments to come to the aid of the Greeks.

Greek nationalists had begun with cultural projects such as the campaign to purge the modern Greek language of its Turkish and Slavic words and to return it to the classical tongue of the glorious Age of Pericles. More dangerously, a revolutionary secret society was formed in the Russian port of Odessa, patterned after the Carbonari of Italy and headed by Alexander Ypsilanti (1792–1828), who was an officer in the Russian army. In 1821 Ypsilanti led an expedition into the Danubian provinces of the Ottoman Empire; it failed to stir up a major revolt. The conspirators were more successful in the Morea (the ancient Peloponnesus), where they launched a peasant uprising. The ensuing war for independence was a ferocious conflict, with atrocities committed on both sides. When the Turks surrendered at Tripolitsa in 1821 after the first major Greek victory, twelve thousand captives were massacred, hanged, impaled, even crucified. In 1822, when the Turks took the Greek island of Chios, the Ottoman forces retaliated with an equally brutal massacre, killing or selling into slavery thirty thousand Greek inhabitants of the island. The French painter Eugène Delacroix depicted the massacre in a moving painting that won sympathy for the Greek cause while at the same time provoking outrage about the brutal treatment of prisoners on both sides. By 1827, when it appeared likely that an Egyptian force fighting on the behalf of the Ottoman sultan would recapture the last rebel strongholds, Britain, France, and Russia intervened to save the Greek independence movement at its darkest hour.

The three-power action resulted from the combined pressures of public opinion and strategic interests. In Britain, France, and Germany, the Philhellenic (or pro-Greek) movement had won many supporters. Philhellenic committees sent supplies and money and demanded that their governments intervene directly. But intervention presented the European powers with the same difficult quandary Russia was facing in Serbia. At the Congress of Vienna they had all agreed to support legitimate governments against insurgent movements to preserve stability. Support for the Greeks would mean an attack on a legitimate government. Metternich, in fact, opposed the Greek independence movement for precisely this reason. Ultimately intervention hinged on Russia, for Greek patriots had formed their secret society on Russian soil and with Russian backing. Alexander was deterred by Metternich's reasoning; he also feared that an Ottoman collapse would destroy the Concert of Europe. His younger brother Nicholas I (r. 1825–1855), who came to the throne when Alexander died, believed that support for Greece would best maintain stability in the region and protect Russian interests. Russia wished to support the Orthodox subjects of the Islamic empire, but there were important economic interests at stake, as well. The great wheat-producing areas in the south were being developed intensively, and Odessa on the Black Sea had become the major commercial port for the grain trade. Protecting commercial interests in the Black Sea was therefore of the highest importance. Britain and France believed that a three-power intervention would both rescue the Greeks and check the Russians.

In October 1827 Russian, British, and French squadrons sank the Turkish and Egyptian fleet. But the Ottoman military fought back, and Russia had to sustain a costly war in 1828–1829 until Russian soldiers finally threatened Istanbul itself. The subsequent Treaty of Adrianople (1829) allowed Russia to annex outright only a little Turkish territory, but the provinces of Moldavia and Wallachia became a virtual Russian protectorate. After considerable wrangling, the European powers accorded formal recognition to a small independent Greek kingdom, which left most Greeks still within the Ottoman Empire. Greece was finally established as an independent nation in 1832.

The success of the Greek liberation signaled the dangerous weakness of the Ottoman Empire. Nicholas I agreed with his predecessor that the collapse of Ottoman rule would not be serve Russian or European interests. Thus when the governor of Egypt, Mehmet Ali, revolted against the Ottomans in 1832, Nicholas landed a Russian army and got credit for saving the sultan's capital. In 1833 the Turks paid the bill for these services. Instead of wishing to annex large sections of the Ottoman Empire, the tsar, under the influence of a well-argued memorandum from his foreign minister Count Karl Nesselrode (1780–1862), preferred to maintain a weak and friendly Ottoman Empire that would serve as a buffer between Russia and the Habsburg territories. In the Treaty of Unkiar-Skelessi, Nicholas took the Ottoman Empire under his protection, and the Turks agreed to close the Bosporus and the Dardanelles to the warships of any nation.

Alarmed at the control the Unkiar-Skelessi agreement gave to Russia in an area of the world vital to British imperial and commercial interests, British diplomacy was determined to undo the treaty. The next time Mehmet Ali revolted (in 1839), the British were able to put him down with their fleet before he came near a Russian land force. In 1841 all the other important powers joined Russia in guaranteeing the integrity of Turkey, thus ending the exclusive position obtained by Russia at Unkiar-Skelessi.

The Decembrist Revolt in Russia, 1825

Russia, which did so much to determine the outcome of revolutions elsewhere, experienced its own revolutionary upheaval in 1825. Since the end of the eighteenth century, small circles of highly educated, often westward-looking intellectuals had begun to criticize the Russian government for its inability to alleviate the poverty of the majority of the population, half of whom were enserfed to individual noble landowners. Soon afterward, some began to call for the outright abolition of serfdom. Under Alexander I's father, Paul (r. 1796–1801), an extremely arbitrary, repressive ruler who treated even his nobility with contempt, criticism of the serf system had led to criticism of Russian autocracy and hopes for some kind of constitutional government. In 1801 Paul was assassinated in a palace coup. Alexander I came to the throne well known in aristocratic circles as a reformer, a supporter of constitutional government, and a critic of the inhumane serf system. Many members of the educated elite believed that reform was imminent, but they would be sorely disappointed, especially after Alexander offered Poland and Finland constitutions but turned his back on political and social reform at home.

The disappointment turned to bitterness among young officers who had served in the Napoleonic campaigns. Returning home after liberating Europe from tyranny and having seen western freedoms for themselves, many young officers from some of the highest ranked aristocratic families expected Russia to move in the direction of west European democracy. The introduction of Freemasonry during the eighteenth century had enabled nobles to meet on equal terms with men from other ranks of society and establish friendly alliances. As Alexander offered contradictory and increasingly dispiriting signals, secret societies became to form to discuss possibilities for reform.

High-ranking officers in St. Petersburg secretly formed the Northern Society, which aimed to make Russia a decentralized, limited monarchy, with the various provinces enjoying rights somewhat like those of American states. The serfs would receive their freedom but no land. These reforms would be achieved by peaceful means. A second secret organization, the Southern Society, with headquarters at Kiev, included many relatively impoverished officers among its members. It advocated a highly centralized republic, the granting of land to liberated serfs, and the assassination of the tsar.

A hastily planned uprising occurred in December 1825, when the sudden death of Alexander left confusion over the succession. With no male heir, the crown was to pass to the late tsar's brother Constantine. Constantine, however, had relinquished the throne to a still younger brother Nicholas, but in a secret document. Constantine refused to confirm the renunciation in public and Nicholas, following a century of succession crises and palace coups and knowing that secret society leaders were actively encouraging revolt among the Imperial Guards, was reluctant to appear to be usurping the throne. After weeks of uncertainty, December 14/26* was the date chosen for the troops in St. Petersburg to declare their allegiance to Nicholas as the new ruler. Northern Society officers took advantage of the uncertainty to lead their troops to overthrow the tsar and establish a constitutional monarchy. They were well aware that their chances of success were nil, but the impact of this tiny movement on subsequent developments in Russia was monumental. Rebel officers managed to mobilize a minority of the St. Petersburg garrison to occupy Senate Square, where the oath was to take place. Nicholas himself led the loyal troops and, after several efforts to disband the rebels, reluctantly gave the command to open fire. Dozens were killed; hundreds were arrested and interrogated. Five conspirators were hanged, and 284 were sentenced to prison and exile.

Nicholas saw the Decembrist revolt as an attack on the legitimacy of autocracy. Opening his reign by having to suppress a revolt reinforced the monarch's commitment to the traditional principles of tsarist autocracy. But the courage of the conspirators and their dignity in Siberian banishment fixed them in public memory as heroic and patriotic martyrs in the cause of democratic reform. They became an enduring model for successive generations of revolutionaries. Especially important in establishing a model of self-sacrifice was the role of the Decembrists' wives: free to divorce their husbands and retain the wealth and privileges the men had lost, many women chose to follow their husbands into exile instead.

Across Europe in the 1820s, efforts to install some form of constitutional rule or popular sovereignty were resisted by powerful forces in traditionally absolutist societies. Even in the more liberal countries with longer constitutional histories, we see resistance to popular sovereignty among rulers and powerful elites. In the early 1830s, however, another wave of revolutions fanned out from the capital of revolutionary Europe, Paris.

The Revolutions of 1830

France

When he was placed on the throne in 1814 King Louis XVIII (r. 1814–1824) would have preferred to be an absolute ruler; but he knew that returning to the prerevolutionary order was impractical, if not impossible, especially since he was declining in health and suffered from the additional political handicap of having been imposed on the French by their enemies.

The ambiguities of Louis XVIII's policies were most evident in the constitutional charter that he signed in 1814. Some sections sounded like the sev-

---

*The Russian calendar was 12 days behind the west European calendar in the nineteenth century, 13 days behind in the twentieth. I give both dates for Russian events as here.

enteenth-century absolute monarchy of Louis XIV; for example, the preamble asserted the royal prerogative: "The authority in France resides in the person of the king." But the charter also granted a measure of constitutional monarchy. There was a legislature, composed of a Chamber of Peers, appointed by the king, and a Chamber of Deputies, elected on a very restricted suffrage that allowed fewer than a hundred thousand of France's 30 million people the right to vote. The Chambers had no formal right to confirm the king's choices of ministers. Yet since Louis tended to select ministers acceptable to majority opinion in the legislature, this was a functional compromise with parliamentary government. Furthermore, the charter guaranteed religious toleration, a measure of freedom for the press, equality before the law, and equal eligibility to civil and military office. It also accepted the Napoleonic Code and, still more important, the revolutionary property settlement.

The charter, however, greatly irritated the noble and clerical émigrés, knows as ultraroyalists or "Ultras," who had returned to France after their revolutionary exile. They were determined to recover both the privileges and the property they had lost during the revolution. When the election of 1815 gave the Ultras control of the Chamber of Deputies, they proposed to set up special courts to deal with suspected revolutionaries. At the insistence of the allies, Louis XVIII dismissed the Chamber and held a new election, which returned a more moderate majority.

Events, however, soon strengthened the Ultras' hand. Antirevolutionary fears swept France after the Spanish uprising of 1820. When the king's nephew, the Duke de Berri was assassinated the same year, the Ultras accused the liberal opposition of encouraging violence. Louis dismissed the moderate government, and the Ultras won control of the Chamber of Deputies, reimposed censorship of the press, and put through a law giving extra weight to the votes of the wealthiest 25 percent of the already very restricted electorate. In 1821 French education was placed under the direction of the Roman Catholic bishops.

The tempo of the reaction quickened when Louis died, and his brother, an Ultra leader, became King Charles X (r. 1824–1830). Charles greatly extended the influence of the church by encouraging the activities of the Jesuits, whose order had been banned in France since 1764, and by sponsoring a law compensating the émigrés for their confiscated property. The liberal opposition increased in response.

Liberal opponents of the king were primarily wealthy businessmen and professionals, writers, journalists, and artists as well as prosperous landowners. Their grievances were primarily political. The Ultras were desperately trying to reconstruct a society of aristocratic privilege that had long been obsolete. The liberals called for broadening of opportunities, extending the right to vote, constitutional rule of law, and an end to the power of the old aristocracy. Discontent with the status quo was not the exclusive province of well-educated, liberal elites. An economic crisis, initiated by a series of bad harvests in the late 1820s, together with the challenges and uncertainties of early industrialization (to be discussed more fully in Chapter Three) generated bread riots, grain seizures, demonstrations, and other forms of public protest among lower classes in villages, towns, and cities all over France. Areas where mechanized production was beginning to scare artisans who practiced traditional forms of labor saw even more heightened protest as the economic crisis spread.

After a brief attempt to conciliate the liberals, Charles X appointed as his chief minister the ultraroyalist Prince Jules de Polignac (1780–1847). Polignac hoped to bolster Charles's waning prestige by scoring a military victory. He attacked the Bey of Algiers, a largely independent vassal of the Ottoman Empire, who was notorious for his collusion with the Barbary pirates. The capture of Algiers (July 5, 1830) laid the foundation of the French empire in North Africa, but Charles blundered into provoking revolution anyway. On July 25, 1830, without securing the legislature's approval, Charles and Polignac issued the Four Ordinances, muzzling the press, dissolving the newly elected Chamber, ordering a new election, and introducing new voting qualifications that would have disenfranchised the bourgeois mainstay of the opposition. The king and his chief minister believed that public opinion, mollified by the recent victory at Algiers, would receive these measures calmly. They miscalculated utterly. The publication of the decrees on July 26, 1830 turned a parliamentary crisis and artisanal street demonstrations into a revolution.

Liberal journalists, whose newspapers had become quite popular during the previous decade, protested the new laws. Artisans, the unemployed, students, and some radical intellectuals in Paris came out to demonstrate and fought skirmishes with government troops. During *les trois glorieuses* (the three "glorious" days of July 27, 28, and 29) Parisian artisans blocked narrow streets with barricades, captured the city hall, and hoisted the tricolor atop the cathedral of Notre Dame. They shot and threw rocks at soldiers. When Charles realized he could no longer control the situation, he abdicated in favor of his grandson and sailed to exile in England. Divisions among the revolutionaries surfaced quickly.

The revolutionary rank and file in 1830 came mainly from the lower bourgeoisie and urban artisans. Their leadership came from the parliamentary opponents of Charles X and from cautious young liberals like Adolphe Thiers (1797–1877) and François Guizot (1787–1874). Thiers edited the opposition paper *Le National;* he had also written a history of the French Revolution to show that it had not been all bloodshed but had also had a peaceful and constructive side. Guizot, too, had written history, a survey of civilization focused on the rise of the bourgeoisie. The revolutionaries of 1830, like those of 1789, were not agreed on the kind of regime they wanted. A minority would have liked a democratic republic with universal suffrage. But the liberal bourgeois majority, who identified a republic with the Reign of Terror, wanted a constitutional monarchy with a suffrage restricted to the wealthy. The moderate leaders were ready with a candidate for the throne—Louis Philippe, the duke of Orléans.

Louis Philippe (r. 1830–1848) had fought in the revolutionary army, then had emigrated in 1793 before the worst of the Terror. He claimed to have lit-

The Written Record

THE FRENCH CONSTITUTION OF 1830

Louis Philippe, King of the French, to all present and to come, greeting. We have ordered and do order that the Constitutional Charter of 1814, such as it has been amended by the two Chambers on August 7th and accepted by us on the 9th, shall be again published in the following terms:

Public Law of the French

1. Frenchmen are equal before the law, whatever may be their titles and ranks.
2. They contribute, without distinction, in proportion to their fortunes toward the expenses of the state.
3. They are all equally admissible to civil and military employments.
4. Their personal property is likewise guaranteed; no one can be prosecuted or arrested save in the cases provided by law and in the form which it prescribes.
5. Everyone may profess his religion with equal freedom and shall obtain for his worship the same protection.
6. The ministers of the Catholic, Apostolic, and Roman religion, professed by the majority of the French, and those of the other Christian sects, receive stipends from the state.
7. Frenchmen have the right to publish and to have printed their opinions, while conforming with the laws. The censorship can never be re-established.
8. All property is inviolable, without any exception for that which is called national, the law making no distinction between them. . . .
11. The conscription is abolished. The method of recruiting for the army and navy is determined by the law.

Forms of the Government of the King

12. The person of the king is inviolable and sacred. His ministers are responsible. To the king alone belongs the executive power.
13. The king is the supreme head of the state; he commands the land and sea forces, declares war, makes treaties of peace, alliance and commerce, appoints to all places of public administration, and makes the necessary rules and ordinances for the execution of the laws, without the power ever to suspend the laws themselves or to dispense with their execution. . . .
15. The proposal of laws belongs to the king, the Chamber of Peers and the Chamber of Deputies. Nevertheless every taxation law must be first voted by the Chamber of Deputies. . . .

F.M. Anderson, *The Constitution and Other Select Documents Illustrative of the History of France, 1789–1907*, 2nd ed. (Minneapolis, 1908), pp. 507–08.

Eugène Delacroix, Liberty Leading the People, *1831. In this painting the figures of the revolutionaries take the foreground; there is almost no attempt to place them in a realistic setting; the effect is to emphasize the heroic spirit and passionate commitment of those fighting for liberty, including those who died for and against their cause. They include a cross section of society, a worker, an intellectual (probably the painter himself), and a youth, all led by Marianne, the mythical embodiment of the French Revolution. Her nakedness is not meant to be realistic or erotic, but mythical and nurturing.* (Réunion des Musées Nationaux/ Art Resource, NY)

tle use for the pomp of royalty, and he dressed and acted like a sober, well-to-do businessman. However, he accepted the crown at the invitation of the Chamber. The Chamber revised the Charter of 1814 and called Louis Philippe, not the "King of the France" but "King of the French." The new government also replaced the white flag of the Bourbons with the red, white, and blue revolutionary tricolor. The July Monarchy, as the new regime was called, left France far short of realizing the democratic potential of liberty, equality, and fraternity. The liberals who brought Louis Philippe to power were as frightened as anyone by the popular revolution and did not want to see the people gain any political power. After 1830 the franchise was increased by only a fraction: 166,000 men could now vote out of a population of 31 million.

Louis Philippe did little to win hearts and minds of his people, and opposition to the July Monarchy grew almost immediately. The new government did not represent the interests of the poor artisans and lower middle classes who had fought to overthrow Charles and the Ultras. Artisans and workers were angry in 1830 about changes wrought by early industrialization. They

Philipon's satirical journal, La Caricature, *made Louis Philippe an object of derision with constant, inventive, new uses for his pearlike image. They became so common in Parisian satire that the German poet Heinrich Heine noted in 1832 that the pear was the "common standing joke of the people." This new use of public space, both on walls and in publications, helped activate public political debate in France and cost Philipon thousands of francs in court fees and days in jail as the government prosecuted him repeatedly, eventually shutting the doors of the journal in 1835.* *(Print Collection, Miriam and Ira D. Wallach Division of Art, Prints and Photographs, The New York Public Library, Astor, Lenox and Tilden Foundations)*

took part in the revolution not because Charles had revoked constitutional rights or reinstated censorship but because they wanted some control over their economic conditions and some relief for poverty and hunger. When the "glorious" street fighting of the July Days brought the Louis Philippe to power, the poor felt betrayed. Discontented workers and artisans would rise up again in Paris in 1831 and in major disturbances in Lyons in 1831 and 1834. Louis Philippe responded by cracking down on associations and placing restrictions on freedom of the press.

Increasing repression and corruption made Louis Philippe a favorite target for a new class of journalists and political cartoonists, including Charles Philipon (1800–1862) and Honoré Daumier (1808–1879). With his heavy jowls and large paunch, Louis Philippe had the misfortune to resemble a pear, a word that in French can also mean "nitwit." For ten years, French publications were filled with humiliating images of the king's pearlike image, which undermined his authority with ridicule. In addition, peasants and many people from all social classes had strong positive memories, regularly reinforced by new publications, of the glorious and heroic rule of Napoleon. In contrast, Louis Philippe's attempt to simplify the image of the ruler, by dressing in bourgeois style, brought neither democracy nor glory to France. But in the short run, despite the ultimate failures of 1830, the uprising in Paris and the fall of Charles X in France inspired revolts all over Europe.

National Independence in Belgium

The union of Belgium and the Netherlands, decreed by the Congress of Vienna of 1815, worked well only in economics. The commerce and colonies of Holland supplied raw materials and markets for the textile, glass, and other manufactures of Belgium. In language, politics, and religion, however, King William I of Holland exerted power arbitrarily. He made Dutch the official language throughout his realm, including the French-speaking Walloon provinces. He denied the pleas of Belgians to rectify the "Dutch arithmetic" that gave the Dutch provinces, with 2 million inhabitants, and the Belgian, with 3.5 million, equal seats in the States-General. He refused to grant special status to the Catholic church in Belgium, and particularly offended the faithful by insisting that the education of priests be subject to state supervision. All these grievances tended to foster Belgian nationalism and forge common bonds between the Catholic Dutch-speaking Flemings of the provinces north of Brussels and the Catholic French-speaking Walloons of the highly industrialized southern provinces.

Revolution broke out in Brussels on August 25, 1830. Headed by students inspired by the example of Paris, the riots were directed against Dutch rule. The insurgents recruited their fighters chiefly from the industrial workers, many of whom complained of low pay and frequent unemployment. However, the better-organized middle-class leadership soon controlled the revolutionary movement and predominated in the Belgian national congress that convened in November 1830. As in France, the revolution was won because a coalition of workers and notables opposed the status quo. In victory the Belgian elite, like the French elite ignored the grievances of the poor, who felt betrayed.

The Belgian national congress proclaimed Belgium an independent constitutional monarchy. The new constitution granted religious toleration, provided for wide local self-government, and put rigorous limits on the king's authority. Although there was no provision for universal suffrage, the financial qualifications for voting were lower in Belgium than they were in Britain or France. King William stubbornly tried to reconquer Belgium in 1831–1832. A French army and a British fleet successfully defended the secessionists, however, and prolonged negotiations resulted in Dutch recognition of Belgium's new status in 1839. In 1839 also, representatives of Britain, France, Prussia, Austria, and Russia guaranteed both the independence and the neutrality of Belgium.

Nationalist Revolutions in Poland, Italy, and Germany

The course of revolution in Poland contrasted tragically with that in Belgium. In 1815 the Congress of Vienna had reaffirmed the partition of Poland into provinces controlled by Prussia, Austria, and Russia. Tsar Alexander had given the kingdom of Poland the most liberal constitution on the Continent: it preserved the Napoleonic Code and endowed the Sejm with limited legislative power. A hundred thousand men received the right to vote. But Poles had never reconciled themselves to partition, especially to Russian rule. They saw themselves as victims of Great Power politics, their nation "crucified." Censorship, unrest, and police intervention marked the last years of Alexander I. The advent of Nicholas I in 1825 increased political friction, although the new tsar at first abided by the Polish constitution. Secret societies on the Carbonari model arose in the kingdom of Poland and in Lithuania, Belarus, and Ukraine. Romantic nationalism made new converts at the universities of Warsaw and Vilna (in Lithuania). Then the outbreak of revolutions in France and Belgium inspired this new generation of nationalist freedom fighters to act. In November 1830, when Nicholas I threatened to use Polish troops to suppress the revolts in France and Belgium, a secret society of army cadets in Warsaw launched a revolution.

Russian control over Poland dissolved in the winter of 1830–1831 and a government was formed under Polish nobleman Adam Czartoyski (1770–1861). This rebellion was no social or political revolution; leadership of the movement was assumed by a nobility who were reluctant revolutionaries with no intention of emancipating the Polish peasants or sharing political power. Their goal was national independence, not political equality or social justice. In September 1831, when more radical groups in Warsaw and other cities threatened the nationalist government and attacked the royal castle, the Polish nobility chose Russian rule over Polish but popular revolution. Once the Russians were in control again, Nicholas I arrested and exiled movement leaders, scrapped the Polish constitution, imposed martial law, and closed the universities.

In Italy and Germany news of the July Revolution in Paris stimulated abortive revolutionary efforts in which secret societies of students and other young liberal nationalists called for national unification. In 1831 Italian Carbonari insurgents briefly controlled the small duchies of Parma and Modena and a sizable part of the Papal States. Again, as in 1821, Metternich sent troops to suppress revolution and restore legitimacy in Italy. The revolutionaries had mistakenly counted on French assistance, but the July Monarchy had no intention of risking war with Austria.

In Prussia King Friedrich Wilhelm III (r. 1797–1840) had never fulfilled his promise to grant a constitution, though he did set up provincial Diets (elected assemblies). The Karlsbad Decrees succeeded in suppressing open opposition but mild political ferment continued in Germany, and the Burschenschaft reorganized underground. In 1830 and the years following, a few rulers in northern Germany, notably in Saxony and Hanover, granted constitutions. Excited by these minor successes and by the appearance of Polish refugees, thirty thousand revolutionary sympathizers, including many students from Heidelberg and other universities in the region, gathered in the Palatinate in May 1832. There they demanded the union of the German states under a democratic republic. Their ability to take effective action toward unification, however, was another matter. In 1833 some fifty instructors and students tried to seize Frankfurt, the capital of the German Confederation and seat of its Diet. The insurgents, together with hundreds of other students accused of Burschenschaft activities, were given harsh sentences by courts in Prussia and other German states.

The failures of nationalist movements in Poland, Italy, and Germany would deter their adherents only temporarily; nationalism gained momentum and powerful supporters during the next decades.

Reform Without Revolution: Great Britain

In the years immediately after 1815, Britain went through an intense postwar economic crisis. Unsold goods accumulated, and the working classes experienced widespread unemployment and misery. The Corn Law of 1815 increased popular suffering by prohibiting the import of cheap foreign grain until the price of home-grown grain rose to a specified level. This assured the profits of the English grain farmer and but raised the cost of bread for the average English family. Although trade unions were outlawed, workers nonetheless asserted themselves in strikes and in popular agitation. As in France, workers' unrest over economic and social issues helped prepare the way for political reforms, from which they did not benefit.

Britain emerged from the Napoleonic wars with an executive composed of a prime minister and a cabinet of ministers responsible to Parliament (rather than the monarch). The monarch had little real power, but for most of the nineteenth century the throne belonged to Queen Victoria (r. 1837–1901), who enjoyed the patriotic loyalty of her subjects. Victoria was the most popular British ruler since the days of the Tudors, and her name would be used to describe the entire era. Queen Victoria was also the matriarch of European dynasties, as her many children and grandchildren married into the royal families of the Continent.

Still, real power lay with Parliament, which in the early nineteenth century was very far from being a broadly representative body. The House of Lords, which had equal power with the House of Commons except over money bills, was composed of the small privileged class of peers born to their seats, with the addition from time to time of a relatively few new peers, created by the monarch. The House of Commons was made up of elected representatives recruited from the gentry, the professional classes, and very successful businessmen, with a sprinkling of sons of peers. Two parties, Whigs and Tories, dominated Parliament. Whigs were increasingly supported by the new industrial elites and liberal reformers, while Tories tended to be more conservative. The House of Commons was elected by less than one-sixth of the adult male population, voting without a secret ballot. The working classes in both town and country and most of the middle classes were excluded from the franchise.

Proposals to change the structure of representation had come close to being adopted in the late eighteenth century, but the wars with revolutionary and

Napoleonic France postponed reform. Agitation to expand the franchise increased in the difficult years immediately following the return to peace. In wartime and in the immediate postwar years, the Tory government denounced even moderate reformers as revolutionaries. The government feared any kind of public disorder, with memories of the French Revolution still vivid, and sought to suppress public agitation for political reform. In 1819 one such public meeting called to win public support for extending the right to vote ended in disaster. At St. Peter's Fields near Manchester, banners advocating parliamentary reform were displayed and middle-class speakers addressed a peaceful assemblage of nearly sixty thousand people. A clumsy police attempt to disrupt the meeting and arrest a popular speaker led to a riot in which eleven people died and more than four hundred (including a hundred women) were wounded. The debacle came to be called the "Peterloo" massacre, after the famous defeat of Napoleon at Waterloo only four years earlier. Entrenched positions hardened, and class antagonisms became more evident. Postwar repression reached its height with Parliament's approval of six "gag acts," which curtailed freedom of speech, prohibited training in the use of firearms, and imposed a stamp tax on political literature.

In the aftermath, the Tories increasingly moved toward conciliation to avert the dangers of revolution. More flexible leaders were brought into the government, including George Canning and Sir Robert Peel (1788–1850), who lifted the restrictions on civil rights imposed during the long war with France and the postwar crisis. The new leaders permitted laborers to organize into unions, though not to strike; they reformed the antiquated criminal code, so that, for example, the theft of a sheep no longer carried the death penalty; and they began the reduction in protective tariffs that was to lead to free trade (though not yet affecting the Corn Laws).

While the electoral campaign was heating up, an Irish movement to remove civil restrictions on Catholics was also gaining momentum. This movement, led by the charismatic Irish lawyer Daniel O'Connell (1775–1847), was meant to be a step toward the overall goal of Irish independence. The Irish had chafed under English colonization for centuries. A subject population primarily made up of Catholic Irish peasants was subordinated to the English (and Scots) who had settled in the northern Irish province of Ulster in the sixteenth and seventeenth centuries, and had remained as privileged Protestant landowners. Although there were also native Irish among the ruling classes, many of them had been Anglicized Protestants. For three centuries religious, political, and economic conflicts in Ireland had remained unresolved. Early in the nineteenth century the English attempted to address the political problem by a formal union of the two kingdoms, with Irish members admitted to the British parliament. In part to prevent Napoleon from using Ireland to attack England, the United Kingdom of Great Britain and Ireland came into being on January 1, 1801. However, the Irish had never accepted political annexation, especially in as much as they did not enjoy the same civil and political rights as their English counterparts.

Under O'Connell's dynamic leadership of the Catholic Association, the movement for Catholic "emancipation" was transformed from an elite to a mass popular movement that won widespread support in Ireland. When O'Connell legally won election to the House of Lords but was barred as a Catholic from taking his seat, the British leadership feared bloodshed or even civil war. Thus Peel, together with the Tory prime minister, the Duke of Wellington, pressured the House of Lords to pass legislation it had rejected many times before, and in 1829 the Catholic Emancipation Act became law. Now Catholics everywhere in the United Kingdom could enjoy all but the highest offices of state—which were still reserved to the majority Anglican church. But the price of O'Connell's victory was high: the bill raised property qualifications for voting in Ireland, which excluded many peasants, who felt betrayed. Moreover the act failed to resolve the thornier issues of Irish independence. O'Connell was a gradualist, not a revolutionary, and the movement for Irish independence would be taken over by others.

In the meantime, a popular campaign for electoral reform brought intense pressure on the British government. The main advocates for reform were increasingly wealthy manufacturers in rising industrial towns who lacked political power to pass legislation they considered favorable for a modern economy. The House of Lords, dominated by the rural landed elites, twice refused to pass a reform bill approved by the House of Commons. In 1830 the antireform prime minister, the Duke of Wellington, was replaced by Earl Charles Grey (1764–1845), a Whig who favored reform. Public demonstrations in favor of reform began to increase the pressure. One of the most serious incidents occurred in Bristol. Although the city had been represented in the House of Commons since 1295, by 1830 only 6,000 men of the 104,000 people living in Bristol could vote. In 1831 a demonstration protesting the Lords' resistance to reform turned into a riot, during which mobs burned down one hundred houses including the bishop's palace and the customs house and attacked jails, releasing prisoners. Dragoons attacked the crowd killing twelve and wounding hundreds more.

Grey then resorted to drastic tactics, persuading the new king, William IV (r. 1830–1837), to threaten to appoint enough new peers to the House of Lords to win approval of the bill. The pressure worked, and eventually, in the face of this threat, the House of Lords passed the Reform Bill of 1832.

The Reform Bill of 1832 left all women and most men without the vote, but it created an important precedent. The Reform Bill accomplished a potentially revolutionary change without revolutionary violence. In the aftermath of the 1830 uprisings in France and on the Continent, British conservative politicians chose to compromise with liberal reformers to prevent a handful of scattered riots from becoming a revolution. The aristocratic House of Lords, under severe pressure, went along, and Britain gained an expansion of the franchise to middle-class voters through parliamentary politics rather than revolution. Yet by no means did the Reform Bill bring political democracy to Britain. It did diminish the great irregularities of electoral districts, giving seats in the Commons to more than forty unrepresented industrial towns. The number of voters was increased by about 50 percent, so that virtually all the middle class got the vote; but the property qualifications for voting excluded the great mass of workers. Only 20 percent of the male population could vote after 1832, and women were explicitly excluded. Since, however, the bill extended the suffrage in the countryside, which tended to vote conservative, its impact was not as radical as its opponents had feared.

New elections did, however, bring a much larger percentage of business representatives into the government and, for the first time, liberal causes, such as the abolition of slavery, had a voice. In the 1830s Parliament abolished slavery in the British Empire, prohibited child labor, and created elected municipal governments.

The Counterrevolution in Russia

Nicholas I would never forget the threat to autocracy posed by the young Decembrist rebels. He remained committed to principles of autocratic rule and a belief in Russia's unique mission until his death in 1855. He was prepared to make improvements but not to touch the fundamental institution of the autocracy. Though he was uneasy over the dangers inherent in serfdom, he was afraid to reform it in any significant way because he feared that concessions would stimulate revolution among the peasants. Nicholas was deeply worried about the possibility that subversive foreign ideas might penetrate into the universities. Repressive measures drove intellectual life underground, where, against all logic, it flourished. The late 1830s to mid-1840s have been called "the Remarkable Decade" for the appearance of a cluster of extraordinarily gifted thinkers and writers. Inspired by the moral courage and idealism of the Decembrists and by contemporary German political philosophers, highly educated young men (and some women) devoted themselves to "serving society." These intellectuals distinguished themselves from west European thinkers by their intense commitment to social and political criticism aimed at practical improvements of conditions for the impoverished peasantry who comprised the majority of the Russian people. The Russian word for intellectuals—*intelligentsia*—came to stand for this public service ideal. The *intelligentsia* of the 1830s–1840s, Alexander Herzen, Vissarion Belinsky, and others (see Chapter Two) criticized the autocracy for repressing free speech, for oppressing the peasants through support of the serf system, and for excessive and incompetent government interference in everyday life. Herzen and others were forced into exile by suffocating and dangerous conditions at home.

Nicholas responded to the challenges of western economic and political development with his own, quite different attempt to modernize the Russian government: regulation. He created a series of new bureaucratic institutions, codified the laws, and in general tried to introduce into civic life the systematic discipline of the military. These measures strengthened autocracy and gave extraordinary powers to the secret police, but they were not entirely reactionary. A well-trained bureaucracy that rewarded merit and expertise (without revoking the advantages of birth and family connections), prepared the way for the measures known as the Great Reforms that would follow in the next generation. Reluctant to industrialize, Nicholas nonetheless made efforts to improve the lot of peasants living on state-owned lands.

The reign of Nicholas has often been vilified by contemporaries and historians as politically reactionary and socially stagnant, but this is misleading. Nicholas knew that changes in society and politics were necessary, but he was so suspicious of any and all initiative coming from society, and so determined to control the course of events, that even his best efforts met with skepticism. He alienated the most educated and active members of society, and blocked the organic dynamism necessary for ongoing development.

* * *

In light of more decisive events both before and after the revolutions of the 1820s–1830s, historians have dismissed the importance of these mostly failed movements. But they were important historical landmarks for several reasons. First, thousands of men and women risked scandal, prison, and in some cases their lives to challenge the Restoration political settlement that emerged from the Congress of Vienna. Once the French Revolution had made possible constitutional sovereignty, equality before the law, and the abolition of aristocratic privilege, some people refused to let those possibilities die. Yet the majority of activists were wary of grand schemes and fought for specific reforms: the right to vote, national independence and unity, economic reforms, and an end to specific kinds of discrimination. These limited ambitions were both the strength and the weakness of revolutions during this period. Where they mobilized a large percentage of the population, as in France and Britain, they had more success. Where limited goals attracted activists only in specific fractions of the population, as in Spain, Italy, Germany, Russia, and Poland, they could not withstand government suppression.

These revolts are also important for what they tell historians about fissures within society. In France and elsewhere, political campaigns succeeded in effecting revolutionary political change only because they could call upon the pressure of volatile and unpredictable lower-class discontent. But there was in fact very little to bind these very different forces of revolution, and after the dust cleared, the sources of popular discontent remained unresolved. Nineteenth-century revolutions generally would involve uneasy coalitions of antigovernment forces; but the goals of different groups were often entirely incompatible, so even when "successful," the uprisings would always leave some of the participants unsatisfied.

In addition, the revolutionary wave of the 1830s widened the split between the West and the East inherent in the conflicts that emerged after the Congress of Vienna. Britain and France were more firmly committed to support for liberal constitutional monarchies both at home and in Belgium. Russia,

Austria, and Prussia were equally committed to suppressing revolution by force. In 1833 Metternich, Nicholas I, and Friedrich Wilhelm III formally pledged their joint assistance to any sovereign threatened by revolution.

Finally, despite their political differences, the Great Powers remained committed to international stability, the Concert of Europe, and the balance of powers. In most cases, when revolutionary movements threatened that stability, European rulers responded with restraint or were restrained by existing international agreements. This commitment to stability is all the more remarkable in the context of revolutionary challenge and intellectual and economic change.

TWO

Romanticism

The beginning of the nineteenth century was a period of great cultural activity and achievement. Literature, music, painting, and theater, as well as history writing and political thought, all flourished in the first decades of the century as thinkers struggled to come to terms with the challenges posed by modern revolutions. All over Europe artists experimented with new forms of expression, found new audiences, and developed new notions of individuality. An upsurge of artistic activity occurred in countries that had not previously produced much of artistic originality. This cultural flowering took diverse forms, all of which have come to be designated Romanticism.

Romanticism was a broad cultural movement, which rejected the Enlightenment's emphasis on reason and classical forms derived from ancient Greece and Rome, while embracing its idealization of individual self-determination. Romantic writers, musicians, artists, and other public figures sought to replace what they saw as an overly rational and mechanistic view of human nature with the expression of individual imagination, faith, and feeling rooted in the natural world and in national sovereignty and traditions. Romantic writers and artists protested against the oversimplification of the Enlightenment ideal of a thinking, objective, logical individual and insisted on the intricacy and complexity of human nature, recognizing the irrational and emotional elements of human nature and the unique and peculiar history of each individual nation. The Romantics accused their Enlightenment predecessors of being unduly optimistic about the perfectibility of humanity and found that pleasure might also be taken in the grotesque, the disorganized, the morbid. Most Romantics were disturbed by the destruction of nature that had already occurred as a result of early industrialization, especially in England. In some places, especially but not exclusively in eastern Europe, however, Romanticism was linked with a vague ideal of "progress" that included economic development and urbanization. Romantic artists explored "exotic" cultures, which at that time meant non-European cultures; they were preoccupied by death and loss, and highly conscious of change over time.

During the Enlightenment artists and writers had sought "laws of nature" that could be applied universally to all individuals and all peoples. The

Romantics sought uniqueness, spontaneity, extremes of feeling and behavior, and above all, the valorization of the individual's ability to both perceive and convey depth of feeling. This was a rejection of centuries' worth of attempts to perfect an objective, rational, scientific, realistic truth. At least since the Renaissance, artists, scientists and other thinkers, and writers had been trying to distinguish what was real from what they considered to be in some way unreal (superstition, prejudice, witchcraft, scientific errors). They sought ways to represent the real world as accurately as possible, with perspectival drawing, for example, which made the two-dimensional space of a canvas appear to be three-dimensional. In place of the quest for a single objective, perfectible, universal reality, the Romantics developed notions of multiple, conflicting perspectives—multiple, contradictory realities in the drama of the individual's inner life and in the more spontaneous, imperfect, and expressive representation of nature.

Throughout the nineteenth century, however, Enlightenment concepts of human nature and social organization remained extremely powerful and widely accepted as the proud heirs of the Enlightenment promoted notions of rational objectivity and a detached, scientific rationality. The Romantic sensibility evolved through competition with Enlightenment thinking, but the Romantic sense of human nature was less than a thorough break from, and more a repositioning of, the Enlightenment individual. The Romantic individual was endowed with an Enlightenment sense of empowerment based on advances in science and technology, a sense of civic responsibility, and an acute ability to observe the world and change it for the better. The Romantics added feeling, faith, a presence in the natural world, an appreciation of exotic and supernatural worlds, and a respect for national history to the Enlightenment's arsenal of tools for making the world a better place.

Romanticism was, however, much more than an artistic movement; it contained a crucial political element as well. Ideas about individual uniqueness and expression stimulated movements for national awakening and national self-determination everywhere in Europe. As such, Romanticism came to characterize the worldview of a whole generation of European intellectual elites in the early nineteenth century. In eastern Europe, where its liberal nationalist goals were achieved much later, the visionary ideal of the committed intellectual lasted much longer.

An Age of Feeling and Poetry

Literary romanticism may be traced back to the mid-eighteenth century—to novels of "sensibility" like *La Nouvelle Héloïse* by Jean-Jacques Rousseau (1712–1778) and to the sentimental "tearful comedies" of the French stage. In the 1770s and 1780s a new intensity appeared, for example, in the morbidly sensitive *Sorrows of Young Werther* by Johann Wolfgang von Goethe (1749–1832), and *The Robbers,* a drama of social protest by J. C. F. von Schiller (1759–1805).

Goethe, considered by many to be the greatest German writer of modern times, is difficult to categorize. Like other late eighteenth-century writers, Goethe was both an exponent of Enlightenment rationality and an explorer of irrationality, faith, and feeling, above all in his masterpiece, the poetic drama *Faust*. Begun in 1808 and not published until after the poet's death in 1832, this long poetic drama was a philosophical commentary on the main currents of European thought. According to the traditional legend, the aged Faust, weary of book learning and pining for eternal youth, sold his soul to the devil, receiving back the enjoyment of his youth for an allotted time, and then, terror-stricken, going to the everlasting fires. Goethe partially transformed this legend: Faust makes the same infernal compact with Mephistopheles, who points out how disillusioning intellectual pursuits are, but Faust is ultimately saved through his realization that he must sacrifice selfish concerns to the welfare of others. A drama of sinning, striving, and redemption, Goethe's *Faust* took the reader on an emotional journey through exotic, supernatural realms to explore the conflicts his readers faced in an age of great change and spiritual crisis. Goethe decried the Enlightenment attack on Christian morality and religion but could not quite endorse those values either; as such *Faust* remains a work that spoke to the soul-searching complexity of the period.

The Enlightenment had also glorified poetry based on strict forms, like the heroic couplets of Racine and Pope. The Romantics rejected this neoclassicism as artificial and praised the vigor, color, and freedom of the Bible, Homer, and Shakespeare. The result was a great renaissance of poetry all over Europe, especially in England, which produced a galaxy of great poets: William Wordsworth (1770–1850), Samuel Taylor Coleridge (1772–1834), George Gordon, Lord Byron (1788–1824), Percy Bysshe Shelley (1792–1822), Felicia Hemans (1793–1835), John Keats (1795–1821), and others.

Wordsworth and Coleridge pressed furthest in their reaction against classicism and rationalism. In 1798 the two men published *Lyrical Ballads*, to which Coleridge contributed "The Rime of the Ancient Mariner," a supernatural tale of the curse afflicting a sailor who slays an albatross. Later he created "Kubla Khan," which has a surrealistic quality, probably induced by narcotics.

Wordsworth, who had lived in France during the early years of the Revolution and had been disillusioned by the failure of rational reform and the French Enlightenment's confidence in human perfectibility through reason, put his faith in the "immortal spirit" of the individual. In place of the light shed by Newton's laws, he found "a dark, inscrutable workmanship." Like many other Romantics, Wordsworth considered nature to be the inspiration for all true art, spirituality, and human imagination. Not only did he sing the beauties of nature in his local Lake District of England, but he denounced the destruction of nature and commercialization that had come with industrialization. Wordsworth and other Romantics looked to the natural world and preindustrial society for a more humane and organic way of life. Nature's wildness and fecundity offered a model for individual experience.

A Closer Look

British Romantic Poetry

The World Is Too Much with Us (1807)

William Wordsworth celebrated nature and called into question the value of the modern world of commerce; in this poem, he compares the present unfavorably with the past: ancient and pagan though it was, but in thrall to the mysteries of nature

The world is too much with us; late and soon,
Getting and spending, we lay waste our powers;
Little we see in Nature that is ours;
We have given our hearts away, a sordid boon!
This Sea that bares her bosom to the moon,
The winds that will be howling at all hours,
And are up-gathered now like sleeping flowers,
For this, for everything, we are out of tune;
It moves us not.—Great God! I'd rather be
A Pagan suckled in a creed outworn;
So might I, standing on this pleasant lea,
Have glimpses that would make me less forlorn;
Have sight of Proteus rising from the sea;
Or hear old Triton blow his wreathed horn.

We'll Go No More A-Roving (1817)

George Gordon, Lord Byron, captured deep feelings in simple accessible language. This poem of melancholy at the passing of love and cooling of sexual passion conveys Byron's musicality and his play on his own celebrity.

So we'll go no more a-roving
So late into the night,
Though the heart be still as loving,
And the moon be still as bright.

For the sword outwears its sheath,
And the soul wears out the breast,
And the heart must pause to breathe,
And Love itself have rest.

Though the night was made for loving,
And the day returns too soon,
Yet we'll go no more a-roving
By the light of the moon.

England in 1819 (1819)

The Romantics' focus on feelings did not make them unworldly. On the contrary, most of them wrote poems on contemporary political issues, such as this heartfelt critique by Percy Bysshe Shelley. The "king" of the first line is a reference to George III.

An old, mad, blind, despis'd, and dying king,
Princes, the dregs of their dull race, who flow
Through public scorn—mud from a muddy spring,
Rulers who neither see, nor feel, nor know,
But leech-like to their fainting country cling,
Till they drop, blind in blood, without a blow,
A people starv'd and stabb'd in the untill'd field,
An army, which liberticide and prey
Makes as a two-edg'd sword to all who wield,
Golden and sanguine laws which tempt and slay,
Religion Christless, Godless—a book seal'd,
A Senate—Time's worst statute unrepeal'd,
Are graves, from which a glorious Phantom may
Burst, to illumine our tempestuous day.

When I Have Fears that I May Cease to Be (1818)

Many of the Romantics were preoccupied with death and among other things sought a form of immortality other than Christian salvation. John Keats found consolation in the endurance of great art, as in this poem.
When I have fears that I may cease to be

Before my pen has glean'd my teeming brain
Before high-piled books, in charactery
Hold like rich garners the full ripen'd grain.
When I behold, upon the night's starr'd face
Huge cloudy symbols of a high romance
And think that I may never live to track
Their shadows, with the magic hand of chance
And when I feel, fair creature of an hour,
That I shall never look upon thee more,
Never have relish in the faery power
Of unreflecting love;—then on the shore
Of the wide world I stand alone, and think
Till love and fame to nothingness do sink.

Thoughts During Sickness

Women Romantic poets often outsold men. Felicia Dorothea Browne Hemans began publishing poetry at age 14 and became one of the most popular of the British Romantic poets. In this poem she celebrates imagination as a gift of divine and intellectual inspiration. How might male and female poets differ in their attitudes towards the divide between emotions and reason?

THOUGHT! O Memory! gems for ever heaping
High in the illumined chambers of the mind,
And thou, divine Imagination! keeping

Thy lamp's lone star 'mid shadowy hosts enshrined;
How in one moment rent and disentwined,
At Fever's fiery touch, apart they fall,
Your glorious combinations!—broken all,
As the sand-pillars by the desert's wind
Scatter'd to whirling dust!—Oh, soon uncrown'd!
Well may your parting swift, your strange return,
Subdue the soul to lowliness profound,
Guiding its chasten'd vision to discern
How by meek Faith Heaven's portals must be pass'd
Ere it can hold your gifts inalienably fast.

The New Penguin Book of Romantic Poetry, eds Jonathan and Jessica Wordsworth (London, 2001) pp 432, 397–398, 662, 440

George Gordon, Lord Byron, exemplified the Romantic spirit in poetry. Byron was born into a family of aristocrats with a long history of mental instability and extreme behavior. His periodic uncontrollable rages (begun in childhood) alternating with periods of dark, suicidal depression, his sexual voraciousness, his physical recklessness and eccentricities, his brutal selfishness and extravagant generosity all found expression in his poetry and attracted a great deal of attention (and misunderstanding) to his life as well as to his work. Byron's private miseries added power and depth to his poetry and made him one of the first public celebrities of the modern age. The "Byronic hero" was adventurous, melancholy, defiant, and prodigal, and while such characters were associated with Byron personally, they only partly reflected his experience. Byron used his wealth and rank to speak out for liberal causes in England and abroad. And despite his profligate behavior and very short life, Byron wrote unceasingly and produced a large body of poetry. His work includes lyrics and satires, the best known of which are *Childe Harold's Pilgrimage* (1812–1818), which followed Byron's own travels in Europe and the Middle East and created the "Byronic hero," and *Don Juan* (1819, unfinished at his death), a long poem that satirized people and events of his day with pointed humor. Byron became ill and died at age 36 while in Greece aiding its war of liberation.

Percy Bysshe Shelley and John Keats were poets of greater philosophical depth and poetic accomplishment than Byron, but they shared his destiny of a tragic early death. Shelley was also an outspoken liberal who criticized religious and social conventions and lived a life of free-thinking unconventionality. His poetry embodied the spontaneity of Romanticism, its search for a spirituality more personally fulfilling than the rigid institutional religion of his day; but his liberalism was squarely rooted in Enlightenment ideals, and he looked to classical Greece for his vision of democratic civic life. One of his greatest poems, "Prometheus Unbound" (1820), updated the story of the mythical Greek hero who had been punished by the gods for stealing fire for people to use. In Shelley's hands, Prometheus is humanity, chained and tormented by the tyrannical power of kings and modern institutions. Prometheus is freed by Hercules and reunited with his wife to begin a world where human love and beauty rather than power reign. Shelley died in a boating accident when he was 29 years old.

Keats was the least political of this generation of poets and the most philosophical and literary. His odes exploring the power of beauty and its representation in art, from "On First Looking into Chapman's Homer" (1816) to "Ode on a Grecian Urn" (1819) are considered among the richest in the English language. Keats's sensuous lyrics venerated nature as a source of goodness and beauty (in contrast to Enlightenment images of nature as a great machine), and he was drawn to the melancholy and supernatural. Keats, son of a stableman, an orphan at 14 and ill most of his life, died of tuberculosis at age 26.

Literary Romanticism appeared later in France, where the Enlightenment thrived and classicism long retained its hold. Victor Hugo (1802–1885), who defined Romanticism as "liberalism in literature," challenged tradition in poetry, plays, and novels. *Notre Dame of Paris* (1831) and *Les Misérables* (1862) exposed the lives of the poor to middle-class readers. Hugo's direct challenge to the classical tradition led to sensational public spectacles and showed how debates over language and the proper subjects for art could be deeply divisive and provocative. Hugo's most notorious play, *Hernani* (1830) broke the rules of classical drama by including lines of vernacular speech, contradictory elements of plot, and conventions drawn from melodrama. When, on opening night, one of the characters in *Hernani* violated classical theatrical conventions by uttering a line ending in the middle of a word, traditionalists in the audience set off a riot. Debates about language, art, and innovation, were fought in the press for weeks, and were followed all over Europe.

Where Romanticism appeared later in the century, it was often blended into realism, especially the realist, social novel (see Chapter Five). Honoré de Balzac (1799–1850), France's greatest social novelist of the nineteenth century, combined meticulously detailed depictions of contemporary society with the passionate extremes of Romantic plots and characterizations. In writing that explores the dark and seamy sides of the social life of his times, Stendhal (pseudonym of Marie Henri Beyle, 1783–1842) combined the Romantic attachment to dramatic emotional plots and characterizations with a commitment to liberal social criticism. *The Red and the Black* (1830) and *The Charterhouse of Parma* (1839) exhibit both a fascination with the complexities of social and moral life and a pessimistic rejection of the Romantics' love of beauty. The early work of Russian writer Fyodor Dostoevsky (1821–1881) likewise combines social realism with emotional and narrative elements of Romanticism.

In Russia, Romanticism was instrumental in the creation of Russian as a modern literary language and led to the so-called Golden Age in poetry. Romanticism was also associated with the liberation of authentic individuality from the artificial conventions of aristocratic social life. The Decembrists' politics were rooted in Romantic (as well as Enlightenment) ideas of individual dignity, civic responsibility, and liberal democracy, and several of the Decembrist leaders were also poets. Kondraty Ryleev (1795–1826), one of the five Decembrists who would be hanged for their roles in the uprising, had written poems about heroes from Russian history who fought against tsarist tyranny, often sacrificing their lives. After the failed revolt, Ryleev and the other Decembrist rebels faced their interrogators with defiant pride inspired by Romantic heroes in works by Byron and Schiller, and by Russia's own great poet of the period, Alexander Pushkin (1799–1837).

Like Goethe, Pushkin is hard to classify, and like Byron, whom he admired and surpassed as a poet, Pushkin lived a short dramatic life in which success and tragedy figured in equal measure. Public scandals, outrageous behavior, and sexual escapades; gambling, drinking, hypochondria, and suicidal depression; social alienation and defiant political provocation characterized his early years in society in St. Petersburg and in exile (for writing political verse) in the southern borderlands, the Caucasus, and provincial Russia. But the young man who appeared to observers to be a wastrel and a dandy was writing constantly and with great discipline. Pushkin's profoundly innovative imagination led him to write literature free from adherence to rigid neoclassical genres and archaic literary language. He experimented in every genre, broke down barriers among them, appropriated new subjects for literary exploration, and almost single-handedly created a modern literary language by introducing the living spoken language to the archaic written word, making Russian more supple, accessible, and expressive.

Pushkin's father was descended from one of the oldest noble families in Russia, and the future poet grew up in world of frivolous aristocratic decadence. On his mother's side Pushkin possessed a very personal source of Romantic exoticism, as he was the proud great-grandson of an African servitor of Peter the Great. He entered the world of letters while still in school, an overnight sensation at age 15. Between 1823 and 1831, Pushkin wrote his most famous work, the "novel in verse," *Evgeny Onegin,* an ingenious blend of strict poetic form and free-flowing language depicting a deceptively simple tale of love and loss, fickleness and dignity, falsity and authenticity among the cultured Russian elite. Inspired by and often compared to Byron's *Don Juan, Onegin* contains satire less biting and more personal, in a slice of life less sweeping and more emotionally profound. Pushkin's huge appetite for every detail and every nuance of life as it was lived and his ability to convey complexity in purest poetic form give *Onegin's* reader the illusion of seeing and feeling Pushkin's entire world. Pushkin's command of form and language gives his greatest works a clarity and lightness of touch that makes them unusually accessible and readable.

Though never directly involved in political opposition, Pushkin wrote about tyranny, serfdom, and liberty throughout his career and paid for it dearly. He lived directly under the eye of two tsars and his entire adult life was shaped by the indignities (and privileges) of autocracy: exile, surveillance, censorship, and the onerous burden of state patronage. His mature works, such as the play *Boris Godunov* (1825–1831) and poem "The Bronze Horseman" (1833), treat the paradoxical nature of political power: its allure and its potential, both creative and destructive. Pushkin typified the romantic style in his refusal to draw explicit moral or other conclusions or even to end his tales with much in the way of closure. His narrative works typically begin in medias res and end inconclusively.

In eastern Europe, Romantic literature combined the social idealism of French Romanticism and the liberal nationalism of German and Italian Romanticism. In Italy, the greatest exponent of Romanticism was Alessandro Manzoni (1785–1873), who saw literature as a means for promoting nationalist sentiment, as well as for exploring morality, politics, and character. Manzoni's masterpiece, *The Betrothed* (1827), is a sprawling historical novel set in the seventeenth century, intended to show the ways in which divine providence and divine inspiration operate in everyday life. The novel helped develop the Italian literary language and offered historical material for imagining a glorious Italian past.

The Romantic period, which arose in the context of revolutionary change was a response to change and its possibilities; as such, it also contributed to an important rethinking of gender roles. Liberal individualism, the belief that each individual was unique, along with a defiant and unconventional (if small) counterculture, created possibilities for women to live unconventional lives and take on new, different, and more active roles in European culture and society. During the eighteenth and early nineteenth centuries, women's writing began to reach a wide public; at the beginning of the nineteenth century at least half of the literature published in England was written by women. The male writers' idea that emotions were as important as reason suggested that the eighteenth-century gender stereotypes of women as emotional and men as rational needed some revision. Women's writing shows that Romanticism was not entirely devoted to celebrating feelings. Like their more famous male contemporaries, women writers endorsed ideas about individual uniqueness and imagination, and they tended to support liberal political causes such as the abolition of slavery and extension of democratic rights; but women also wrote about woman's essential rationality and intellectual capabilities, as complementary rather than contrasting the capacity for feeling. Felicia Dorothea Browne Hemans became one of the most popular of the British Romantic poets. Her writing sold well enough to support her family, and she took pride in her success as a professional writer. Her poems celebrate traditional female domestic roles as well as the power of reason and intellectual inspiration.

In France, George Sand (1804–1876, pseudonym of Amandine Aurore-Lucile Dupin) rebelled against the conventions that valued women's lives only for marriage and childbearing. She left her husband, supported herself by writing, and had stormy affairs with numerous famous men, including Romantic poet Alfred de Musset and composer Frédéric Chopin. Sand's public persona attracted as much attention as her writing. She cultivated her own celebrity by smoking and wearing men's clothing in public. But her antics did not slow her productivity. A prolific writer, Sand is best known for a steady stream of confessional novels of romantic passions, often autobiographical, that questioned social conventions of the day, protested the social constraints on women, and revealed her own successes and failures to lead the life of an independent professional *and* passionate woman. Sand was also an active republican and socialist, publicly calling for an extension of political rights to women and the poor.

The most important novel of the Romantic period was written by a woman, Mary Godwin Shelley (1797–1851). *Frankenstein, or the Modern Prometheus,* (1818) contains many characteristic Romantic motifs and techniques. Mary Godwin was the daughter of famous political radicals William Godwin and Mary Wollstonecraft. Her mother died shortly after giving birth to her and she was raised by her father in a household that was stimulating intellectually but not emotionally. In 1814 Mary met and fell in love with Percy Shelley, a married man; they ran off together soon after, though they married only after Shelley's first wife committed suicide. Death stalked Mary and Percy Shelley, and they stalked it back. Before eloping they spent their courtship walking about the cemetery where Mary's mother was buried. Three of their own four children died young. Shelley himself died in 1822, when he was 29 and Mary was only 25. She wrote six more novels and several volumes of critical and biographical work.

Frankenstein, unlike the conventional horror movies based on the novel, was a serious work of social critique haunted by the mysteries of birth and death, in which a scientist, Victor Frankenstein, believes he can construct a living being out of body parts found in graves. The laboratory creation of a living creature is shown in the novel as a crime against nature, a monstrous, purely scientific "birth," lacking not only in romantic love but also in parental responsibility. Shelley's biting critique of scientific arrogance was not a universal rejection of technological or scientific progress. The Romantics, Mary Shelley and Percy included, were well read in the scientific advances of their day and applauded discoveries that were in harmony with or did not alter the natural world. But Victor Frankenstein seeks power *over* nature and flees from responsibility for the creature he produced. It is this corrupt use of reason, detached from feeling and responsibility, that makes his creation a monster. In addition, Shelley's criticism of science is specifically a criticism of *male* scientific rhetoric. Shelley was fully aware of the gendered metaphors used by scientists to describe their conquests over nature. Ever since the scientific revolution of the seventeenth century, scientific experimentation was portrayed as virile male activity intended to "penetrate" and "subdue" a passive, female Nature. Frankenstein's desire to control nature is likewise represented as a desire to control the feminine, but he goes further. His attempt to create life from inert matter is not only an effort to subdue the female but to usurp woman's unique ability to bear children and eliminate the biological need for women altogether. In *Frankenstein,* Shelley invested the Romantic critique of reason and fascination with death with her own desire for and fear of childbirth, and her own experience of a lonely, motherless childhood. Frankenstein, the creator, is destroyed by his attempt to isolate reason from feeling and nature, while his creation is at least partly humanized by his openness to experience in the world.

Music

Romantic composers, like romantic poets, sought to free their compositions from classical strictures as a means of emphasizing the music's emotive qualities; they sought to convey something of the natural and mysterious supernatural worlds in musical forms; and they used music to tell stories, represent human beings and human states, and encourage nationalist sentiment. Often they looked to the popular ballads and tales of the national past. Composers of opera and song turned to literature: Shakespeare's plays, Scott's novels, Byron's poetry, and the poems and tales of Goethe and Pushkin provided the basis for musical compositions and operas. Yet, although literature and music often took similar paths during the romantic era, there were significant differences. Romantic musicians did not revolt against the great eighteenth-century composers as Wordsworth and Coleridge revolted against their predecessors. Rather, romantic music evolved out of the older classical school.

The composer who played the commanding role in this evolution was Ludwig van Beethoven (1770–1827), who lived most of his life in Vienna. Where earlier composers had indicated tempo with a simple "fast" or "slow," Beethoven added such designations as *appassionate* and "Strife between Head and Heart." Part of the color and passion of Beethoven's works derived from his skill in exploiting the resources of the piano, an instrument that was perfected during his lifetime, and his use of more instruments—especially winds, percussion, and double basses—than was traditional. In his Ninth (and final) Symphony, Beethoven introduced a chorus in the last movement to sing his setting of Schiller's "Ode to Joy."

After Beethoven, orchestral works took on increasingly heroic dimensions. The French composer Hector Berlioz (1803–1869) projected an orchestra of 465 pieces, including 120 violins, 37 double basses, and 30 each of pianos and harps. The *Symphonie Fantastique,* which he supposedly based on Goethe's *Werther,* was completed in 1830. Berlioz's *Requiem* called for a full orchestra, a great pipe organ, four brass choirs, and a chorus of two hundred. The romantic propensity for bigness also affected the presentation of J. S. Bach's choral works, like *the Passion According to St. Matthew;* composed originally in 1727 for relatively few performers, it was revived with a full orchestra and a large chorus in a precedent-setting performance directed by Felix Mendelssohn (1809–1847) in 1829.

Music for the human voice reflected both the increased enthusiasm for instruments, particularly the piano, and the general romantic nostalgia for the past. In composing songs and arias, Romantic musicians devoted as much skill to the accompaniment as to the voice part itself. Franz Schubert (1797–1828), Beethoven's Viennese contemporary, made a fine art of blending voice and piano in more than six hundred sensitive *lieder* (songs), seventy of them musical settings of poems by Goethe. Meantime, Carl Maria von Weber (1786–1826) was striving to create a fully German opera, taking an old legend as the libretto for *Der Freischütz* (the freeshooter, 1821). Its plot ran the romantic gamut of an enchanted forest, a magic bullet, and an innocent maiden outwitting the devil, and its choruses and marches employed folklike melodies.

In Russia, Mikhail Glinka (1804–1857) cast aside the Italian influences that had dominated the secular music of his country to base his opera *Ruslan and Liudmila* (1842) on a poem by Pushkin, embellishing it with dances and choruses imitative of Russian Asia.

Perhaps most romantic of all was the Polish-French composer Frédéric Chopin (1810–1849). Writing almost exclusively for the piano, drawing heavily on the melodic forms of Polish popular music, Chopin best combined Romantic music with national idioms, especially in his polonaises, which were written to accompany traditional Polish dances. His work was passionate and stirring, and he made the piano the most popular instrument of the century.

Painting

The virtual dictator of European painting during the first two decades of the nineteenth century was the French neoclassicist Jacques-Louis David (1748–1825). David became a baron and court painter under Napoleon, then was exiled by the restored Bourbons. No matter how revolutionary the subject, David employed traditional neoclassical techniques, stressing form, line, and perspective.

The next generation of painters included those who adopted David's revolutionary passion but rejected his attachment to classical forms and Renaissance perspective. Painters joined poets and writers in stressing individual expression and the heroism of the contemporary life. They experimented with forms meant to convey authenticity, spontaneity, and depth of feeling, rather than realistic verisimilitude. The most important French Romantic painter was Eugène Delacroix (1798–1863), whose paintings often represented major events of his day, commemorating popular victories such as his *Liberty Leading the People* (1831, see Chapter One) celebrating the 1830 revolution, or denouncing tragedies, as in the *Massacre at Chios* (1824). Here and elsewhere, his style seems more conventional than that of some of his contemporaries in that he retained certain aspects of classical form, imagery, and a use of great mythic figures to convey ideas. But Delacroix's paintings reject classical rules of perspective and composition, and his revolutionary experiments with color, shadow, and movement laid the foundation for Impressionism later in the century. Delacroix's writing about the expressive qualities of color were important formulations not only for painters of his own era but for those who followed.

The works of Spaniard Francisco de Goya (1746–1828) represent many aspects of the Romantic temperament in painting: passionate, defiantly radical in form, politically committed, and devoted to depicting a broad range of emotional experience, including the irrational and fantastical as well as the brutally real. In 1810 Goya produced his first great series of etchings, *The Disasters of War,* based on personal observation of Spain's military defeat and occupation by Napoleon's forces. In 1814 Goya returned to the subject in two powerful paintings of French soldiers executing Spanish guerrilla fighters who had resisted the occupation. Entitled simply *May 3, 1808,* one painting depicts an impromptu French firing squad shooting groups of men dressed in ordinary clothes in the dead of night. Rough paint strokes and radically simplified forms heighten the spare drama of the scene. The soldiers' faces are turned away from us; only the next victim is clearly visible, lighted by some technologically advanced lamp that highlights his simple defiant heroism, his arms outstretched as if about to be crucified. In *Absurdities* (1820–1823), a later series of prints, and the *Black Paintings* (1820), Goya introduced images of the supernatural, dreams, hallucinations, superstition and witchcraft that seem to plumb the deepest recesses of human feeling and their expression in social life of both the elite and the poor.

Two English painters would take another radical Romantic approach to form and feeling by painting directly from nature and finding the same inspiration there that Wordsworth and the Romantic poets used. John Constable (1776–1837) and J. M. W. Turner (1775–1851) painted landscapes and seascapes that seem almost abstract in their attempt to evade realistic depiction and speak directly, authentically to our emotions. But Constable based his radically romantic vision on an Enlightenment endorsement of scientific knowledge as basis for representation and perception. "It is the soul that sees," Constable wrote, but to depict the *ways* that the soul sees, he studied modern optics. "Painting is a science and should be pursued as an inquiry into the laws of nature." Turner's painting were even more radically unconventional. The actual objects in his paintings almost disappear in explosions of light and color. He did not care whether his paintings were well received; he cared about expressing his own authentic imagination and exercising his own creativity. Turner saw artistic creativity as a force of nature and sought to convey that on canvas.

The German Romantic painter Caspar David Friedrich (1774–1840) also took nature for his primary subject and also turned his back on the realistic depiction of nature. Friedrich's paintings were considered very strange during his lifetime, bathed as they are in moody moody, eerie light, and displaying highly personal visions of nature. He is appreciated today for the psychological and spiritual expressiveness of his landscapes, which invest each scene with an emotional response to life's mystery and ephemerality. Friedrich believed that only isolation from modern life—noisy, congested, commercial cities—allowed true feeling and self-expression, so his paintings often convey a disquieting sense of aloneness. As in the early Middle Ages, Europeans were fascinated once again with death, and especially with dying

Caspar David Friedrich, Monastery Graveyard in the Snow *(1817–1819). Friedrich was neither a social critic nor a secular anticlerical. In this painting both nature and the church are in danger of perishing, visited only by ghosts of the past, but both still retain their soaring grandeur and their ability to inspire reverence, awe, and terror.* *(Staatliche Museen zu Berlin, National-Galerie)*

heroically. Two immensely popular paintings of the time captured the *frisson,* the chill of pleasure down the spine, that merged Romanticism and a form of social realism. Friedrich's depiction of the wreck of the *Hope* showed a vessel trapped in ice, never to escape from its destiny. Another, earlier work, by the French artist Théodore Géricault (1791–1824), showed the fate of passengers from the frigate *Medusa,* whose passengers, 149 in all, were put onto an open raft and cut adrift at sea; a handful lived to tell the tale. Before painting *The Raft of the Medusa,* Géricault devoted himself to studying corpses in a morgue so that he might capture this horrific moment of both realistic and romantic revelation.

Russian Romantic painters almost all began their careers by painting portraits of the hundreds of dashing young military officers who defended Europe from Napoleon. These portraits departed from classical style in emphasizing individual characteristics, especially eyes, rather than turning the men into ideal or social "types." Alexei Venetsianov (1780–1847), the son of a petty merchant who sold flowers and shrubbery in Moscow, got his start in the military portrait business, but he sought a means to express something quintessentially Russian. Around 1818, long before Russian writers turned their attention to the peasants who made up 80 percent of the population, Venetsianov began to chronicle peasant life in paint. These works were Romantic in the sense that they idealized peasant life and peasant work as noble and in harmony with the natural world, but they still managed to convey genuine emotions and authentic experiences of overworked peasants toiling in the fields. Many Romantic painters sought authenticity in an idealized premodern society, which they perceived to exist still in rural, peasant culture. The idea that the peasant and the medieval were unspoiled by modernity was very widespread in Europe.

Architecture

In architecture, Enlightenment classicism flourished alongside Romanticism during the first half of the nineteenth century: the neoclassical looked to Greek and Roman antiquity, and the Romantic neo-Gothic looked to the Middle Ages. Many architects of the early 1800s mastered both styles, not so much copying ancient or medieval structures as adapting them to the needs and tastes of the day. At the beginning of the nineteenth century the Roman vogue, firmly set by the French Revolution, reached its peak in Napoleonic Paris with triumphal arches, columns, and churches patterned after Roman forms. Yet by the second quarter of the nineteenth century neo-Roman was yielding to Greek revival, stirred in part by a wave of enthusiasm for the Greek independence movement. Often, the classical and Gothic were combined, with fundamental designs classical in their proportions, while decoration was medieval. The Houses of Parliament in London were Gothic in their spires and towers, but they also embodied classical principles of balance and symmetry. At other times the neo-Gothic and the neoclassical came into conflict.

At Oxford University two important new museums were built in the mid-nineteenth century in dramatically different styles. The Ashmolean Museum of Art and Archeology was built in the neoclassical tradition between 1839 and 1842. When a number of influential scholars began to argue for the construction of a museum of natural sciences as well as for the teaching of the natural sciences, those who saw in the sciences an attack on religion resisted both proposals fiercely. John Ruskin (1819–1900), the art and architecture critic, and Henry Acland (1815–1900), professor of medicine and main force behind the museum campaign, pushed for a museum that would link past and present, scientific knowledge and faith. The neo-Gothic, they argued, especially its ornamental style which was rooted in nature, would provide the essential blend of science, art, and faith that Ruskin and Acland saw at the heart of their enterprise. The neo-Gothic also embodied a national style in as much as it provided continuity with the great buildings of the nation's past and represented a time when religion was unsullied by secularism and materialism. Ruskin and Acland prevailed, and the Oxford University Museum of Natural History is considered one of the best examples of nineteenth-century neo-Gothic architecture.

St. Pancras Railway Station, London. George Gilbert Scott, completed 1876. Epitome of the Gothic revival in architecture: medieval Catholicism in service to secular modernity. (Hornsey Historical Society)

Religion and Philosophy

The Romantic religious revival was marked at the institutional level by the pope's reestablishment in 1814 of the Jesuit order, whose suppression in 1773 had been viewed as one of the great victories of the Enlightenment. Catholicism gained many converts among romantic writers, particularly in Germany, and the Protestants also made gains. Pietism found new strength in Germany and Russia. In England Coleridge vigorously defended the established church, while also introducing the new German idealist philosophy. Chief among these romantic German philosophers was G. W. F. Hegel (1770–1831). Like Kant in the eighteenth century, Hegel attacked the tendency of the Enlightenment to see in human nature and history only what met the eye. Human history, properly understood, was the history of efforts to attain the good, and this in turn was the unfolding of God's plan for the world. For Hegel, history was a *dialectical* process—that is, a series of conflicts. The two contending elements in the conflict were the *thesis*, the established order of life, and the *antithesis*, a challenge to the old order. Out of the struggle of thesis and antithesis emerged a *synthesis*, no mere compromise between the two but a new and better way—a combination that was another step in humanity's slow progress toward the best of all possible worlds. In turn, the synthesis broke down by becoming conventional and unproductive; it became locked in conflict with a new antithesis, and the dialectic produced another synthesis—and so on and on.

The dialectical philosophy of history was the most original and influential element in Hegel's thought; it would help to shape the dialectical materialism of Karl Marx. Still, Hegel was once even more famous as a liberal idealist. His emphasis on duty, his choice of Alexander the Great, Caesar, and Napoleon as "world-historical" heroes, his assertion that the state "existed for its own sake"—all suggest a link with authoritariansim. Yet Hegel foresaw the final synthesis of the dialectic not as a brutal police state but as a liberalized version of the Prussian monarchy.

Romantic Nationalism

The rise of the nation as a source of modern identity is one of the major innovations of the nineteenth century. Try to imagine a world without *nations*. Kingdoms, principalities, grand duchies, empires, and the like were defined by acknowledged borders, but each political entity contained a profusion of people with diverse local customs, languages, traditions, religions. Such diversity was assumed and accepted, even prized. Central and local governments demanded taxes from their poor and service from their elites, but no sense of unified action or purpose motivated them. Rulers required military service for an army ready to expand their territory and protect themselves from invaders, but no posters or propaganda of any kind encouraged people to fight for a unified political cause. People of a single village were so insulated that they distrusted visitors from neighboring villages even when they spoke the same language, planted the same crops, and practiced the same religion. Peasants on the Loire had more in common with peasants on the Rhine and the Volga than they did with anyone in Paris, Cologne, or Moscow. Before there were nations there were no International Olympics or soccer World Cups for peaceful competition among people fiercely loyal to a national team, there were no national flags or anthems.

Romanticism in the arts was everywhere connected with new ideas about the nation. The French Revolution and Napoleon's rise and fall awakened feelings of fear and pride all over Europe. Soon afterward, those feelings would come to be associated with the modern nation, and Europeans would develop a powerful modern ideology—nationalism. A number of historical paths could lead to the construction of a modern nation and a number of stages were required. The dissemination and discovery of nationalism, the changes it underwent, and different ways of interpreting and explaining the rise of nations and nationalism were critical elements in the revolutions of the 1820s and 1830s and will be important themes in the rest of this book. At the outset it is important to remember that nations as we know them did not always exist. Even the ingredients that go into making a nation—common culture or language, form of government, economic networks—were all as artificial as the boundary lines that divide plains and mountain chains on a map. The first stage of nationalism relevant here is the appearance of ideas about nationalism connected with Romanticism.

The French Revolution had given ordinary French men and women a belief that the government they supported was an entity they had created, which made it worth fighting for. Napoleon had shown how powerful a national political ideology could be—both militarily and in cultural terms. Political activists and intellectuals throughout Europe began to look to their nation's past in search of cultural uniqueness with which to generate the same kind of power, the same claims to independence. In the countries defeated by Napoleon and then responsible for his defeat, people began to take new pride in their contribution to their reemergence from foreign domination. In eastern Europe and the Balkans, feelings that would undermine the Austrian empire were spreading. Liberation movements discussed earlier were often motivated by new ideas about national sovereignty, in the Greek fight for independence from Ottoman Empire, for example, and in the Polish struggle against Russia. All these early nationalist movements were colored by Romanticism.

The belief that each nation is unique was related to the Romantic belief in the uniqueness of the individual. The desire to express that uniqueness in independence and national sovereignty was linked to the Romantic emphasis on personal expression. Like artistic Romanticism, nationalism was at first an intellectual movement confined to members of Europe's educated elite. Gradually nationalism spread through middle-class and lower-class society.

There are two very different ways of explaining the rise of nationalism in the nineteenth century. Some historians see nationalism as an emotional, almost mystical force and the nation as an entity *discovered* by people looking to the past. The Romantic return to the national past, though intensified by French expansionism, had begun before 1789 as part of the repudiation of the Enlightenment. These pioneers of Romanticism tended to cherish what the philosophes detested, notably the Middle Ages and the medieval preoccupation with religion. The German writer Johann Gottfried von Herder (1744–1803) developed one of the earliest theories of nationalism based on shared cultural heritage. Each separate nation, he argued, had its own distinct personality, its *Volksgeist*, or "folk spirit," and its own pattern of growth.

Stimulated by Herder, students of medieval German literature began to collect popular ballads and folk tales in search of a unique German national spirit. The most famous of these were the brothers Jacob Grimm (1785–1863) and Wilhelm Grimm (1786–1859), who began publishing their German folk tales in 1806. In 1782 the first complete text of the *Nibelungenlied* (Song of the Nibelungs) was published, a heroic saga of the nation's youth that had been forgotten since the later Middle Ages.

By putting a new value on the German literature of the past, Herder helped to free the German literature of his own day from its reliance on French culture. Herder himself was no narrow nationalist, however, and he asserted that the cultivated person should also study other cultures. So he also helped to loose a flood of translations in Germany beginning about 1800: of Shakespeare, of *Don Quixote,* of Spanish and Portuguese poetry, and of works in Sanskrit. Despite Herder's own respect for and interest in cultures other than his own, cultural nationalism did not lead to cultural pluralism in Europe, but rather to cultural competition as nationalists everywhere sought to prove their own cultural superiority.

In Herder's view, nations appeared naturally, organically, often after years of development and struggle; modern nations arose inevitably, and the peoples of modern nations developed national allegiances naturally, based on cultural and linguistic similarities and a desire for national independence. Recently however, historians have argued that nations and nationalism appeared for specific political reasons arising from the politics and economics of the nineteenth century. Herder thought nationalism was there to be discovered; recent historians have shown that nationalism was constructed. Modern politics, whether democratic or autocratic, required communication and commitment to a central, unified set of institutions and ideas. So intellectuals and political actors searched for common cultural heritage, common histories, and common ethnicities on which to base a claim for autonomy. But more often than not, these cultures and ethnicities had to be invented or exaggerated.

Herder's cultural nationalism had an especially profound impact on peoples whose cultures had been diluted by centuries of Austrian or Ottoman domination. Not only did German students go looking for their national spirit in peasant folk culture; Polish, Czech, Slovak, Serb, Slovene, Bulgarian, and Hungarian collections of folk tales and songs were also published in the first decades of the century. It soon became clear to would-be nation builders that a modern nation also required a modern literature, and that required a modern literary language, flexible enough for prose and understandable to all. In many parts of Europe, however, standardized national languages did not exist. Even in France, a country with relatively clear and relatively old national boundaries, only a small percentage of the population spoke French in the early nineteenth century. In Italy, the elite often spoke French better than Italian, and Italian itself was fragmented into dialects only barely intelligible to all. At the beginning of the century, Czech did not exist at all as a distinct language and had to be reconstructed altogether. In much of eastern Europe, official and vernacular languages differed, as did written and oral languages. German was the official language in the Czech lands; Latin and German were used by the nobility in Hungary; only peasants spoke Hungarian or Magyar, as it was then called.

Language reform, regeneration, and standardization served the goal of building a national culture as a prelude to national sovereignty. The languages we know today in eastern Europe are the result of Romantic language reform and standardization. As the Bulgarian Romantic nationalist, Ljuben Karavelov, wrote, "One may see a nation in its language, as in a mirror. . . . Every nation should take pride in its language . . . [and] purify it of foreign garbage." Thus the process of making nations as political entities was accompanied by the appearance of new dictionaries, grammars, new professional vocabularies, as well as new literary societies, an explosion in the publication of newspapers and magazines, all of which contributed to the flourishing of new literatures. The mid-nineteenth century also saw the revival or invention of popular festivals and rituals, flags, national anthems, and celebration of historical events. In all these cases, some elements of national cultures preexisted their nineteenth-century form, but especially in regions without a nation state, such as the German principalities of central Europe, or the non-German regions of the Austrian empire, some political driving force was necessary to activate the cultural ingredients of nationalism and mobilize them into a source of common identity.

The next major episode in the history of nationalism came with the adoption of individual national identities among young revolutionaries after 1830. Movements for national unification in Italy, Germany, and Poland, and for independence in Ireland, the Czech lands, Hungary, and elsewhere, established revolutionary brotherhoods under such names as Young Germany, Young Italy, and Young Ireland. Despite shared tactics and shared goals, when the young people of Europe sought "freedom for suffering peoples" in the new language of nationalism, they took the first steps toward replacing international appeals for democracy with nationalist justifications.

Giuseppe Mazzini (1805–1872) founded Young Italy as a secret society for mobilizing the people of the Italian peninsula to unite on the basis of shared culture and history and to fight for their independence and national sovereignty. Influenced by Herder, Mazzini looked to the glorious Roman past and believed that God intended Italy to be a united and free, democratic republic.

Mazzini's Young Italy linked national liberation with revolutionary individual liberty rooted in a selective reading of national history. This would be a powerful model for young intellectuals in other countries. Such movements appeared almost everywhere in Europe, but their "brotherhoods" and "societies" remained small in number. All of them were made up primarily of intellectuals or members of the educated elite, and all owed their growth to the opening of educational opportunity and social mobility that had begun during the Napoleonic period. Nationalist movements developed most rapidly where nationalist or democratic aspirations were most forcefully repressed: the Austrian, Russian, and Ottoman empires during the period of autocratic restoration after 1815.

Romantic nationalism had conservative as well as radical elements. The search for cultural uniqueness was motivated by a desire to establish cultural independence; but the search for that uniqueness in a premodern, suppos-

The Written Record

Mazzini's Romantic Nationalism

Giuseppe Mazzini was the foremost spokesman for liberal Romantic nationalism and the sovereign rights of individuals and nations. He formed an underground society, Young Italy, for the purpose of uniting Italy as a nation.

Young Italy is a brotherhood of Italians who . . . are convinced also that Italy is destined to become one nation. . . .

Young Italy is Republican and Unitarian.

Because all true sovereignty resides essentially in the nation, the sole progressive and continuous interpreter of the supreme moral law. . . .

Because our Italian tradition is essentially republican; our great memories are republican; the whole history of our national progress is republican; whereas the introduction of monarchy amongst us was coëval with our decay, and consummated our ruin by its constant servility to the foreigner, and the antagonism to the people, as well as to the unity of the nation.

Young Italy is Unitarian—

Because, without unity, there is no true nation. . . . National unity, as understood by Young Italy, does not imply the despotism of any, but the association and concord of all.

Both initiators and initiated must never forget that the moral application of every principle is the first and most essential; that without morality there is no true citizen; that the first step towards the achievement of a holy enterprise is the purification of the soul by virtue; that, where the daily life of the individual is not in harmony with the principles he preaches, the inculcation of those principles is an infamous profanation and hypocrisy; . . . and that Young Italy must be neither a sect nor a party, but a faith and an apostolate. . . . As the precursors of Italian regeneration, it is our duty to lay the first stone of its religion.

Giuseppe Mazzini, "General instructions for the members of Young Italy," in *Life and Writings*, vol. I (London, 1891), pp. 117–28.

edly more orderly world was a conservative reaction to social change. Herder's theory was intended to free all peoples from cultural hegemony to find their own cultural identity. But no country in Europe was entirely ethnically homogeneous; all existing countries and all regions hopeful of achieving autonomy contained significant ethnic minorities. The unintended consequences of Herder's cultural nationalism were to create both a pretext for excluding those minorities and a source of conflict between peoples of divergent cultures.

Those who see nationalism as constructed and those who see it as discovered would agree that nationalism arose, like so many other intellectual systems and artistic trends, to assist people in establishing a meaningful sense of their lives in a rapidly changing world. Just as poetry helped people create a viable individual identity in a new complex cultural world, identification with a nation gave an increasing number of people a comfortable sense of collective identity. National identity joined people with a community of similar people, distinguished them from others and connected them with a specific past and a hoped-for future.

Melodrama and Popular Romanticism

In the first half of the nineteenth century, Romantic nationalism and poetry were produced by and for Europe's small educated elite, but everyone in society needed help finding their moorings in a world undergoing radical change. In popular culture Romanticism had a counterpart in the new genre of melodrama. Once reason and secularization had proved inadequate to resolve the moral conflicts of modern society, people from all social backgrounds found guidance as well as entertainment in melodrama.

Melodrama's emotional extremism has often been derided as crude fare, pandering to coarse people needing simplistic, escapist entertainment. But in fact, melodrama, just like Romantic poetry and prose, arose as a rejection of Enlightenment rationality and the eighteenth-century culture of elegance and restraint. In both cases, artists chose to portray a more complex response to the new problems of the postrevolutionary, industrial, urban world. And just as Romanticism established new ways of seeing and portraying the world that would reverberate throughout the century that followed, melodrama quickly came to infiltrate almost every genre of popular cultural entertainment, including that produced by the educated elite. Beginning as a specific kind of staged drama in the 1790s, melodrama entered everyday life as a distinct mode of behavior. Like Romanticism or the realist novel (which often incorporated melodramatic elements), melodrama offered its audiences a means for making sense of lived experience.

Rousseau coined the term *melodrame* for the theatrical dramas to which he added music, but it was another Frenchman, René-Charles Guilbert de Pixérécourt (1773–1844), who produced the first corpus of plays that launched the genre's wild popularity. Pixérécourt, despite writing "for those who don't know how to read," as he put it, attracted the educated as well. He wrote about sixty melodramas, the first of which appeared in 1800 and earned the playwright praise as "the man who made all France weep." Borrowing from a tradition of boulevard theatrics, he used special light and sound effects to engage spectators on a fundamental sensory level that complemented the intense emotionalism of the situations that entangled his characters. His *Victor, or Child of the Forest* (1798) established the conventional properties identified with melodrama: an aesthetic of excess, a formulaic plot, false identities, suspense about whether virtue or vice would be rewarded, strained coincidences and the repeatedly delayed emergence of the truth, and a clear-cut binary moral system in which pure good does battle with pure evil, resulting in a happy ending where justice triumphs. Plots usually revolved around virtuous females preyed upon by cosmopolitan male villains, usually noblemen, in a narrative that exaggerated everyday realities and illustrated the instability of both gender and class relations. The formulas, the excess, the deceptively simple morality, and melodrama's mass popularity made intellectuals criticize melodrama as a simplistic form of escape for those who most needed to be enlightened. But these critics missed the point. Melodrama exaggerated the circumstances of time and place, of social mores and behavioral clichés, to be able to offer a uniquely accessible means for uneducated audiences to think about the rapidly changing world around them, to perceive interactions among politics, art, and everyday life. No more (nor less) escapist than the wanderings of Byron's Childe Harold or the trials of Shelley's Frankenstein, nor more flamboyant than Sand's racy novels, melodrama in fact shared several fundamental features with both Romanticism and realism. However, it was distinguished from the other two genres politically in that its requisite happy ending supported the conservative status quo in social relations, which Romanticism and realism critiqued.

Melodrama captured the uncertainties of life in revolutionary France, and later, industrializing Europe, where traditional markers of identity, social and political institutions, and religion were all undergoing fundamental changes. The popular plays offered models of virtuous behavior in confusing new situations produced by modern cities and their social life. From the French stage, melodrama raced across Europe, not because it was entertaining escapism but because it was entertaining engagement with the real world outside the theater. The plays appealed to audiences because they offered a moral compass in a secularizing world, because they engaged directly with the moral uncertainties of everyday life, in the context of emotionally satisfying dramatic thrills, with a tidy resolution at the end.

* * *

The early nineteenth century was a period of dramatic change. When the French Revolution suggested that the people could determine their own political destinies, artists and writers of all kinds looked inside themselves and asked what else people could do, think, say, and be. Such freedom brought a cultural explosion of personal artistic expression. It also brought anxiety. Artists and writers would help the people, including the very middle classes the Romantics contemptuously dismissed and commercial writers embraced, by offering new models of thought and behavior in a world of unimaginable flux. The peace that came in the aftermath of the French Revolution with the defeat of Napoleon brought massive unemployment, new governments, and new lines of political conflict, as some hoped to restore the past and others could hardly wait for the future. Romantic and melodramatic art and culture reflected the excitement and anxiety that came with change, and they offered news ways of seeing and behaving in the world. As the pace of economic change began to match that of political change, new challenges and new solutions would be necessary.

THREE

The Industrial Age Begins

When the Liverpool and Manchester Railway line opened in September 1830, a rival railway train drawn by the Rocket, the fastest and strongest of the locomotives, struck and killed William Huskisson, a leading British politician and an ardent advocate of improving transport and communication, who had underestimated the locomotive's speed. This, the first railway accident in history, was symbolic of the new age to come: powerful machines with unpredictable consequences benefited many, brought destruction to others, and transformed society far more rapidly than anyone had predicted. Each advance in industrial technology produced rippling effects that inspired new inventions and adaptations, shifted populations from village to city, and changed the ways people worked, creating new jobs and making others obsolete.

The industrial revolution was truly revolutionary. Although it took decades to occur and most people recognized its impact only after those decades had accrued, industrial production radically transformed the lives of millions of people, including those who lived far from manufacturing centers or were apparently unconcerned with the changes industry brought to society. The industrial revolution was not just a matter of economic growth and technological innovation. The changes that occurred were revolutionary because each innovation set off chain reactions of demand and innovation in related and unrelated fields of production. Those chain reactions were possible because the technology involved was continuously improvable, and therefore the processes of innovation and rising productivity developed a self-sustaining momentum of their own. The mechanization of one stage of textile manufacturing virtually demanded mechanization of the next stage; changes in the relationships between stages of production led to changes in the organization of labor, the structure of families, and the levels of nutrition and treatment of disease, which in turn provoked radical changes in domestic politics, international competition. Industry made possible the production of a multitude of new commodities in ever-increasing numbers. Today it is hard to imagine the world without the things that industry made. The word itself, "industry," comes from this period, as do such terms as factory, railroad, middle class, capitalism, scientist, and engineer. Industrialization would create new kinds of freedom: from velocity to modern democracy. It would also create new kinds of chains: factory work, modern warfare, imperialism, and the discipline and standardization of modern life. The industrial revolution changed the world in concrete ways and in the ways people experienced and thought about their lives.

How is this new world so different from the old preindustrial one? What is revolutionary about the industrial revolution?

The industrial world is first and foremost a world of *machines*. In the eighteenth century, the machine was still something exotic. Before the industrial revolution clothes were made by hand, even the fabric used to make clothes was woven by hand from thread that was spun by hand, made from plants that were sown and harvested by hand. Most people before the nineteenth century did not wear underwear—cotton was too expensive, wool too itchy, linen hard to wash. Machine production made cotton cheap and durable clothing became widely available. Before industrialization, if people traveled, they traveled by human or animal power—slowly. Few people had friends in distant cities, and relatives or acquaintances who moved might as well have disappeared. Preindustrial recreation meant no recorded music or amplified sound, no cinema. Entertainment usually consisted of live performances: theater for the rich, wandering minstrels for the poor. Religious services, holidays, community rituals provided the most common public performances. In the nineteenth century machines began to manufacture everything people used and to change the way traditional activities were done. Machine manufacturing made it possible for more of everything to be produced. The abundance of newly affordable objects is staggering: clocks, clothes, underwear, furniture, dishes, tools, toys, buttons, paper, and later in the century, photographs, books, newspapers, saddles, guns, tea and coffee, once luxury items, became widely available.

The industrial world is a world of *cities* rather than farms and villages. Increasingly, large numbers of people lived and worked closer together where they could be organized around the machines. Production was concentrated in factories, where new forms of work organization arose. Ultimately even rural areas were transformed by machine production and urbanization. On the national level, industry replaced agriculture as the main focus of the economy. The industrial world is also a world of clocks. Time, as a human construct, literally changed with the industrial revolution. People began to sleep and rise according to the clock because they needed to get to work, and they stayed at work, according to the clock. Machines are indifferent to the cycles of the sun, so factories could be run "around the clock." The sheer increase in the number of clocks produced shows how important they became. In 1800 about 350,000 pocket watches were made each year in Europe. In 1875, 2.5 million were produced. Industry literally increased the pace of modern life by increasing the speed with which people could travel and communicate with one another.

The industrial world introduced new forms of power and power relationships. Power over the machine offered power over other people. Factory owners who controlled the clock and the machine could regulate the lives of the people they employed in new ways. The first forms of worker resistance to factory labor were not strikes seeking shorter hours or higher pay, but machine-breaking rampages by workers taking out their frustrations on the symbols of all that industry did to change their lives. The concentration of people in cities and of workers around machines led to new kinds of mass mobilization for political activity. The rise of modern professional organizations, trade unions, even political parties is connected with changes in production.

Machines, cities, factories, and clocks are all real signs of new forms of life in the modern industrial world, in particular they are signs of human control over nature. The world of nature, where things are grown and hundreds of tasks are performed by animal or human power according to the natural cycles of seasons and days, was being replaced. As a result, industrialization changed the way people thought about themselves as individuals, as societies, and as part of a natural world. Throughout the nineteenth century, roughly two models of cultural outlook confronted one another. Industry and Enlightenment rationalism idealized practical, applied sciences, secular human nature, and the power of human beings to transform, organize, and improve the natural world. The Romantic, and later modernist, worldview idealized art above science, valued the intuitive, spiritual, even irrational sides of human nature, and responded to the industrial city aesthetically, either with horror at its unnaturalness or in thrall to the beauty of industrial forms.

Industrialization in Europe also marked one important stage toward the "globalization" of our own century. It bound the nations of Europe in dense international networks of trade and commerce and, by the second half of the century, had created an international capitalist economy. However, at the same time that Europeans came to depend on one another economically as never before, successful industrialization depended on the organization of discrete, powerful nation-states. Industry and nationalism would reinforce one another in the second half of the nineteenth century, as the people of different nations competed for everything from international power and colonies to athletic trophies. The rise of modern European power and wealth, Europe's ability to control colonies in far-flung parts of the globe, the Europeans' sense of cultural superiority, all are partly rooted in the industrial revolution.

The industrial revolution began in England, but there is little consensus among historians about its exact causes or why it occurred in England first. The ingredients that produced this dramatic transformation were many, but reliable statistics are few. Economic, technological, political, social, demographic, military, geographic, and cultural developments all came into play in complex combinations, which makes the process difficult to analyze and explain.

Recent research, however, has modified two long-standing beliefs about the industrial revolution. First, there was no clear, identifiable moment of "takeoff," but rather a relatively extended, steady period of accelerating growth; and second, England's experience was unique but it was unique in surprising ways. At the end of the eighteenth century, conditions similar to those that existed in England on the eve of industrialization existed in a number of other regions of the world. Those conditions include an agricultural revolution that supported a rapidly increasing nonagricultural population; an increase in family-oriented, hand-powered manufacture of luxury and common household goods; and the multiplication of market networks for distributing agricultural surplus and new manufactured products. In Holland, northern Germany, and the Atlantic coast of North America, as well as in China's Yangzi Delta, India's Gujarat, Japan's Kanto plain, and parts of the Ottoman Empire, an agricultural revolution had occurred, population pressure and domestic production had increased, technology had progressed, and commercial networks had spread in such a way that each of these regions was poised on the same brink as England.

On the other hand, industrialization, which is often imagined as a process occurring throughout Europe, did not occur anywhere in Europe in the same way that it occurred in England. Once machine production had been introduced and the urban organization of production begun in England, its various constituent parts were adopted or rejected by entrepreneurs and governments in other regions of the world in accordance with their respective prevailing needs. It could be imposed on weaker regions through economic coercion and military force. It could be imported by governments or privileged elites. It could arrive wholesale or piecemeal. England led the way, but because it was first, its industrial revolution was atypical. In the decades that followed, second- and third-generation industrial newcomers would fashion their own unique paths or have those paths fashioned for them.

Precursors: Agriculture, Demography, and Markets

There would have been no industrial revolution if not for the agricultural revolution that preceded it. Land was the single most important source of wealth in Europe before the industrial age, and it remained a major commodity and sign of status for the elite whose income derived from the hard labor of others. Even in the nineteenth century the majority of people in Europe earned their livelihood by working the land or paying others to do so. But crucial changes had taken place in the methods and organization of farming in the century before industrialization, which raised the productivity of farming, creating enough surplus food to support a large population who did not work the land.

Agricultural labor was backbreaking work, and the people who performed it rarely had much control over the product of their labor, being instead almost entirely dependent on the erratic rhythms of nature. Sometime in the seventeenth century a transition got under way that would finally begin to give farmers some control over nature. The agricultural revolution had three important components: increased agricultural productivity, based in part on the consolidation of landholdings, called "enclosure," the expansion of market-oriented practices in the countryside, and population increase. Together these changes would put pressure on the production of food and fuel that would lead to industrial revolution.

Before enclosure, most farms were tended communally and even the poorest families had access to common land. Communal farming provided a social safety net for everyone in a village, especially during years of crop failure and for those on the margins of society: the unmarried, the aged, and the disabled. But communal agriculture was risk averse. Poor farmers were unlikely to try planting new crops or to experiment with new technologies when they lived on the edge of subsistence. Wealthy landowners, on the other hand, began to see the profits to be made in producing for the market. In England and Holland, and then later across the Continent, landowners sought to consolidate their holdings, forcing small landowners to work for them for wages or pushing people off their land altogether. Enclosure was fiercely resisted in England, but Parliament supported it with legislation. By the late eighteenth century, governments in France and Prussia followed suit.

By contrast, peasant communal farming in Russia lasted into the twentieth century. Until then, the commune was seen as a convenient method for the state to maintain order among the many thousands of peasant villages spread across the vast territory of the Russian empire. In the eighteenth century, Peter the Great encouraged the peasant commune for ease of tax collection and in the nineteenth, Alexander II saw the commune as the institution most likely to maintain order during the upheaval that accompanied the emancipation of the serfs in 1861. Noble landowners in Russia had long produced grain for the international grain trade even when Russian peasants went hungry, but most of that agricultural production was carried out communally by peasants working as serfs or as wage laborers on noble estates. There was little incentive for noble landowners to try to increase production, and by the late nineteenth century, government officials came to believe that communal land tenure inhibited ambitious peasants from instituting more productive farming methods. Still, for most officials, control over the population trumped economic development. Only in 1906 were Russian and Ukrainian peasant farmers allowed to consolidate their holdings, leave the peasant commune, and set up independent family farms.

Consolidation, whether by large landowners or small, allowed farmers to produce enough surplus food to sell on the market. Here English agriculture had a distinct advantage. Landed elites, who owned 70 to 75 percent of the land during the eighteenth century, were motivated to increase productivity. Their power, wealth, and prestige depended on the size and success of their lands (unlike Russian noble landowners, whose prestige rested on size alone and who, until the very end of the nineteenth century, considered the actual work of farming, or even thinking about farming, to be beneath their station).

English farmers stood to benefit from renting out their land to the most productive, innovative, adaptive tenant farmers, who could increase productivity and pay rents. Well-off farmers looked for ways to increase the yield of their crops to make more money, which led to one of the major innovations of the agricultural revolution. In England and Holland first, farmers began to use a form of crop rotation that restored nutrients to the soil as the crops grew. Fields depleted of nutrients did not need to be left fallow but could be used continuously, and animals could be fed nutrient-rich crops like clover and turnips. The ability to feed more animals further increased the productivity of farming. Horses and oxen could work harder and on less food than people could; and the animals produced more and better manure for fertilizer, further increasing production.

In France, even where peasants won significant property rights during the revolution and grain yields were comparable to English grain yields, farming was carried out on family-owned farms, which were devoted to subsistence rather than surplus production. Any surpluses were spent on enlarging holdings rather than increasing productivity. French peasant agriculture was also much less adaptive than the tenant farms of England to rapidly increasing needs of urban populations for food and hand-produced manufactured goods. English agrarian productivity continued to grow into the nineteenth century as industrial cities increased demand for foodstuffs. Increased productivity meant that fewer hands were necessary to produce a surplus of food. Labor was released to go look for wage work in cities, and surpluses could be sold on the market. Cash profits could be used to buy foodstuffs produced elsewhere and transported to markets so farmers could specialize in the crops best suited to their region. Economies of scale and efficiency further increased productivity. In 1840 one economic historian has estimated, English male farmers produced 50 percent more than the French and more than twice that of Swiss, German, Swedish, or Russian agricultural workers.

Though demographic trends are notoriously difficult to explain, it seems likely that increased agricultural productivity in England in the eighteenth century supported a dramatic increase in the population. The increase in population then probably stimulated further productivity by increasing demand for food, clothes, and fuel. Between 1680 and 1820 the population of Great Britain more than doubled, from approximately 4.9 million to 11.5 million people. By 1850 it had nearly doubled again.

Other countries in both western and eastern Europe would catch up with England's rate of population growth in the later nineteenth century, and there too population growth probably increased demand for agricultural products and manufactured goods.

The benefits of population growth were unexpected, and in the late eighteenth and early nineteenth centuries, economists and social observers would fear a crisis of overpopulation. In earlier centuries, increased population usually strained people's ability to feed and clothe themselves to such an extent that population would begin to decline again. But during the industrial revolution a new momentum was created, in which increased demand could be

Estimated Population Totals and Percentage Growth

	Population (in millions)		Percentage growth 1680–1820
	1680	1820	
England	4.9	11.5	133
France	21.9	30.5	39
The Netherlands	1.9	2.0	8
Spain	8.5	14.0	64
Italy	12.0	18.4	53
Germany	12.0	18.1	51
Western Europe	71.9	116.5	62

Source: E. A. Wrigley, *People, Cities and Wealth* (Oxford, 1987), p. 216.

met by increased production. Extra hands were first put to work spinning and weaving, and later sent off to work for wages in industrial factories in towns and cities. In the early stage of industrialization, domestic production of manufactured goods helped ease the population pressure. As a result, the modern market entered the countryside through the door of the peasant's hut.

A significant increase in population and a rising demand for manufactured goods, especially cloth, during the eighteenth century forced people to look for new kinds of income. Merchants and contractors turned to individual peasant families to spin and weave at home in their own cottages, and the "cottage industry" was born. As the population continued to grow, the peasants' need for cash and cloth increased. Merchants throughout Europe began to organize systematic production of cloth. Entrepreneurs "put out" or provided raw materials; unmarried women ("spinsters") and surplus underemployed sons provided the cheap labor for spinning and weaving. The cottage industry became the "putting-out system." In some regions domestic putting-out manufacturing became the primary occupation, bringing a cash, market-oriented economy into villages all over Europe, in some regions even overtaking the primacy of farming. In England, unlike much of Europe, the entrepreneurs who supplied raw materials and sold finished goods on the market were not restricted by guild or other regulations.

The agricultural revolution was disruptive to traditional communities and practices throughout Europe. It brought unquestionable benefits, in that more people were better fed and had more cash to spend on increasing number of manufactured goods. By creating new markets and profits for agricultural goods, it produced the financial capital necessary to invest in new manufacturing enterprises. By making agriculture more concentrated and efficient, the agricultural revolution produced the human capital necessary to run the machines of those new enterprises. And the advance of the market economy along with the rising population created a market for simple manufactured goods. But at the same time, millions of people were forced out of their ancient communities and compelled to rely on the dubious charity of the government for their livelihood or to work for wages on large farms, or, increasingly, in the dark slums of towns and cities.

The agricultural revolution created some of the necessary resources for the industrial revolution to come, and it created problems whose solutions would spur industrial innovations. In particular, the expansion of the putting-out system and of domestic manufacturing of textiles created a large demand for raw cotton in a country with no extra arable land.

Momentum

Growing population, growing food supply, and growing cash supply led to demands for more food, jobs, and things. More people demanded more cloth for clothes; they wanted food transported to markets more quickly; and they needed new sources of energy to run the primitive manufacturing processes they had. The eighteenth century saw an energy crisis that was solved with machines that would revolutionize the production of energy and create momentum for the changes that fueled the industrial revolution. The technological process was revolutionary because mechanized forms of production created their own self-sustaining momentum. Innovations in one sector of the economy created demands in other sectors, which led to new innovations and new demands in yet other areas. The pace of innovation increased as a result of this unusual joint momentum between previously unrelated industries. The key areas of joint momentum were textiles, iron, and transportation, which together faced an energy crisis in the eighteenth century: English manufacturing could not keep up with demand, but at the same time was depleting accessible sources of timber and coal.

The textile industry was the first to exploit the potential of machine-driven energy. In many ways, the putting-out system was especially favorable for the spinning and weaving of cloth. It involved just enough steps for an entire family to work efficiently, and there was just enough demand for the cloth for it to be reasonably profitable. But there was a problem inherent in the system that, ironically, stimulated invention: spinning yarn was slower than weaving cloth. This meant that the women who spun worked continuously, while the men who wove spent some time sitting idly by, or even doing "women's work," waiting for the women to catch up. In 1767 James Hargreaves (1720?–1778), an illiterate carpenter and farmer invented (or perfected) the "spinning jenny," which made it possible to spin on eight spindles at a time instead of one. Improvements quickly made the jenny able to accommodate over a hundred spindles at a time, greatly multiplying the amount of yarn one woman could produce. The spinning jenny solved the problem of supply but created a problem of quality: the yarn spun on a jenny was too weak for weavers to use as both weft and warp. In 1769 Richard Arkwright (1732–1792) invented the water frame, which used water mill power to stretch the cotton before it was spun, resulting in much stronger yarn. Then in 1779 Samuel Crompton (1753–1827) combined the two devices in a new machine he called

Mechanized spinning in a Lancashire cotton factory, 1834. *(The Granger Collection)*

the "mule." The mule was three hundred times as productive as one spinning wheel, and it spun yarn of higher quality. The mechanization of spinning eventually concentrated production in factories or cotton mills. But the consequences of mechanized spinning did not stop there.

Innovations in technology that seem to be great achievements in retrospect are often a more mixed blessing at the time of their introduction. The changes produced by the new spinning machines disrupted many peoples' lives. When new machines make old skills obsolete or elevate people previously considered marginal, conflict and resistance are common. When spinning was mechanized, it quickly outpaced the weaving process. So much yarn was being produced in England at the beginning of the nineteenth century that weavers were in great demand. Their wages rose, and weavers became the elite of early industrial production. Then, in 1787, Edmund Cartwright (1743–1823) invented a power-driven loom, which could be operated by only a fraction of the number of existing weavers. By 1830 Britain operated more than fifty thousand power looms, and machine production made this superior but inexpensive cotton fabric available to people of all classes. But large numbers of highly skilled working men—the laboring elite—suddenly lost their jobs. Once cotton was exported in large volume—accounting for 70 percent of Britain's exports by 1850—the national wealth increased, opening up new opportunities and new jobs. But in the process large numbers of workers had their livelihoods destroyed and their dignity undermined by the power of a machine.

In the eighteenth century most of the machines that revolutionized textile production were powered by waterwheels in mills situated on the banks of

A Closer Look

A Day at the Mills

Frequently, entire families had to work as a matter of sheer economic necessity. A factory worker testified before a British parliamentary committee in 1831–1832:

At what time in the morning, in the brisk time, did those girls go to the mills? *In the brisk time, for about six weeks, they have gone at 3 o'clock in the morning, and ended at 10, or nearly half-past, at night.*

What intervals were allowed for rest or refreshment during those nineteen hours of labour? *Breakfast a quarter of an hour, and dinner half an hour, and drinking of ale a quarter of an hour.*

Was any of that time taken up in cleaning the machinery? *They generally had to do what they call dry down; sometimes this took the whole of the time at breakfast or drinking, and they were to get their dinner or breakfast as they could; if not, it was brought home.*

Had you not great difficulty in awakening your children to this excessive labour? *Yes, in the early time we had to take them up asleep and shake them when we got them on the floor to dress them, before we could get them off to their work; but not so in the common hours.*

What was the length of time they could be in bed during those long hours? *It was near 11 o'clock before we could get them into bed after getting a little victuals, and then at morning my mistress used to stop all night, for fear that we could not get them ready for the time. . . .*

So that they had not above four hours' sleep at this time? *No, they had not. . . .*

Were the children excessively fatigued by this labour? *Many times, we have cried often when we have given them the little victualling we had to give them; we had to shake them, and they have fallen to sleep with the victuals in their mouths many a time.*

Did this excessive term of labour occasion much cruelty also? *Yes, being so very much fatigued the strap was very frequently used.*

What was the wages in the short hours? *Three shillings a week each.*

When they wrought those very long hours what did they get? *Three shillings and sevenpence halfpenny.*

From *English Economic History: Select Documents*, ed. A. Bland, P. Brown, and R. H. Tawney (London: Clarendon, 1915), pp. 510–13.

rivers. Before the decades of the 1830s and 1840s, the increase in production and drop in the price of cotton cloth was gradual if dramatic. Another leap in productivity and fall in production costs was possible only when a new source of energy was applied to textile production. The centerpiece of this new form of mechanized production was the steam engine, developed and refined by James Watt (1736–1819) in the middle of the eighteenth century and first put to use in England. The steam engine not only would provide continuous momentum to textile production but would lower production costs and increase productivity in a whole range of other interconnected industries.

The development of steam-powered engines is a classic example of the interlocking relationship between different economic and technological processes in the industrial revolution. The agricultural revolution, which allowed more land to be cultivated for longer periods of time, created a market for sturdier and more expensive iron plows, iron horseshoes, and iron hubs for wagon wheels. Wood turned into charcoal, which had been used as fuel for smelting iron, was expensive and inefficient (and in England, rather scarce). So coal, which was plentiful in Britain, replaced wood. But as surface coal was exhausted, deeper and deeper mines had to be drilled, and these coal mines were continually being flooded by water. The mines were pumped out by hand or by horse-driven machines, which were also very inefficient. The first steam engines were invented to pump water out of the mines. But steam engines had been pumping mines for decades before their use became revolutionary and self-sustaining. It was only after coal smelting made iron production more efficient that iron could be used in the steam engines, which in turn allowed high-quality steam engines to be widely distributed, which coming full circle now, made coal mining more efficient, which made it easier to produce the coal to run steam engines.

Steam engines were adopted gradually even in England, but by 1800 efforts made to adapt the mule to steam-powered engines were successful and there were approximately twelve hundred steam engines operating in Britain. The steam-powered mule still required the attention of a skilled operator. The main introduction of steam power to textiles came after 1830, when Richard Roberts (1789–1864) developed an automatic steam-powered mule. Roberts, unlike the self-taught inventors Hargreaves, Arkwright, and Crompton, was trained as an engineer and machine maker. Over the next three decades, steam engines would be adapted to almost every industry, but it would be late in the century before it made water power obsolete. Between 1840 and 1850 the number of steam engines in Britain doubled, but even so, water power remained the basis of more than a third of Britain's woolen textiles industry and one-eighth of cotton production. One of the paradoxes of the industrial revolution is that the application of technological advances like steam power was matched by the technological improvement of water power. In France, where water was abundant and coal was scarce and expensive, steam engines were adopted even more slowly. In 1832 Benoit Fourneyron patented the precursor of the modern turbine engine. And in the 1860s, of the more than a hundred thousand industrial enterprises outside Paris and Lyons, 60 percent used water power.

Trains: The Ultimate Machine

The one machine that tied the whole process together, both literally and symbolically, was the railroad train. Steam, coal, and iron brought the railway

Capacity of All Steam Engines (in Thousands of Horsepower)

	1840	1850
Great Britain	620	1,290
France	90	270
Germany	40	260
Belgium	40	70
Czech lands*	20	n/a
Austria	20	100
Russia	20	70
Italy	10	40
Spain	10	20
Netherlands	—	10

*Ivan Berend, *History Derailed: Central and Eastern Europe in the Long Nineteenth Century* (Berkeley, 2003), p. 147.
Source: Carlo Cipolla, ed. *The Fontana Economic History of Europe: The Industrial Revolution*, vol. 1 (London, 1973), p. 165.

age. Coal powered the railways and the railways carried coal. Demand for railroad building stimulated coal mining and steel production, spreading steam engines throughout Europe and fueling the industrial revolution.

Though railways based on wooden rails were known from the sixteenth century, iron and steel rails made it possible to carry great weights and mount giant locomotives to pull long trains. Improved canals and hard-surfaced roads in Europe and North America had been important means of transportation for the early increases in trade and manufacturing. A Scot, John McAdam (1756–1836), had devised a means of surfacing (called "macadamizing") roads so that they could be traveled in all weather. But extraheavy shipments broke the road's surface, and increasing demand for such heavy materials as coal and steel called for a new form of transportation. George Stephenson (1781–1848) and others put the steam engine on wheels and created the modern locomotive. Coal-burning steam engines were far faster than horse-drawn carriages and canal boats. Soon railroads were popular means of transporting people as well as goods.

The first British railroad opened in 1825; the rest of Europe was not far behind. By the 1840s major railway-building projects were initiated in a number of European countries, and by the 1860s trains were making their way into the most remote parts of the Continent.

The lines differed in one important respect. In Britain, traffic for railways existed before they were built, and railroad companies could easily find private capital for finances. In western Europe, however, lines were built as traffic grew to require them, and private capital needed a government guarantee or subsidy, since the profit margin was precarious. In eastern Europe lines were built well before there was enough traffic to make them profitable, and state financing was necessary. Thus a varying pattern of private capital, state-aided capital, foreign capital, and state-controlled capital developed. In

A. F. Whiteley's viaduct, Manchester and Leeds Railway, 1845. The building of the railroads inspired a huge number of representations in everything from jig saw puzzles to series of lithographs to great paintings: most depictions show the railroad as a monumental achievement, the triumph of modern engineering and control over nature. Rarely is the actual work of construction depicted. When workers are shown, they are often tiny (like other humans and animals) in comparison with the great bridges and tunnels, as they are here. Note also the size and solidity of the stone and iron bridge, towering above the obsolete horse-drawn cart and canal boat. (Yale Center for British Art, Paul Mellon Collection)

Britain the railways boosted an industrial revolution already in progress; in western Europe the railways often sparked the revolution; in eastern Europe, to which the iron, rails, locomotives, engineers, and capital all had to be imported, the railway boom led governments into debt and threatened ruin while stimulating economic development.

Railroads were a major stimulus for new sectors of economic growth. They created new jobs in carriage-making, upholstery, and glass production. They required the construction of station houses, signal lights, and new bridges, and the engineering advances to build bridges strong enough to carry heavy trains on iron rails. New industries and factories appeared to support the production of trains, provide them with fuel, and move along the tracks bringing fuel and manufactured goods to new sites of production.

Railroads marked the first major change in speed since the Roman Empire. In 1815 Napoleon could move no faster than Caesar had, which is to say no faster than the horse. Just fifty years after Napoleon, the countries with the best railroads had superior military power as well. Rail travel contributed to

Spread of Railways: Length of Line Open (in Kilometers [1 km = 5/8 mile])

Country (1914 boundaries)	1830	1840	1860	1880	1900
Great Britain	157	2,411	14,603	25,060	30,079
Germany	—	469	11,089	33,838	51,678
France	31	496	9,167	23,089	38,109
Belgium	—	334	1,730	4,112	4,591
Austria-Hungary	—	144	4,543	18,507	36,330
Italy	—	20	2,404	9,290	16,429
Netherlands	—	17	335	1,846	2,776
Russia	—	27	1,626	22,865	53,234
Spain	—	—	1,917	7,490	13,214
Sweden	—	—	527	5,876	11,303
Romania	—	—	66	1,384	3,100
Serbia	—	—	—	—	929

Source: Carlo Cipolla, ed., *The Fontana Economic History of Europe: The Emergence of Industrial Societies*, vol. 2 (London, 1973), pp. 789–94.

Prussia's victory over France in 1870 and Russia's lack of railroads was a primary cause for its humiliating defeat in the Crimean War (see Chapter Seven).

By the middle of the nineteenth century trains had become symbols of the modern age. The power of trains was depicted in painting and, at the very end of the century, became the subject of the first motion pictures. Trains spread new ideas about the natural world. Some people complained that Europeans were losing their appreciation for natural beauty because trains moved them too quickly through the landscape. On the other hand, almost everyone could afford a train ride. The first trains carried only cargo, but soon people could ride too: the rich inside the carriages and the poor on top. By the 1840s even fourth-class carriages were covered and prices made cheap enough to get peasants to cities to work in factories. The new railroad stations were as important in changing the urban landscape as factories themselves. As Claude Monet shows in his series of paintings of the Gare Saint-Lazare in Paris, the play of steam, steel, glass, and light made modern railway stations objects of a strange new kind of beauty, and they were the forerunners of twentieth-century modernist architecture.

Even more than clocks and factories, the train helped spread modern concepts of time. Before the nineteenth century, every little town had its own local time, bound to differ by at least a few minutes from clocks in neighboring villages. In preindustrial society, local self-sufficiency made coordination unnecessary. But when trains began running by schedules, the need for uniform concepts of time appeared. Even in a small country like England, train conductors had to carry massive schedules that told only what local time their trains would arrive. Competing railroad companies had competing time schedules. When profit and efficiency became strong enough motives, this chaotic situation was systematized. In 1847 all British train companies agreed to coordinate their schedules around what was called Greenwich

A Closer Look

Railroads and the Modern Imagination

Early trains traveled at about 20 to 30 miles per hour, which was approximately two to three times faster than a horse-drawn stagecoach. The increase in speed (which reached 40–50 miles per hour in the 1850s) and the flat, straight, hard path needed for the rails created an entirely new experience of time and space. How did this experience change perceptions about nature and human nature?

Surely an inanimate power, that can be started, stopped, and guided at pleasure by the finger or foot of man, must promise greater personal security to the traveler than a power derivable from animal life, whose infirmities and passions require the constant exercise of other passions, united with muscular exertion to remedy and control them.

—*Anonymous, 1825*

It is really flying, and it impossible to divest yourself of the notion of instant death to all upon the least accident happening.

—*Thomas Creevy, after a ride on Stephenson's locomotive, 1829*

The flowers by the side of the road are no longer flowers but flecks, or rather streaks, of red or white; . . . the grain fields are great shocks of yellow hair; fields of alfalfa, long green tresses; the towns, the steeples, and the trees perform a crazy mingling dance on the horizon; for time to time, a shadow, a shape, a spectre appears and disappears with lightning speed: it's a railway guard.

—*Victor Hugo, 1837*

The communal journeys on trains and steamships, and the great gatherings of workers in the factories, inspire, to a great degree, the sentiment and habits of equality and liberty. By causing all classes of society to travel together and thus juxtaposing them into a kind of living mosaic of all the fortunes, positions, characters, manners, customs, and modes of dress that each and every nation has to offer, the railroads quite prodigiously advance the reign of truly fraternal social relations and do more for the sentiments of equality than the most exalted sermons of the tribunes of democracy.

—*Constantin Pequeur, 1839*

A providential event . . . which swings mankind in a new direction, and changes the color and shape of life. . . . Space is killed by the railways and we are left with time alone. . . . Just imagine what will happen when the lines to Belgium and Germany are completed and connect up with [French] railways! I feel as if the mountains and forests of all countries were advancing on Paris. Even now, I can smell the German linden trees; the North Sea's breakers are rolling against my door.

—*Heinrich Heine, 1843*

All cited in Wolfgang Schivelbusch, *The Railway Journey* (Leamington Spa, U.K., 1977), pp. 14, 23, 37, 56, 70–71.

mean time. By then, telegraphs existed to transmit the exact Greenwich time around the country instantly. Eventually Greenwich mean time became an international standard, as it remains today. But it took more than thirty years, until 1880, before even the whole of Great Britain adopted it. The United States followed in 1883, Germany in 1893; France held out until 1911. The domination of the Greenwich clock symbolized Britain's power: the first to industrialize was the first to control nature.

Steam-powered engines affected other forms of transportation including water transport, though at a less revolutionary pace. Robert Fulton's (1765–1815) steamboat, the *Clermont,* made a successful trip on the Hudson River in 1807, and soon paddle-wheel steamers plied the inland waterways of the United States and Europe. However, when the Scot Samuel Cunard inaugurated the first regular transatlantic steamer service (between Liverpool and Boston in 1840), the coal required for the voyage took up almost half the space on his vessels. Consequently, only passengers and mail went by steamship, most freight being handled by sailing ships. Finally, in the 1860s, the development of improved marine engines and the substitution of the screw propeller for the paddle wheel forecast the doom of commercial sailing.

Communications also experienced radical improvement. In 1840 when Great Britain inaugurated the penny post, a letter could go from London to Edinburgh at the cost of one penny, less than a tenth of the old rate. More dramatic was the utilization of electricity for instantaneous communication, beginning with the first telegraph message from Baltimore to Washington in 1844. Then came the first submarine cable (under the English Channel) in 1851, the first transatlantic cable in 1866, and the first telephone in 1876. This communications revolution was not limited to Britain. Belgium also used the turnpike principle, establishing all-weather roads financed by tolls, so that by 1850 most major centers were reachable even in the worst weather. The Ruhr River, made navigable by 1780, was tied in by roads and canals to the rest of Germany, France, and the Low Countries. But canals were frequently built too soon, before there was enough traffic to pay for them. It was the railways, which could transport goods, passengers, and armies, that truly transformed the Continent as they had Britain.

Why Britain?

The agricultural precursors and technological developments that transformed the British economy so dramatically would not have been enough to sustain economic growth and continuous innovation. Other factors came together to make Britain the launch site of industrialization: politics, natural resources, and established markets and economic institutions.

In Britain, the effects of the agricultural revolution came at the right time and in combination with other factors that differentiated it from most of the rest of the world. By the end of the eighteenth century Britain had the ingredients that would enable the rise of an urban, commercial, manufacturing society: surplus capital to invest in building new enterprises, a large and mobile labor force, which was accustomed to wage work either on farms or in the putting-out system, almost enough food to feed those workers and their employers, and a surplus of goods to be sold on expanding markets.

These conditions, however, were not unique to Britain. At the end of the eighteenth century the Yangzi Delta in China had undergone a similar agricultural revolution, with extensive specialization and production of luxury and common goods. A similarly stimulating potential crisis of increased population led to widespread trading between the Yangzi Delta and interior, less productive parts of China. The Yangzi also had extensive investment capital as silver from the New World became available. The Kanto plain of Japan, India's Gujarat, parts of the Ottoman Empire, as well as the Netherlands in Europe all also had relatively free and highly developed markets, trade with less developed regions, extensive hand and water-powered manufacturing, and commercialized and specialized agriculture. India's cotton industry was far more advanced than England's, especially in textile dyeing and weaving. Even in the early nineteenth century, British observers claimed that Indian iron bars were superior to English iron and less expensive.

Up until the very end of the eighteenth century, conditions in England were nothing special. Only in the first decades of the nineteenth century did its strengths really come into play. Economic historian Kenneth Pomerantz argues that the key difference between England and the rest of the world was its access to an enormous reservoir of underused resources in the Americas and its proximity to an abundance of coal. Just when Chinese regional trade was declining because the Chinese hinterlands began to become more self-sufficient and saturated with Yangzi commercial goods, Britain was able to take greatest advantage of its own vast overseas hinterland for fuel, food, and raw materials like cotton. C. A. Bayly argues that South India, like China, experienced a form of equilibrium, in which regional economies traded people, resources, and capital without entering the self-sustaining momentum created by unequal trade advantages and technological improvability. In the Ottoman Empire, political conflicts between regional efforts at economic autonomy and centralizing efforts at control hamstrung commercial development. In the relatively long run, British economic conditions benefited from specific forms of disequilibrium and from its access to the resources of the Americas, but in the short run, political and social contexts were also important in placing Britain's proto-industrialization in a more advantageous position over the rest of Europe and Asia.

Britain had strong geographical advantages. Water protected the islands from invasion and political instability. Inland water routes provided an important transportation network, augmented by an extensive system of canals. And transportation around Great Britain was unhindered by regional tariffs as in France or Germany. Mineral geography also favored Britain: its coal deposits were great, conveniently located, and therefore relatively less expensive to excavate and transport.

In the political sphere, Britain also had advantages over the rest of the world. At the simplest level, while France was undergoing revolution and then waging war across continental Europe, Britain was politically stable and far less disrupted by war, occupation, and revolution. Security of this kind allowed for risky, innovative activities. In addition, England had broken free of restrictive feudal social structures and absolutist monarchy a full century before any other European country. Throughout the eighteenth century Parliament had authority to decide a wide range of economic issues, reaffirming the elite's commitment to property rights and public order. Furthermore, since the end of the seventeenth century, landowners had control over minerals found under their land, giving them an automatic interest in what would become the fuel of industrialization. These facts had an impact on the way people (especially people with surplus wealth for investment capital) thought about themselves and their society. There was in Britain a long-established tradition of aristocratic elites—and not just middling commercial classes—seeking to improve their lot in the world, rather than being content to enjoy the privileges of status. In England this notion of improvement and profit seeking had become a part of government policy. The government encouraged and protected economic development. It was in the interest of both the British monarchy and the British parliament to increase the country's wealth.

Political stability and economic activism also produced the first professional public finance system and financial institutions. A stable tax collection system and a sense of public service among the elite who were represented in Parliament minimized resistance to taxation. The exploitation of new developments required a constant flow of fresh capital. From the first, the older commercial community supported the young industrial community. The Bank of England, founded in the late seventeenth century, offered a stable and free-flowing source of financing. Banks further assisted economic expansion by promoting the use of checks and bank notes in place of coins. During the Napoleonic wars, when the shortage of coins forced some British millowners to pay their workers in goods, the British government empowered local banks to issue paper notes supplementing the meager supply of coins. But whenever financial crises occurred—and they came frequently before 1850—dozens of local banks failed, and their notes became valueless. Parliament therefore encouraged the absorption of shaky banks by the more solid institutions, and in 1844 it gave the Bank of England a virtual monopoly on issuing banknotes, thus providing a reliable paper currency. It also applied the principle of limited liability (indicated by "Ltd" after the name of British firms). Earlier, the shareholders in most British companies were subject to unlimited liability, and they might find their personal fortunes seized to satisfy the creditors of an unsuccessful enterprise. The practice of limiting each shareholder's liability to the face value of that person's shares encouraged investment by diminishing its risks. By contrast, in eastern Europe and Russia, the Middle East, Asia, and Africa, private property was much less secure. Financial institutions and commercial companies, being less open, and more secretive, operated in an environment of far less public trust.

Finally Britain had force and the willingness to use force to protect and exploit its resources. The value of its Caribbean slave labor production in the eighteenth century stimulated constant improvements in shipbuilding as well as systems of military readiness for maintaining the navy's ability to protect the islands. When international trade became a possibility, Britain was best prepared to take advantage of it.

By the mid-nineteenth century, the tangible signs of Britain's economic predominance were evident on every hand—in the teeming docks and thriving financial houses of London; in the mushrooming factory and mining towns of the Midlands, the north of England, and Scotland; and in other quarters of the globe as well. But most striking of all in the comparison of these early stages of industrialization are the similarities with other world regions: Britain, much less Europe as a whole, had no monopoly on economic dynamism. Britain's exceptional success at moving into machine production was based on a largely accidental combination of a multitude of factors that were present in many other parts of the world, though not concentrated in any other single country.

The international economy also favored Britain in the early stages of industrial development. The mechanization of the cotton industry was propelled by a huge and growing worldwide demand for cotton and other manufactured goods and by the free labor extracted from slaves. The willingness of Europeans to kidnap or purchase, transport, and employ slaves from Africa funded the industrial revolution in Europe, though historians still debate the exact role the slave trade played in European industrialization. High profits were also were made possible by the availability of cheap raw materials, which could be transported to Britain, turned into manufactured goods, and transported to international markets. During the two centuries prior to mechanization of cotton production, Britain had gained control of an economic system known as the Atlantic Triangle. Other countries traded and shipped in the Atlantic, but none achieved power and profit to equal Britain's. British ships took slaves from the coasts of West Africa across the ocean to ports all over the Americas. The money made on the slave trade was used to buy raw materials, especially cotton, to take back to Britain to be manufactured and then sold on the world market. World demand for cotton stimulated technological innovations in cotton production, but that demand could not have been met if the Atlantic economic network had not existed. The Atlantic Triangle worked because of the relative underdevelopment of Africa and the Americas for the interlocking economic relations that the British had developed and exploited.

Britain's cotton industry became so dominant in the nineteenth century, and its manufacturers so ruthless, that it could destroy competitors, even when the competition's product was of higher quality. When British cotton production boomed at the end of the eighteenth and beginning of the nineteenth centuries, Britain simply shut down cotton trade with India. Before this, India's cotton industry was the most productive in the world. The Indian textile industry was devastated without British demand, and Britain could exploit the demand for cotton that already existed.

This was a major turning point in European and global economic history. Until the industrial revolution, European countries had always imported more from Asia than they had exported. Until the early nineteenth century India and China had their own self-sufficient cultures and economies. There was little demand for European goods in return for the spices, silks, jewels, and cottons sent west from Asia. The deliberate destruction of the Indian cotton industry was an important step in the British domination of India and opened the way for Britain to colonize other regions of Asia. China held out against European domination, but only until European money and guns forced it to open to trade in the mid-nineteenth century (see Chapter Nine). The British were determined to maximize their profits by making use of their competitive advantage. In both Europe and in the rest of the world, Britain would act to undermine protective tariffs elsewhere, prevent competition with its products, and exploit weaker economies. Cheap British goods dominated Continental markets; advanced British machinery was patented and even after the patents lapsed could not be easily adapted or replicated everywhere. Through a combination of force, threat, diplomacy, and commerce, Britain sought to maintain its economic lead.

Finances, markets, political stability, fuel, a surplus of food, mobile labor that was cheap or free, investment capital, and a moral system that condoned the exploitation of slavery, no one of these factors was enough to launch an industrial program of sustainable innovation and growth with revolutionary consequences. Britain had the right combination at the right time.

The Challenge of Industrialization in Western Europe

In the first half of the century the British industrial revolution could be neither ignored nor escaped. People from all over Europe traveled to Britain to see the miracle for themselves. "I am here in the center of the most advanced industry of Europe and of the Universe," wrote one young French textile entrepreneur visiting in 1842. And according to Friedrich List, a German liberal activist and writer who linked industrial progress with cultural and politics, "Industry is the mother and father of science, literature, the arts, entertainment, freedom, useful institutions, and national power and independence." Further east, the absence of economic growth discouraged István Széchnyi and Miklós Wesselényi, two young Hungarian aristocrats traveling west in 1822. Wesselényi found the filthy, bleak, factory towns so deplored by Romantic poets to be more appealing: "One glass factory, coal mine, and ironworks next to the other. The entire area covered by fire and smoke like the scenery of the Last Judgment. . . . The steam engines are used everywhere, and they are exquisite." On returning home, Széchnyi wrote a book entitled *Credit*, became an advocate for industrialization, called for the abolition of feudal privileges and restrictions, and established the first steam mill in Hungary.

Britain came to the continent in numerous forms. To maximize profits and maintain its competitive edge, Britain exported manufactured goods, especially cheap cotton, machinery, expertise, and entrepreneurs. The first mech-

Raw Cotton Consumption, Approximate Annual Averages (in Thousands of Metric Tons)

Country	1801–1814	1815–1824	1825–1834	1835–1844	1845–1854
Great Britain	31.8	54.8	105.6	191.6	290.0
France	8.0	18.9	33.5	54.3	65.0
Russia	0.9	1.0	1.8	6.1	21.5
Austria	—	—	6.8	14.3	26.5
Germany	—	—	3.9	11.1	21.1
Sweden	—	—	—	1.1	3.1

Source: Carlo Cipolla, ed., *The Fontana Economic History of Europe: The Emergence of Industrial Societies*, vol. 2 (London, 1973), p. 780.

anized textile factory in Bohemia was established by an Englishman in 1801; two Englishmen brought wool spinning machines to Moravia in 1802. In France, British industrial spies posing as mechanics, engineers, and entrepreneurs broke laws against sharing technology to bring the new spinning jenny and water frame across the Channel. In 1843, when such arrangements became legal, British industrialists imported machinery to France to set up ironworks and gasworks.

Once Britain showed the profits to be made in industry, people everywhere had to decide whether and how to respond. In Europe, and later in Asia and Africa, people like Széchnyi and Wesselényi welcomed industrialization and sought to mimic Britain's achievement. But everywhere industry took its own time and its own form based on local conditions, histories, cultures, and politics. Everywhere industrializers would come into conflict with those who sought to preserve the indigenous and the traditional, or simply to resist outsiders. Everywhere new people would benefit, and new hierarchies of geography and class would appear. Many Europeans saw industrialization as inevitable, as central to what they thought of as modern. They might deplore its impact, but advocates of industry were more disdainful of the nonindustrial world around them, which they saw as "backward" and "primitive." As Wesselényi put it in 1822 watching the frenetic activity on the London docks, "I feel like a small-town tradesman in his Sunday suit, ludicrously stiff and afraid to move." But others saw British industry as an assault on national or "natural" traditions and cultures and tried to minimize its impact.

No other region possessed all the factors that made industry so profitable and transformative in Britain; everyone else was in (at least) second place. All industrializing societies, therefore, had one feature in common: competition with and catching up to Great Britain. By the 1830s, when the first signs of continental industrialization were becoming visible, Britain had had a fifty-year head start. Its cotton industry was almost entirely mechanized; its iron production output exceeded that of the rest of the world combined; and the opening of the first railway lines in 1825 and after provided a powerful boost that led immediately to advantages for British industrialists.

This unevenness of development had a profound and lasting impact. Industrialization would always be a *regional* process, with an infinite number of regional comparisons and variations. Even in Britain and the most industrialized countries, industry intersected with traditional agrarian economies or other nonindustrial ways of life. This was true *within* countries, where wealthier, industrialized sectors would dominate poorer agrarian ones, and where rural–urban conflict would become increasingly acrimonious; and it was true within Europe as a whole. Wherever industry flourished, the distinctions between industrial and nonindustrial became more pronounced, whether within or across national boundaries. Regional economic distinctions would become sharper as the advantages of industrial wealth and power became clear.

In the first half of the nineteenth century, continental Europe remained predominantly agrarian. But everywhere in Europe, people knew the world was changing.

France

Industrial growth took place in France in the first half of the nineteenth century but with a much smaller role for the mechanized, factory-oriented production pioneered in Britain. This made it seem to earlier historians that France experienced no industrial revolution until much later in the century. But in fact, rates of per-capita economic growth during this period were high. France did not have the same demographic pressures as England, so agriculture could become more productive without creating a large, mobile, factory-bound labor force. As a result of slower population growth, the demand for mass-produced goods that fueled the British textile industry was much lower in France; nonetheless between 1806 and 1851 French rural economic productivity increased by about 29 percent per capita. In France economic growth combined mechanized industries, to meet lower but still considerable demand for cloth, with a great expansion of existing handicraft manufacturing and improved agricultural productivity.

French artisanal production had been responsible for a large percentage of Europe's luxury goods. And as one eighteenth-century defender put it: "Our merchandise . . . is sought after all over Europe for its taste, its beauty, its finesse, its solidity, the correctness of its design, the perfection of its execution, the quality of its raw materials." For some decades, at least, French furniture, jewelry, tapestries, silk, and porcelains would be enough to spur growth and make France the second biggest economy in Europe. But mechanization of textiles and heavy industry also made inroads in France.

Mechanized textile production increased fivefold between 1820 and 1860, and the mechanization of woolen production was even more noticeable, competing easily with British exports. Railroads also spread quickly in France. Locomotives were entirely imported until 1838; in 1842 French locomotive production equaled the number of those imported and by the 1850s importation had stopped and France was exporting its own locomotives to Italy,

Spain, and Russia. By midcentury, French industry was no longer dependent on British imports.

French industrialization highlights both the extreme degree of British advantage and the possibilities for success at a slower pace. But if France had become an industrial power, it was far from being an industrial country in the first half of the century. Seventy-five percent of the population was still rural and predominantly agricultural in 1851. And even the majority of industrial workers (about three-quarters) were employed in establishments with fewer than ten workers. Increased productivity on farms and artisanal workshops along with a small but successful mechanized industrial sector made France competitive with Britain in the early stages of European industrialization, but these factors would all become liabilities later in the century, when there were more players and harsher rules.

Germany

German industrialization would become the economic miracle of the second half of the nineteenth century, but there were signs of what was to come before 1850 as well. A sleepy village like Moabit in Prussia could be transformed by the presence of two large machine works. In Leipzig's suburbs, twenty-three new manufacturing enterprises appeared before 1850, including two textile mills, a steam-powered rolling mill, a gasworks, a railroad yard, and a boxcar plant.

Railroad building, as everywhere, spurred production in coal, steel, and related industries. This was apparent to municipal leaders and investors in the 1840s, who advocated railroad building as a way to create jobs for the growing population. The first line, all of 6 kilometers long, opened in 1835. But this was quickly followed. By 1850 German states, cities, and industrial sites were linked by 5,875 kilometers of track, more than twice the amount in France. But while industry grew, especially after the 1830s, it grew slowly and in scattered locales. As in France, the numbers of people engaged in putting-out manufacturing also grew: from 1 million to 1.5 million between 1800 and 1850. Unlike France, however, the population grew faster, and there were not enough manufacturing jobs for all the men and women who wanted them. The number of weavers grew from 315,000 in 1800 to 570,000 in 1850, but 90 percent of those worked at hand-operated looms. Artisans found it increasingly difficult to move up from journeyman to master, and everyone found it difficult to compete with cheap British imports; yet industry had not expanded sufficiently to absorb the underemployed. The mechanization of textile production was partial, regional, and socially disruptive. So, for example, new textile centers appeared in the Rhineland for wool, silk, and linen production. In many of these industries, spinning was mechanized, while weaving was still done by hand. But even the partially mechanized Rhineland production depressed demand for Silesian linen, throwing an entire region's skilled artisanal workers out of work.

During this period Germany lacked Britain's political unification and stability, its large store of coal, and its control over the international raw materials trade. But the main factors were in place for rapid expansion of industry: desire was spurred by British competition and supported by imports of British technology, and investment capital existed, as shown by private investment in railroad building, as well as a mobile, skilled labor force.

Italy

Italy should have entered the nineteenth century with everything necessary for modern industry. It had a long history of trade, finance, and especially extensive silk textile production. But its resources were concentrated in a few regions (Piedmont, Lombardy, Liguria, and Campania); and it shared Germany's lack of political unity, which weakened both policy making and concerted commitment to industrialization. Urban and rural poverty, deeper than in France or Germany, weakened demand for mass-produced goods. Communications were undeveloped, especially in the south. The wealthy were uninterested in investing in industry, and national fragmentation made it more difficult to devise a coherent policy of railroad building. Despite these disabilities, some industry survived and flourished and provided the basis for further development in the last third of the century. Flour milling was mechanized. Locomotives were produced in Naples, steam engines in Genoa; printing presses and farm equipment were made in Turin, Milan, and Naples; and the paper industry was established in Naples, Tuscany, Lombardy, and Piedmont. Lombardy saw growth in cotton spinning. Overall, the north would be far more industrialized than the south.

The Challenge of Industrialization in Eastern Europe

Austria

Discussion of Austrian economic development is complicated by the difficulties of defining the area under discussion. To some extent industrialization, where it occurred, was a result of policy made in Vienna and concerned the whole of the Habsburg realm, and to some extent each region must be discussed independently. In the aggregate, industrialization across the Austrian empire was relatively feeble, its policies divided, and its financial situation precarious. Nevertheless, there were pockets of economic growth and industrial development, alongside regions where resistance to change inhibited industrialization.

If we first look at the whole Habsburg realm, one of the main factors was the government's attempt to isolate the empire and make it self-sufficient. Remember that the main political power during this period was Metternich, whose overriding interest in preventing political change and suppressing political dissent had meant the closing of Austria to intellectual movements of western Europe. In Vienna, economic policy makers hoped to exploit the low wages and abundant raw materials of the eastern portion of the empire to fuel the industrialization of the western portions. But this policy limited the ability of food suppliers to find the best markets and maximize their profits, hindered manufacturers from selling goods outside the country where there was greater demand, slowed railroad growth, and in general made Austria less competitive internationally.

Railroad growth was also hampered by Metternich's desire to build primarily strategic rather than commercial railroad lines. In addition to politics, Austria suffered from the French preference for high-quality, traditional handicrafts. Viennese shawls, gloves, shoes, silks, and Bohemian glass were all of the highest quality. Frustrated entrepreneurs complained that Austria produced for the very rich or the very poor (luxury goods or shoddy textiles and ceramics), while Germany produced for the middle classes (high-quality textiles, earthenware, porcelain, leather, instruments, and machinery). In every index of growth, Austria lagged behind the other second-generation industrializers: France, Belgium, and Germany.

The most important reason for Austria's relatively poor showing was its financial weakness, which limited credit. The Austrian National Bank made credit available only to the wealthiest clients, which effectively prevented risk-taking entrepreneurial activity. Private banks filled the void, most famously that of the Rothschild family, but they could not meet the need for loans that an industrializing economy required. Furthermore, state expenditures on the military drastically curtailed spending on economic development. Metternich's fear of revolution and the expensive foreign policy he practiced to prevent it brought Austria to the brink of financial collapse. By the late 1840s, when railroad building and mechanized cotton spinning were expanding elsewhere, Austria was reduced to begging for a large loan from the Rothschild financiers to keep the government itself afloat. Metternich told Solomon Rothschild that they both stood on the brink of the abyss: "If the devil fetches me he will fetch you too."

Despite such weaknesses, individual regions of the Austrian empire were among the strongest early industrial economies of eastern Europe. Western Austrian provinces and the Czech lands—Bohemia and Moravia—accounted for seven-eighths of the industrial output of the empire and helped stimulate growth in agricultural productivity in the eastern regions.

The Czech lands had well-developed putting-out manufacturing of textiles in the late eighteenth century, as well as nearby coal deposits and considerable glass and iron production. In 1798, out of a total 4 million inhabitants, almost 700,000 people were involved in textile production and 200,000 in glass, iron, and paper industries. Investment came from local well-off peasants and from merchants as far away as Saxony and Silesia, as well as England and Holland. The Czech nobility was also atypical in their investment in textile, glass, and iron proto-industrial production on their estates. In many cases they exploited serf labor and their rights to serf products to reap especially high profits. For raw materials, often they had to look no further than their estates, where coal, wood, wool, timber, and agricultural products were plentiful. The share of aristocratic investment in Czech industrialization (as opposed to joint stock and limited liability companies or state sponsorship) was extraordinarily high and would remain so through the nineteenth century. In the 1830s almost a third of all coal mines and half of all sugar refineries were owned by noblemen; in the 1870s a full two-thirds of industrial enterprises were owned by noble families. Austrian state policy discouraged joint stock companies by taxing them at a much higher rate than personally owned enterprises. Noble industrial investment was not uncommon in other Habsburg lands (Poland and Hungary, for example), but Czech noble industry differed from the others in having at its disposal a developed putting-out system.

Second-generation industrialization in the Czech lands, therefore, got an early start: steam engines were introduced in the 1820s and by 1841 there were 156 steam engines there. Combined Czech and Austrian horsepower ranked fifth behind Britain, France, Germany, and Belgium. Cotton factories contained 435,000 spindles in 1828 and twice that many in 1841. The Czech cotton industry grew rapidly between 1800 and 1850, though it was still primarily powered by water. Railway construction began in the 1830s, which further benefited development in the Czech lands as there were rich coalfields in Ostrava, Kladno, and Podkrušnohorí. The first railroad lines radiated out from Vienna and were financed by the Viennese Rothschilds. By 1850, the Habsburg realm was linked by more than 4,500 kilometers of track, placing it fourth in Europe.

In contrast to Austrian provinces and the Czech lands, Hungary struggled unsuccessfully to introduce industry in the first half of the century. The Hungarian Diet began to debate economic reform as early as 1825, but ran into entrenched feudal elites, lack of modern credit institutions, and serfdom. Lajos Kossuth (1802–1894), soon to become a central political figure in Hungary, called for a tariff system that would protect Hungarian products from stronger Austrian–Czech economies, but in 1841 there were only nine steam engines in all Hungary. A few financial institutions were created—a commercial bank in 1841, a railway line beginning to link Budapest with Vienna in 1846—but successful industrialization did not occur there until the second half of the century.

The Balkans

The Balkan provinces of the Ottoman empire faced even more daunting obstacles to industrialization. In medieval times, Ottoman occupation had brought stability and settlement to nomadic cultures in southeastern Europe, repopulating sparse regions and encouraging cultivation of underused land. The Muslim Ottomans were relatively tolerant of ethnic and religious differences and offered incentives to local peoples to convert to Islam. Those incentives included bureaucratic positions as local representatives of the sultan in the European colonies.

Ottoman influence began to have increasingly negative effects, however, as Ottoman authority in the Balkans faltered in the eighteenth and nineteenth centuries. Local governors took advantage of the power vacuum to increase their grip on local populations and secure their power. They recruited their own armies, fought each other, and raised taxes to levels that were disastrous for the economy. At the same time, they gave up on providing basic services like road building, protection against crime and banditry, and famine relief in hard times. Not only was there was no population pressure to kick-start agricultural innovation or cottage industry, there was underpopulation. Arable land lay fallow and unoccupied through much of Ottoman Europe.

Some market-oriented farming appeared in Bulgaria, Macedonia, and northern Greece on the outskirts of regional commercial towns. In the late eighteenth and early nineteenth centuries in Bulgaria, a region that escaped the worst Ottoman warlordism, cottage industry appeared, stimulated by demand for cloth for military uniforms. With minute exceptions, there was no railroad building until the 1880s, no banking until the 1860s, and no foreign investment until the latter part of the century. In the Balkans, sparse settlement, banditry, warlordism, rapacious fiscal policies, and famine combined to slow economic growth.

"Core–Periphery" Industrialization

Eastern Europe was not left out of the industrialization process, but its role was secondary, dependent, and far less profitable than in the west. As people in industrializing countries moved from farming to factory work, food production declined and production of consumer goods increased beyond local demand. East Europeans exported food and raw materials to the industrial powers and imported cotton clothes and mass-produced goods back again. In some cases, where there was the highest demand and the least poverty, this led to modest economic growth in nonindustrial or proto-industrial regions, but it was a dependent growth, not capable of sustaining the kind of economic momentum that so sharply distinguished industrial economies. Such a dependent dynamic also characterized the Scandinavian and Mediterranean economies. Sweden and Spain exported iron ore to the foundries of England, France, and Germany. But not until the end of the century would such exports fund railroad building and domestic development. Until they could begin to mechanize their own production, these regions were dependent "peripheral" economies. Economic historians Ivan Berend and György Ránki see a classic "core–periphery" relationship at work here. The European economy at this time was not a mutually beneficial integrated system but a fundamentally unequal one, in which the weaker periphery was exploited to benefit the core: "its foreign trade, balance of payments, and production development tied to, influenced by, and subordinated to the core countries." This core–periphery relationship was repeated within some countries, where powerful urban core economies like London and Vienna created dependencies of their surrounding rural peripheries. The Russian empire affords a complex example because it played periphery in relation to the west European core, while at the same time the Russian metropole played core to its own imperial possessions.

Russia

In Russia (and parts of eastern Europe) traditional communal agriculture was a brake on industrial development. This was true to a lesser extent in parts of western Europe as well, but in the East, it was rare to find enclosed, private property, cultivated or managed by individual families. Peasants worked in varying degrees of servitude or as outright serfs throughout much of the Austrian and Russian empires in the first half of the century. In Russia there was increasing pressure to abolish serfdom, but the calls were more often based on humanitarian than economic grounds, and they came from the intelligentsia rather than the landed elites. The government of Nicholas I intentionally chose not to industrialize for political and cultural reasons. Russian wealth and power and the Russian elite's identity had always been rooted in land ownership. In the 1830s and 1840s, there seemed no reason to gamble on a risky transformation. The overwhelming majority of Russians lived in the countryside and earned their bread by working the land or, in the case of the noble serfowners, living off those who worked the land. Industrial cities in western Europe were already scenes of working-class discontent and open protest, and Russian officials were loath to flirt with the new dangers of proletarianization. And despite all the potential advantages of railroad building, tsarist officials considered railroads dangerous because, according to Nicholas's minister of finance, Egor Kankrin (1774–1845), the mobility trains afforded would make people hard to control. All these decisions would have devastating consequences during the Crimean War, when Russia was unable to mobilize and transport men and materiel to battlefields on the Crimean peninsula. Russia's defeat in that war led directly to the abolition of serfdom and eventually to industrialization.

Nonetheless in the early nineteenth century there were scattered pockets of industrialization in Russia, which should not be overlooked. Russia had some of the biggest mechanized textile factories in the world in the 1830s; by 1861 Russian factories were operating 2 million spindles and several thousand mechanical looms. This was only one-tenth the number of British spindles and half that of France, but Russia was sixth in world textile production. Quantity did not, however, equal quality, and there were no lucrative foreign markets for the inferior Russian cotton. Furthermore, Russia's cotton production was dependent on imports of English yarn and U.S. raw cotton via England, which added to the industry's precariousness. Metals had an equally mixed record. In the late eighteenth century, Russia exported a full one-third of the world's iron ore, but in the beginning of the nineteenth century, the industry fell into a slump that lasted until the 1840s. A lack of government investment in industry, an enserfed and uneducated population, and the country's vast size and great distance from western Europe (raising transportation costs), all hampered industrialization. Each of these factors would be overcome by the late nineteenth century, when Russia experienced its own economic miracle.

* * *

The industrial revolution that began in England affected life around the globe. Industrialization raised the stakes for international competition, and it transformed everything from work, food, dress, and leisure to national power politics. Like all major developments in history, the industrial revolution had mixed results, benefiting some more than others. By the late nineteenth century, when some workers would begin to live in decent housing, dress well, and have money for leisure activities, millions of new recruits to the factories would be occupying the very bottom of the economic order. At the same time, Europeans would use industrial technology and the wealth it brought to dominate nonindustrial nations overseas.

By the 1840s the last great non-European powers had been subjugated and the world economy was ruled by Europeans. India's thriving economy was destroyed by British machine production and military force, and the Opium War of 1839–1842 showed China unable to withstand the onslaught of European military and economic power. For the second- and third-generation industrializers, and for all the countries like Russia and eastern Europe that became peripheral to the European core, industrialization would be accompanied by deep cultural challenges. While at least some people in most countries welcomed industry as the herald of modernization, there would always be large numbers who suffered in various ways, sometimes disastrously. And even among the advocates of industrialization and modernization, the challenge to national identity and culture would be painful.

Even in Great Britain and the most prosperous regions of the second generation, the early industrial economy brought change and insecurity. The first half of the nineteenth century saw repeated and entirely unpredictable booms and crashes. The British and west European economies experienced crop failures in 1816, accompanied by recession. The early 1830s saw another sudden recession, followed by expansion and then another downturn in 1840–1842. Great business prosperity was followed by the Hungry Forties: crop failure, potato famine, bankruptcies, massive unemployment. Excitement about change and progress was often shadowed by anxiety and insecurity for some, and destitution for others.

FOUR

Social Change and Social Life

European society in the nineteenth century witnessed the appearance of new social roles, social hierarchies, and social mobility. The French Revolution had removed many of the obstacles to social and political change, and a long process of democratization began when the revolution abolished aristocratic monopolies on economic opportunity and privilege. In the aftermath of the French Revolution, the rest of Europe experienced pressures of varying degrees to make (or resist) similar changes. Industrialization created new job opportunities and new sources of wealth that created new social groupings and changed the ways people thought about their positions in society. Sometimes imagined changes preceded actual change, motivating people to seek ever greater opportunity and new alliances and creating new kinds of social conflict.

The three most dramatic changes were the growth of cities and the expansion of their cultural influence; the rise of the middle classes in wealth, influence, and power; and the appearance of the urban working classes and the challenge of their collective power. But these developments came gradually and unevenly. While cities were growing and urban culture was coming to symbolize all that was right and wrong about nineteenth-century "progress," the majority of people in Europe continued to live in rural places. In the first half of the century and even on the eve of World War I, traditional rural elites continued to hold political and economic power. City and village were often viewed during the nineteenth century as two opposite poles of European social life, but they tended to be more interdependent than they might have seemed. Distinctions between town and village became more marked as cities grew exponentially, and as urban inhabitants stopped raising chickens or keeping cows. But rural life, especially in the last decades of the century, also responded to currents of change as urban jobs and markets beckoned and urban newspapers, politics, fashion, and entertainment reached the countryside along the railroads and through new trading networks.

Class

The social structure described in this chapter takes for granted that the reader is familiar with the word "class," so it is important to emphasize that it was precisely in this period, the early nineteenth century, when the word appeared and people began to think of themselves as belonging to classes. People identified themselves with others based on their experiences, alliances, enmities, and self-images. The social structure that had dominated European society previously was based on rigid legal categories known as "orders," which were determined by states and imposed on populations. One was born into the noble, clerical, or peasant (or other) order and acquired legal rights and responsibilities as a result. Ideas about class arose in the early nineteenth century as people found they needed new categories to identify new social groupings. At first, class was used to distinguish the productive or useful classes from the privileged aristocracy and clergy. At the same time, it was becoming clear that in between the privileged elite and the unprivileged poor were loosely defined "middling" people, who became the middle classes.

Karl Marx (1818–1883), one of the first to recognize the significance of the new social groupings of early industrial capitalism, saw a connection between the appearance of classes and the way the industrial economy organized people in new social groups. One's place in the economy, or as he put it, one's relationship to the "means of production," determined one's class. But Marx also understood the role that ideas played in shaping class identities. The kind of work one did and the life experiences or culture that resulted shaped what Marx called consciousness. Developing "class consciousness" was a process by which workers, for example, would come to think about and talk about their role in the economy, their place in the social hierarchy, the interests they shared with other workers, and the conflicts those interests created with members of other classes. So the rise of classes in the nineteenth century, itself a new phenomenon, produced another new phenomenon, class conflict: a process by which people came to identify both with and against other people in the new context of postrevolutionary industrial capitalism.

The lines between classes or orders, while quite clear and unbreachable at times, could be more flexible than Marx believed. Throughout the century, most people constructed their sense of themselves within a compound of identities based on the old orders, new classes, particular skill or occupation, gender and family roles, age, region, nation, empire, and religion. Each of these categories underwent change during the nineteenth century. Class identification itself could be voluntary, even if laboring for wages was not, and the meanings associated with each class were developed by people in interaction with each other, with conflicting classes, and with the state and other institutions. Not only was society changing as classes were coming into being, but change in every social grouping, old and new, was based on conflicts of interests with other groups.

In this chapter the people of Europe will be categorized in several somewhat rigid ways: rural/urban, male/female, and above all, upper, middle, lower class. But readers should keep in mind that none of these categories was ever very stable. Not only did ideas about masculinity and femininity change in different times and contexts, and not only did rural and urban peoples mix in significant ways, but classes themselves were never entirely coherent, homogeneous groupings with clear boundaries between them. There was not a great deal of social mobility from poor to rich until late in the nineteenth century; but an individual's sense of belonging to one or another class might be both settled and fluid at the same time, depending on whether one was at work or at the pub, on a Sunday or a Monday, at age 16 or age 60 and, perhaps most important: in an era of revolutionary conflict or one of routine and stability.

Population Growth and Redistribution

The most basic social change of the nineteenth century was the population explosion. The remarkable rise of population transformed society and tested the earth's resources even before people thought in these terms. Perhaps ten thousand years ago the total population of the globe was under 10 million. By 1750, when the modern rise was beginning, the figure was 750 million. By 1930 it was 2 billion, and only forty-five years later, in 1975, it was double that. Today the figure is close to 6.6 billion. Thus, human population expanded to reach its first billion over hundreds of thousands of years; the second billion was added in a single century; the third in only thirty years, and the fourth in only fifteen. Today we take population growth for granted, but sustained and spectacular population growth was unprecedented in the nineteenth century. This uncontrollable explosion in population was made evident as people flocked to the cities, which grew far more rapidly than sanitation, police, or schools could provide for, creating teeming slums that bred disease and discontent.

Population trends are notoriously difficult to explain. The data, especially for the first half of the century, are extremely sketchy and must all be considered estimates. There is some consensus, however, that the population explosion of the nineteenth century was the result of a rare coincidence of increasing birth rates and decreasing mortality rates: more children were being born and were living healthier, therefore longer, lives.

The rise in population did not necessarily mean that individual couples were having more children; it could also mean that there were more people available to have children. Birth rates probably increased originally in response to the rise in agricultural productivity. Then, individuals could safely begin to take measures to control birth rates. Russia, for example, had one of the highest birth rates on the continent, and by the end of the century overpopulation in many rural areas was perceived to be a problem. Many Russian peasant women had as many babies as they could, because they faced a high infant mortality rate. But this was a vicious cycle: the high mortality rate probably existed because parents could not adequately care for the large number of children they bore. Where birth rates were lower (not just in

Population Estimates of Selected Countries (in Millions)

Country	1800	1850	1900
Austria	14.0	17.5	26.2
Austrian Empire	19.0	30.7	45.5
Belgium	3.1	4.4	6.7
Bulgaria	—	—	3.5
Denmark	0.9	1.4	2.5
Finland	0.8	1.6	2.7
France	27.4	35.7	38.9
Germany	23.0	35.2	56.4
Greece	0.9	1.0	2.5
Hungary	5.0	13.2	19.3
Ireland	5.2	6.6	4.5
Italy	17.2	24.4	33.0
Norway	0.9	1.4	2.2
Poland	9.0	—	15.1
Portugal	2.9	3.5	5.4
Russian Empire	40.0	68.5	130.0
Spain	10.5	14.0	18.6
Sweden	2.4	3.5	5.1
United Kingdom	17.5	27.2	41.0

Source: Raymond Pearson, *European Nationalism, 1789–1920* (New York, 1994), p. 237.

Russia), parents could feed and care for infants better so their offspring tended to survive longer. Then when more children began to survive infancy, people began trying to limit family size.

Ironically, wealth as well as poverty provided reasons for controlling family size. Aristocratic and well-off families began limiting the size of families in the eighteenth century. Upper- and middle-class families began to concentrate wealth and attention on their individual children, viewing them not as potential sources of income but as creatures in need of special nurturing and shelter from the outside world. At the other end of the spectrum, historian Boris Mironov has discovered peasants practicing birth control in some of the most impoverished Russian villages; birth rates declined and infant death rates declined as well. Birth rates, after reaching a peak in Britain in the 1860s and in Scandinavia in the 1880s, fell everywhere in Europe at the end of the nineteenth and beginning of the twentieth centuries. The exception was France, where growing acceptance of contraceptive methods and a rise in abortions, despite church opposition to both practices, contributed to an early decline in the French birth rate. The French population continued to grow but at the slowest rate in Europe.

Declining birth rates, however, did not mean declining overall population size. The declining death rate of children was even more important than fluctuating birth rates in soaring population growth.

In 1800 in France and Britain one in five children died during the first year of life; in Germany one in four; in Russian and eastern Europe one in three.

By midcentury, France had reduced infant mortality to 173 per thousand, and by the end of the century, close to 132 per thousand. In Sweden at the end of the century only one out of every ten infants died in the first year, whereas in Russia and Italy one in four babies still died in childhood.

Death rates are also often hard to explain, but it seems that the absence of major warfare, the decline in famines, and improvements in food quality and supply offset the deaths due to raging epidemic diseases and malnutrition. The last major famines in western Europe occurred in 1816–1817 and 1844–1846; famine hit Russia in the 1890s, but it was at least partly the result of government malfeasance. Major outbreaks of infectious diseases occurred from the early 1800s through the 1880s: cholera took 100,000 lives in France in the 1830s and 50,000 in Great Britain; in Russia cholera hit in 1831, and then killed 700,000 people in 1848, but tapered off in second half of the century.

Health was also influenced by great strides in the practice of medicine, especially in the latter part of the century. A vaccine for smallpox was discovered in the mid-nineteenth century, quinine helped control malaria, treatments for tuberculosis were improved, and for reasons no one understands, typhus, typhoid, diphtheria, and smallpox appeared in less virulent forms. The use of antiseptics may have made childbirth itself less dangerous.

Many diseases seem to have been connected with the urban crowding that everywhere accompanied the first decades of industrialization. Based on new ideas about germs and hygiene, in the second half of the nineteenth century urban planners improved water supplies, cleared out swamps, provided better sanitation, and reduced overcrowding. Purification of water and efficient disposal of sewage (both requiring public measures, usually by municipalities) helped reduce the incidence of typhus. So did the introduction of the water closet, or flush toilet; more frequent bathing, as water became more readily available; and washable cotton fabrics, which made it easier to clean clothes and bedding. Because surgery was increasingly performed in well-equipped hospitals with antiseptics and effective anesthesia, especially after the introduction of ether in 1846, certain medical problems no longer led to death—except on the battlefield, where far more soldiers died of disease and infection after surgery than from their wounds.

From the time of Hippocrates to the nineteenth century, few significant new drugs had been developed, and often treatment for a specific disease was harmful according to present-day medical knowledge. For example, sufferers from malaria were subjected to leeching, which caused dehydration at a time when patients' bodies needed all their strength and an increase in liquids. But the kind of large-scale research that can be conducted only on the battlefield or in a hospital led first to the isolation of infectious patients in separate hospital wards after 1875, and then to specific studies of specific diseases. While the incidence of some diseases increased, notably cancer, the chances of surviving childhood to die of old age were materially greater at the end of the century than at the beginning. However, since access to such improvements in health often depended upon the ability to pay, death rates varied substantially according to class.

In the early 1800s the key factor in both rising birth rates and declining deaths rates was the increase in agricultural productivity, which meant that there was more and more varied food available. The food supply would fluctuate, and the poorest would still suffer hunger in hard times, but in the aggregate, better food meant greater resistance to disease, and more people living to childbearing age. By the second half of the century (in western Europe), a rise in grain prices no longer brought famine in its wake.

In general then, the nineteenth century witnessed a major transition in demographic patterns. Until that time, high birth rates and high mortality rates balanced each other out, producing at most very slow growth. In especially good times, the population rose more quickly, but limited food supplies and economic opportunities would increase mortality rates and produce population decline. In the nineteenth century, a significant drop in mortality increased the number of healthy people of childbearing age, so that when birth rates began to fall at the end of the century, population continued to grow even while individuals were practicing birth control and limiting family size. This occurred most dramatically in France, where declining birth rates occurred first and slowed (but did not reverse) population growth.

Rural Society

Peasants

Even in the middle of the nineteenth century, Europe was primarily a world of peasants. The population in most European countries was at least half composed of those who made their living by farming. England was the only country that had reached approximately 50 percent urban by midcentury. At the other extreme, Russia, Poland, and Spain had at least 85 percent of their people engaged in agriculture, and even in France at midcentury, almost two-thirds of the population was rural; in Prussia, it was close to three-quarters. Eastern Europe was far more rural than western Europe: in 1910 Serbia's rural population was 89 percent, Bulgaria's 82 percent, Romania's 83 percent, Bosnia-Herzegovina's 87 percent. Since definitions of "urban" vary and many rural people worked in the putting-out system, a better indicator is the number of people who support themselves by farm work, as in the following table.

Peasant life differed substantially from middle-class and city life. From Russia to England, elites commented on that difference in stark terms. In 1845 future prime minister Benjamin Disraeli (1804–1881) wrote of Britain as two nations "between whom there is no intercourse and no sympathy." Adolphe Blanqui claimed that of urban and rural civilizations, "nowhere is the distance separating them greater than in France." Harsher observers all over Europe referred to peasants as savage, cretinous, beastly, and subhuman. Peasant life also varied tremendously from region to region within any one country and between countries across the Continent. The conditions that

Agricultural Workforce in Relation to Total Active Population

United Kingdom	1841: 22%	1901: 9%
Germany	1871: 45%	1895: 36%
France	1886: 52%	1901: 43%
Italy	1850: 70%	1901: 59%
Austria	1869: 65%	1900: 60%
Hungary	1869: 70%	1910: 64%
Spain	1860: 66%	1900: 68%
Russia	1890: 87%	1910: 86%

Source: Clive Trebilcock, *The Industrialization of the Continental Powers, 1780–1914* (London, 1981), p. 435.

shaped particularities of individual rural communities included the degrees of peasant servitude, the crops grown, the proximity of farms to urban markets, and the vagaries of nature from year to year.

In much of western and central Europe, the French Revolution had abolished serfdom and established private landownership and free market. In France, Spain, Switzerland, and west German states, peasants had the right to own land. In France the revolution had greatly diminished elite landowning and increased the number of peasants who owned small farms.

In the beginning of the nineteenth century, in eastern Germany, the eastern regions of the Austrian empire, and Russia, peasants worked as serfs bound either to individual seigneurs or states. Though markets existed in the East, profits from them were reaped by the landowners, not by the growers of food. And those same seigneurs had extensive powers over their serfs, from arranging marriages to carrying out justice to administering the whip or the knout to miscreants. In some regions in between these extremes, including Scandinavia and parts of Germany, peasants were free to own land and move independently, but they were forced to pay landowners fees of various kinds, and peasants were excluded from hunting and forestry in many areas. In some parts of the Austrian empire, peasants enjoyed personal freedom, but they paid such onerous fees and dues to landowners as to be nearly enslaved.

While servitude was being abolished or modified through much of western and eastern Europe, in Russia the institution of serfdom formed the basis of the entire social and political structure until it was abolished in 1861. Noble wealth and status were determined by the extent of land and serf ownership, but noble landowners considered the work of farming beneath them. Nobles depended entirely on their serfs' labor (or tsarist loans) to pay for the luxuries to which they felt entitled. The nobility's exclusive right to own serfs was the bedrock of noble political status and identity. Since medieval times, Russian noblemen had enjoyed the right to own land with serfs in return for service to the tsar, and they clung to that right tenaciously even after service was no longer compulsory.

The tsars in their turn depended on noble service. When rumors about the mildest possible reforms in serf obligations spread through Russian society in the first decade of the nineteenth century, the noble response was panic and outrage, postponing indefinitely discussion about the far more radical steps necessary for abolishing serfdom altogether. Those same rumors raised hopes among Russian peasants, who had always experienced serfdom as a grave injustice, and spread increasing bitterness when reform was postponed. Though they seemed to outsiders to be a people with a deep capacity for suffering and resignation, Russian peasants fought bondage with periodic outbursts of massive violence and with everyday weapons of resistance such as feigned laziness, poaching in the landowner's forests and fields, and defiance of his orders.

Elsewhere in Europe, for all their vast diversity, peasant cultures had much in common with Russian peasant culture. For example, even among heavily enserfed peasants in Russia, many everyday decisions were made collectively by local elders, so peasants had some autonomy in village life. And at the other end of the spectrum, most French peasants were free landowners, but at midcentury they were practicing the same risk-averse subsistence agriculture favored in France for generations. The agricultural revolution that spurred change in England came to some regions of France and Russia only in the late nineteenth century. Before industrialization, the European peasant village was isolated, indifferent to city life, suspicious of outsiders whether from the distant capital or the next village, and well aware of its distance from tsar and king. Religion was invoked as habit (Sunday churchgoing), as ritual (at births, deaths, and weddings) and as magic, as much for morality as for healing and protection. Clothes were homemade, culture was oral, and news was local. Roads, railroads, schools, and in eastern Europe and Russia, emancipation, would begin to transform village isolation, but only in the 1880s did these changes really become visible.

Whether peasants worked as free landowners, sharecroppers, or serfs, farming everywhere was backbreaking and unpredictable labor. Even in food-exporting countries, nature was capricious. New crops provided more food for the growing population, but food supplies still could not always keep up with hunger. In Russia, historically, one in four years brought crop failure. And every innovation had its cost. The most tragic example of this is the Irish potato famine of 1845–1849.

Potatoes were easy to grow and nutritious and gained popularity quickly, especially in countries where small plots and poor soil inhibited cultivation of other grains (but not in Russia, where the risk-averse peasantry had to be forced by government decree to plant them). In Ireland, dependence on potatoes was a blessing that became a curse. For three years, from 1845 through

1847, the potato crop was invaded by a fungus that raced from village to village, destroying the only crop grown in many areas. The British government was slow to provide famine relief. At least a million people died from starvation and disease, and another 1.5 million Irish emigrated to the Americas during the famine.

Such large-scale natural disasters were relatively rare in the nineteenth century. Economic disruptions confined to a single region or economic sector were not uncommon, however, as the profound changes connected with industrial development reached into traditional economies.

Rural Elites

The rise of commercial classes and industrial wealth occurred in a world still dominated by old aristocracies, nobilities, and landed gentry. The urban, industrial, capitalist world was not isolated from the semifeudal, rural, and agricultural one; rather, it grew by exploiting and integrating elements of the old to make the new.

Everywhere, from England to Russia and Spain to Sweden, land was a major source of wealth and income in the nineteenth century. Large landowners in the West ran their farms with modern methods and equipment; they diversified to include food processing and lumbering; they produced for an urban market; they often won favorable economic subsidies and waivers because they could pull political strings; they also often owned significant city properties and participated in the industrial economy. In Russia, landowning among the nobility decreased by almost half after emancipation, and it was not until the very end of the century that a new generation of Russian landowners accepted the consequences of emancipation and tried their hands at modern farming. Despite the noble attrition, extremely large estates were still to be found: 155 seigneurs in the Russian Empire owned more than 270,000 acres of land each, compared with one such landowner in Germany. Almost half the land of many small provinces of the Austrian empire were owned by aristocrats. Large landowners remained the wealthiest people in Europe on the eve of the First World War, followed by those in the oldest capitalist professions: banking and transport, followed at some distance by new industrial capitalists in manufacturing.

Aristocratic culture also continued to exert a dominant influence as new commercial elites aspired to adapt aristocratic ways and be accepted into aristocratic circles. In England, Germany, and elsewhere, large landed proprietors and the wealthiest financiers began to socialize together, send their children to the same schools, and intermarry. Some industrialists were offered noble titles, and exceptional wealth was a ticket into noble society, even occasionally for a handful of Jewish financiers and entrepreneurs. Social-climbing commercial elites sought to display their new status by imitating the old regime's aristocratic culture. The novelist Gustave Flaubert (1821–1880) immortalized this desire for aristocratic privilege in his portrait of a bored provincial housewife in *Madame Bovary.* The fashionable world

Emma Bovary longs for and reads about in the new mass circulation press is the world of the Parisian aristocracy. Even in France where the revolution had eliminated aristocratic legal privileges, high diplomatic and military posts still went to members of old aristocratic families, and many members of the old families sought to buttress their fortunes by engaging in careers in finance and commerce. Successful European financiers and industrialists built enormous rural estates to rival those of the old aristocracy.

As landholding decreased and landed wealth was challenged by industrial wealth, the nobilities of Europe increasingly augmented their income with capitalist investment and their power with state service positions. Politics will be discussed later on, but here it is important to note that for most of the nineteenth century and certainly in the first half, every European government civil service was staffed primarily by members of the landed elites. Positions were increasingly open to talented and ambitious members of the middle classes, but at the end of the century the majority of positions and almost all the highest posts were held by men of noble birth. This was true even when those same governments were passing legislation to nourish industry that undermined noble economic and social privilege. European monarchies clung to their noble elites as bulwarks against the very forces of change that were making both aristocracy and monarchy obsolete: encroaching democracy, popular radicalism, industrial capitalism. Though titled elites held onto authority on the eve of the First World War, they also perceived the threats to their wealth and power represented by the new forms of wealth and power around them.

In northeastern Europe, aristocracies exerted special influence and continued to play leading roles in societies as in the west, but with greater security because industrial capitalism had not advanced far enough to produce a powerful middle class. Even late in the century, middle classes did not seriously impinge on noble political power, and the nobility continued to dominate the economy as large landowners. In Russia, Austria, and most of the Habsburg provinces, the aristocracy completely dominated the highest rungs of the government and the highest ranks of the military. In Hungary the aristocracy also ran most of the country's banks and large industries. The entire country of Romania has been described as "a big estate, administered like an estate." The Polish nobility was numerous, economically powerful, but frustrated politically, especially after the uprising in 1830.

According to Ivan Berend the preservation of the status and power of the old noble elite in eastern Europe provided a source of ethnic and cultural continuity among people without nations. Without independent states, society as a whole looked to its traditional economic and military leaders. This became problematic when traditional noble elites were called upon to provide leadership in unfamiliar modern economic and political circumstances. In Russia, however, with its later serf emancipation, its earlier and larger critical intelligentsia, and its somewhat more established national identity, the noble elite did not retain the same kind of following. Many noble families lost their estates entirely after Emancipation; many others sent their children to be educated in a profession, and many entered the ranks of Russian professional middle classes. These offspring of the nobility were not a true bourgeoisie in the political or economic sense, but in cultural and social terms they were similar in outlook, behavior, and cultural influence to their counterparts in western Europe. However, in both eastern Europe and Russia, the nobility was associated with an anticapitalistic ethos that was thought to characterize their nations more broadly.

In contrast to Russia and the Habsburg realm, in southeastern Europe a national aristocratic elite was almost completely absent. In both former and current provinces of the Ottoman Empire, national elites had been decimated or converted when Ottoman rule was established centuries earlier. Under Ottoman rule, the land was owned by the sultan and administered by a local military–bureaucratic class, made up of Turkish representatives of the sultan. Subordinated to these were local Bosnians, Albanians, and Bulgarians who had converted to Islam. As countries became independent, Turks fled and their places were taken by their military and administrative subordinates. But these new elites were neither ancient aristocracies nor new middle-class servitors, and they quickly replicated the corrupt, exploitative patterns of the old administrative–bureaucratic imperial rulers. Village and town chieftains, military heroes and popular outlaws, the handful of literate servitors, all rushed to get rich from bureaucratic sinecures and bribes. Such conditions did little to encourage native economic growth, education, or social welfare.

Cities

London, Paris, Berlin, Vienna, Madrid, Stockholm, Rome, Prague, Warsaw, Budapest, Moscow: the great modern cities of Europe have medieval, even ancient, histories, but in the nineteenth century they grew at an unprecedented pace. They were joined by a new kind of city. Manchester, Birmingham, and Liverpool; Lódz, Brno, and Donetsk were all created by industry. Steam-engine powered, machine manufacturing concentrated production in the places where people congregated. Factories were situated in cities, or cities grew up around big manufacturing sites, because they were central hubs of transportation, trade, and finance. When factories made millions of new jobs available, millions of people moved to cities to work in them. "Traditional" manufacturing did not necessarily die out, as artisans and tavern owners found business in meeting the daily needs of tens of thousands of new inhabitants. Professional classes grew as the rising population increased demand for everything from beer to legal services to health care to newspapers. City populations became more heterogeneous as they grew and as their economy diversified.

Like so much connected with nineteenth-century "progress," the rise of modern cities had contradictory consequences. Some observers whose ideas date back to the eighteenth-century French Enlightenment thinker Voltaire (1694–1778) saw the city as the best environment for fostering democracy. Voltaire believed that the concentration of people from different backgrounds, engaged in diverse activities, would facilitate the free exchange of ideas and contacts among people that would encourage creativity. Voltaire and his nineteenth-century followers were not blind to the problems of urban centers, especially the poverty of the laboring populations, but the philosophe had been optimistic about the ability of human reason to solve social problems and bring progress. He believed, for example, that the exposure of poor people to the wealthy and well educated would inspire the poor to emulate the rich, and to adopt the culture he considered superior. Adam Smith (1723–1790) also influenced nineteenth-century ideas about cities. His *Wealth of Nations* (1776) was the foundation of capitalist economic theory and liberal politics. Smith believed that all individuals are guided by self-interest to compete with one another for self-improvement. If individuals were left to their own devices, without government interference and without obstacles such as aristocratic monopolies on social privileges, he wrote, the natural laws of the marketplace, "the invisible hand," would produce a natural social order. Similarly, if the economy were allowed to develop without government interference, it would produce the greatest "wealth of nations." The free exchange of goods and capital, like Voltaire's free exchange of ideas unfettered by artificial laws, would produce enough wealth for all people to better themselves.

Smith's theory supported the early industrialists' inclination to provide as little as possible in the way of wages and social services for the workers they employed. It justified the belief that a natural economy would benefit everyone eventually, and it justified keeping municipal governments' roles to a minimum. The state policy based on Smith's theory became known under its French name: *laissez-faire.* This sort of thinking, based on the Enlightenment tenet that human problems could be solved by the application of reason, was also behind the early nineteenth-century style of city building.

Many of the city's great advocates would see cities first and foremost as places where the primary organizing principles were efficiency and profitability. Consequently they built for the convenience of the machine rather than the human beings who both worked the machines and lived next door to them. This modern idea of rational efficiency had a dehumanizing impact. New industrial cities like Manchester and Donetsk were built for the machine; even older cities like London and Paris were crowded in the early nineteenth century with new structures built for usefulness rather than visual pleasure or human benefit. City planners of the first decades were proud of the new human ability to control nature, and accordingly they did what they could to eradicate nature from the cityscape, to make cities as different as possible from the countryside. Lakes were filled in, marshes covered up, hills razed, and buildings concentrated wherever human planners wanted them. This made city life all the more wrenching for job seekers arriving from their villages.

The new industrial city created a new sense of space. But what some praised for efficiency and rationality, others damned for cold dehumanization and illusion. Friedrich Engels, author of a highly detailed exposé of the new industrial life in Manchester, declared that he had "never seen so badly built a town

"Capital and Labor," Punch, *1843. The findings of the Children's Employment Commission, released in 1842, provoked great public outcry and one of the first attempts to regulate child labor. This cartoon satirizes the hard labor and poverty of the workers that supported the ease and prosperity of the new middle classes, as revealed in that report. The mine shafts sketched diagonally in the background are replicas of the reports' widely circulated drawings showing small children "hurrying" coal in carts strapped to their foreheads through the horrifyingly claustrophobic shafts. (Provost and Fellows of Worcester College, Oxford)*

in [his] life." The middle-class industrialist that he addressed "listened patiently and at the corner of the street at which we parted company, he remarked, 'And yet there is a great deal of money made here. Good morning, Sir.'" Manchester, like many industrial towns that followed in its footsteps, grew so rapidly based on the construction of factories that no effective municipal government existed to regulate building, health, or growth. The squalor there was so shocking, and the wealth to be made from it so great, that Manchester came to symbolize both extremes. Alexis de Tocqueville visited in 1835 and concluded that in Manchester "humanity attains its most complete development and its most brutish; here civilization works its miracles, and civilized man is turned back almost into a savage." In the 1830s Manchester possessed no distinguished buildings, and even its admirers admitted it was filthy. Not surprisingly the symbol of industrial "progress" was also a center of social strife. In 1819 the *Times* reported that the workers' "wretchedness seems to madden them against the rich, who they dangerously imagine engross the fruits of their labour without having any sympathy for their wants."

The first critics of city life were not political radicals. Many were from the same social class as the laissez-faire industrialists and city planners, but they viewed the city through a different lens. Influenced by Romanticism, they rejected rationalist and Enlightenment justifications for unregulated growth and poverty. The Bavarian journalist William Heinrich Riehl (1823–1897), for example, lamented the artificiality of the city because it robbed city dwellers of the spirituality they absorbed through contact with nature in the countryside. Riehl was more disturbed by the numbers of urban poor who had left their families in the village to live alone than by the squalor in which individual workers lived. He was alarmed by the seasonal migration of urban labor and the impermanence that migration contributed to the city life.

Like Riehl, many critics of modern cities were first of all alarmed at the rate of urban growth and the major transformation this growth represented. Old capitals swelled quickly: the population of London had already reached close to one million at the beginning of the century; it more than doubled by 1851. Between 1801 and 1851 Manchester and Liverpool more than quadrupled in size. Vienna quadrupled to a population four hundred thousand in 1847. Berlin tripled in size by 1848. St. Petersburg more doubled during this period, but the phenomenally rapid growth of Russian cities would come primarily between 1890 and 1914. Many of the achievements and problems western cities faced in midcentury would be repeated in eastern Europe and Russia at the end of the century.

Unlike the Romantics, who mourned the loss of rural culture and tradition, midcentury critics focused on the deplorable quality of city life itself. Urban population growth outstripped municipal preparedness everywhere in industrial Europe. Urban concentrations of people created problems that did not exist when people lived in small villages or scattered on farms. Many of the urban services we take for granted today had to be invented to meet the challenge of growing cities. Housing construction never kept up with demand, so overcrowding was endemic. Meager sanitation services, water supply, traffic, streetlighting, garbage disposal, and medical care were quickly overwhelmed by growing populations. In most cities, authorities were slow to recognize the need to provide services to people living in new urban slums. Diseases such as cholera, typhoid, and tuberculosis spread rapidly in the overcrowded, filthy, and polluted working-class neighborhoods.

What one liberal social reformer wrote of London in 1883 could apply to cities all over Europe and throughout the century: "Few who read these pages have any conception of what these pestilential human rookeries are, where tens of thousands are crowded together amidst horrors which call to mind . . . the middle passage of the slave ship. To get into them you have to penetrate courts reeking with poisonous and malodorous gases arising from accumulations of sewage and refuse scattered in all directions and often flowing beneath your feet." Parisian working-class quarters were equally appalling. As one disgusted physician wrote: "Look at Paris: all these windows, doors and apertures are mouths which need to breathe. . . . Paris is a great manufactory of putrefaction, in which poverty, plague and disease labor in concert,

Urban Growth of Selected Cities, 1800–1850 (in Thousands)

City	1800	1850
London	1,117	2,685
Istanbul	570	600
Paris	547	1,053
Moscow	250	300
Vienna	247	444
St. Petersburg	220	485
Lisbon	180	240
Berlin	172	419
Madrid	160	270
Barcelona	115	175
Prague	75	118
Warsaw	60	114
Budapest	54	156
Belgrade	20	25

Source: Raymond Pearson, *European Nationalism, 1789–1920* (New York, 1994), pp. 240–41.

and air and sunlight barely enter. Paris is a foul hole where plants wilt and perish and four out of seven children die [of cholera] within the year." Crime, like disease, seemed to increase in cities; to middle-class and professional observers, crime and disease were linked. When the cholera broke out in Paris in 1832, the public assumed it had emerged from the prisons.

In most cities, as much as possible, the middle and upper classes moved away from overcrowded working-class neighborhoods. When the well-off looked at the life of the poor, it was usually from a distance, the only exceptions being journalists and social reformers, women offering charity and, outnumbering all of these, men seeking prostitutes. From London to Moscow and Rome to Stockholm middle-class curiosity about the poor made newspapermen rich by the publication of hundreds of reports like those just quoted. Mass circulation newspapers attracted millions of new readers with crime chronicles, serial potboilers, heart-tugging melodramas, and muckraking exposés about life in the slums. Almost always these publications described the poor denizens of the city as foreigners with alien customs. Judging both from a distance and face to face, the well-off came to assume that the people who lived in filthy quarters among raw sewage on crime-ridden streets were themselves filthy and criminal by nature.

Fears of disease and crime finally moved municipal officials to begin to improve the standard of living for the inhabitants of their slums. As industrialization and urbanization spread across the Continent, such campaigns usually followed mass urban in-migration by two or three decades, and improvement was far from universal. Beginning in the 1850s in western Europe and the 1910s in eastern Europe, local governments brought sanitation facilities, running water, and electricity to at least some of their workers.

Streets were widened and new housing was constructed. The dehumanization of the early nineteenth-century city was never entirely reversed, but in the second half of the century efforts were made to bring nature back into cities (see Chapter Seven).

Before turning to the people who suffered from city life, it is important to remember that for people who could enjoy them, cities were more than centers of industrial production. With rare exceptions, mid-nineteenth-century cities were also bustling centers of culture, civic pride, and entertainment. In the mid-nineteenth century, at the same time that factory districts and slum housing were spreading, old outdoor markets were being replaced by specialized shops with decorative advertising. Municipal halls, new government agencies, banks, stock exchanges, and post offices were being constructed. Roads were paved and sidewalks built for increased traffic and Sunday promenading. Libraries, schools, and universities were founded, along with new museums, opera houses, theaters, and music halls. Hotels, cafes, and restaurants were beginning to attract a tourist trade as well as local patrons.

Railroads changed the face of cities as profoundly as they affected the overall economy, for good and ill. In Germany railway lines broke down the medieval walls that had surrounded most cities at the start of the century. Railway tracks created new neighborhood boundaries wherever they appeared. New bridges created new perspectives, which were hated by many, who regarded most of them as eyesores. Where great railroad stations were built, commerce and industry followed. When London's King's Cross station opened in 1851, it demolished "the awful rookery at the back of St. Pancras Road," as a contemporary noted, improving the neighborhood, but displacing thousands of workers (who were given discounted train tickets as compensation).

Even during periods of the most utilitarian building, major cities held urban dehumanization at bay by making them symbols of national pride and centers of national culture. European capitals were filled with sculptural and architectural monuments to national heroes and achievements, often government funded or commissioned. The city became the symbol of cultural achievement and national power at the same time it was harboring the dregs of humanity, providing thousands of new jobs and opportunities, eradicating nature, and subordinating the majority of its citizens to the tyranny of the machine.

Workers

The European working classes were highly diversified—by profession, family situation, skill level, opportunity, religion, gender, and age. Nationality and culture also divided workers, but the most important factor in shaping working-class life in any given country or decade was the advance of industrialization. All across Europe, patterns of working-class life were remarkably similar at similar stages of industrialization. Working-class experience in England at the beginning of the century was repeated as industrialization moved eastward. As the century progressed, working conditions, labor legislation, gender and age distributions, and class stratification were reproduced in Paris, Berlin, Warsaw, and St. Petersburg, usually with variations only in degree. The initial stages of industrialization were highly disruptive socially and politically. Even after some workers were able to take advantage of improvements in skill, education, and social policy, new waves of workers migrated to industrial cities to begin the process again.

The working classes included laborers in a variety of professions. Artisanal workshops for ancient crafts with highly skilled artisans using hand tools and producing goods for luxury trades coexisted with large machine-powered factories that employed both highly skilled and unskilled workers to produce everything from steel and weapons to candy and cigarettes.

Some seasonal industrial workers, usually the least skilled, spent as much time in agricultural work as in factory work, migrating from village to city after the harvest. In the countryside, more and more peasants entered manufacturing, even full time. In Germany, as noted earlier, in the first half of the century, the number of putting-out workers increased by half a million between 1800 and 1850; and the number of skilled craftsmen increased from 1.23 million to 2 million. France saw the same increases. Some workers lived in rural areas but others—women in the needle trades, men in glassmaking, both in furniture making—could just as likely have been primarily urban. Often locally produced artisanal handicrafts could not compete with cheaper imported British goods. And the population growth increased the numbers of putting-out workers and craftsmen more quickly than it increased demand for their products. All of these workers, and all wage workers faced a new problem of unpredictable boom-and-bust business cycles, or the sudden appearance of a new factory or new technology, which could throw thousands out of work. The Silesian textile industry, fell victim to all of these. In the 1840s, the number of textile workers had increased, but British imports forced prices lower, which lowered wages below subsistence levels. In 1844, the weavers of Silesia rose up in a desperate violent revolt.

Higher up the skill ladder, the arrival of mechanized factories, whether in town or village, did not immediately put traditional craftsmen out of work but in fact increased demand for their products: shoes, leatherwork, tools, construction, and so on. In the Rhineland (Prussia's westernmost province), industrialization occurred early, but the construction of steam-powered spinning factories doubled the number of artisans required for weaving on hand looms. But in most countries, artisans could see the writing on the wall; the unskilled work of tending machines seemed to insult a dignity they had worked years to earn, and they often *feared* competition and obsolescence before actually encountering them.

Some people migrated permanently to the city and were quickly rooted there, while others labored in mobile jobs like construction or transportation, which took them from city to city. Skilled machine operators were paid far more than construction workers or unskilled miners so could live in cleaner and safer environments, dress well, even fashionably, and educate them-

The Written Record

MAN AND MACHINE

Some workers did not hate the factory but derived a sense of dignity and pride in mastering the machine. Semën Kanatchikov describes following his curiosity as a young man and watching steam engines being constructed. He worked 11.5 hours a day at the Gustav List machine-building factory in St. Petersburg, having started his apprenticeship there in 1895 at age 16.

Two years of my apprenticeship at the List factory passed. By now I was already an accomplished draftsman and designed uncomplicated patterns on my own. I loved my craft, and I put a lot of 'spirit' and initiative into it. . . . In order to acquaint myself with the entire process of producing a complete machine, I often made the rounds of the factory's various shops, where I spent hours standing and watching how this or that part of a machine was made. [After describing the initial steps in the process, he describes the last stages of workers finishing a steam engine.] Then, after a few more weeks or months, depending on the size of the machine, I could see the workers in the assembly shop painting the powerful beauty—with its poised bronze and steel parts sparkling—the completed steam engine.

Workers would look with a loving glance at its massive iron body as they passed by. As for me, I began to be gripped by the poetry of the large metal factory, with its mighty metallic roar, the puffing of its steam-driven machines, its columns of high pipes, its rising clouds of black smoke that sullied the clear blue sky. Unconsciously, I was being drawn to the factory, to the people who worked there, who were becoming my near ones, my family. I had the feeling that I was merging with the factory, with its stern poetry of labor, a poetry that was growing dearer and closer to me than the quiet, peaceful, lazy, poetry of our drowsy village life.

A Radical Worker in Tsarist Russia: The Autobiography of Semën Ivanovich Kanachikov, trans. and ed. Reginald E Zelnik (Stanford, 1986), pp. 50–51.

selves and perhaps some of their children. Such improvement was seen by the middle classes as a hedge against working-class radicalism. On the contrary, however, the skilled labor elite were just as likely as the unskilled and more impoverished to become aware of the social inequalities of nineteenth-century society, to protest for better wages and conditions of work, and to develop independent political ideologies.

Factory work universally meant dangerous conditions, long hours (12–16 per day), and low pay. The machinery operated continuously and without safety features; accidents were common. Children who fell asleep at their machines were most vulnerable to losing a finger or a limb, women with long hair could have a piece of their scalp ripped off. Even a minor injury could lead to serious illness, loss of limb, or death due to infection and malnutri-

Average Age of Death in Manchester and Rutlandshire by Occupation:
Report on the Sanitary Condition of the Labouring Population of Great Britain (1842)

Occupation	Manchester	Rutlandshire
Professionals, gentry, and their families	38	52
Tradesmen and their families (in Rutlandshire, farmers and graziers are included)	20	41
Mechanics, laborers, and their families	17	38

Source: Asa Briggs, *Victorian Cities* (New York, 1963), p. 101.

tion. Midwives reported that factory women had a much higher rate of difficult births and fatalities: endless hours tending machines caused bone deformities that affected childbirth. Textile production took place in such damp conditions that workers might stand all day in pools of water, breathing fluff and dust, which led to asthma, bronchitis, and other lung problems. Subsistence wages and irregular employment contributed to the ill health of urban workers. Food, clothes, and medicine all had to be paid for or done without: malnutrition and diseases like rickets, which were related to malnutrition, were common.

In mines, conditions were even more perilous than in factories. Children had jobs navigating in terrifyingly narrow chutes, pulling coal carts strapped to their foreheads along underground railways. Accidents, dirt, and diseases were all multiplied there. But, in the early stages of industrialization, the simplicity of machine work (especially in textile factories) and the machines' sudden insatiable demand for unskilled workers meant that women and small children were often employed in dangerous work for long hours. Sixty percent of the workers in mechanized cotton factories in England in the 1840s were women, including girls as young as 10; in France, women made up 45 percent of textile workers, 41 percent in rubber and paper, and 20 percent in fine metalworking. In most countries protective legislation was eventually passed, restricting the hours and types of work women and children might do. Such legislation was often greeted with mixed feelings, since it protected children, including destitute orphans, from exploitation but it also denied them the ability to contribute to their families' income. In England such legislation followed the courageous testimony of women miners, who felt betrayed when their testimony led not to improved conditions but to unemployment.

The dangerous and unpredictable life of the urban worker caused many men to leave their wives and children home in their native villages for decades, sending cash and visiting infrequently, while others worked in mines and quarries where whole families might be hired as a unit. Women of the working classes most often labored out of public view as "home workers" or "pieceworkers." They rolled cigarettes, made lace, stitched gloves, or sewed other items of clothing. Home work might allow pieceworkers to watch their own children, but they were paid miserably, and by the "piece"

A Closer Look

THE SONG OF THE SHIRT

"The Song of the Shirt," by the minor English poet Thomas Hood (1799–1845), was prompted by a London news report about the arrest of a seamstress for pawning articles belonging to her employer. Paid by the piece, she could earn at the maximum seven shillings a week, on which she was expected to support herself and two young children.

Work—work—work
Till the brain begins to swim;
Work—work—work
Till the eyes are heavy and dim!
Seam, and gusset, and band,
Band, and gusset, and seam,
Till over the buttons I fall asleep
And sew them on in a dream!

O! Men, with Sisters dear!
O! Men! with Mothers and Wives!
It is not linen you're wearing out,
But human creatures' lives!
Stitch—stitch—stitch
In poverty, hunger, and dirt,
Sewing at once, with a double thread
A Shroud as well as a Shirt.

Thomas Hood, "The Song of the Shirt," in *British Poetry and Prose*, ed. Paul Robert Lieder, Robert Morss Lovett, and Robert Kilburn Root, vol. II (Boston: Houghton-Mifflin, 1936), p. 171.

rather than by the hour. In some Ukrainian mining towns, where the majority of men had left families back in Russian villages, a single woman might be hired to migrate from the village as well, to cook, wash, and provide sex for a group of men. By far the most common form of employment for poor women was domestic service. Servants were poorly paid, but they were fed and housed, though their shelter might consist of a cot in a hallway. In addition, female servants were vulnerable to the sexual predations of their male employers, from teenaged sons to elderly masters. Pregnancy almost always meant immediate dismissal and frequently proved a path to the fate a job as a domestic servant had only postponed: prostitution.

Prostitution grew in every nineteenth-century city, where it symbolized the physical and moral dangers of modern life and the hypocrisy of bourgeois sexual practices. Prostitution was a stratified profession, in which a few women were paid well to be the lavishly dressed companions of wealthy men, but most prostitutes worked in dangerous conditions with little control over their lives. Although shunned by most of society as "fallen women," they were occasionally chosen by well-meaning charitable societies to be reeducated and sent out to work in respectable employment. However, respectable wages were usually lower than a prostitute's income, and respectable jobs did not protect young women from being forced to perform the same sexual services as prostitutes, only for free. So a sizable minority of prostitutes (no one knows how many) chose prostitution as a full-time occupation that provided some autonomy and decent wages or as a part-time supplement to factory labor or piecework. This "casual" prostitution was especially appalling to elite observers. With prostitution came venereal disease, a genuine epidemic. As a result, the social and moral disorder became a medical matter to be regulated and policed. A prostitute, but not her clients, needed a license to ply her trade and could be arrested for practicing without one.

Women's work, even in acceptable public professions, was considered a threat to the "natural order" of things. That natural order was based on a fundamental contradiction in eighteenth-century Enlightenment thought which produced in the nineteenth century gender-specific "separate spheres." Enlightenment thinkers believed that all human beings were equally subject to natural laws, which endowed all of us with certain, specific rights (the U.S. Declaration of Independence contains the transatlantic version). Those specific natural rights were differentiated by sex. Nature endowed men and women with different biological structures, which favored different activities or social functions. Women's smaller brains and muscles, larger hips, and "lack" (or internal positioning) of genitalia conditioned them for reproduction. As such, their natural social functions would be connected with reproduction: private, domestic life, religious and moral education, and dependence on physically stronger men. Men's greater physical strength made them coarser and therefore able to cope with the hard, dirty, public work of the industrial city, managing employees, maneuvering in the rough and ready new world of capitalism. Though men and women both breached the divide that separated these spheres, the two classifications remained powerful ideal types that affected women of all classes by assigning jobs and activities to one or the other gender, and tainted all women who worked outside the home. Such clearly defined social roles created stability and security as well as resentment and protest, however. Some women in all classes would champion and some would challenge the restrictions placed on them by nineteenth-century ideal types. By the middle of the century, increasing public roles for women would create new cultural and social conflicts.

Social Mobility

Great new wealth was produced in the nineteenth century, but while it did not flow evenly into everyone's pockets and did not erode the power of old elites or end poverty, historians generally agree that people in most social groups had a higher standard of living at the end of the century than at the beginning, and higher than they had had as peasant farmers, even if most workers still had many reasons to protest. Evidence for such improvement, however, is scarce, and much of it does not take into account the great variety among workers of different industries and locations, nor can it account for the psychological effects of poverty, uncertainty, and instability.

The transition from farm to factory must have been a wrenching one psychologically, even if it was only from one form of poverty to another. The switch from a life dominated by natural rhythms and from the variety of farm work to a world dominated by the clock and the noisy, repetitive machine must have been disorienting. But for all the difficulties of city life, for some workers, mastering this world and leaving the farm behind was a source of great pride. And it also seems clear that at least some workers earned more in real wages, ate and dressed better than their rural counterparts, and were more literate.

The *belief* that workers were worse off living in the city than in the countryside was very widespread. As George Sims, a popular British writer, put it in the 1880s, "the story of one slum is the story of another, and all are unrelieved by the smallest patch of that colour which lends a charm to pictures of our poorest peasantry. God made the country, they say, and man made the town; and wretched as is the lot of the agricultural laborer, the handiwork of Heaven still remains to give some relief to the surroundings of his miserable life." In part this belief was supported by the fledgling science of economics, which sustained the middle classes in the belief that poverty was inevitable and poor relief systems were a waste of precious resources because they could never eradicate poverty.

Even the staunchest defenders of laissez-faire urbanization did not imagine that workers lived comfortable lives. But they tended to agree that some people were forced to sacrifice for the benefit of progress for society as a whole and that ultimately their labor would benefit them in terms of lower prices and more available goods. The line that divided those indifferent to workers' fates from those moved by their plight was based on individuals' beliefs about workers as human beings. The popularity of utilitarian city-building shows how easy it was for employers to regard their workers as less than human, as almost another species. Reformers, on the other hand, often blamed *laissez-faire* economics for causing or at least aggravating working-class poverty and the squalor in which workers lived. These observers were moved by the plight of workers as individuals with whom they shared the city. They were unwilling to sacrifice some classes of people for the prospect of future prosperity. Advocates of *laissez-faire* growth viewed the poor as instruments of social policy and believed that industrial development benefited the nation as a whole. Enthralled by the power industry had tapped and believing that it contributed to the progress of all humanity, they saw themselves as civilizers rather than elitist, selfish monsters. Finally they believed

Derby Day, *by William Powell Frith, 1858. One of the most popular paintings of nineteenth-century Europe,* Derby Day *shows an event at which rich and poor might mingle and contains a catalog of midcentury dress and social interaction, both highly idealized. (Tate Gallery)*

that economic freedom nurtured political and intellectual freedom and that poverty itself would be eradicated with economic progress.

The difference here is one of focus: on the future and the nation as a whole or on the present and the individual. There is also a difference in positions on the nature of social responsibility. When prosperity or even comfort failed to reach the slums decades after the cities began to overflow, reformers and workers turned to political protest to effect change. The difference is also one of psychology and sensibility: middle-class observers of the poor, especially lower-middle-class observers in danger of being confused with or descending into the working classes, tried hard to distinguish themselves culturally from workers. They clung tenaciously to the outward signs of middle-class respectability and were often the harshest critics of working-class family life and social habits. But the vulnerable clerk and *laissez-faire* businessman were not the only ones to see the poor as fundamentally different from the middle class. Sigmund Freud (1856–1939) showed a typically bourgeois mentality when he wrote to his fiancée that "the 'people' are quite unlike us in the way they judge, believe, hope and work. There is a psychology of the common man that is rather different from ours."

Though the nineteenth century is often described as "the bourgeois century," and many historians cite the rise of the middle classes as the century's most characteristic development, it is crucial to remember that the rise of the urban poor was equally dramatic and influential. And most important, it was the perpetual comparison and observation of each other that shaped the mentality, the culture, and ultimately the politics of the middle and lower classes, and of the nineteenth century itself.

Middle Classes

The middle classes were as diverse as the working classes, though like workers, they shared some salient characteristics as a class. Together the French and industrial revolutions paved the way for the numerical growth of the middle classes by abolishing aristocratic monopolies, expanding government functions, stimulating economic growth, and creating the need for new professions or transforming old ones. As the industrial revolution picked up steam and spread geographically and economically, the pace of expansion also increased.

There were a number of paths in the nineteenth century into the bourgeoisie.

First, the military officer class was open to nonaristocrats for the first time after the French Revolution. However, this path to success faded in importance after the Napoleonic Wars ended. The top ranks of the military would remain primarily, though not exclusively, aristocratic.

The arts also offered opportunities as new arts institutions opened all over Europe and the structures for funding them changed. With the general increase in wealth and growth of cities, the audience for public displays of visual arts increased. Museums for painting and sculpture, and halls for opera, symphony, and theater, were opened by municipalities in every major and many minor cities in Europe. These institutions offered a wide variety of public entertainments that had previously been the exclusive preserve of royalty or the very wealthy. Audiences at many classical theater and music performances were mixed for much of the century, but inexpensive music halls, theaters, and public fairgrounds offered rowdier fare for the poor. Advances both in printing technology and in literacy meant that newspapers and literature, especially the novel, flourished as never before. All these offered employment to artists, whose income would be based on audience-generated revenues, rather than on royal or aristocratic patronage.

The arts represented a way for people to support themselves without the financing of patrons because the growth and distribution of industrial wealth created a market for theater, opera, music hall, magazines, and novels. A large segment of the arts-consuming population were women. The bourgeois ideal of liberating frail females from the rigors of public labor gave women more leisure time to read, to go the theater and concerts, and also to the law courts, whose trials were as entertaining as their television counterparts are today. Still while many more people (women included) could become artists and earn a middle-class income, participation in the arts remained limited to a fairly small social group.

Government service was a much more common, if equally precarious, route to the middle class. In the first half of the century most government expenditures increased dramatically: by 25 percent in Spain, 40 percent in France, 44 percent in Russia, 50 percent in Great Britain, 70 percent in Austria. Police forces appeared in France in 1798, in Ireland in 1823, in England in 1829, in Spain in 1844. Judicial systems and postal services grew and public railroad systems spread. An army of clerks was required to document these new government functions. By the latter decades of the century, these new functions included managing social welfare, poor relief, and labor legislation. The number of state civil servants in France increased from 225,000 to 304,000, from approximately 100,000 to 400,000 in Britain, and from 200,000 to 400,000 in Germany. At the lowest levels, the work required not much more than literacy, as it mostly involved endless copying of documents, and it was very poorly paid—at wages often lower than those of skilled workers. But clerks worked in clean offices and prided themselves on the status conferred by their "white collars." In some countries (notably Italy, Spain, and Russia), enterprising clerks had the possibility of supplementing their income by receiving bribes.

Moving up in government service required more education, which was not very easily acquired in the early nineteenth century. Elementary and secondary education was generally not available to the lower classes. But for those with some means and more talent, university students were chosen by merit (and of course family influence). A university education provided entrance into a variety of occupations, new and old. There was a growing need for professionals in medicine, law, engineering, and the sciences, as well as the higher ranks of government service.

The most important sector of the new middle classes was, of course, the new economy: business, banking, trade, and commerce. Here the middle classes ranged from the wealthiest bankers to the smallest shopkeepers and poorest, harried shopclerks. At the top of the heap were the bankers and merchants who had grown rich in the earliest days before the industrial revolution. They were in a position to invest in and profit handsomely from the growing industrial economy. These were the elites who would merge with and identify with the old aristocracies, adopting their habits and customs and looking down on the newcomers of the nineteenth century. Next in wealth and power were the new industrialists and entrepreneurs: those who exploited the new technology earliest and entered factory production when huge profits were to be made, before the first business slumps and political crises brought prices down or cut off supplies of raw materials. Below the entrepreneurs are the shopkeepers, their sales staffs, and perhaps skilled artisans, who straddled the lines between middle and working classes. Shopkeepers and artisans often began as wage earners but managed to invest in a small shop catering to the needs and desires of the newly wealthy. They made and sold clothes and hats, foodstuffs of all kinds, tobacco products, linen and textiles, soaps and perfumes, musical instruments, books, furniture, and of course clocks, until big new department stores put some of them out of business at the end of the century.

In the middle of the century, according to historian Peter Gay, a skilled artisan in France earned around 1,800 or 2,000 francs a year; quite a bit more than a schoolteacher, who made about 1,500. A successful shop might produce for its owner between 4,000 and 5,000 francs. Professionals earned over 8,000 francs a year; the more successful and better located could multiply that several times. A higher civil servant earned at least 12,000 francs but could expect regular raises from beneficent superiors. Bankers, entrepreneurs, publishers, and speculators earned far more. A successful artist might begin living hand to mouth in a garret, but might eventually fare better than most: early in his career Claude Monet sold paintings for 300 francs each, more than two months of a teacher's annual salary.

Differences within the middle class were not restricted to standards of living. The French middle class tended to be more oriented toward leisure and luxury in their consumption habits; the Germans and Swiss more sober and ascetic and more likely to provide paternalistic protections for their workers. The earliest Russian middle classes tended to be members of dissident religious sects but by end of century came to resemble in culture and diversity the middle classes of central and western Europe. Alongside national and other differences there are a number of important cultural similarities, shared in various degrees from nation to nation and up and down the middle-class social hierarchy. Most of these attributes were pairs of contradictions forged in conflicts over class, gender, religion, and nationality.

The new European bourgeoisie was a supremely self-confident class; material success made them so. History, science, and religion combined to make the world theirs to conquer. Pride in past accomplishments and optimism about the future were common. Though social mobility from working to middle class or from middle class to aristocracy was a great rarity, the middle classes strongly believed in self-improvement. They embraced respectability, which meant sober and proper public behavior, financial independence, and family stability, as well as such habits as reading for cultural and moral edification. Respectability joined with property entitled the middle classes to political power and social leadership, and they sought to instill their values in the rest of society (and later in the peoples of Europe's colonies). At the same time the middle classes developed fears of all kinds: fears of the lower classes and their behavioral excesses, fears of international instability, and by the end of the century, fears that all their sober hard work would be undermined by socialism, nihilism, and feminism. Social fear was so pervasive and reason so revered that this generalized anxiety acquired the status of a disease: neurasthenia. Women seemed so prone to physical symptoms of anxiety and depression that many contemporaries attributed the disorder to female frailty. Freud blamed sexual repression. But Peter Gay has persuasively shown that sexual pleasures were widely enjoyed among both men and women of the European middle classes and that anxiety was as much a male malady as a female one.

Middle-class anxiety, it seems, was a response to the one inescapable fact of the nineteenth century: change. Whether one welcomed or deplored the century's transformations, change brought anxiety. Poet and critic Matthew Arnold observed that "There is not a creed which is not shaken, not an

A Closer Look

CLASS AND CULTURE

Baroness Germaine de Stael (1766–1817) was one of the most prolific and successful writers of the early nineteenth century. In novels like *Corinne,* she described the ways that local culture might mean more than class in determining social customs.

Lord Edgarmond was my father. I was born in Italy; his first wife was a Roman. . . . I lost my mother ere I was ten years old, and as it was her dying wish that my education should be finished ere I went to England, I was confided to an aunt at Florence, with whom I lived till I was fifteen. My taste and talents were formed ere her death induced Lord Edgarmond to have me with him. He lived at a small town in Northumberland, . . . My mother from my infancy impressed on me the misery of not living in Italy; I set forth with an explicable sense of sadness. . . .

Lady Edgarmond met me politely, but I soon perceived that my whole manner amazed her, and that she proposed to change it if she could. Not a word was said during dinner, though some neighbors had been invited. I was so tired of this silence that, in the midst of our meal, I strove to converse a little with an old gentleman who sat beside me. I spoke English tolerably, as my father had taught me in childhood; but happening to cite some Italian poetry, purely delicate, in I which there was some mention of love, my step-mother, who knew the language slightly, started at me, blushed, and signed for the ladies, earlier than usual to withdraw, prepare tea, and leave the men to themselves during the dessert. I know nothing of this custom, which 'would not be believed in Venice.' Society agreeable without women! For a moment I thought her ladyship so displeased that she could not remain in the same room with me; but I was reassured by her motioning me to follow and never reverting to my fault during the three hours we passed in the drawing-room waiting for the gentlemen. At supper, however, she told me gently enough, that it was not usual in England for young ladies to talk; above all, they must never think of quoting poetry in which the name of love occurred.

In the morning. . . . I met my father, who said to me: 'My dear child, it is not here as in Italy; women have no occupations save their domestic duties. Your talents may beguile your solitude and you may win a husband who will pride in them; but in a country town like this all that attracts attention excites envy and you will never marry at all if it is thought that you have foreign manners.

Corinne, or Italy (Paris, 1807), cited in Susan Groag Bell and Karen M. Offen, *Women the Family and Freedom: The Debate in Documents,* vol. 1 1750–1880 (Stanford, 1983), pp. 65–66.

accredited dogma which is not shown to be questioned, not a received tradition which does not threaten to dissolve." And Karl Marx, whose influential theory of history and revolution was based on change, noted that with the coming of bourgeois society, "All that is solid, melts into air."

The bourgeoisie idealized the family as a social institution and emotional refuge, for better or worse. Though conflict and abuse of family members were always possible, the nineteenth century saw the evolution of marriages based on choice rather than parental contract. Increasing prosperity made it possible for bourgeois families to devote more time and resources to raising their children. The ideology of "separate spheres," the strict division of gender roles and separation of the dangerous public and secure private life, made the home a haven for men and their children. New laws and beliefs at the end of the eighteenth century idealized motherhood and domestic life. In the preceding century some women did assist their husbands in a shop or other workplace, but it now became a source of middle-class pride for women to leave the public sphere.

Women had extensive power inside the home, based on the belief that women's natural strengths were limited to the domestic and emotional. They supervised their children's religious and secular education and organized the family's entertainment and socializing. The woman of the house was also often responsible for managing the family economy, and even in families with a servant or two, this was a large job. Barred from politics and all higher education (except in rare exceptions, in medicine), deprived of independent control of finances (except in Russia), legally dependent on their fathers and then their husbands, women in the bourgeois family were bound to their homes. These conditions were very widespread in Europe; one finds only differences in degree between southern and northern, eastern and western Europe.

Though most women apparently accepted the characterization of their abilities as domestic, those women of the middle class who did not were far less proud of their accomplishments and less self-satisfied than their husbands, and more likely to press for the right to education, to vote, to exert more control over their own lives.

The idealization of the family, the "cult of domesticity," gave the bourgeoisie a sense of their superiority to working-class families. Exposés of lower-class urban life depicted neglected children, divided families, rampant illegitimate births, and divorce and abandonment. Bourgeois observers and social reformers generally agreed that lower-class family instability was a sign of lower-class degeneracy and the cause of a variety of social ills, especially crime. Few observers in the nineteenth century spent much time thinking about the structural obstacles to raising a family on working-class wages in the new industrial city. The afflictions of slum life already discussed made it impossible to construct the kind of cozy domesticity so prized by the bourgeoisie, even when workers aspired to do so. Economic cycles often forced workers to move from place to place in search of work, dividing families. Poverty and unpleasant living conditions in cities encouraged men to leave their wives and children behind in the countryside. When workers did marry

Portrait of a middle-class family in Florence. In southern and eastern Europe the middle class grew more slowly but lacked nothing in style. (Fratelli Alinari)

or bring wives to the city, the usual result was reproduction. But in the absence of public schools or day-care institutions, working wives were forced to leave their children unsupervised. Illegitimate births soared in the early nineteenth century, but these were not always a sign of instability or even abandonment. As in the countryside, a child might be a planned prelude to marriage, rather than an embarrassing mistake.

Despite these problems, middle-class observers misjudged the demise of the working-class family and erred in attributing to it responsibility for urban crime and disorder. In western Europe in particular, the family remained central to working-class culture and economic survival. Women who worked for wages were usually young and unmarried. When women married, they usually left the public labor force and took up piecework at home. In Germany, home garment workers organized their family and work life around husbands' factory schedules, guaranteeing family leisure time in the evening. This robust working-class family life was rarely glimpsed by the middle class. Those bourgeois who valued hard work were unable to recognize it in conditions unlike their own.

Religious Minorities

There were two significant minority populations in nineteenth-century Europe. Jews and Muslims were both defined by their religious beliefs but were treated like members of distinct ethnic groups. Jews formed significant and visible minority populations in cities all over western Europe and in villages and towns of eastern Europe and Russia. Muslims were almost exclusively found in southeastern Europe. Jews and Muslims suffered under similar sets of prejudices and legal barriers, with important regional variations.

In many west European countries legal restrictions on Jewish citizenship were lifted after the French Revolution, but legal emancipation did not immediately bring cultural assimilation, social integration, or improvement in the lives of west European Jews, the majority of whom lived in terrible poverty. Like people in villages elsewhere, Jews were resistant to giving up their own language, Yiddish, for Dutch, French, or German, and they were further hindered from assimilation and improvement by continued restrictions on economic activity. When major economic changes occurred with the spread of on industry to the continent, these restrictions were gradually lifted, and educational policies forced Jews to learn the national language. During the Enlightenment significant numbers of Jews resolved to assimilate into the secular world around them. In countries where Jews were relatively small percentages of the population—England, France, the Netherlands, German principalities, and Italy—progress toward constitutional rights and middle-class status was relatively rapid. In the Austrian Empire, integration was slower. Entering national public economic life had mixed benefits for Jews. Competition for jobs in increasingly nationalist and ethnically self conscious societies made Jews vulnerable to new forms of scapegoating, prejudice, and violence. The achievement of social integration never matched the acquisition of legal political rights, but the middle decades of the nineteenth century were marked by relative acceptance and toleration.

In Russia and eastern Europe, Jewish life was further restricted and poverty extensive. Within the Russian Empire, the majority of Jews in Russia, Poland, Belarus, and Ukraine were restricted to the Pale of Settlement on the southern and southwestern borderlands of the empire. There they were forced to reside in villages rather than cities. Not allowed to own property, they made their living in small commerce, services, and trade. Early in the century aggressive efforts were made to force Jewish integration into the service state through conscription and special Russian-language schools. After a horrific series of pogroms in 1881 the tsarist government decided that integration was not desirable. As in western Europe, though on a smaller scale, Jewish assimilation was rather successful in St. Petersburg during the middle decades of the century, but many gains were wiped out by the resurgence of anti-Semitism after 1881.

Muslims were a numerical minority in southeastern Europe, but they dominated society in the Ottoman territories, and Islamic culture was visible everywhere. There was considerable tension between Christians and Muslims in southeastern Europe, and frequently Christians viewed the Turks as alien oppressors. But at the same time there was a significant amount of interaction and cultural symbiosis. By and large, the Ottoman rulers were tolerant of Jews and Christians, but non-Muslims suffered some legal discrimination, paid higher taxes, and were prohibited from such activities as riding horses.

In the nineteenth century, Muslims in Bulgaria, Bosnia-Herzegovina, Macedonia, Albania, and elsewhere were either ethnic Turks or converted Slavs.

Elite conversion began even before the Ottoman victory over Constantinople in 1453 and continued for centuries to produce the empire's Balkan ruling class. Peasants also converted to Islam, sometimes en masse, to avoid various forms of persecution. Women sometimes converted to escape unhappy marriages. Peasant converts continued to speak their native Slavic languages, and Turkish was used only by administrative elites. Intermarriage was not uncommon, and in everyday life cooperation across religious lines was as familiar as conflict. In many regions there was more animosity within Balkan ethnic groups between people of the mountains and people of the plains than there was between Muslims and Christians.

The nineteenth century brought developments with contradictory consequences. Capitalism and higher education introduced secular ideas, middle-class associations, and forms of sociability that cut across religious lines, enabling Muslims, Jews, and Christians to socialize and do business with one another. But religious difference was always there to be called upon or exploited in moments of strife. The appearance of modern nationalism had the effect of hardening lines of difference.

The presence of Jews and Muslims in Europe raised the question of what it meant to be a "European." Many Europeans viewed Europe as fundamentally Christian. A Muslim empire on its border with Asia, and a Jewish population scattered throughout the continent complicated that definition. Even in an age of secularization and assimilation, Jews and Muslims were identified as alien.

Southeastern Europe seemed to be a frontier of semibarbaric exoticism for most of the rest of Europe for most of the nineteenth century. Western as well as eastern Europeans who visited the Balkans routinely identified anything familiar as "European" and anything unfamiliar as "oriental." As nationalism and a penchant for scientific classification arose, northern Europeans were disconcerted by the commingling of Christian and Muslim, modernity and tradition, and urban and rural that they found in the Balkans. To travelers as well as to politicians and diplomats, even the European, Christian Slavs of the region seemed semi-Asiatic in appearance and behavior, which made them either unattractively or enticingly mysterious, depending on one's point of view. The Muslim Turkish administrators were viewed at times as beautifully mannered and at times as brutally repressive of the Christian population. A well-informed and sympathetic British traveler, Viscountess Emily Strangford, writing in the 1870s, found the Bulgarians (Christians) "burning with the desire for progress," and possessing "a curious mixture of industry and thrift with laziness and apathy; at one time [the Bulgarian] appears so Oriental, at another so Western." Many accounts were more disdainful, but sympathy for the people of the Balkans was often based on abhorrence of their Ottoman Muslim oppressors.

To many west Europeans, Ottoman tyranny was a model of "Asiatic despotism," and Muslims were presumed to be especially barbaric. During the Greek war for independence, most west Europeans acknowledged only Ottoman atrocities, though as we have seen, equally pitiless cruelty was visited by the Christian Greeks on their Ottoman Muslim enemies. In the nineteenth century Christianity and Islam were seen by many west European Christians as incompatible, which was not always true in earlier centuries. In 1829 the Russian F. P. Fonton concluded that "the coexistence of Muslims and Christians is the epidemic sin of the present situation." This in itself overshadowed the Balkan reality that as Ottoman power was slipping, and power was locally falling into the hands of dangerous and corrupt officials, there were Muslim as well as Christian Slavic victims. During the Bulgarian war for independence, to take the most notorious example, Russian and Bulgarian forces massacred ten times as many Muslims as Ottoman forces slaughtered Christians. Some estimate that as many as 5 million Muslims were driven out of southeastern Europe beginning in 1821 and between 1 million and 2 million more migrated voluntarily after 1878.

Among southeastern Europeans as well, as nationalism came to serve as the primary justification for liberation from Ottoman imperial rule, it became increasingly important to distinguish who did and who did not belong to each ethnically defined nation. Were Muslims in Bulgaria members of the Bulgarian nation? Similar questions complicated Christian attitudes toward Jews in the latter nineteenth century. After several decades of toleration and Jewish social mobility, the rise of mass nationalism would lead people to ask: Are the Jews who live among us in Berlin (or Vienna, Paris, Rome, and Prague) Germans? Do they deserve citizenship in the German (Austrian, French, Italian, or Czech) nation? Such questions would not be easy to resolve.

* * *

In his history of the origin of the word *class*, Raymond Williams wrote that its appearance in the early nineteenth century was rooted in "the increasing consciousness that social position is made rather than merely inherited." The belief that one might improve one's position in the world rather than accepting one's lot in life fueled a number of complementary and contradictory trends. First, ideas about social mobility came into conflict with ideas about unchanging ethnic and religious identities: uncertainty about whether Jews and Muslims could or could not become Europeans is relevant here. Second, ideas about social progress, whether through ascending the ladder or joining together with one's peers, were tied to ideas about popular sovereignty and contributed to the new political ideologies just then being articulated about how societies as a whole could be improved. Third, the idea that one *could* change led people to think that they *should* change, and that led further to the notion that there was something lacking in those who did not change: the "undeserving" poor and the "idle" rich. Charles Dickens (1812–1870) perfectly captured both the promise and the uncertainty of nineteenth-century social identity by beginning his great novel *David Copperfield* with the words: "Whether I shall turn out to be the hero of my own life, or whether that station will be held by anybody else, these pages must show."

FIVE

Ideas and Ideologies

The modern political party system was born in the first decades of the nineteenth century. People began analyzing politics in a systematic way in response to the overthrow of absolutism in France and the revolution's violent denouement, to the Declaration of Independence and creation of constitutional government in North America, and to the rising pace of industrialization. The French and American revolutions had shown that government did not have to be based on tradition or hereditary dynasty. Instead, a people (or the educated and determined elite of a people) could construct a government of their own making, based on their own ideas, and in accordance with what they believed to be the laws of nature and society. These events threw down a political and intellectual gauntlet to the peoples of the European continent.

Jean-Jacques Rousseau had formulated the intellectual challenge in his many writings during the mid-eighteenth century. First, he asked a revolutionary question: "What is the nature of government suitable for forming a people that is the most virtuous, the most enlightened, the wisest, in short, the best?" In other words, governments are to be constructed by people, not received from a divine power. In *The Social Contract* (1762) Rousseau argued that "the best" government would be based on a contract, freely entered into. Natural law guaranteed, he believed, that all men were born free and equal, and therefore free and equal individuals (women were still excluded) could come together to devise a government that would protect the natural rights of one and all.

Not everyone in Europe agreed with Rousseau, and not everyone agreed that the French Revolution's subsequent experiments with liberalism, radicalism, and nationalism had been a success. In the years that followed, every thinking person had to arrive at a personal assessment of *The Social Contract.* Europeans debated the meaning and implications of the revolutions, and in so doing they invented new sets of political ideas, which they offered in the public marketplace for consumption and further discussion. New forms of communication made publicizing political ideas an international phenomenon. Prominent writers on liberalism, conservatism, socialism, and nationalism came from Ireland, France, Scotland, Poland, Italy, Wales, Hungary, and Russia. In countries with minimal censorship, new institutions arose to facilitate those discussions: newspapers and journals, book publishing, clubs and other voluntary associations. In countries where censorship operated, these institutions were far more restricted but they existed nonetheless, in private salons, study groups, underground circles, and in coded discussions in published journals. The ideas that resulted formed the first modern political ideologies and laid the groundwork for the birth of modern political parties.

Liberalism, conservatism, and socialism were separate responses to Rousseau's theoretical challenge and the practical challenge of the French and American revolutions. Nationalism also appeared at this time, not in competition with liberalism, conservatism, or socialism, but rather as an element of each.

Like romanticism and nationalism, the new political ideologies arose within the context of new ideas about individuals and individual human nature. The Enlightenment had idealized individual reason, classical culture, and the symmetry and logic of science. Just as scientists had discovered crucial laws of nature in the preceding centuries, Enlightenment social thinkers believed that logical, reasoning individuals could discover laws of society and create governments that would protect all individuals' rights. They placed reason, science, and progress above faith, nature, and tradition in their thinking about politics, just as they had in their thinking about art and culture. A variety of people found this portrait of humanity troubling or incomplete. The Enlightenment application of reason and science to thinking about politics and society was challenged by views that cherished tradition, faith and feeling and who did not believe that the dark sides of human nature could be conquered by social laws or social contracts. One's position on individualism and human nature influenced one's choice about political allegiance.

If ideologies were in large part responses to past events, they took shape in the context of ongoing political events. Between the 1810s and the 1840s each of these major intellectual systems congealed into one or more political movements and acquired the names by which we know them today. They found a political voice in state formations, popular protests, and intellectuals' discussions. This chapter will examine new political ideas, new kinds of political activity associated with those ideas, and the social and economic contexts for the rise of modern politics.

Conservatism

As a political ideology, conservatism predates the restoration of monarchies and aristocracies at the Congress of Vienna. Many people were horrified by the turmoil and violence of the French Revolution. Conservatism arose to defend the old regime that the revolution had set out to destroy. As early as 1790, Edmund Burke (1729–1797) set the tone for counterrevolutionary conservatism. Burke, an Irishman born in Dublin, studied law and later became a representative in the British parliament. In *Reflections on the Revolution in*

France he provided a thoughtful response to the excesses of revolution, an intellectual defense of tradition, order, and stability. Burke's criticism began with an attack on the Enlightenment, which many people at the time blamed for revolutionary excesses. Like the Romantics, Burke objected to the Enlightenment's overconfidence in reason. He argued that reliance on human reason interfered with the natural evolution of humanity and society, especially when reason was used to justify innovations or reforms of society. Burke argued that the society and government of the old regime had evolved over a long period of time and were therefore tested and true; individuals should not try to meddle with that natural, organic social evolution. In contrast to Enlightenment thinkers and many later liberals, Burke believed that change brought not progress but anarchy.

Burke was also opposed to Enlightenment individualism. He believed that an individual's life had meaning only in the context of a community. Burke favored a society of orders, in which one was born as a member of, and remained legally tied to the nobility, clergy, or peasantry; such a society was unchanging and socially paralyzing but secure. Burke believed that people in these societies benefited more from their sense of belonging to a community than from their identity as individuals. Burke also deeply opposed the revolution's attack on religion, which he saw as the cement that held the various social groups together, despite other differences of wealth, status, and culture. Burke feared that the attack on the church was an attack on all morality and blamed Enlightenment secularization for the violence of the revolution.

Burke's conservatism appealed to many people looking for security in times of change. It appealed particularly to those who had the most to lose from revolutionary change. But his was not an entirely defensive ideology. Burke had a genuine affection for the variety and mystery of tradition. He was not opposed to all reform, but felt it should be approached with caution to prevent wanton destruction and preserve what was valuable from the past. Rage and frenzy, he observed, "pull down more in half an hour, than prudence, deliberation and foresight can build up in a hundred years." Like the Romantics, he saw people as complex beings who often acted on the basis of feeling rather than reason, but the conclusions he drew from that observation differed from those of Romantic rebels and radicals. Precisely because people were often driven by passions, constraints were necessary to control the free will of individuals.

Burke's doctrines were especially welcomed by the émigrés. Among them was Joseph de Maistre (c. 1753–1821), a diplomat in the service of the king of Sardinia, who had been forced into exile when the French overran Savoy and Piedmont. De Maistre combined Burke's conservatism with a belief in the viciousness of the state of nature and a traditional Catholic view of human sin and the need for discipline. The French Revolution, he believed, had been God's punishment for the philosophes' arrogance in believing that society could be remade without divine assistance. The postrevolutionary world needed firm control by an absolute monarch and inspired guidance from the church.

A Closer Look

Gender and Ideology: Conservatism

Conservatism had female advocates who wanted to preserve a gendered order, just as male theorists wanted to preserve social rank and historical traditions. Here Hannah More, one of the most popular writers of her day, justified "separate spheres." On what assumptions about human nature and society does she base her arguments?

The chief end . . . in cultivating the understandings of women, is to qualify them for the practical purposes of life. Their knowledge is not often, like the learning of men, to be reproduced in some literary composition, nor ever in any learned profession; but it is . . . to be exhibited in life and manners. A lady . . . is to read the best books, not so much to enable her to talk of them, as to bring the improvement which they furnish . . . ,and to be instrumental to the good of others. . . .

But they little understand the true interests of woman who would lift her from the important duties of her allotted station, to fill with fantastic dignity a loftier but less appropriate niche. Nor do they understand her true happiness, who seek to annihilate distinctions from which she derives advantages, and to attempt innovations which would depreciate her real value. Each sex has its proper excellencies, which would be lost were they melted down into the common character by the fusion of the new philosophy. . . . Is it not, then, more wise, as well as more hounourable, to move contentedly in the plain path which Providence has obviously marked out to the sex, and in which custom has for the most part rationally confirmed them, rather than to stray awkwardly, unbecomingly, and unsuccessfully in a forbidden road? Is it not desirable . . . to be the best thing of one's own kind, rather than an inferior thing, even if it were of an higher kind?

Hannah More, "The Practical Use of Female Knowledge. . . ." In *The Works of Hannah More*, vol. III (London, 1853), 187–88, 199–201.

In Russia, similar political ideas arose in response to the same challenges and some additional ones. Widespread rural poverty, the persistence of serfdom, and the government's unwillingness to alleviate peasant conditions led Russians into a debate that would become almost universal in the later nineteenth and twentieth centuries. Russians looked to the west European industrial economy and liberal democracy and wondered whether they should or could follow the same path. How could Russia maintain its cultural identity if it embraced European capitalism and individualism? Many Russians, including tsar Nicholas I, believed that Russia's special characteristics significantly distinguished the country from western Europe and endowed it with a special role in history and even a special mission. As a traditional, autocratic, agrarian, and Christian nation (with an Orthodox culture unsullied by the Enlightenment), Russia was, according to this "nativist" way of thinking, superior to the materialistic, secular, chaotic, revolutionary, bourgeois West and could lead Europe on a path of spiritual renewal.

While many nativists shared official beliefs in Russia's unique culture, they did not necessarily support the government's entire position. A group of intellectuals who later came to be known as "Slavophiles" believed in Russia's special spiritual path but were opposed to serfdom, to government interference in intellectual life, and to the bureaucracy and militarism of Nicholas's regime. They shared with western conservatives an idealization of medieval times, which they believed to have been characterized by "natural," "organic" relationships between tsar and people and among the people of all classes. This communalism, or *sobornost,* was embodied in the peasant commune, which seemed to them to be an ideal model for modern forms of community. Slavophiles believed that this happy state of affairs had been ruptured by Peter the Great, who introduced modern bureaucratic political relationships and a servile admiration for the west. *Sobornost,* embodied by the commune, would bring Russians together across class lines on the basis of shared history, religion, and cultural traits.

The political goal of conservatism was to retain as much as possible of the prerevolutionary (or in Russia's case, pre-Petrine) social and political order. This program was given a powerful boost by the resurgence of religion and aristocratic privilege after 1815. The Congress of Vienna had restored not only monarchies and dynasties but some of the traditional rights of aristocracies as well. Autocratic regimes in Russia, Prussia, and Austria were able to exploit fears of the extremes of liberalism to justify their continued power. Friedrich Wilhelm IV of Prussia, for example, argued that only autocracy could provide Christian charity and protect the poor from the predations of laissez-faire liberals. The same regime, on the other hand, heavily supported landed and business interests that were hardly innocent of exploiting the poor. Conservative employers during this period of early industrialization often tried to provide a "familylike" atmosphere in their factories and promoted an image of themselves as paternalistic guardians. All evidence suggests that these industrialists sincerely believed in the benevolence of their paternalism and that their workers did not object to the benefits of such situations and developed a certain amount of loyalty to their employers. But when issues of economic and political conflict emerged, workers in such factories often fought just as hard for their rights as workers in more liberal, modern factories.

In political terms, under the "Metternich system" conservative ideas were translated into a rigid absolutism opposed to any political change. Metternich idealized what he thought of as social "equilibrium," embodied in the prerevolutionary social order. Any challenge to that delicate balance should be suppressed at all costs. But it was too late: European society was already too dynamic to preserve a social structure designed for a preindustrial, static society. Challenges to the conservative order began gathering steam almost immediately.

Liberalism

Liberalism was the nineteenth-century's political adaptation of the Enlightenment, the heir of its confidence in progress and commitment to individual freedom. Liberals believed that progress, generally speaking, would result from their ability to observe and understand society and, through the application of reason, to resolve social problems and improve life for everyone. Some liberals derived their ideas about freedom from a concept of natural rights. They believed, as the Declaration of Independence put it, that by virtue of being human "all Men are created equal, that they are endowed by their Creator with certain unalienable Rights, that among these are Life, Liberty and the Pursuit of Happiness." Other, more extreme liberals believed that individuals should be free to pursue their rational aims, unhindered by any government interference or traditional restrictions, and that all would benefit from the freedom of each. They were particularly opposed to government interference in the economy, and this more mechanistic view of rational individualism was expressed first and most clearly by economists, including Adam Smith.

Economic Liberalism

Economic laissez-faire, based on Smith's argument that economic systems benefited from unfettered individual activity, was developed by two nineteenth-century writers, Thomas Malthus (1766–1834) and David Ricardo (1772–1823). Along with Smith, they were the first to theorize about unhampered economic freedom, claiming that their speculation was based on scientific evidence and pointing to the continued growth of the British economy for proof. But their optimism related only to the middle classes. In their hands, economics became known as "the dismal science" because the benefits of the expanding economy prophesied misery for the working poor.

Educated for the ministry, Malthus was perhaps the first professional economist in history. In 1798 he published his *Essay on Population,* an alarming warning that the human species would breed itself into starvation. In the *Essay,* Malthus formulated a series of natural laws:

> The power of population is indefinitely greater than the power in earth to produce subsistence for man.
> Population, when unchecked, increases in a geometrical ratio.
> Subsistence only increases in an arithmetical ratio.

Misery and vice would spread, Malthus believed, because the unchecked increase in human numbers would lower the demand for labor and therefore lower the wages of labor. The reduction of the human birth rate was the only hope held out to suffering humanity. It was to be achieved by "moral restraint," that is, by late marriage and by "chastity till that period arrives."

Ricardo, too, was a prophet of gloom. He attributed economic activity to three main forces: rent, paid to the owners of great natural resources like farmland and mines; profit, accruing to enterprising individuals who exploited these resources; and wages, paid to the workers who performed the actual labor. Of the three, rent was the most important in the long run. Farms and mines would become depleted and exhausted, but their yield would continue to be in great demand. Rent, accordingly, would consume an ever-larger share of the "economic pie," leaving smaller portions for profit and wages.

Ricardo did not believe that the size of the economic pie was necessarily fixed, and thus did not subscribe entirely to the mercantilist idea that the total wealth of humanity was severely limited, so that more for one person meant less for another. And yet he did predict eventual stagnation. Whereas Adam Smith had cheerfully predicted an increasing division of labor accompanied by steadily rising wages, Ricardo brought labor and wages under the Malthusian formula. Ricardo's disciples hardened this principle into the Iron Law of Wages, which bound workers to an unending cycle of high wages and large families, followed by an increase in the labor supply, a corresponding increase in competition for jobs, and an inevitable slump in wages. The slump would lead workers to have fewer children, followed by a resulting shortage of labor and rising wages; then the whole cycle would begin again. Ricardo himself, however, regarded the cycle not as an Iron Law but simply as a probability. Unforeseen factors in the future might modify its course and might even permit a gradual improvement of the workers' lot.

The classical economists as these early theorists were known proved to be wrong. The size of the economic pie expanded far beyond the expectations of Ricardo, as did the portions allotted to rent, to profit, and to wages. Malthus did not foresee that scientific advances would make the output of agriculture expand at a nearly geometrical ratio. Nor did he know that the perils of increasing birth rates would sometimes be averted by contraception or by emigration.

Laissez-faire liberalism won particular favor with the new industrial magnates. The captains of industry were perhaps disturbed by Ricardo's prediction that profits would inevitably shrink; but they could take comfort from the theory that suffering and evil were "nature's admonitions." It was consoling to the rich to be told, in effect, that the poor deserved to be poor because they had indulged their appetites to excess.

In policy terms, however, middle-class liberals did not always agree on what economic policies would best serve them. In England they called for (and won in Parliament) reduced tariffs in order to foster free trade. French and Hungarian entrepreneurs, on the other hand, wanted high tariffs to protect them against British manufactured goods. The German *Zollverein,* or customs union, provided some protection against British goods, but opened up trade within the German provinces to unfettered commerce. By midcentury commercial interests everywhere wanted government help in building roads and improving communications.

Middle-class liberals widely agreed that they wanted no interference in their contractual relationships with their employees. They fought to prevent the legalization of unions and any law regulating hours and wages. Working-class leaders attacked supporters of the classical economic doctrines for acting without heart and without conscience and for advancing economic theories that seemed only to rationalize their own interests. Many middle-class liberals, however, also came to see laissez-faire economics as heartless.

Utilitarian Liberalism

One path of retreat from stark laissez-faire doctrines originated with Jeremy Bentham (1748–1832), an eccentric philosopher. Bentham founded his social teachings on the concept of utility: he believed that the goal of any action should be to achieve the greatest good for the greatest number. Ordinarily, he believed, governments could best safeguard the well-being of the community by governing as little as possible. In social and economic matters, they should act as "passive policemen" and give private initiative a generally free hand. Yet Bentham realized that the state might become a more active policeman when the pursuit of self-interest by some individuals worked against the best interests of other individuals, since the goal was the greatest good for the greatest number. If the pains endured by the many exceeded the pleasures enjoyed by the few, then the state should step in.

Twentieth-century doctrines of the welfare state owe a considerable debt to the utilitarianism of analysts like Bentham. By the time of his death, Bentham was already gaining an international reputation. He had advised reformers in Portugal, Russia, Greece, and Egypt, and his writings were to exert a broad influence. His most important English disciples, the Philosophic Radicals, pressed for reform of court procedures, local government, and poor relief to free humanity from the artificial constraints of the society. The argument over whether nature (genetic inheritance) or environment (education, family, and state) most determined one's fate was now fully joined.

Humanitarian Liberalism

John Stuart Mill (1806–1873) grew up in an atmosphere dense with the teachings of utilitarianism and classical economics. From his father, James Mill (1773–1836), a utilitarian colleague of Bentham's, he received an education almost without parallel for intensity and speed. He began the study of Greek at age 3, was writing history at 12, and at 16 had organized an active Utilitarian Society. At the age of 20 the overworked youth suffered a breakdown. He turned for renewal to music and the poetry of Wordsworth and Coleridge; presently he fell in love with the married Mrs. Harriet Taylor, to whom he assigned the major credit for his later writings. They remained friends for twenty years, until the death of Mr. Taylor enabled them to marry. The intellectual partnership was important to them both, and they endowed the liberal creed with the warmth and humanity it had lacked.

Mill's humane liberalism was expressed most clearly in *On Liberty* (1859), *Utilitarianism* (1863), *The Subjection of Women* (1869), and his posthumous *Autobiography* (1873). But it is evident, too, in his more technical works, notably *Principles of Political Economy* (1848). He revised this enormously successful textbook several times, each revision departing more and more from the "dismal science" of Ricardo and Malthus.

Mill outlined schemes for curbing overpopulation by promoting emigration to the colonies and "elevating the habits of the labouring people through education." This one example is typical of the way in which Mill's quest for positive remedies led him to modify the laissez-faire attitude. He asserted that workers should be allowed to organize trade unions, form cooperatives, and receive a share of profits. However, these changes could best be secured within the framework of private enterprise, and not by public intervention. But Mill also believed that there were some matters so pressing that the state would have to step in—to protect laboring women and children and to improve intolerable living and working conditions.

Mill made universal suffrage and universal education immediate objectives. All men should have the right to vote; all should be prepared for it by receiving a basic minimum of schooling, if need be at state expense; women should have the same rights. He proposed the introduction of proportional representation in the House of Commons so that political minorities might be assured of a voice. Protection of the rights of the individual became the basis of his essay *On Liberty.*

Based on a combination of utilitarian and humane liberalism, activists in England began to campaign for the alleviation of some of the poor's suffering. Liberals in western Europe called for an end to serfdom in eastern Europe and campaigned actively for the abolition of slavery in Africa and the Americas. The reform that stirred up public opinion most thoroughly was the New Poor Law in England, passed in 1834. This bill made more coherent a system of public relief that had originated in the Elizabethan Poor Law of 1601 and in earlier Tudor legislation. But it also transformed the concept of relief. The old methods of "outdoor relief" had permitted supplementary payments from the parishes to able-bodied poor working for low wages, as well as supplements for children and "doles" paid directly to families living in their own homes. The New Poor Law permitted greater supervision by the central government in London and supplied poorhouses in which able-bodied paupers were made as uncomfortable as the limits of decency would allow. In the past, poverty was seen as an inevitable fact of life, to be alleviated by charity. Under the new law, poverty was assumed to be the fault of the poor, who either did not work hard enough or squandered their income through laziness or drinking and vice. The poorhouse stigmatized the indigent, and it became shameful to be in need of relief. Poorhouses offended humanitarians in the upper classes, but to middle-class business interests, they had the merit of making poor relief more efficient—or so it was alleged. The ideology behind the law—that the Poor Law commissioners would teach discipline and restraint to the poor, including restraint in the size of families—was challenged by many, while the inefficiency of the operation of the law was challenged by even more. Clearly, the New Poor Law did not work. In 1838 in England and Wales there were over 80,000 workhouse inmates; by 1843 the figure was nearly 200,000.

A Closer Look

The New Poverty: Discipline and Punishment in the Workhouse

The passage of the New Poor Law (1834) in England signaled a shift in views of poverty that emphasized the moral deficiency of the impoverished in place of earlier ideas about their misfortune and bad luck. Work houses were intended to retrain the poor by instilling work discipline. Not surprisingly, the poor resented these attitudes and this treatment. Workhouse punishment books record the severity of punishments meted out to inmates in an effort to instill work discipline. Some chilling examples of this can be seen in the "Pauper Offence Book" from Beaminster Union in Dorset. Which offenses received the harshest punishments?

Name	Offence	Punishment
Elliott, Benjamin	Neglect of work	Dinner withheld, and but bread for supper.
Rowe, Sarah	Noisy and swearing	Lock'd up for 24 hours on bread and water.
Aplin, John	Disorderly at Prayer-time	Lock'd up for 24 hours on bread and water.
Mintern, George	Fighting in school	No cheese for one week.
Greenham, Mary, and Payne, Priscella	Quarreling and fighting	No meat 1 week.
Bartlett, Mary	Breaking window	Sent to prison for 2 months.
Park, James	Deserted, got over wall	To be whipped.
Hallett, Isaac	Breaking window	Sent to prison for 2 months hard labour.
Staple, John	Refusing to work	Committed to prison foı 28 days.
Johnson, John	Refusing to work	Cheese & tea stop'd for supper. Breakfast stop'd altogether.
Soaper, Elizabeth	Making use of bad language in bedroom Trying to excite other inmates to insubordination. Refusing to work.	Taken before the Magistrate & committed to prison for 14 days hard labour.

Source: http://users.ox.ac.uk/~peter/workhouse/life.html.

The utilitarian reform with the greatest long-term impact was the repeal of the Corn Laws in 1846, following a long campaign by the Anti-Corn Law League. The Corn Laws were tariffs that protected British farmers by limiting imports of cheap grain, which kept the price of bread artificially high. This pressure group wanted Britain to adopt free trade so that it might export manufactured goods to pay for imports of raw materials and food, which as we have seen was key to the success of the industrial revolution in Britain. In 1846 the Irish potato famine made urgent the need for massive imports of cheap grain, and the Anti-Corn Law League persuaded Tory prime minister Robert Peel to abandon traditional Tory protectionism.

Still another series of reforms were the Factory Acts, begun very modestly in 1802 and 1819. The Act of 1819 applied only to the cotton industry, forbade night work for children, and limited day work to twelve hours; it did not provide for effective inspection and was violated with impunity by many employers. The Act of 1833—forbidding child labor entirely below the age of 9 and restricting it to nine hours for those below 13, and twelve hours for those below 18—also provided for salaried inspectors to enforce the law.

The passage of these and subsequent acts required the support of both conservative Tory and liberal Whig parties, as well as demands from below and paternalistic or self-interested concern from above. Such a political alliance ultimately led to a series of acts that established a basis on which later reformers could build. The major architects of this legislation were Richard Oastler (1789–1861), a Tory; Sir John Cam Hobhouse (1786–1869), a radical; Michael Sadler (1780–1835), the parliamentary leader behind the bill of 1833; and the liberal Lord Shaftesbury (1801–1885). Oastler led the Anti-Poor Law movement and together with Shaftesbury achieved the passage of the Ten Hours Act, which in 1847 limited the normal workweek to ten hours a day, six days a week. Shaftesbury himself sponsored legislation that took women and children out of coal mines and provided for institutionalized care for the mentally ill. The single greatest intervention against the concept of personal property and for universal human rights was the emancipation of slaves throughout the British Empire, passed in 1833. It had the united support of liberal humanitarians and the hard-headed calculations of many business and plantation owners that slavery was no longer economically sound.

Liberals all over Europe spearheaded movements for popular sovereignty and civil rights. Their political aspirations were shared even by many among the working poor. Liberals called for constitutional guarantees of freedom of religion, freedom of speech, and freedom of assembly. They called for the equality of all citizens before the law, the replacement of laws that guaranteed different privileges for people in different social orders. They called for governments to be responsive to the people in elected, representative assemblies with legislative powers. The middle classes supported these ideas in varying degrees. Since everywhere in Europe the bourgeoisie feared popular tyranny as much as they feared the tyranny of kings they often fought for their own right to vote without supporting the same rights of all men (much less women or members of racial and religious minorities). But arguments based on natural rights and individual freedom were taken up by disenfranchised men and women in country after country as the nineteenth century progressed. In southern and eastern Europe, where authoritarian political systems dominated, the liberal goals of a written constitution, limited monarchy, and representative government were paramount. In England and France, where institutions based on limited liberal ideological principles

A Closer Look

Gender and Ideology: Liberalism

Women's advocacy of liberalism was rooted in their own experiences and interests, at times corresponding to and at times differing from men's liberalism. The revolutions of the 1830s opened a floodgate of protest against "female enslavement," and the founding of societies and journals devoted to political and social reform. How were these ideas influenced by Romanticism? Enlightenment rationalism? How do assumptions about similarity and difference shape these women's liberalism?

In her first novel, *Indiana* (1832), George Sand captured a woman's assertion of independence:

Madame Delmare, when she heard her husband's imprecations, felt stronger than she expected. . . .

"Will you condescend to inform me, madame," he said, "where you passed the morning and perhaps the night? . . ."

"No monsieur, I do not propose to tell you. . . . I know that I am the slave and you the master. The laws of this country make you my master. You can bid my body, tie my hands, govern my acts . . . but you cannot command my will, monsieur; God alone can bend it and subdue it. Try to find a law, a dungeon, an instrument of torture that gives you any hold on it! . . ."

"Hold your tongue you foolish impertinent creature; your high-flown novelists' phrases weary me."

"You can impose silence on me, but not prevent me from thinking."

Eliza Sharples was a radical writer, editor, and activist. The following is from a speech she made in 1832:

O Liberty! Though abuses have been committed in thy name—though vice shelters itself under thy angel-wings, yet thou are virtue's God . . . I have left a happy home and comparative affluence to launch the frail bark of my intellect, my soul, my genius, my spirit, on the ocean of politics; . . . And to you, ladies, sisters, with your leave, I would say, I appeal, and ask in what way are you prepared to assist me? . . . Will you not be offended at this step of mine, original to my understanding, but, I think, not unworthy of us, nor unbecoming in me? Are you prepared to advance as I have already advanced . . . and seek that equality in human society which nature has qualified us for, but which tyranny, the tyranny of our lords and masters, hath suppressed? . . . we are as men in mind and purpose; . . . we may make ourselves [their help-meets] on the condition that . . . we shall be free to all the advantages, all the privileges, all the pleasures of human life.

Marion Kirkland Reid (1843) based her argument for equal political rights on views that included sameness and difference.

The ground on which equality is claimed for all men is of equal force for all women; for women share the common nature of humanity, and are possessed of all those noble faculties which constitute man a responsible being and give him a claim to be his own ruler. . . . We are aware that it is said, that woman is virtually represented in Parliament, her interest being the same as those of man; but the many laws which have been obliged to be passed to protect them from their nearest male relatives, are a sufficient answer. . . . but the manifestly unjust nature of the laws which this necessity has produced, . . . [show] most distinctly, that no sentiment, either of justice or gallantry, has been sufficient to ensure anything like impartiality in the laws between the sexes. . . . [and] that woman requires representation, and second, that she is not represented.

Louise Otto (1851), a German journalist, wrote that the differences between man and woman are complementary:

We insist on the equality of women with men. . . . Man and woman appeared through the hand of God or creation . . . as two complete creatures of equal rank; but the difference in their physical characteristics are also maintained in the life of the spirit. The union of both produces a balance of these differences. The man in himself and the woman in herself are equally significant individuals. . . . Women ought to be able to act in common for the common good, as well as for their own development, with the same freedom as men. In the struggle for woman's freedom it is particularly important to rescue what is truly womanly; to liberate it from that one-sided despotism of judgment that has been developed by men by degrees and from which not only the female sex, but the entire better part of mankind suffers. . . . My speaking "more from the heart than from the head" is neither reproach nor praise—it is the essence of woman. I have never desired anything else, never striven to change this. I have offered myself with my heart for the fatherland, for humanity—and the more I participate in and work for public affairs, the more I recognize how much better it would be if in all matters of state or of society the heart played a great part than it now does.

Women, the Family, and Freedom: The Debate in Documents, vol. 1, *1750–1880*, ed.Susan Groag Bell and Karen M. Offen (Stanford, 1983): Sand, pp. 148–49; Sharples, pp. 131–32; Reid, pp. 233, 236; Otto, pp. 297–298

already existed, liberals worked to make government more inclusive and representative.

Liberals supported the idea of a thriving "public sphere" (though the term was not used at the time). The public sphere is an open uncensored arena for discussion of all issues affecting society. The public sphere included institutions such as newspapers, clubs, and voluntary associations that arose to support everything from literacy education for the poor to amateur scientific experimentation, musical performance, philosophical debates, and sports teams. These public, community activities were notable for their autonomy from the state and from traditional institutions like church or family and modern ones like a person's job or business. For people trying to establish individual and collective identities and personal political beliefs, the institutions that made up the public sphere were as important as the foundational ideological ideas themselves.

Liberalism took a somewhat different forms in Russia. The 1830s and 1840s were a period of intense political debate among intellectuals. Censorship and Nicholas I's attempt to prevent any kind of criticism of his reign confined these debates to carefully coded publications and discussions in private salons, known in Russia as *kruzhki,* or circles. In contrast to the Slavophiles mentioned earlier, who believed that Russia could forge its own path, Russian "Westernizers" looked to western Europe for models of development. The Westernizers harshly criticized the tsarist government for ignoring the plight of the Russian people. They saw Russia as "backward" in comparison to the West and believed that the only solution to Russia's problems lay in introducing liberal individualism, democratic reform, a constitution, the rule of law, and popular education. They were not wholly uncritical of western Europe, however.

Both Westernizers and Slavophiles deplored the crass commercialism of industrial society and saw the western bourgeoisie as mercenary and uncultured. In fact, the divide between these groups in Russia was far less rancorous than in other countries. Not all Slavophiles were opposed to economic modernization, and Westernizers found as much in the West to criticize as to admire. Both groups passionately favored freedom of speech and press, and both were opponents of autocracy. These similarities are rooted in the fact that Russia faced two serious problems on which most thinking people could agree: serfdom and autocracy. They differed in some of their solutions, but they all had to take into account Russia's enormous agrarian population and its intransigent and resilient tsarist authoritarianism. Looking back, Alexander Herzen would say of the Slavophiles and Westernizers: "We looked in different directions but one heart throbbed within us."

Toward Democracy: The Vote

Political representation and constitutional protection of individual rights did not come anywhere without a struggle. In Britain in the 1820s, the rising middle classes had small opportunity to mold national policy. Booming industrial cities like Manchester and Birmingham sent not a single representative to the House of Commons. A high proportion of business leaders did not belong to the Church of England but were nonconformists who still suffered discrimination when it came to holding public office or sending their sons (not to speak of their daughters) to Oxford or Cambridge. Even in France, despite the gains made since 1789, the bourgeoisie often enjoyed only second-class status.

In Great Britain, middle-class liberals won the place they felt they deserved in the Reform Bill of 1832. But the middle classes were not the only people who wanted the right to vote and were willing to work for it. When laborers tried to win the vote, the limits of Parliament's inclination to share power were exposed. The London Workingmen's Association for Benefiting Politically, Socially, and Morally the Useful Classes was founded in 1836. Its founders wrote a charter that called for universal male suffrage, the secret ballot, annual elections, and other reforms, including salaries for members of Parliament so that working men could afford to serve. Workers wanted direct representation in Parliament to press for legislation that would mitigate the hardships brought on by the industrial revolution. Millions of men signed the Great Charter, as it came to be called, before the document was delivered to Parliament in 1839. The Chartists' strength lay in the urban industrial proletariat, particularly the unions, and the movement was supported by many intellectuals of varied social and economic backgrounds. Parliament refused even to consider the Charter. When workers presented it a second time in 1842, accompanied by 3.3 million signatures, Parliament again rejected it out of hand. A small group of workers in northern England threatened strikes and insurrections to press for reform, but for the most part in the 1830s millions of working-class "Chartists" used the same tactics the middle classes had used for the same ends, and failed. It would take decades more for British working men to get the vote.

As the Chartist movement shows, popular sovereignty was harder to win for some than others, and across Europe liberal electoral reform came in fits and starts. Many members of the middle classes wanted the vote for themselves but believed that only people with education and property should be enfranchised. Workers and women had to struggle much harder to win rights that middle classes achieved more easily. And some countries, from Ireland to Poland, remained imperial properties of one of the Great Powers. Some liberals, often called radicals, pressed harder for more extreme political reform. In the 1830s and 1840s radicals in many countries began working for universal male suffrage, an end to monarchy, and the establishment of a republic. Radicals shared most other liberal goals. They were not socialists. They believed in legal constitutional guarantees of civil and political rights, but they thought everyone in society should share those rights.

To conservative Europeans, liberal principles and politics seemed extreme. But others found that even radical liberalism did not satisfy their hopes for political rights and social justice. When the right to vote proved elusive or insufficient to meet their economic goals, working men and women and national minorities turned to new ideologies: socialism and nationalism.

Socialism

Constitutional government and the right to vote were only the first steps towards what some people saw as genuine equality.

In the 1830s and 1840s, workers and middle-class social observers were critical of liberalism for several reasons. Liberalism seemed to favor the middle classes at the expense of the poor. As the politics of capitalism it was used by some to justify the inhumane treatment of workers. In the 1830 revolutions, for example, French liberals benefited from the mass display of working-class discontent to win political concessions for themselves. Dissatisfied with the political settlement of 1830, workers in Paris rebelled in 1832 and in Lyons in 1831 and 1834. Both workers and middle-class liberals wanted political representation in order to make governments support their economic aspirations and protect their civil rights. Workers in factories and shops wanted the right to vote in order to defend their own interests against their bourgeois employers, who kept them poorly paid, ill fed, and badly housed. Liberal political goals created unanticipated conflicts between these social groups. Workers would continue to share many liberal political aims; but they began to see that voting in and of itself would not alleviate the conditions in which they lived and worked. And while they shared liberal political goals, they had little sympathy for the members of middle class who kept them impoverished.

Criticism of liberalism was often linked to criticism of industrial capitalism. Although the potential of the industrial revolution to transform everyday life and make some people very wealthy was becoming evident in western Europe by the 1830s and 1840s, it was also clear that that wealth was not distributed evenly. In fact it seemed at that time that the industrial system had some serious flaws: periodic business crises, unpredictable patterns of unemployment, and fluctuating wages. The people who produced the goods that made the few wealthy were working 14 or 16 hours a day, receiving near starvation wages, and living in filthy, dangerous, pestilential slums. By the 1830s mass urban poverty seemed to be the main result of industrialization. Liberals had criticized capitalism for these reasons as well, but socialists went further in their analysis of the causes for these shortcomings and in proposing means for rectifying them to create a better society. Unlike liberals, socialists proceeded from the belief that society was not a mere accumulation of autonomous individuals, put on earth to compete with one another in the pursuit of self-interest. Socialists believed that people are social creatures, whose lives derive their meaning from cooperating with one another. The socialist, Robert Owen (1771–1858), wrote that "The primary and necessary object of all existence is to be happy, but happiness cannot be obtained individually."

Workers criticized middle-class businessmen and factory owners as parasites who did not understand the nature of hard physical work. They valued community and associations of various kinds rather than individual competition. Some intellectuals who shared their critique of capitalism and liberalism invented a new ideology, socialism.

In his later years J. S. Mill referred to himself as a socialist; by his standard, however, most voters today are socialists. Universal suffrage for men and for women, universal free education, the curbing of laissez-faire policies in the interests of the general welfare, the use of the power to tax to limit the unbridled accumulation of private property—all these major changes foreseen by Mill are now widely accepted. But modern socialists did not stop, as Mill did, with changes in the distribution of wealth; rather, they went on to propose changes in arrangements for the production of goods. The control of the means of production is to be transferred from individuals to the community as a whole, which is then to share in the profits and benefits of production.

Historically, socialism denotes any philosophy that advocates the vesting of production in the hands of society and not in those of private individuals. In practice in the twentieth century, as in China or the Soviet Union, for example, socialism usually meant that the state, acting as the theoretical trustee of the community, owned at least the major industries, such as coal, railroads, and steel. Socialism in its most complete form theoretically involved public ownership of almost all the instruments of production, including the land itself, virtually eliminating private property. To varying degrees in the late twentieth century, most European states engaged in some practices derived from original socialist theories: control of some industries, some utilities, some forms of transportation. Canada, Australia, and Sweden are examples of what are referred to as "mixed economies."

In the twentieth century, countries with revolutionary socialist governments often called themselves communist, but in the nineteenth century the terms *socialism* and *communism* were used almost interchangeably.

Utopian Socialism

The earliest socialist theorists were called "utopian" socialists because many of them not only criticized societies undergoing industrial revolution but also drew up blueprints for ideal (utopian) societies. Above all they shared a revulsion at extremes of individualism and based their plans on the human capacity for cooperation rather than competition. Their consideration of religion, psychology, and basic human feelings shows the influence of Romanticism, but they also believed that rational human beings could solve the problems society posed. In many cases, the utopian socialists not only dreamed up plans for harmonious communities, but organized them, sometimes in the Americas. Their theories sound quaint today, but they attracted the support of thousands of workers in the early nineteenth century, especially in France and later in Russia.

Count Claude-Henri de Saint-Simon (1760–1825), considered the first such utopian, does not fit easily into any pigeonhole, which probably suits a socialist who descended from one of the oldest aristocratic families in France. Educated by Enlightenment philosophes, the young Saint-Simon fought with the French army in the American War of Independence. During the French Revolution he made and lost a large fortune, but despite his reverses he never lost his enthusiasm for the enormous potential of the industrial age. He admonished the members of the new capitalist elite: "Christianity commands you to use all your powers to increase as rapidly as possible the social welfare of the poor!" Saint-Simon was not opposed to social hierarchies, but he called for society to reward those who produced the most rather than those who owned the most. Productive workers—farmers and laborers, but also artists and intellectuals—would top the hierarchy in his ideal society. Saint-Simon sought a form of social organization that would guarantee individual freedom, but that society he believed would incorporate individuals into a rationally organized, scientifically managed community.

"Organization," "harmony," and "industry" were three of Saint-Simon's catchwords. When all three elements were coordinated, humanity would achieve some of the major improvements he proposed, among them great networks of highways and waterways, and would become a single, rational society. After Saint-Simon's death, his followers focused on the strain of social Christianity in his teaching. Prosper Enfantin (1796–1864) combined local railroads into a Paris–Lyons–Mediterranean trunk line, and another Saint-Simonian, Ferdinand de Lesseps (1805–1894), promoted the building of a Suez Canal and made an abortive start at digging across the Isthmus of Panama.

The vagueness of Saint-Simon's concepts permitted almost every kind of social thinker—from laissez-faire liberal to communist—to cite him with approval. Among his disciples were Giuseppe Mazzini and Louis Blanc, the Russian revolutionary pioneer Alexander Herzen, and the French positivist philosopher Auguste Comte. What was socialist about Saint-Simon was his goal of reorganizing and harmonizing society as a whole, rather than merely improving the well-being of some of its individual members.

Saint-Simon and most of the other utopian socialists tended to have positive views about women's capacities, and there was greater scope for women's accomplishment and independence in most of their ideal communities. Saint-Simon became known for his advocacy of extramarital sex, or "free love," as its detractors called it. As a result, many educated women and some working women were drawn to Saint-Simonism. The *Saint-Simoniennes* represented a range of views, but most called for women's suffrage and some kind of marriage reform, sexual freedom, and legalized divorce. Some French working-class followers of Saint-Simon succeeded against all odds in organizing a women's newspaper and engaging in other forms of social activism.

Saint-Simon's compatriot and contemporary Charles Fourier (1772–1837) also extolled harmony and drew up an elaborate blueprint for achieving it. At the French textile center of Lyons, Fourier was appalled by the contrast between the wealth of the silk manufacturers and the misery of their workers. In Paris he was shocked when he found that a single apple was selling for the same price a hundred apples would cost in the countryside. Clearly, he concluded, something was amiss in a society that permitted such disparities.

Just as Newton had found the force holding the heavenly bodies in a state of mutual attraction, so Fourier claimed to have discovered the force holding the individuals of human society in a state of mutual attraction. This force was *l'attraction passionnelle;* that is, human beings were drawn to one another by their passions. Fourier drew up a list of passions—sex, companionship, food, luxury, variety, and so on, to a total of 810. Since existing society thwarted the satisfaction of people's passions, Fourier proposed that it be remodeled into units he called *phalanges* (phalanxes), each containing 400 acres of land and accommodating 500 to 2,000 (though ideally 1,620) persons. Volunteers would form a phalanx by setting up a community company and agreeing to split its profits three ways—five twelfths to those who did the work, four twelfths to those who undertook the management, and three twelfths to those who supplied the capital.

Fourier's phalanx, with its relatively generous rewards to managers and capitalists, fell short of complete equality. Yet it did assign to labor the largest share of the profits, and it foreshadowed many other features of socialist planning. Each phalanx would be nearly self-sufficient, producing in its own orchards, fields, and workshops most of the things required by the inhabitants. Adult workers who performed the most dangerous or unpleasant tasks would change their jobs eight times a day because "enthusiasm cannot be sustained for more than an hour and a half or two hours in the performance of one particular operation." They would work from four to five in the morning to eight or nine at night, enjoying five meals. They would need only five hours of sleep, since the variety of work would not tire them. All would become so healthy that physicians would be superfluous, and everyone would live to age 140.

Both to eliminate the evil of prostitution and to allow human association the fullest possible scope, Fourier advocated complete sexual freedom in the phalanx; he recommended marriage only for the elderly, whose passions had begun to cool. While colonies sprang up in which Fourierism was tried, especially in the New World, public opinion, including working-class opinion, remained hostile to surrendering the privacy of the family.

The utopians made significant contributions to socialist theory and social psychology. Some of Fourier's recommendations, including higher pay for dangerous jobs and the use of devices for relieving the tedium of work, have become common practice in modern business.

In 1800 self-made British businessman and utopian socialist, Robert Owen, took over the large cotton mills at New Lanark in Scotland and found conditions that shocked him. A large part of the working force consisted of children who had been recruited from orphanages in Edinburgh when they were between 6 and 8 years old. Although the youngsters did get a little schooling after hours, Owen found many of them "dwarfs in body and mind." Adult laborers at New Lanark fared little better.

Remaking New Lanark into a model industrial village, Owen set out to show that he could increase profits and the welfare of his laborers at the same time. For the adults he provided better working conditions, a 10.5-hour day, higher pay, and improved housing. He raised the minimum age for employment to 10, hoping ultimately to put it at 12, and he gave his child laborers time off for schooling. A properly educated nation, Owen believed, would refute the gloomy predictions of Malthus, who "has not told us how much more food an intelligent and industrious people will create from the same soil, than will be produced by one ignorant and ill-governed."

In the 1820s Owen visited America to finance what would be a failed effort to set up a colony at New Harmony, Indiana. Undaunted by this failure, he spent the rest of his career publishing and supporting projects for social reform. He advocated the association of all labor in one big union—another experiment that failed, though the call was taken up later in the United States; and he sought to reduce workers' expenditures by promoting the formation of consumers' cooperatives—an experiment that succeeded. He, too,

The Institute for the Formation of Character, New Lanark, Scotland. Robert Owen insisted that all children have equal capabilities if they are properly educated from an early age. All working-class children in his model community went to school. Owen was proud of the school and loved showing it off, as can be seen in this drawing, which includes an audience. Owen also believed in using visual stimulation, also shown here, which he considered more natural for children than reading books. (New Lanarck Conservation)

offended many with his attacks on established religion and his enthusiasm for spiritualism.

Both Owen and Fourier relied on private initiative to build their model communities. In contrast, Louis Blanc (1811–1882) developed Saint-Simon's vaguely formulated principle of "organization" into a doctrine of state intervention to achieve utopian ends. Blanc outlined his scheme for social workshops in a pamphlet, *The Organization of Labor* (1840), which began with the statement, "The other day a child was frozen to death behind a sentry-box in the heart of Paris, and nobody was shocked or surprised at the event."

"What proletarians need," Blanc wrote, "is the instruments of labor; it is the function of government to supply these. If we were to define our conception of the state, our answer would be that the state is the banker of the poor." The government would finance and supervise the purchase of productive equipment and the formation of social workshops; it would withdraw its support and supervision once the workshops were on their feet. As the workshops gradually spread throughout France, socialistic enterprise would replace private enterprise, private profits would vanish, and labor would emerge as the only class left in society, thereby achieving a classless society.

Much of Louis Blanc's socialism was characteristically utopian, particularly in his reliance on workers to make their own arrangements for communal living. The real novelty of his plan lay in the role he assigned to the state and in the fact that he began to move socialism from philanthropy to politics. Ironically, politics was to prove his undoing. Alarmed conservatives identified the national workshops of 1848 as an effort to implement his social ideas, and he was forced into exile.

The utopian socialist with the largest working-class following was Étienne Cabet (1788–1856). His widely read novel, *Voyage to Icaria* (1840), applied Christian principles to social organization and described a society in which harmony ruled. In the 1840s as many as 50,000 workers, mostly tailors, shoemakers and other skilled artisans (whose jobs in small workshops were threatened by mass production) counted themselves "Icarians." Cabet's newspaper had 4,500 subscribers. Some of his followers set out with Cabet for the Americas, where he founded colonies in Iowa and Texas.

Utopian socialism appeared slightly later in Russia, after 1848, though its origins lay in the Westernizer and Slavophile debates of the 1830s and 1840s. Alexander Herzen, the former Westernizer and outspoken critic of Nicholas's regime, combined elements of Westernism and Slavophilism to create what became Russia's unique brand of utopian socialism. Like other radical intellectuals of his day, Herzen called for the abolition of serfdom and the overthrow of autocracy; but he came to believe that the revolutionary spirit in Russia and the model for the future society lay in its vast countryside among its peasant population. Most Westernizers had seen the peasant commune as a pit of backwardness and stagnation, but for Herzen it was a native Russian model of egalitarian organization. He wanted to see the establishment of a communal society organized around the peasant commune but with all the constitutional protections for individual civil rights provided by a rule of law. Russian utopian socialism had pronounced Romantic and liberal–nationalist elements. During the 1850s "peasant socialism" would become a popular idea, and successive generations of young radicals would look to the peasantry (usually from afar) for a source of Russian authenticity, simple wisdom, and revolutionary zeal. Just as often, they were disappointed with the real world of peasant poverty and resignation.

Frustration with such dreamy visions led some young critics to espouse more radical and hard-nosed forms of socialism.

Karl Marx and Marxism

It was Karl Marx (1818–1883) who lumped together all the other socialists of his day under the label "utopian." He was intent on distinguishing his own critique of capitalism and his theory of social organization from theirs. Marx not only analyzed industrial capitalism, but he studied the history of economic, social, and political structures and subjected that history to rigorous philosophical analysis. He then constructed his theories according to what he thought were "scientific" laws of historical evolution. Marx's ultimate socialist society was no less utopian than that of contemporary theorists, but his analysis of capitalism gave the workers and radical intellectuals of his day much stronger weapons for confronting their employers and authoritarian governments. In the mid-nineteenth century, his ideas were just one intellectual system among many others. But in the second half of the century Marxism became a powerful force for change, attracting millions of followers in Europe and around the world.

Born in the Rhineland to a middle-class family, Marx attended the University of Berlin, where he studied Hegelian philosophy and became involved in radical politics and journalism. In 1843 the Prussian government drove him from the country after it had had enough of his radical newspaper's criticism. He went to Paris, where he encountered the utopian socialists and studied histories of the French Revolution. Soon the French government also tired of his biting attacks and open atheism and expelled him as well. Marx settled in London in 1849 and spent the rest of his life there. In 1844 he had met and befriended another young middle-class German, Friedrich Engels (1820–1895). Engels had worked in his family's textile mill in Manchester, England, and in 1844 wrote a penetrating exposé of industrial exploitation, *The Condition of the Working Class in England.* Marx traveled around industrial England with Engels to collect observations of capitalism firsthand. In many ways, the two German socialists made a striking contrast. Marx was poor and quarrelsome, a man of few friends; except for his devotion to his wife and children, he was utterly preoccupied with his economic studies. Engels, on the other hand, was the son of a well-to-do German manufacturer and represented the family textile business in Liverpool and Manchester. He loved sports and high living, but he also hated the evils of industrialization.

Both Engels and Marx took an interest in the Communist League, a small, secret international organization of radical workers. In 1847 the London office of the Communist League requested that they draw up a program. Engels wrote the first draft, which Marx revised; the result, the *Communist Manifesto,* remains the classic statement of Marxian socialism. In fewer than fifty pages, Marx and Engels laid out a concise version of their critique of capitalism, a historical analysis of the origins of capitalist exploitation, a forecast of the future (based on the same "scientific laws of history"), and a call to arms. At the time, it was only one of a hundred radical pamphlets, but it would go on to become perhaps the most influential and widely read political document of the nineteenth and early twentieth centuries.

The *Manifesto* opens with a dramatic announcement: "A spectre is haunting Europe—the spectre of Communism." It closes with a stirring and confident appeal:

> Let the ruling classes tremble at a Communistic revolution.
> The proletarians have nothing to lose but their chains. They have a world to win.
> Working men of all countries, unite!

In between it narrates a communist view of history: "The history of all hitherto existing society is the history of class struggle." Changing economic conditions determined that the struggle should develop successively between "freeman and slave, patrician and plebian, lord and serf, guildmaster and journeyman." The guild system gave way first to manufacture by large numbers of small capitalists and then to "the giant, modern industry," which would inevitably destroy bourgeois society. Industry creates mounting economic pressures by producing more goods than it can sell; it creates mounting social pressures by depriving more and more people of their property and forcing them down to the lowest class, the proletariat. These pressures would increase until a revolutionary explosion would occur. Landed property would be abolished outright; other forms of property would be liquidated more gradually through the imposition of crushing income taxes and the abolition of inherited wealth.

Eventually, social classes and tensions would vanish, and "we shall have an association in which the free development of each is the condition for the free development of all." The *Manifesto* provides only this vague description of life after the revolution. Since Marx defined political authority as "the organized power of one class for oppressing another," he apparently expected that "the state would wither away." After having created a classless, conflictless regime, the state would become irrelevant. He seems to have assumed that the great dialectical process of history, having achieved its final synthesis, would then cease to operate in its traditional form.

Marx's writing combined Enlightenment faith in natural law and the scientific analysis of social life with Hegel's Romantic philosophy of history. Marx found three laws in the pattern of history. First, *economic determinism:* he believed that economic conditions largely determined the character of all other human institutions—society and government, religion and art. Second, *the class struggle:* he believed that history was a dialectical process, a series of conflicts between antagonistic economic groups, ideas, and practices. In his own day the antagonists were the "haves" and the "have-nots"—the bourgeoisie against the proletarians. Third, the *inevitability of communism:* he believed that the class struggle was bound to produce one final upheaval that would raise the victorious proletariat over the prostrate bourgeoisie. As he wrote to a friend in 1852, "What I did that was new was to prove (1) that the *existence of classes* is bound up with *particular historical phases in the development of production,* (2) that the class struggle necessarily leads to the *dictatorship of the proletariat,* (3) that this dictatorship itself only constitutes the transition to *abolition of all* classes and to a *classless society.*"

From Adam Smith's labor theory of value, Marx concluded that the worker should receive the profits from the sale of a commodity, since the value of the commodity should be determined by the labor of the person who produced it. The Iron Law of Wages, however, confirmed Marx's belief that capitalism would never permit workers to receive this just reward. And from observing the depression of the late 1840s, he concluded that economic crises were bound to occur again and again under a system in which capital produced too much and labor consumed too little.

Marx oversimplified human nature by trying to force it into the rigid mold of economic determinism and ignoring nonmaterial motives and interests. Neither proletarians nor bourgeois have proved to be the simple economic mechanisms Marx supposed them to be. Labor has often assumed a markedly bourgeois outlook and mentality; capital has eliminated some of the worst injustices of the factory system. Like Malthus, Marx did not foresee the notable rise in the general standard of living that began in the mid-nineteenth century and continued well into the twentieth.

Since Marx also failed to take into account the growing strength of nationalism, the *Manifesto* confidently expected the class struggle to transcend national boundaries. In social and economic warfare, nation would not be pitted against nation; the proletariat everywhere would join to fight the bourgeoisie. In Marx's own lifetime, however, national differences and antagonisms were, in fact, increasing from day to day.

It is easy to point out the errors of judgment and analysis Marx made, but some of his predictions turned out to be true in ways he may not have expected. The *Communist Manifesto* anticipated the strengths as well as the weaknesses of the communist movement. First, it foreshadowed the important role to be played by propaganda. Second, it anticipated the emphasis to be placed on the role of the party in forging the proletarian revolution. The communists, Marx declared, were "the most advanced section of the working-class parties of every country." In matters of theory, they had the advantage over the great mass of the proletariat of "clearly understanding the line of march, the conditions, and the ultimate general results of the proletarian movement." Third, the *Manifesto* assigned the state a great role in the revolution. Among the policies recommended by Marx were "centralization of credit in the hands of the state" and "extension of factories and instruments of production owned by the state." Today it is hard to avoid the conclusion that economic globalization has made apparent the large role played by governments in protecting the economic interests of increasingly large corporations.

From 1849 until his death in 1883, Marx lived in London, where, partly because of his own financial mismanagement, his family experienced the misery of a proletarian existence in the slums of Soho. After poverty and near starvation had caused the death of three of his children, he eventually obtained a modest income from his own writings and Engels' generosity. Throughout this time he revised his writings producing the first volume of *Capital* in 1867. Two further volumes of *Capital,* pieced together from his notes, were published after his death.

In *Capital* Marx spelled out the labor theory of value according to which the workers created the total value of the commodity they produced, yet received in the form of wages only a small part of the price. The worker's wages constituted *surplus value,* something actually created by labor but appropriated by capital as profit. It was the nature of capitalism, Marx argued, to diminish its own profits by replacing human labor with machines and thus gradually choking off the source of surplus value. Thus would arise a mounting crisis of overpopulation and underconsumption. Marx considered *Capital* his greatest work and a serious contribution to the ongoing struggle to improve human society. Although Marx may have overestimated the book's value in effecting social change, he was correct in his evaluation of the work's analytical value:

Capital was the first thoroughgoing analysis of the fundamental mechanisms of modern economic systems. It showed the ways that advantages accrue to property owners and employers through wage and price systems, while workers have little but their ability to work to trade for wages.

Apostles of Violence and Nonviolence

The various forms of liberalism and socialism did not exhaust the range of responses to the economic and social problems created in industrial societies. Nationalists reinvigorated old mercantilist ideas, not only advocating tariffs to protect agriculture and industry but also demanding that colonies abroad provide new markets for surplus products, new fields for the investment of surplus capital, and new settlements for surplus citizens. Others advocated anarchy and violence, while nonviolent preachers of mutualism, goodwill, and good works sought to return to primitive Christianity.

Tradition assigns the honor of being the first modern socialist to Gracchus Babeuf and his fellow conspirators under the French Directory in 1796–1797. The egalitarianism of Babeuf was too loosely formulated to be called truly socialist, however; the only direct link between him and later socialist doctrines derives from his followers' belief that human nature could change only through immediate violent action in the manner of the Reign of Terror. The leader of these new terrorists was Auguste Blanqui (1805–1881), a professional revolutionary who participated in every Paris revolt of the nineteenth century. Blanqui believed that the imposition of a dictatorial regime by an elite vanguard of conspirators would be the only way to deal with a bourgeois capitalist society. An inveterate plotter of violence, he spent forty of his seventy-six years in prison. When his movement died out in the 1870s, his followers tended to join the Marxian socialists.

Anarchists

Other proponents of violence called themselves anarchists, believing that the best government was no government at all. For them it was not enough that the state should wither away at some distant time, all such instruments of oppression should be annihilated at once. The anarchist ideal exerted an important influence on the proletarian movement. The Russian revolutionary Prince Peter Kropotkin (1842–1921) made the most complete statement of anarchist theory in his book *Mutual Aid: A Factor in Evolution* (1902). Kropotkin foresaw a revolution that would abolish the state as well as private property and would lead to a new society of cooperating autonomous groups within which workers would need to labor only four to five hours a day. Kropotkin's countryman and fellow anarchist Mikhail Bakunin (1814–1876) helped to shape the Russian revolutionary movement and won the attention of workers from many countries by his participation in the First International. Bakunin contributed to the formation of the program known as anarchosyndicalism (from the French word *syndicat,* which means an economic grouping, particularly a trade union). The anarchosyndicalists scorned political parties, especially Marxist ones. They believed in direct action by the workers culminating in a spontaneous general strike that would free labor from the capitalistic yoke. Meantime, workers could rehearse for the great day by engaging in acts of anticapitalist sabotage. In 1908 these theories received their most forceful expression in *Reflections on Violence* by a French engineer and anarchosyndicalist, Georges Sorel (1847–1922), who declared that belief in the general strike constituted a kind of false hope that would convert all workers into saboteurs. But the writer most frequently cited by the anarchosyndicalists was the French publicist Pierre-Joseph Proudhon (1809–1865). "What is property?" Proudhon asked in a pamphlet in 1840. "Property is theft," he answered.

Christian Socialists and Christian Democrats

Still other efforts to mitigate class antagonisms came from the Anglican and Roman Catholic churches. In England the Christian Socialists urged the Church of England to put aside theological disputes and direct its efforts toward ending social misery. The Christian Socialists attacked materialism and championed brotherly love against unbrotherly strife, and association and cooperation against exploitation and competition. They relied far more on private philanthropy than on state intervention, however, as did their Catholic counterparts on the Continent, who advocated what they called Christian democracy or social Christianity.

By the second half of the nineteenth century an atmosphere of crisis was enveloping the Roman Catholic church. A thousand years of papal rule in central Italy ended when the government of Rome passed to the newly unified kingdom of Italy in 1870; anticlerical legislation threatened traditional Catholic bulwarks in Italy, France, and Germany; and the materialism of the industrial revolution and the new ideologies of science, nationalism, and socialism were all competing for the allegiance of Catholics. The church initially responded to these problems by seeking refuge in the past. Pope Pius IX (r. 1846–1878) issued the *Syllabus of Errors* in 1864, condemning many social theories and institutions not consecrated by tradition. While Pius also condemned the materialism implicit in laissez-faire, socially minded Catholics were disturbed by his apparent hostility to trade unions and democracy.

His successor, Leo XIII (r. 1878–1903), recognized that the church could not continue to turn its back on modernity without suffering serious losses. He knew that Catholicism was flourishing in the supposedly hostile climate of the democratic and largely Protestant United States. Moreover, his study of St. Thomas Aquinas convinced him that the church had much to gain by following the middle-of-the-road social and economic policies Aquinas recommended. Accordingly, Leo XIII issued a series of modernizing documents, notably the encyclical *Rerum novarum* (Concerning New Things, 1891).

In *Rerum novarum* Pope Leo described the defects of capitalism as vigorously as any socialist, but attacked with equal vigor the socialist view of property and the doctrine of class war. Leo believed that the workers must help themselves, and *Rerum novarum* concludes with a fervent appeal for the formation of Catholic trade unions.

These Catholic unions exist today, but they are only a minority in the realm of organized labor. Neither the Christian democracy of Leo XIII nor the Christian socialism of the Anglican reformers has achieved all that their founders hoped. Yet the Christian democrats eventually came to play a central part in the politics of Germany, Italy, and other European states. In Britain at the beginning of the twentieth century, both Marxism and Christian socialism attracted workers and middle-class intellectuals to the developing Labour party.

Mass Political Movements

The nineteenth-century preoccupation with analyzing society, and attempting to forge an ideal one, produced a large number of competing political programs and dreams. At one time historians thought that conservatives were primarily drawn from privileged elites, that liberals were all bourgeois, and that socialists included a handful of intellectuals and a mass of workers. There is some truth to this generalization, but its shortcomings are worth examining. Certainly people who were politically inclined aligned themselves with ideologies that protected their interests. But the stress on community was shared by conservatives and socialists, the desire for constitutions was shared by many workers with the bourgeoisie, and the middle classes disagreed among themselves about whether republican or constitutional monarchy was the better option. Various kinds of people favored a rule of law for its impersonal justice and practical protections. Opponents to a rule of law ranged from supporters of autocracy who thought the harshness of modern life required personal relationships between rulers and their subjects to Marxists who believed that law, far from being impersonal, served the interests of the "ruling class." Finally, many people favored political programs that seemed to run against their interests. Young aristocrats and bourgeois activists formed the core of socialist movements; peasants in many countries erroneously believed that their monarchs would protect them from landlord exploitation and oppression. More often than not peasants voted against people they identified as urban no matter what their political programs promised. During periods of heightened political activity, social class is only one of the factors that determines an individual's choice of allegiance. The political ideas discussed here were like lightning rods, around which masses of people collected at points of acute political tension.

* * *

This chapter began with a question: what is the best government "for forming a people"? Educated Europeans answered the question first by developing new intellectual systems for writing the social contract between government and people. The revolutionary wave that swept across Europe in 1848 tested the ideologies that appeared in the first half of the century in response to the French Revolution. The 1848 revolutions would establish institutions and a "public sphere" in which people of all classes could freely debate political issues and apply ideology to the pressing concerns of their own lives. Revolutions are often called "crucibles" for their concentration of diverse streams of ideas and events, and subsequent transformation of those streams into something new. After 1848, the loose sets of ideas discussed in this chapter would be transformed into modern political parties capable of acting in modern political systems.

SIX

The Revolutions of 1848

In the year 1848, dozens of revolutionary uprisings broke out all over continental Europe, unleashing a storm of mass political protest. In retrospect we can see that 1848 was a key turning point in the nineteenth century. The mass accumulated anger toward the disruptions of industrialization together with the desire for more power and control over work and government triggered a cascading series of dramatic, interlocked events. In the short run the revolutions failed to achieve almost all their aims; when the dust settled in 1850–1851, it seemed that little had changed. To the historian, however, it is clear that the revolutions were truly revolutionary. They transformed the great ideologies of the early nineteenth century from a set of inchoate ideas into the foundation of powerful political parties. They made nationalism and nation building a cause that would be attractive to many new groups of people, including the powerful statesmen who originally fought against them. Hundreds of thousands of people in Europe had their first opportunity to participate in politics, to debate political ideas and programs, to conceptualize and articulate their beliefs about political rights, and to take direct action based on those beliefs. And the revolutions made it clear that state rulers could ignore the voices of popular protest only at their own peril unless they were prepared to use force. In the decades after 1848, the most stable European states co-opted the classes that made the revolution, appropriated some of their programs, and found new, modern ways to control the discontented.

As important as the revolutions were, there was nothing inevitable about them. As logical as they seem when we examine their causes, the revolutions were as much the product of accident and coincidence as determination and choice. We look for and find remarkably similar patterns among them, but the revolutionary events unfolded without a roadmap, as a series of ad hoc experiments based on guesswork, hope, and rage, in a time of intense pressure. The unpredictable nature of revolutionary events is one of the things that makes them complex. In 1848 the revolutions were complicated by the multiple conflicting forces that fueled them. Initially differences were overcome to call for change in what seemed to be a single voice, but they undermined each other once changes began to occur. How people dealt with those conflicts determined the outcome of events.

Any narrative of the revolutions of 1848 necessarily includes a bewildering array of names, places, and events. The account that follows is meant to show the importance of the events discussed thus far in this book: the challenge to the Congress of Vienna state system, the impact of machine production on urban and rural society, the changing social context, and the influence of ideologies and cultural movements. Each of these contributed to and was transformed by the revolutionary events as they unfolded in each national context.

Causes

Inevitable or not, many people in the 1840s believed that they were living on the eve of a great cataclysm: from professional observers like diplomats and journalists to the radicals who welcomed change and the conservatives who feared it. The writer Gustav Freytag (1816–1895) spoke for many: "We lived then like people who feel under their feet the pressures of an earthquake. Everyone . . . declared that things could not remain as they were." Metternich himself declared, "I am not a prophet and I don't know what will happen, but I am an old physician and can distinguish between temporary and fatal diseases. We now face one of the latter. We'll hold on as long as we can, but I have doubts about the outcome." Three major trends combined in the 1840s to make upheaval seem imminent: the spread of nationalist programs, the upsurge in liberal political activity, and the terrible economic crisis that branded the decade the Hungry Forties.

Nationalism in the 1840s

Romantic nationalism—the concept that each people deserves its own sovereign nation—had gained considerable currency by the 1840s. France seemed to have gone a long way toward achieving national unity, a national system of law and administration, the extension of markets, and through the spread of public education, a common language. People all over Europe looked to France as a model for their own nationalist ambitions. However, no other nation, or "proto-nation" had the ingredients for the kind of unity France had already achieved, and in most countries, existing governments were opposed to both liberalism and nationalism. The authoritarian monarchies and empires of eastern Europe based their claims to power on tradition, dynasty, and religious authority. They ruled over countries that were made up of multiple ethnic groups, multiple "nations," and they believed that only a supranational form of government could maintain peace and stability in countries where ethnic groups were geographically scattered all over the map. And they adamantly opposed the liberal political reforms that accompanied Romantic nationalism and threatened to undermine traditional monarchies and semifeudal social orders with a polity based on individual rights.

Italian and German nationalists faced particular problems. Both Italy and Germany were made up of diverse, autonomous states, with governments whose priorities did not include national unification or liberal reform. Nationalism remained a movement of middle-class intellectuals. Peasants and others in both countries had local loyalties or supranational ones, to the Catholic pope, for example, or the Habsburg monarchy. Few peasants anywhere thought of themselves as members of the ethnically or even geographically defined nation in which they lived. In Italy, moreover, the two northern provinces of Venetia and Lombardy were under Austrian control, so any hope of national unity would mean a two-stage battle: first to liberate Piedmont and Lombardy from Austria, then to persuade the rest of Italy to accept a unified political state. Despite the difficulties, nationalists in secret societies and public forums sought to create links with their counterparts in other provinces. Moderate Italian nationalists put their hopes in national scholarly groups and other voluntary associations, and growing commercial ties. Rejecting the gradualism of such programs, Giuseppe Mazzini reestablished Young Italy in 1840 after years in exile; other radical nationalists staged uprisings in Romagna and Calabria in 1843 and 1844 that were easily suppressed at the time, but frightening to Italy's elites and rulers. At the other extreme, a Piedmontese priest, Vincenzo Gioberti, made the cause of national unification a topic of general conversation with a conservative proposal: to unite the nation under the pope with the support of the small army of northern Piedmont-Sardinia. Another conservative plan for stabilizing the situation and unifying Italy was presented by Piedmontese liberals to King Carlo Alberto, the one clearly anti-Austrian monarch, who surprised everyone by showing interest in the plan. The conservatism of these nationalist proposals together with the failure of the radical uprisings left liberal nationalists frustrated but ready for more concerted action. The prospects for reform in Italy seemed to brighten in 1846, when a new pope, Pius IX (r. 1846–1878), was elected. His initial progressive actions, such as the release of political prisoners and steps to modernize the administration of the Papal States, aroused hopes that would be bitterly disappointed.

Germany faced an even more complicated challenge from the Habsburg monarchy. Austria was predominantly German speaking and a member of the German Confederation. It was almost impossible to imagine a unified German state without including Austria. But 80 percent of the Austrian Empire was not German speaking, and it was equally impossible to imagine a unified Germany that included the whole of the Austrian Empire. Most of the liberal nationalists in Germany began to put their hopes in Prussia, where there had been sympathy within the bureaucracy for liberal reform and national unity, but a Prussian-led unification of Germany presented additional problems. Among other things, Prussia was the dominant economic power as well as a Great Power in the European state system. And it was predominantly Protestant. Southern Catholic German states wanted Austria, predominantly Catholic and another Great Power, included in any unified state to balance Prussia.

Within Austria, nationalist issues presented even stickier problems. The Romantic cultural activities of east European nationalists stirred up the nationalist political aspirations of young people in every region of the empire. These movements were still paradoxical in their effects, in that many of the young nationalists who invested so much in the defining importance of language in constructing the nation were still learning their national languages. And their search for unique national cultural attributes among their peasants showed that the peasants themselves, as in Italy and Germany, had little interest in nationalist programs. In Poland, nationalists faced triple the problem Italians faced, in that the country was divided and under the control of three Great Powers: Austria, Prussia, and Russia. So to gain national unity and independence, Poles would have to fight three Great Powers. Also, the "nation" in Poland (as in Hungary) had a history stretching back to medieval times but was traditionally associated with the aristocratic elite; so Polish nationalists also were obliged to fashion a new nationalist ideology that included the Polish peasantry. They had already failed at both challenges in the uprising against Russia in 1830, and again in 1846, when peasants in Polish Galicia refused to join with noble insurgents against Austria and Prussia. For Polish peasants, class trumped nationality, and they identified with the Austrian emperor as their only protection against the Polish landlords. When Galician peasants, turning Polish noble rebels over to representatives of the Austrian government, were asked "Aren't you Poles?" they answered, "No, we are imperial Austrians." When asked who Poles were then, they answered, "They are the gentlemen, the stewards, the scribes, the scholars; we, on the other hand are peasants, imperial peasants."

Hungarian nationalists believed that they had many of the necessary ingredients for a successful nationalist movement on the French model. They had a national assembly, the Diet, and all their national territory was united under what was called the Crown of St. Stephen (which was subordinate to the Habsburg monarchy). Liberal nationalists also believed that they had been working for the good of everyone in Hungary since the 1820s, in their efforts to bring liberal constitutional reform, abolish serfdom, spread education, and replace elitist Latin with the vernacular Magyar (Hungarian). The problem there was that not all the people of Hungary were ethnic Magyars. Romanians, Slovaks, Serbs, and especially Croats, a sizable minority, saw the movement for the national sovereignty of Hungary as a movement to suppress their own aspirations toward nationhood. Hungarian nationalists were surprised by this. They could not understand why Croats and Romanians were so resistant to Hungarian nation unity when France had managed to incorporate the Bretons, Basques, Catalans, and Provençals. In all these cases, Metternich's response to agitation for national unity and liberal reform was suppression, though by the 1840s rather ineffective suppression. The weakness of the Habsburg regime, like those of the other monarchies in Europe, was palpable.

Crisscrossing lines of allegiance would contribute to the defeat in 1848 not only of nationalism but of liberalism as well. One of the tragedies of midcentury politics is that the liberal component of nationalist ideologies had good reason to succeed in Europe during the revolutions at the end of the 1840s. The increasing number of people touched by industrial and social changes saw Metternich's stubborn resistance to political change as anachronistic and irrational. Years of fighting for more democratic elections by the middle classes in Britain, and the successful passage of the British Reform Bill in 1832, raised hopes for middle-class liberals in Vienna, Berlin, Munich, Prague, Budapest, Milan, Naples, and elsewhere. But the entanglement of nationalism with liberalism would ultimately prevent either from achieving its goals in 1848.

Political Activism

If the 1830s were years of accelerating industrial and economic growth, the next decade saw the rise of political agitation. In Austria beginning around 1840, despite censorship and police surveillance, political poems were heard in coffeehouses and salons, liberal sentiment sneaked into plays, and the Hungarian press was openly critical of the Vienna government. *Austria and Her Future,* published anonymously by Viktor von Andrian-Werburg (1813–1858), declared the empire "a lifeless mummy." An admirer of the British constitution, he criticized Metternich's political repression and financial policies. In Hungary, where the nobility were the leading liberal nationalists, István Széchnyi called for liberal political reforms both to mobilize the economy and to stave off peasant rebellion. In the 1840s Lajos Kossuth, who would soon become the leader of Hungarian nationalism and the nation's first president, published the *Budapest Gazette,* a newspaper that called for radical political reforms. Kossuth also published translations of works such as de Tocqueville's *Democracy in America,* which spread democratic ideas.

In Prussia, political life also picked up in the 1840s: pamphlets, local clubs and associations, and a spate of new journals were all devoted to the burning political problems of reform. City governments that had been inactive previously began to engage in direct political activities: petitioning the king to grant a constituent assembly, protesting repressive state policies, and propelling leaders into the public eye.

Much of the foregoing activity was encouraged by an outpouring of writing and activity in France, still considered by many the political and cultural capital of Europe. French nationalism was expressed in the liberals' belief that France would lead the rest of Europe to "liberty, equality, and fraternity." For two decades a flourishing school of caricaturists pilloried the government's shortcomings in brilliant political cartoons. Histories appeared that celebrated some of the more radical phases of the French Revolution. *The History of Ten Years,* by the socialist Louis Blanc, condemned the July Monarchy of Louis Philippe for failing to live up to its promise. In the 1846 elections, the tiny elite sector of society possessing the right to vote defeated French liberals at the polls. Turning to a broader public, the liberals embarked on a nationwide opposition campaign. They organized legal banquets in cities and towns, where local and national liberal leaders would make speeches calling for reform, even occasionally calling for a republic with universal male suffrage. Europeans on the Continent also watched the British Chartist movement with great interest.

Everywhere the accelerating pace of intellectuals' political life was partly fueled by an awareness of the social crises occurring around them. Poverty and crime seemed to be on the increase. Governments were unable to respond. In every European capital, literature and journalism shone a spotlight on social ills, increasing labor unrest, and government inadequacy. In the 1840s, the inability of governments to alleviate poverty and strife undermined their legitimacy. In southern Germany, opposition parties won surprising victories in local elections in 1846 and 1847, while by contrast the joint session of Prussia's provincial parliaments, convoked by the king, was able to accomplish little. None of this intellectual political activism in the 1840s called for revolution; everyone involved still hoped for peacefully negotiated change. But the ability of human beings to build cities, light them with gas lamps, and connect them by means of railroad trains gave impetus to those who believed the political system should be subject to the same forces of progress. The misery of those adversely affected by "progress" only highlighted the need for change.

The Hungry Forties

Liberal nationalist agitation occurred within a context of mounting misery and discontent among artisans, industrial workers, and peasants in what became a full-fledged economic crisis by 1848. After the revolutions of the 1820s and 1830s had been suppressed, the effects of industrial revolution in Britain began to be felt on the Continent. While economic growth would eventually benefit an increasing number of people, in the short run it brought massive disruption and hardship. Industrial machine production threatened traditional artisanal crafts production; cheap British manufactured goods threatened to undermine existing industries; and British imports of food and raw materials from the Continent, while stimulating agricultural productivity, tied peasants to the unpredictable business cycles of the British economy and postponed industrialization.

All the horrors of working-class life described in the preceding chapters created widespread if still smoldering anger. But even more important were the disruptions to traditional handicraft production and social life and the *threat* that the degradations of factory work and slum life might soon become everyone's fate. Competition from cheaper, factory-produced goods drove artisanal wages down, and the cities were becoming uglier and more crowded by the year. Economists have persuasively demonstrated that real wages fell significantly throughout the 1830s and 1840s. In the Austrian town of Linz, in 1842, the police director reported that two-thirds of the 26,000 inhabitants were malnourished. Approximately 1,800 people there were living on a daily wage of under 16 kronen (kr), while in Vienna (where wages were probably slightly higher) one egg cost between 6 and 7.5 kr, and potatoes cost 1 to 2 kr each; the price of wood had increased 250 percent in the preceding decade. For the whole empire, children accounted for half the deaths recorded in 1847.

Rural workers in putting-out manufacturing had their own complaints. Overpopulation had not been relieved by migration, so there was increased competition for jobs in putting-out industries. And there were legions of complaints about suppliers cheating the putting-out workers. Outworkers complained that merchants paid less than promised for finished work and that merchants deducted fines based on claims that finished work was of low quality. Some merchants weighed raw materials when wet, to be able to claim that workers had received more material than in fact had been provided. For their part, outworkers could refuse to turn over finished goods. But the workers had leverage only in areas not stressed by overpopulation and enjoying enough prosperity to make it feasible for workers to resist taking whatever terms the entrepreneurs were offering.

Among peasants the main source of discontent was serfdom and the continuation of feudal obligations where serfdom had been only partly abolished. In Austria, peasants were required to pay one-tenth of their crops to the lord and perform labor on his lands. The government also levied land taxes for salaries of priests and schoolteachers, for road maintenance, and such. Feudal dues took up approximately 70 percent of a peasant's income. A contemporary official described the peasants of Galicia and Bukovina (in the eastern portion of the empire), as exploited like "work animals." Most important, very widespread discontent among peasants centered on the communal use of land. Population growth, agricultural innovation, and proto-industrialization put new pressures of common pasture and woodlands. With less land lying fallow, there were fewer places for animals to graze unregulated. With more people, more timber was needed for housing and fuel. Changes in customary communal land uses touched the very heart of peasant life. Laws passed to regulate sales and usage of such land set off angry protests in France and Austria. In Italy, even where the Two Sicilies tried to protect traditional usage, large-scale confrontations occurred in the 1840s. Wood theft was extraordinarily common, though it is not clear that the peasants who took wood from forests considered it "theft."

Documented conflicts between peasants and landowners over communal land were numerous all over France, Italy, Germany, Austria, Poland, Hungary, and Russia. Conflicts took place in courts and village squares, and occasionally erupted into large-scale rioting. The worst such case occurred in connection with the attempt, alluded to earlier, of Polish noblemen to challenge the Austrian government in Galicia in 1846. The Polish peasants in Galicia refused to join the nobility in their effort at national liberation. On the contrary, they saw the nobles' uprising as an opportunity to settle old class and economic scores. They burned and looted manor houses, and killed more than a thousand noblemen and estate managers.

All these troubles were multiplied by the economic crisis that gathered steam beginning in the early 1840s. The business recession in Britain in 1841 turned to full-fledged depression in 1842. The importance of British business and industry for the Continent was such that the depression had a significant impact on unemployment, prices, and growth everywhere. This downturn was followed in 1845 with the first of several disastrous crop failures. The potato blight that brought famine to Ireland also resulted in serious food shortages in much of northern Europe. The following year saw the worst grain harvest in decades. By 1847 food prices had doubled and bread riots spread. Famine on the Continent was averted, but the high price of food depressed the market for manufactured goods, which slowed or even stopped production, resulting in the layoff of thousands of artisans and workers in large cities and manufacturing villages.

Revolution did not flow directly from high food prices or mass unemployment. But these were proof, it seemed at the time, of the harshness of the new industrial climate and the inability of rulers, governments, or social elites to do anything about it. In most cases, popular anger was directed not at specific institutions or individuals, but rather at prevailing conditions. The revolution came about because popular rage, accrued over two decades of deterioration, coincided with elite desires for change, which had themselves reached a fever pitch. By the end of 1847 politics had reached an impasse: governments refused to consider reform, but opposition movements refused to back down.

The Revolutions of 1848

On January 12, 1848, a small band of insurrectionaries took to the streets in Palermo, on the island of Sicily, protesting tax rates and calling for a constitution. Soon agitation spread to Naples, the capital of the Two Sicilies, where the king gave in almost immediately, promising a constitution, civil rights, and a national assembly. The following month, in Paris, similar protests led to street fighting and the abdication of King Louis Philippe. Within two weeks, crowds inspired by these victories and demanding liberal political reform appeared on the streets of Munich, Vienna, Budapest, Krakow, and Venice and many smaller cities in between. All over Italy, the Germanies, and the Austrian Empire, proud monarchs surrendered their exclusive right to power, granting promises of liberal reform. Metternich fled Vienna in disguise, giving hope to reformers in every country.

The success of popular protest in early 1848 was called the "Springtime of the Peoples," and it was celebrated everywhere. Proclamations of "freedom," church bells, and fireworks were heard; there were parades in the largest cities and in the most remote villages. The tricolor flag of the French Revolution was hoisted on public buildings. People wept in streets and kissed strangers. Women wore tricolor petticoats. In many places "freedom" temporarily erased long-standing differences. In Mainz, Protestants, Catholics, and Jews celebrated together. In Prague, Czechs and Germans organized

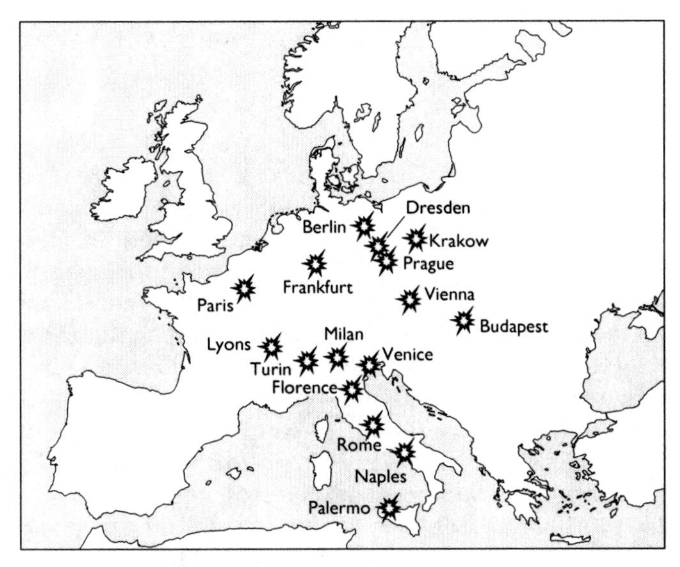

Centers of Revolutionary Activity, 1848–1849

together. It is remarkable that so many uprisings occurred all over Europe within weeks of each other. As Eric Hobsbawm noted, the most rapid information network available at the time (that of the Rothschild bank) could not carry news from Paris to Vienna in less than five days, but once the uprisings began, it took only a few weeks for governments in a huge swath of Europe to be overthrown or transformed. To contemporaries, revolution seemed to engulf all of Europe. It is commonly said that only Britain and Russia were spared, but in fact the revolutions concentrated in the heartland of the Continent, dodging the Iberian peninsula, Scandinavia, and the Balkans as well.

There were similar causes and similar patterns among the revolutions: at the start, liberal middle-class (and noble) mobilization against the current regimes was followed by the swelling of working-class, artisanal, and peasant discontent over economic conditions. Then victory revealed differences between moderates and radicals, and between the middle and lower classes. The persistence of peasant and worker unrest further divided the revolutionary allies, some of whom were responsible for establishing new constitutional monarchies. Where nationalism came into play, revolutionaries in one nation undermined those in its rival nations or were easily manipulated to do so, leading to the defeat of all. Governments proved harder to reconstruct than to destroy.

The revolutions can be broken down into roughly three regional groups, in France, in Italy and Germany, and in the Austrian Empire. The revolutionary wave in each country contained a number of related but different conflicts: the political conflict that pitted liberals against absolutist states, the nationalist conflict that sought national unity or sovereignty, the economic conflict that pitted the downtrodden against the wealthy and privileged, and a multiplicity of social conflicts that pitted village against city, Christian against Jew, and nation against nation.

France

The economic crisis hit France with particular severity. Railroad construction almost ceased, throwing more than half a million out of work; coal mines and iron foundries, in turn, laid off workers. Unemployment increased the discontent of French workers already embittered by their low wages and by the still lower esteem in which they were held by the government of Louis Philippe. The main beneficiaries of the July Monarchy in the 1830s and 1840s were the social and economic elite—aristocrats and bankers, and industrial magnates, who had gained the right to vote. Heading the liberal opposition was Adolphe Thiers, who continued to support the principle of constitutional monarchy. Radicals and republicans formed a second opposition group, which increased in numbers with the growing political awareness and literacy of the working classes. The third and smallest group was made up various socialists, who gained recruits as a result of the economic depression of the late 1840s. Potentially more formidable than any of these, but as yet representing only a vague, unorganized sentiment, were the Bonapartists. The return of the emperor's remains from St. Helena to Paris in 1840 revived the legend of a glorious and warlike Napoleon, so different from the uninspiring Louis Philippe.

The liberal opposition leader Thiers played a major role in organizing the banquet campaign held during the summer of 1847, which brought liberal constitutional monarchists together with republicans; eventually they began calling for the resignation of chief minister François Guizot. The government did not take the campaign seriously until a huge banquet was announced for February 22, 1848, to be held in Paris. When the Guizot ministry forbade the banquet, the Parisians substituted a large demonstration in the administrative sector of the city. The night passed without much incident, but on February 23 crowds grew and became more aggressive. They moved to working-class quarters in the center of Paris, where narrow streets could be blocked with barricades. Cries changed from calls for reform to attacks on the king. Louis Philippe dismissed Guizot and prepared to summon Thiers to the ministry. But his concessions came too late. Supported by workers, students, and the more radical republican leaders, protesters began to clash with government troops, who panicked and fired into the crowd, killing or wounding between forty and fifty of the rioters. Rumors spread that the government planned to massacre workers, who swiftly rose up in revolt. Overnight a million paving stones were torn up, along with 4,000 trees and 1,500 barricades were constructed to protect the neighborhoods of the workers.

On February 24, Louis Philippe abdicated (and escaped in disguise to England). The Chamber declared a republic and set up a provisional government headed by an eloquent, cautious republican, the Romantic poet Alphonse de Lamartine (1790–1869). Popular unrest did not cease, however, but mounted

Honoré Daumier, "The Last Meeting of the Ex-Ministers," Le Charivari, *March 9, 1848. Daumier's drawing shows the triumphant arrival of the Republic by contrasting a confident, personification of revolution striding in through a flood of light, striking terror into the cowardly government officials within.* (*National Gallery of Canada, Ottowa, 1999*)

along with unemployment, and obliged the provisional government to take in a few socialists. Notable among these was Louis Blanc, best known as an advocate of social workshops to be owned and run by workers themselves with the financial assistance of the state. As a gesture toward the "right to work," which meant the ability to earn enough by working to support oneself, and also as a measure to restore calm in Paris, the provisional government authorized the establishment of national workshops in the capital. These workshops, however, were not a genuine attempt to implement the blueprint of Louis Blanc but a relief project organized along semimilitary lines and enrolling more than a hundred thousand unemployed persons from Paris and the provinces.

The future shape of France now hinged on the outcome of the elections of April 23, 1848, when all adult males would be qualified to vote for the National Assembly, which would draw up a constitution for the Second Republic. (The original French republic had lasted officially from September 1792 until Napoleon's coronation in 1804.) In this election, 8 million men, 84

The Written Record

The "Springtime of the Peoples"

In a short-lived moment of euphoria and unity, the revolutionaries of 1848 proclaimed France a Republic (February 26, 1848)

Citizens:

Royalty in any form whatever is abolished.

No more legitimism, no more Bonapartism, no regency.

The Provisional Government has taken all the measures necessary to prevent the return of the old dynasty and the accession of a new one.

The republic is proclaimed

The people are united.

All the forts surrounding the capital are ours.

The brave garrison of Vincennes is a garrison of brothers.

Let us maintain with respect the old republican flag whose three colors traveled around the world with our fathers. Let us show that this symbol of equality, liberty, and fraternity is at the same time the symbol of order, of the most real and most lasting order, since its foundation is justice and its instrument is the whole people. . . .

Documents in the Political History of the European Continent, 1815–1939, ed. G. A. Kertesz (Oxford, 1968), p. 86.

percent of the potential electorate, went to the polls. The more conservative peasants, who still made up the bulk of the population, approved the fall of the July Monarchy but dreaded anything resembling an attack by the socialists on the private property they had recently acquired. Of the almost nine hundred deputies elected, therefore, most were either monarchists or conservative republicans.

The Paris radicals refused to accept the results of the elections. Demonstrators invaded the National Assembly and proposed the formation of a new provisional government. Alarmed moderates arrested the radical leaders. They also decided that the national workshops threatened the finances of the new government as well as law and order (though in fact, by keeping tens of thousands of unemployed workers engaged in productive activity, they probably contributed to stability). The Assembly decreed the closing of the workshops; their workers could either enlist in the army or accept work in the provinces.

Two revolutions came into conflict here. The liberal revolution of property owners, worried about social misery but more worried about order and the proper functioning of a legitimate government (supported by the peasantry), faced the impatience of the urban poor, who had gone to the barricades to win economic security and social equality. The poorer districts of the capital

The Written Record

THE RIGHT TO WORK

One of the first acts of the new government that came to power after the February uprising was in response to workers' demands. Louis Blanc's treatise, *The Organization of Labor,* was one of the foundations of radical thought in the 1840s, and many of its ideas were adopted by working-class radicals. Therefore, Blanc was asked by the Provisional Government to draft a proposal for "The Right to Work."

The Provisional Government of the French Republic undertakes to guarantee the livelihood by work of the workers.

It undertakes to guarantee work for all citizens;

It recognizes that workers must combine in order to enjoy the legitimate benefits of their labour. . . .

Documents in the Political History of the European Continent, 1815–1939, ed. G. A. Kertesz (Oxford, 1968), p. 86.

responded by launching another revolt, which led to some of the bloodiest fighting of that revolutionary year. From June 23 to June 26, 1848, workers, artisans, students, the unemployed, some socialists, and some liberal republicans fought a futile battle against a revived military led by General Louis-Eugène Cavaignac (1802–1857), the energetic minister of war.

These June Days were a landmark in modern history, the first large-scale outbreak with clear overtones of class warfare. Most of the insurgents seem to have been people who had tried vainly to enroll in the workshops and were still unemployed and desperate. Most were artisans—masons, locksmiths, cabinetmakers, wine sellers, and other craftsmen of the type who had been prominent in the capture of the Bastille in 1789 and in the uprising of 1830. Among them were also workers of the new industrial age—mechanics, railroad men, dockworkers. The prospect of a social revolution infuriated and terrified the propertied classes and those who felt that Parisian workers were undermining the new order. Peasants, shopkeepers, landowners, and apparently some workers poured into Paris on the new railroads to quell the uprising. About 1,500 people were killed during the fighting, but in the days that followed the repression was even more ferocious. Three thousand rebels were shot on the spot and another 12,000 were arrested, of whom approximately 4,500 were subsequently deported, chiefly to Algeria. Socialist clubs and newspapers were padlocked, and Louis Blanc fled to England. France became a virtual military dictatorship under General Cavaignac.

The fears of the middle-class moderates were evident in the constitution of the Second Republic, which the National Assembly completed in November 1848. The Assembly declared property inviolable and refused to include the "right to work" among the fundamental rights of French citizens. The president was to be chosen by popular election every four years, and the single-chamber legislature was to be elected every three years.

When elections for president were held in December 1848, the least likely candidate won twice as many votes as the other three combined: Louis-Napoleon Bonaparte (1808–1873) was the nephew of the emperor Napoleon, but he was not an impressive figure. The magical name of Bonaparte, however, allowed him to tap the glamour of the Napoleonic legend. In reflecting back on this election, Karl Marx would famously write that all great events occur twice in history: "the first time as tragedy, the second as farce." In 1848 Louis-Napoleon staged a clever campaign to identify himself with the cause of order, stability, and democracy. Unlike Louis Philippe, he was a master of public image, an important quality for the exercise of modern politics. He sold himself to the propertied as a protector of property, and to the common people as a protector of voting rights (unlike the liberals, who wanted to limit voting to property owners and had turned on the urban poor in June). Over the next two years, the institutions of liberal political culture would be systematically suppressed. Radical clubs were closed, networks of underground secret societies in towns and villages around France were disbanded, and the word "republic" was no longer permitted in public. Thousands of revolutionaries were arrested, tried and sentenced; thousands more were shot without trial. Louis-Napoleon promoted generals who supported him and sent the hostile to Algeria. In May 1850, universal male suffrage was abolished.

The crowning blow came in a coup d'etat in December 1851, when Louis-Napoleon declared himself president for life. Signs placed around Paris announced the dissolution of the legislature. There was massive resistance, this time not in Paris but in villages and towns all over France, but it was no match for the military. Louis-Napoleon resurrected a phony imitation of universal male suffrage in calling a plebiscite, held to approve the coup and grant the president the authority to issue a new constitution. The new government would have elections by universal male suffrage but no public debate, no press discussion of political issues. A year later, tired of pretending to be the president of a republic, he declared himself Emperor Napoleon III; another plebiscite was held to ratify proclamation of the empire.

The revolution of 1848 failed to bring democratic reform to France and made people more aware of the conflicts that had been growing under the surface of modern industrial society. But despite its ultimate failure, just as in 1830, the French uprising inspired and sparked similar movements elsewhere.

Italy

By 1848 three movements were competing for the leadership of Italian nationalism. One of these groups, based in the north, favored the domination of Piedmont; its leader, Count Camillo di Cavour (1810–1861), was an admirer of British and French liberalism and an ardent advocate of constitution. Cavour was the editor of an influential Turin newspaper, *Il Risorgimento* (resurgence, regeneration), which gave its name to the movement for unification. A conservative nationalist group was led by Vincenzo Gioberti, author of the plan to unite Italy under the pope. The third group was Mazzini's radical Young Italy, which favored a republic. These divisions would be multiplied and complicated once the revolution got under way.

The monarchies of Italy collapsed no less quickly than that of the French. When the uprising in Palermo spread to Naples, Ferdinand II agreed to grant a constitution and basic civil liberties and to call elections for a legislative assembly. In mid-February the grand duke of Tuscany was forced to follow suit. News of the rising in Paris quickened the pace of the Italian revolutions, as King Carlo Alberto of Piedmont-Sardinia and Pius IX, the pope and political ruler of the Papal States, agreed to become constitutional monarchs. Next came Lombardy and Venetia, where the ideas of Young Italy had inspired revolutionary movements. Ever since January 1 citizens of Milan, the capital of Lombardy, had been boycotting cigars as a protest against the Austrian tax on tobacco. News of revolution in Vienna touched off five days of heavy fighting in Milan, which forced the Austrians to withdraw their forces, to the great embarrassment of the commander there, Field Marshal Count Josef Radetzky (1766–1858). Lombardy declared itself independent of Austria, as did Venice, the capital of Venetia, Austria's other Italian province. Both declared themselves in favor of joining a united Italy. This rapid collapse of Habsburg rule in Lombardy-Venetia inspired a national crusade against the Austrians.

Once the nationalist cause was out in the open, all the divisions previously concealed by repression also came out into the open. Carlo Alberto, clearly anti-Habsburg but never a liberal, reluctantly assumed command of the Italian forces. Like other rulers of smaller Italian states Carlo Alberto had granted a constitution in order to prevent a revolution, but he refused an offer of help from republican France, fearing the possibility of radicalizing the liberal movements in Italy. As town and country had opposing views and the Austrians exploited these divisions well, the decision to "go it alone" proved unwise. Once Carlo Alberto had committed Piedmont to fight for the independence of the northern provinces, nationalists in the rest of Italy demanded that their governments join in. At first the pope agreed to support the Piedmont forces, but as leader of all Catholics, including Austrian Catholics, he was in a difficult position. On April 29, Pius IX announced that his "equal affection" for all peoples obliged him to adopt a neutral position in the war with Austria and to recall his soldiers; the pope could not act both as an Italian patriot and as an international spiritual leader. The pope's announcement dealt a fatal blow to those like Gioberti, who were hoping for a moderate path to unification under the leadership of the pontiff. It was also a turning point in the fate of the revolution. In Naples, radicals demanded that the king send troops to aid the war against Austria and that the new assembly receive control over foreign affairs. King Ferdinand II regained enough nerve to resist this demand and sent troops to suppress street fighting that arose in the conflict. Liberal government ministers resigned in protest, but Ferdinand replaced them with conservatives more to his liking.

In the meantime the revolution in Italy had moved from the capitals to the countryside. As would happen everywhere in Europe, long-standing disagreements broke out in open conflict during the summer of 1848 and continued well afterward, in some countries until the summer of 1849. In Italy, peasant conflicts over communal land and forest use took a revolutionary form as peasants seized control of disputed lands. Forests in mountainous regions were occupied. State foresters, who administered forest use, were harassed or beaten and driven away. Illegal usage was common everywhere in Europe. Jonathan Sperber's recent study of 1848 concludes that "if we were to ask how [1848] was experienced, we would have to say that more than any other way, it was the time when the peasants could do what they wanted with the forest." Such incidents give us a good sense of what revolution meant to ordinary people. In one case, in the Two Sicilies, a crowd of ragged, thin, and haggard people numbering in the thousands, carried the revolutionary tricolor flag and shouted slogans of the kind one expected from urban radicals: "Long live the constitution; long live Italy!" At the same time their demands were not conventionally considered political: the crowd demanded bread and land to farm. For peasants, the revolution signified political rights, a vague sense of Italy as a nation, and access to common lands. Urban intellectuals often dismissed peasant views as backward, but they were no less legitimate than their own similar desires for political unification or the right to vote.

In the meantime, the fate of the revolution in Italy was decided on the battlefields of the north. Milanese revolutionaries forced Austrian troops under Field Marshal Radetzky to withdraw from the city in March. But then Piedmont-Sardinia overplayed its hand. First, in both Lombardy and Venetia, Carlo Alberto won plebiscites in which a huge majority of voters agreed to join Piedmont-Sardinia under a constitutional monarchy, a result that signaled defeat for republican nationalists like Mazzini. The Piedmontese government further lost popular support when it announced that suffrage would be restricted to property owners and that peasant demands for forest and farm land would be denied. Next, in April Radetzky sent a detachment of soldiers to wipe out a community of nationalist insurgents in Venetia. His extremely brutal instructions—to burn the village and kill every man, woman, and child there—quickly undermined what remained of the peasants' support for the revolution in northern Italy.

Carlo Alberto's troops might still have had a chance to beat the disorganized and underfunded Austrian forces, but the southern and central states withdrew their support for the war. Piedmont's annexation of Lombardy and Parma and Modena, two small north Italian duchies, made the other Italian states fear the imperial ambition of Piedmont more than they desired the unification of Italy. In the Two Sicilies, the king followed the papal example in withdrawing his troops from the war. The Austrians, taking the offensive, reconquered Lombardy and crushed the forces of Carlo Alberto in July.

The Italian revolution was not, however, defeated yet. In November 1848, in Rome, radical adherents of Young Italy and a crowd of ten thousand led by the city's democratic intellectuals rose up against the political power of the pope. After Pius IX fled to the Two Sicilies, the rebels transformed the Papal States into a democratic Roman republic headed by Mazzini. The republicans hoped to set up a national assembly in Rome, with which to unify all of Italy and renew war against Austria. By February 1849, four major states—Piedmont-Sardinia, Tuscany, Rome, and Venice—were all working cautiously toward unification, though without unanimity. Catholic clergy refused the sacrament to anyone voting in elections for the constituent assembly, and in more than one town, Catholic peasants refused to enter the army, tore down republican flags, and raised the papal flag instead. Some provinces came close to civil war. In March 1849 Carlo Alberto reluctantly agreed to renew the war with Austria, but within the month Austria prevailed and the king abdicated.

In August 1849 the Austrians put an end to Venetian independence after a prolonged siege and bombardment of Venice. Rome, however, was still in the hands of the republicans who had forced the pope into exile. Austria threatened to move further into Italy after its success in the north. Both republicans and Catholics begged Louis-Napoleon to intervene on their behalf, to save the revolution or the Catholic church, something of a contradiction. Louis-Napoleon was sympathetic to Italian nationalism: he had fought against the pope in the Papal States in the 1830 uprising, and he was opposed to the augmentation of Austria's power in Italy. The French army arrived on Italian soil and was promptly defeated by forces led by the talented Giuseppe Garibaldi (1807–1882) at the beginning of his career fighting for Italian unification. But in June the French came back to capture Rome, and Mazzini's republic surrendered to French troops.

All three paths to unification had been defeated. Piedmont, however, had emerged as the leader of Italian nationalism and liberalism. It had defied the hated Austrians and was the only Italian state to retain the constitution granted in 1848. When Carlo Alberto abdicated, the crown passed to Vittorio Emanuele II (1820–1878), who later was to become the first king of unified Italy.

Germany

The German revolutions in 1848 roughly paralleled those in Italy. In Germany, too, liberalism and nationalism won initial victories and then collapsed before internal dissension, popular unrest, and Austrian resistance. The revolution in Germany had three main threads: a liberal reformist movement that sought reform of central political institutions, a popular movement that sought some economic relief, and a nationalist movement seeking to unify Germany into a single state. The failure of all three was the more surprising because the revolutionary movement had begun to recruit support among industrial workers, artisans fearing industrial competition, and peasants intent on abolishing the relics of serfdom. The efforts aimed at national unification were doomed by divisions between the popular uprising and the liberal parliamentary movement.

In Prussia in 1847 it had seemed as if Friedrich Wilhelm IV (r. 1840–1861) was moving toward reform on his own; he promised to carry out his father's unhonored pledge to give Prussia a constitution and an elected assembly. Having decided to compromise with wealthy liberal industrialists on political reform to obtain loans needed to invest in railroad building in the poorer eastern portion of the province, the king agreed to call a united (or national) Diet. However, as mentioned earlier, the meeting of representatives from the provincial diets that he finally convoked in 1847 did little.

In Bavaria, discontent had spilled out onto the streets even before the Paris uprising. An aged King Ludwig I had taken up with a flamboyant dancer, Lola Montez, who exercised power on her own, a situation that epitomized the corrupt obsolescence of dynastic rule. Demonstrations in January and February in Munich were radicalized by the news from Paris, and people began calling for a republic. The king abdicated and revolutionary pressures spread: demands for constitutions and civil liberties fanned out rapidly. Immediately, peasants all over southwestern and western Germany rose up against landowners, tax collectors, moneylenders, and other rural elites. Journeymen in towns rebelled in March in the Rhineland and Saxony. There was machine breaking, as well as attacks on steamships and railroad lines. By mid-March most of the rulers of the smaller German states had yielded to the pressure, and in Berlin demonstrators were mobilizing.

The stature of Prussia gave its revolution special significance for Germany. Friedrich Wilhelm took a dual approach: he offered concessions to protesters (abolition of censorship, a constitution, and a united Diet), but he backed these up with a show of armed force. On March 18, peaceful demonstrators enthusiastically listening to the king's reformist decree were enraged to see soldiers massed around them. The people demanded the withdrawal of troops; when this did not happen, panic ensued. Then soldiers shot into the crowd; angry and frightened demonstrators dispersed to erect barricades, and artisans and others fought the king's troops for what they thought the king had just given them. More than two hundred rioters, primarily craftsmen, were killed. To avoid further bloodshed, Friedrich Wilhelm agreed to withdraw his troops. He summoned an assembly to draw up a constitution, declared Prussia "merged in Germany," and proclaimed himself "king of the free, regenerated German nation." The Prussian government set about making liberal reforms.

Liberal political reform, however, did little to alleviate the economic and social problems of peasants and workers, who now engaged in their own revolution. Popular violence actually increased after the liberal political settlement in Berlin. This "social revolution" undermined political reform by revealing the liberals' lack of a political base. At the same time it weakened the chances that peasants and workers might achieve their aims by showing that they had no representation in government, and no political organization of their own. The disarray on the left gave conservative groups a chance to regain their nerve. One group tried to persuade the king to reassert his authority, others gained influence in politicizing the military, others launched a new conservative journal, the *Kreuzzeitung,* which conservatives used to enter the "public sphere" that had been monopolized by liberals before 1848. Finally, moderates in the liberal government and in society wearied of popular violence and gave support to conservative voices calling for stability. By the fall the Prussian government regained its confidence. On November 2 Friedrich Wilhelm announced the formation of a new government and appointed a conservative career military officer, Count F. W. Brandenburg, as prime minister. A week later fifty thousand troops marched into Berlin. On December 5 Parliament was dissolved and a new, very moderate constitution, which eventually reconsolidated the power of the king, was issued.

In the meantime, since May a constitutional convention had been meeting in Frankfurt, the capital of the Confederation, to begin the work of creating a unified German state. Its 830 members were elected throughout Germany; the representatives were almost entirely members of the middle classes and lacked a broad popular base. Moreover, these men to whom it fell to decide the geographical limits of Germany lacked political experience and talent for practical statesmanship. The existing German Confederation included Austria proper but excluded most of the non-German Habsburg territories. The Austrian issue divided the assembly into two camps: the "Big Germans," who favored the inclusion in the projected German state of Austria and of Bohemia, with its large Czech population, and the "Little Germans," who opposed the inclusion of Austria.

In March 1849 the Frankfurt Assembly adopted a liberal national constitution for a unified Germany. The constitution was based on the American federal system and British parliamentary practice. Individual states were to surrender many of their powers to the German federal government. The federal legislature would consist of a lower house, elected by universal male suffrage, and an upper house, chosen by the state governments and the legislatures. Ministers responsible to the legislature would form the federal executive. Over all would preside a constitutional monarch, the German emperor. The assembly elected Friedrich Wilhelm of Prussia to be the first emperor of a unified Germany. Twenty-eight of the smaller German states agreed to accept the constitution, and it seemed possible that Friedrich Wilhelm would accept it, as well. The constitution was similar to the one he had issued for Prussia in December, and he would have gained enormous power and territory.

The king, however, waffled for a month, refusing to answer Frankfurt's offer. In the end, although pressure from Austria played a role, more important was Friedrich Wilhelm's regret over having given in to the liberal revolutionaries in 1848, coupled with the deeply conservative views that made it difficult for him to countenance such a major political transformation or to rule at the behest of an elected assembly. He refused to accept "a crown from the gutter," as he so delicately put it, launching a new round of demonstrations denouncing him. Many of the protestors concluded that the only answer to the king's rejection was a republic. Two provinces, the Palatinate and Baden, established revolutionary governments in the spring of 1849, but they were defeated in July, marking the end of the revolution in Germany.

The forces of order were more powerful than any of the revolutionaries had realized in the spring of 1848. The forces of revolution were far more divided, unsure of themselves, and lacking in decisive leadership.

The Austrian Empire

The Austrian monarchy was more seriously wounded in the spring of 1848 than any other government. Opposition to Metternich's rule was long-standing and well developed. Emperor Ferdinand I (r. 1835–1848) was mentally incompetent. The Habsburg government was ill prepared to deal with open protest, even less so after Metternich exited the scene. Yet Austria, too, managed to ride out the storm.

There were three main sites of insurrection in the Habsburg realm, their fates all intertwined: Vienna, where the revolution pitted students, workers, and middle-class liberals calling for constitutional reform against the absolutist government; Prague, where liberal reform was mired in a struggle between Czechs and the powerful German-speaking minority; and Budapest, where the struggle for a Hungarian nation pitted Hungarians against Vienna as well as against minorities inside Hungary, especially Croats. All these movements were complicated by the geographical distribution of Austria's ethnic populations. In the Hungarian part of the empire—which had large minorities of Slovaks, Romanians, Serbs, Croats, and Germans—the dominant Hungarians fell just short of a majority. Throughout the empire, moreover, the German element, chiefly bureaucrats and merchants, predominated in most towns and cities.

Among the peoples of the Habsburg realm in 1848, nationalism ran strongest in the Italians of Lombardy and Venetia, the Czechs of Bohemia, and the Hungarians (or Magyars as they were then called) and Croats. The antagonism between Croats and Hungarians revealed an all-important fact about the nationalistic movements within the Habsburg Empire. Some groups—Italians, Hungarians, Czechs, and Poles—resented the German-dominated government in Vienna. Others, notably the Croats and Romanians, were less anti-German than anti-Hungarian. In this situation, the central government in Vienna could apply a policy of divide and conquer, pitting anti-Hungarian elements against Hungarian nationalists and subduing both. This was substantially what happened in 1848. In the same way that peasants often preferred the protection of the Austrian Crown to alliance along ethnic lines with nobles, Czechs, Croats, and other minorities would chose to support Vienna at moments that critically strengthened the hand of counterrevolution.

The news of the February revolution in Paris shook the empire to its foundations. Four separate revolutions broke out almost simultaneously in March 1848: in Milan and Venice, in Hungary, in Vienna itself, and in Bohemia. In Hungary, Lajos Kossuth gave an electrifying speech: based on claims that Hungary was a free country, with its own ancient constitution, he demanded political autonomy, parliamentary government, and an elected legislature to replace the Diet of feudal Hungary. These concessions were won; the Hungarian Diet passed a law calling for a separate, self-governing state, with its

The Austrian Empire

own army, budget, and foreign policy, though the Habsburg emperor would remain the official monarch. Laws were passed abolishing serfdom and censorship, and ending the immunity of the aristocracy from taxation. On the other hand, Transylvania (with a Romanian majority) and Croatia were incorporated into Hungary without their consent. A law was passed declaring all religions equal, but when voting rights were legislated, the property qualification excluded most Slavs and Romanians, and a special qualification excluded Jews.

In his speech Kossuth also said that Hungary could not be free while the emperor ruled as an absolute monarch over the rest of his domains; and he demanded constitutional rights for the rest of the empire. Aroused by the Hungarian revolt, Viennese university students and unemployed workers rose up on March 12. Metternich's subsequent resignation brought a liberating hope for change all over the empire. Although the imperial government repeatedly promised reforms, the constitution it granted seemed woefully inadequate to the Viennese insurgents. By May the political atmosphere was so charged that Emperor Ferdinand and his family were whisked away from the capital for their protection. Pending a meeting of a constituent assembly in July, a revolutionary council ran affairs in Vienna. In the meantime, Austrian forces were distracted by war in Piedmont. In September a constituent assembly, meeting in Vienna and representing all the Habsburg provinces except the Italian and the Hungarian, emancipated the peasants from their obligation to work for the landlords.

Meanwhile, in Prague, Czech nationalists were demanding rights similar to those granted the Hungarians. In June 1848 the Czechs organized an assembly called the Slavic Congress to promote the solidarity of Slavic peoples against "Big German" encroachments. However, the Czech nationalists wanted only autonomy *within* the Habsburg multinational empire, not to overthrow it, and took pains to exhibit that loyalty by flying the Austrian flag at the Slavic Congress. Nonetheless, by calling for constitutional monarchy and political reform, the Slavic Congress had challenged Habsburg absolutism. In June this act of defiance set off a series of demonstrations during which the wife of the commander of the Austrian garrison in Prague was accidentally killed.

In late spring 1848, the Austrian Empire appeared to be on its last legs. Governments in Vienna, Budapest, and Zagreb each claimed sovereign authority; Polish, Romanian, Slovak, and Serb movements had the same aspirations; Germany was threatening to exclude Austria from any German nation; the king was in hiding; and the Italian provinces were fighting for independence (and not yet losing). But then the tide began to turn as figures emerged who were not opposed to using harsh military force. The counterrevolution began.

First to be brought under control was Prague and the sequence of events there was a herald of things to come. Prince Alfred Windischgrätz (1787–1862), the recently widowed commander of the Prague garrison and

The Written Record

NATIONALISM IN 1848
THE SLAVIC CONGRESS, PRAGUE

The Slavic Congress in Prague is an unprecedented event. . . . For the first time since history gave us a name, we, scattered members of a large family of peoples, have met in large numbers in order to acknowledge our brotherhood and to discuss peacefully our common concerns; we have understood each other not only through our majestic tongue, spoken by eighty millions, but also by the harmony of our heartbeats, through the identity of spiritual interest. . . .

The Latin and Germanic nations . . . have for thousands of years not only secured their independence with the might of the sword, but also satisfied their thirst for domination. Their policy was mainly based on the right of the stronger, . . . [the upper classes] ruled by privilege and assigned only duties to the people. It is only now, that public opinion has succeeded in shattering the fetters of feudalism, in regaining for the individual the eternal rights of man. Among the Slavs, however, . . . one tribe after another fell into subjection, and demands with a loud and resolute voice his inheritance: liberty. . . . He wants no domination, no conquest, only liberty for himself as for all . . . unconditional equality before the law, the same measure of right and duty for everyone . . . the liberty, equality and fraternity of all citizens.

[But we make demands not only for the individual.] No less sacred than the human being with his inherited rights is the people in the totality of its spiritual interests. . . . Nature . . . has not destined one to rule over another. . . . But at present . . . the free Briton denies the Irishman his national equality, the German threatens many a Slavic race with force . . . the Hungarian is not loath to claim nationality rights for his own nation alone. We Slavs condemn all such presumption unconditionally. . . .

In the belief that the powerful spiritual stream of today demands new political forms and that the state must be reestablished upon altered principles, . . . we have suggested to the Austrian Emperor, . . . that he transform his imperial state into a union of equal nations, which would accommodate these demands no less fully than would a unitary monarchy.

. . . . The enemies of our nationality have succeeded in frightening Europe with the specter of political Pan-Slavism . . . but we know the magic word that alone can exorcise this specter and promote freedom, culture and humanity. . . . The word is justice! Justice for the Slavic peoples in general and for its oppressed peoples in particular.

In the name of the liberty, equality, and fraternity of all peoples!

Documents in the Political History of the European Continent, 1815–1939, ed. G. A. Kertesz (Oxford, 1968), pp. 127–29.

the epitome of the absolutist regime the revolutions had overthrown in March, bombarded the city to end a week of radical demonstrations and street fighting. Windischgrätz declared martial law, which he used to crush the Czech national movement. Although the Czechs were openly loyal to the Habsburg empire, their calls for liberal political reform of the empire were anathema to Windischgrätz.

The defeat of the Czech liberal nationalists was a double defeat because German nationalists in Prague, Vienna, and throughout Germany supported the suppression of the Czech movement. Though these Germans shared the Czechs' liberal politics and their nationalist aspirations, they believed that Czech nationalism threatened their own German national goals. For these Germans, national politics trumped liberal politics, and they were willing to sacrifice the latter (liberalism) for the former (nationalism). Windischgrätz's ability to use national differences to divide the liberal movement would be the key to the Austrian Empire's resurrection from the ashes.

The other key was military victory against the Italian insurgents in Venetia and Lombardy. Here Austria benefited from Carlo Alberto's ambition to take control over northern Italy rather than press Radetzky when his troops were retreating in disarray. When the two armies finally met the Italians were easily defeated.

In August a revived Viennese government tried to revoke the concessions made to Hungary in March, and in September imperial troops marched against Hungary under the leadership of the Croatian governor (or ban) Josip Jelačić. Ban Jelačić had the same kind of nationalist aspirations for Croatia that prevailed in Prague—autonomy but within the framework of empire—therefore his allegiance was with Vienna over Budapest. When an angry mob in Budapest captured and murdered the new commander in chief of the imperial army, Jelačić was appointed in his place, and civil war began between Hungary and Austria. It was to be the longest military conflict of the revolutionary years.

At first Jelačić's forces had the advantage of organization and experience, but his brutal occupation and massive looting of the Hungarian countryside provoked a partisan war among the Hungarian peasantry. The war was complicated by divisions within the peasantry and among Austrians. While many Hungarian peasants fought against the imperial troops, in Galicia and elsewhere peasants fought against local nobilities. In the meantime radicals in Vienna revolted again, proclaiming their support for the Hungarians and declaring Austria a democratic republic. But the Habsburg armies crushed the Vienna revolution in October after days of fierce street fighting, comparable to the Parisian June Days. The radical leaders of the insurrection were executed.

In November 1848 the energetic and unscrupulous Prince Felix Schwarzenberg (1800–1852) became the Austrian prime minister. Schwarzenberg arranged the abdication of Ferdinand I and the accession of Ferdinand's nephew, the 18-year old Franz Josef (r. 1848–1916). He then declared that the promises made by the old emperor could not legally bind his successor and

Mór Than, Hungarians Fight for Independence at Tápió *(1848) (Hungarian National Museum)*

shelved the projects of the constituent assembly, though he honored the emancipation of the peasantry. The Hungarians fought on. In April 1849 the parliament of Hungary declared the country an independent republic and named Kossuth its new president. Russia now offered Austria military assistance. In August 1849 Russian troops helped to subjugate the Hungarian republic. But fighting continued until the end of December when the Hungarian revolutionary government was finally evicted from Budapest, bringing to an end the European revolutionary movement.

Great Britain and Russia

Revolutions did not occur in either England or Russia, and it is worth taking a moment to consider why. The conventional answer is that England was already too liberal and Russia was still too authoritarian for revolution, and there is some truth to this. England and Scotland (but not Ireland) had stable economies that had already made a transition to urban industrialization, so economic causes of discontent, while still extensive, were less explosive. The British parliament was just barely willing to compromise with middle-class liberals to avoid revolution, so liberals had some hope that legal reform was possible. The Chartist movement for enfranchising the workers was losing steam by 1848, so workers were disillusioned by mass politics just when they might have been galvanized for active opposition. The artisanal workers were already far weaker than their counterparts on the Continent, and the skilled workers who often led in radicalism either were demoralized Chartists or could see the possibility of making material gains in the existing system. Finally, the poor in England had more resources to fall back on in hard times, such as trade unions and mutual aid societies.

Ireland was not as fortunate. In Ireland economic decline was as severe as anywhere in Europe leading into the 1840s and then the potato famine struck, with its widespread starvation and out-migration. Hunger of course breeds discontent, and there was no lack of unhappiness in Ireland at the time; but starvation weakens the oppositional spirit. The huge English police force in Ireland further hampered demonstrations of discontent. There were, nonetheless, sparks of radical opposition in the 1840s. A group arose called Young Ireland, modeled less on the republican politics of Mazzini's Young Italy than on the cultural, medieval, and linguistic revivalist nationalism of Prague or Budapest. At the same time Daniel O'Connell had perfected the mass political rally, attracting perhaps a million people at a time to meetings calling for repeal of the union with England. But O'Connell was no revolutionary, and he was outmaneuvered by the British, who called his bluff. More aggressive Irish and English working-class leaders, less averse to violence, were in fact planning a joint insurrection in 1848, but the British police uncovered their plans and arrested hundreds of conspirators before the uprising could take place.

In terms of both resignation and repression, Ireland had more in common with Russia than with the rest of Great Britain. Determined to stamp out radicalism, including radical discourse, the Russian government of Nicholas I created an extensive secret police force (though not as extensive as the phrase "police state" suggests). Russia had yet to embrace industrialization; a decision made to preclude the kind of social disruption and radical demands seen in the West in 1848. The overwhelming majority of the population were still peasants living in remote hamlets. Half of those peasants were still enserfed to individual noble landowners, and many of the rest were under obligations to the state. There was a small group of liberal and radical intellectuals in the 1840s, but their numbers were quite limited. Although the influence of radical thought in educated society was impressive, the activists were yet tiny drops in the ocean of the Russian Empire as a whole. Russia's contributions to 1848 were isolated and perhaps incidental. Most famously, Nicholas I sent troops to Austria to suppress the Hungarian revolution, though they were far from decisive in bringing the civil war there to a close. Less well known, the young writer Fyodor Dostoevsky was arrested for his part in a revolutionary ring and sent to Siberia, where he abandoned radicalism and converted to a kind of conservative, Christian Gothic populism. Finally, tsarist political repression persuaded the young, radical writer, Alexander Herzen, to go into voluntary exile in Western Europe. He arrived in Paris in 1848 and presently became the finest chronicler of the 1848 revolutions.

Consequences of 1848

Not one of the revolutionary movements of 1848 stayed in power after toppling existing monarchies. Yet politically, socially, and culturally much had changed. Perhaps the most important legacy of the revolutions was their mass political mobilization and far-reaching expansion of the public sphere.

Frédéric Sorrieu, The Universal Republic of Democracy and Equality *(1848).This painting celebrating the victory of popular revolution in 1848 sanctifies the scene with apocalyptic imagery, as Christ and his angels preside over the procession as over an assembly of the saved after the Day of Judgment. The flag waving at the front of the procession is the red, white, and blue French revolutionary tricolor, followed by a German tricolor in black, red, and yellow and a green, white, and red one for Italy; flags of Hungary and the Czech Lands follow. People of every class and age are represented; the procession winds past the Tree of Liberty in the rear and a monument to the Republic in the foreground.* *(Bildarchiv Preussischer Kulturbesitz/Art Resource, NY. Musee de la Ville de Paris, Musee Carnavalet, Paris, France)*

The news of revolution created an unprecedented hunger for newspapers. In the Austrian Empire, before 1848 there had been 79 newspapers of which only 19 were permitted to discuss politics. In 1848 the total number jumped to 388, of which 306 printed political news without any censorship. In Paris alone, 171 newspapers appeared between February and June. In many places newspapers were read aloud and in groups, both to accommodate the illiterate and to share the news as a collective experience. But people wanted not only to read about events, they wanted to debate and demonstrate the positions they were taking. Clubs sprang up in every city and town for people to get together and talk about the news. In Paris there were 200 such organizations with around 70,000 members. In German-speaking Europe between 1 million and 1.5 million people joined a political club in 1848, one out of every 9 or 10 adult men. Clubs existed to turn people into citizens, educating them about issues and ideas, defining civic duties and obligations, and organizing campaigns to elect rafts of candidates. Most clubs were secular and democratic, but there were also large Catholic clubs. Gradually the clubs evolved into groups associated with specific points of view: liberal, radical, nationalist, and so on. In Germany, the club movement was the source of one of the most important developments to emerge from 1848: the organization of conservative politics. By the middle of 1849 conservative clubs in Germany outnumbered liberal clubs. And the *Kreuzzeitung,* launched in 1848, would remain the major conservative newspaper in Germany. Conservatism would play an important role in mass participatory politics after 1848 and is an important result of revolutionary political mobilization.

In addition to newspapers and clubs, millions of people participated in mass meetings and processions. Large political meetings would be planned ahead of time and advertised. A series of speakers, sometimes national leaders along with locals, would appear. In the fall of 1848, Lajos Kossuth traveled around Hungary from village to village, encouraging the newly liberated serfs to fight against the imperial armies. Thousands attended such meetings in beer halls and churches. Flags, banners, and posters decorated large halls or stages set up in fields and plazas. Some of these mass meetings were organized to directly challenge the government, others to convey new political ideas and establish the contours of new political communities. These events, the first large, secular mass meetings held in Europe, took place in towns and villages in every country where revolution occurred.

The organization of labor also originated in revolutionary organizations. Trade associations arose during 1848 with a multitude of functions (not just to negotiate with employers or organize strikes, as in later unions). Workers founded producers' cooperatives, and consumers' cooperatives. Associations usually included a mutual benefits program, which collected small sums from each member and helped support those in need. Large-scale organizations, intended to represent the craftsmen or workers of large regions and diverse crafts, were primarily found in France and Germany. Further east, such organizations tended to be smaller and more localized.

Women were active in both political clubs and labor associations, and demands for women's rights were a significant part of the revolutionary agenda. The outspoken journalists and writers of the 1830s and 1840s became leaders in 1848. Women were highly visible at mass meetings and demonstrations and were to be found on the barricades fighting alongside men in Prague, Paris, and Vienna. The most active women were in Paris, where they organized women's political clubs and women's newspapers. They called for a right to public education, the right of married women to control their property, and a "right to work" equal to men's rights. Women in Paris also called for the right to vote, and one woman, Jeanne Déroin (1805–1894), ran for a seat in the Legislative Assembly in 1849 even though she was not legally eligible.

Peasant participation in the revolutions was extremely widespread and could be extremely contradictory. Peasants contended both violently and peaceably, both for and against their governments. In Hungary peasants assaulted manor houses, refused to pay feudal dues, and made free use of noble forests; they also supported the noble-dominated Hungarian Diet and National Assembly for programs beneficial to peasants and joined the Hungarian army against the imperial troops. In Romania, nobles mobilized tens of thousands of peasants to fight the Hungarians, while next door the Slovaks failed in the same effort.

These were not irrational contradictions or irresponsible positions (usually), but rather practical and sensible. Where nobles' aims seemed to coincide with peasant aims, the nobles could mobilize peasant support. Where peasants were less economically desperate, as in wealthier grain-growing regions, they tended to be conservative supporters of order. Such peasants fought against radical urban workers and filled the ranks of the armies of Austria, Prussia, and Napoleon III. Where crops like grapes and olives were more market oriented and less predictable, and where peasants were more dependent on nobles' forests, the people tended to be more radical and more prone to violent acts, which they viewed as retaliation for years of humiliation and injustice.

The personal significance of participating in public mass movements cannot be underestimated. The mobilization of mass political communities was an experience that was widely shared and never forgotten, leaving memories of community, empowerment, and mass identity often across class lines. Mass movements on the same scale would not occur again in Europe in the nineteenth century, but everyone who took part in or observed the revolutions gradually came to understand that a new kind of power had been born. Utilizing the advances in communications and transportation, in political thought and organization, mass public bargaining for power would only increase in the decades to come.

In the aftermath of the revolutions, class and an awareness of the political divisions between classes was one of the main legacies of 1848. The fundamental differences in liberal and lower-class outlooks was visible to all. Most liberals were committed to constitutional monarchy, which meant working with the monarchies they had so long opposed, often a painful paradox. They did not directly challenge the aristocracies they sought to supplant. As men of property and commerce, they did not support peasant claims against noble landowners, nor were they willing to commit the resources of the state to providing the "right to work" or the kinds of economic regulation necessary to meet workers' demands for economic security. Most liberals did not favor universal male suffrage, and when popular protest, violence, and demonstrations continued to disrupt the political process of writing constitutions and founding national assemblies, they could neither support the popular revolution nor muster the forces to suppress it. In the end they had to rely on the militaries of the regimes they hated and, in so doing they gave the keys to the castle back to the old regime. French workers and some peasants came away with an enduring commitment to republicanism, the right to vote for representatives who would support their interests. The rift between middle and lower classes was significant. After 1848, liberals became partisans of stability, seeking to protect their gains from working-class socialist challenge.

In political terms, monarchies returned, but they did so with a full awareness of the lure of constitutions and the power of national unity. Prussia and Austria adopted moderate constitutions that left most power in the hands of their rulers; once the precedent for the rule of law and national representative assemblies was established, however, it would be broadened. Constitutional rule would now develop under the leadership and with the participation of far more conservative forces than those who pushed for reform in the 1840s and made the revolutions in the spring of 1848. As one of these rising stars, Otto von Bismarck (1815–1898), would put it, "The great questions of the day will not be settled by speeches and majority decisions—that was the mistake of 1848 and 1849—but by blood and iron." But after 1848 and 1849 even Bismarck would not be able to ignore public opinion, electoral representation, and mass politics.

Finally, the cause of nationalism received an enormous boost from the revolutionary experience. Demands for national self-determination appeared for the first time on a mass scale in 1848. The unmet goals of that year in Italy, Germany, and Hungary would shortly return, to be achieved in the decades that followed. The nationalist aspirations of minorities within those countries and on their borderlands would be far more complicated and would continue to contribute to bloody national and international conflicts.

* * *

In the aftermath of the revolutions of 1848, the challenge for governments in the second half of the century would be to catch up with the industrial progress made by England without succumbing to another round of revolution. The challenge for the people of Europe would be to use the lessons they had learned in 1848 to press for improvements, rights, and nationhood without having to resort to violence. The result was the building of the modern nation-state.

SEVEN

The Modern Nation-State

The Romantic ideas that inspired the midcentury revolutions were discredited when revolutions failed. Disillusionment with utopian ideals brought about a withdrawal from politics of much of the middle class and an appreciation for the practical among the rest. This shift took a variety of forms, from the compromise politics underlying parliamentary procedure to the manipulative realpolitik of the more authoritarian systems. The new realism also transferred the attention of many in the liberal middle classes from their politics to their businesses, linking the two more intimately than ever before. Conservatives made their peace with constitutional politics and learned to use the endowments of the public sphere to their advantage. Even in countries with few of those endowments, a new awareness of competing interests within society and a role for active government regulation arose. Together these developments led to the rise of the modern nation-state.

In the twenty or so years after 1848, state rulers became actively involved in regulating and stimulating national economies for a number of reasons: to compete with England, to build prosperity, and to distract the middle classes from disruptive political postures. Rulers who restored their powers after the revolutions developed a new respect for well-armed internal police forces. The popular unrest taught European rulers to improve living and working conditions for the poor to prevent turmoil. These activities required the expansion of the state itself and led to the spectacular growth of bureaucracies to collect and classify information, to regulate conflicts, and to plan for the future.

All these new initiatives were held together by the state's gradual appropriation of nationalism. Rulers learned to use the image of a national community to their advantage as a stabilizing (usually) area of consensus that cut across class and political lines. Today's use of "nation" and "state" as more or less interchangeable can be misleading. The "state" refers to organized institutions of government, while "nations" are communities of people. National identity was a new source of pride, but it was also an economic and political necessity. Nation-state building after 1848 took a variety of forms, but they all included some state initiative together with the popular clamor; nationalism created a field for political unity between state and society and among contentious social groups. Economically, the nation-state was the most effective unit for accelerating industrialization.

Together these new functions of state activity and the new justifications on rationalist and nationalist grounds are sometimes referred to as "modernization." The term has been criticized, however, for its implication that the history of a few tiny countries on the western tip of the European continent provided the only model for development in the "modern" world. There were obvious differences between Britain and Bulgaria in the nineteenth century, between France and Russia, between Norway and Italy and Albania. But those differences cannot all be reduced to a contrast between the "modern" and the "backward," to the level and pace of industrialization, or even to the penetration of Enlightenment thought. There was, at the time, a widespread belief in the "modern West" as the advance guard of civilization based on economic and cultural superiority, and that belief colors much historical writing. But, in retrospect, the differences among nation-states in the nineteenth century seem as significant as their similarities. England, France, and Germany, Europe's great modern powers, each found its own path to modernity, as did every other country in Europe. More important, the evolution of political systems in the direction of democracy or dictatorship is too complex to be reduced to a question of modernity or backwardness. Modern European nation-states took every conceivable form, combining elements of popular sovereignty with coercion. In fact, it is precisely this *conflict* between the striving of activated societies for popular sovereignty and prosperity on the one hand and for stability and security on the other that marks this period as modern. That conflict existed everywhere in Europe in the second half of the nineteenth century, and it was embodied in the rise of the modern nation-states.

One more point should be made about the aftermath of 1848. Despite the universal unrest and instability in Europe during the year of revolutions, no international wars broke out. No single power tried to use the weakness of its neighbors for its own territorial advantage. No government tried to shift attention away from its domestic strife by mobilizing its armies and a national consensus against a foreign enemy. In fact, the revolutions were initially successful because since 1815 all European states had committed themselves to the preservation of stability through peace, and security through negotiation. Once governments decided to use force to halt internal conflict, the revolutions were brought under control. These facts had important consequences for the nation-states that emerged from the midcentury crisis. Most of Europe's most powerful leaders would continue to place international stability above gross expansion of state power. Most were, most of the time, committed to maintain a rough balance of powers by diplomacy, negotiation, and treaty. Most still believed, as their predecessors at Vienna had believed, that war is as grave a threat to national stability as revolution. But there would be exceptions. The revolutions of 1848 produced the first cracks in the Concert of Europe that had emerged from the Congress of Vienna. The pragmatic and ambitious nation-state builders of the mid- to late nineteenth century would only partially share their predecessors' belief in the inherent value of limited ambition and commitment to mutual rules and restraints. They would remain only partially loyal to the aims of the international order when these ends came into conflict with the aims of their own states. Ultimately the complete breakdown of the Concert of Europe would bring the nineteenth century to an end; its first failure came on the heels of 1848.

The Crimean War

In the early 1850s Britain and Russia were the most powerful countries in Europe. Avoiding revolutionary turmoil convinced people in both countries of the essential correctness of the paths they had chosen and the nations they had become, different as they were. Russia's military self-confidence still lay in its thirty-five-year-old defeat of Napoleon. Nicholas I and his ministers firmly believed that Russian autocracy and Russian culture would prove to be the salvation of Europe. During the revolutions, both Russian and British policy was to take whatever steps were necessary to preserve international stability, though this did not prevent Nicholas from sending troops to put down the Hungarian revolt.

In the meantime, two areas of international affairs concerned diplomatic negotiators in western Europe: the apparent growth of Russian power and the increasing weakness of the Ottoman Empire. Throughout Nicholas's reign, Russian policy had been to preserve Ottoman authority on the assumption that a weak country on its southern frontier was preferable to a power vacuum, which would attract the interests of the Great Powers. The Treaties of Adrianople (1829) and Unkiar-Skelessi (1833, renewed 1841) involved all the powers in protecting the integrity of the weakening Ottoman Empire. In addition, Russia had serious instability on its other southern frontiers. The northern Caucasus had never accepted Russian imperial rule, and in the 1840s opponents there found a charismatic guerrilla leader in Imam Shamil (1797?–1871), the legendary "Lion of Dagestan." Shamil led the people of Chechnya and the northern Caucasus in a war of resistance that prevented Russian control of the region until the 1860s, when Shamil himself was captured. At the same time Russia was gradually extending its hold on the central Asian frontier that bordered British territories in Afghanistan and India.

Britain opposed Russia's increasing influence in the Near East and central Asia, where its own colonial ambitions might be threatened. As a result of these other conflicts and lingering fears dating back to the preceding century, British and Russian diplomats misunderstood each other's ambitions: both, in fact, wished to preserve stability in southeastern Europe and the heartland of the Ottoman Empire on the Black and Mediterranean seas. However, Nicholas was beginning to think that the Ottoman collapse was inevitable, and he wanted to be prepared to take advantage when it came. For twelve years (1841–1853) the Russians tried to reach an agreement with Britain on what should be done with Ottoman territory if and when the empire collapsed. The British did not believe that such a breakdown was imminent and hoped to prevent Russia from doing anything to hasten it. By 1853, however, the tsar mistakenly believed that Britain was not opposed to Russian action inside Ottoman territories, and Britain mistakenly believed that the tsar would not act there without consultation.

Russian relations with the Ottomans were further complicated by religion. The tsar saw himself as the protector of the Orthodox Christians against the Ottoman Muslims. The Russian Empire in the Caucasus region was composed of diverse nationalities, several of them followers of Islam. While the Georgians and Armenians were Christians, the Muslim inhabitants of neighboring Azerbaijan and the Tatars in Crimea and Kazan (though themselves quite diverse historically and culturally) were all strongly influenced by developments in the Ottoman Empire. Turmoil in the Caucasus and the resistance to Russian rule were taking on new significance in an age when nationalism was on the upsurge and the major Muslim power in western Asia was declining. The Slavs of southeastern Europe began to appeal to the Russian tsar to protect them from the Ottoman Muslims. Thus, when a dispute arose pitting Orthodox Christians against Roman Catholics under Muslim rule in the Holy Land, the tsar had a religious pretext as well as political motives to assert his authority over the Christian population in Ottoman territories.

The dispute concerned the right to perform religious rituals at sites considered holy by Christians in Palestine, which was then still part of the Ottoman domain. The conflict was between Roman Catholics, backed by Napoleon III, and the Orthodox clergy, backed by the tsar. This dispute was the immediate cause of the Crimean War, since the Ottomans ruled in favor of the Catholics. But the underlying cause was Great Power conflict. When Napoleon III asked the sultan to make concessions to Catholics in Palestine, both knew that Nicholas would object, so France had to promise the Ottomans French support if those objections escalated into war. Russia proceeded to open negotiations with Britain and Istanbul to settle the dispute amicably, but all sides acted without much restraint. Russia expected its longtime ally Austria to fight on its side, but Austria, which like the rest of the Great Powers, entered war very reluctantly, chose this moment to change sides and throw in its lot with Britain and France. Still that decision was so difficult and momentous that it was late in coming, and Austria gained very little from it. Nicholas was astonished by the end of an alliance that dated back to the early eighteenth century, and the animosity that ensued was one of the main factors leading to the First World War.

In 1853 Nicolas sent troops into the European Ottoman territories, Moldavia and Wallachia (roughly present-day Romania), ostensibly to protect the Orthodox population there as well as to enforce his demands in Palestine. Despite many months of elaborate diplomatic negotiations, the Ottoman Empire declared war on Russia and soon lost its fleet. A full year later Britain, France, and eventually the Italian kingdom of Piedmont-Sardinia then fought the Russians, ostensibly to protect the Ottoman Empire, though in fact to preserve the balance of power. The resulting war was a disaster of outmoded strategy, humiliating defeats, and great loss of life for the western powers, and a further diminishing of Ottoman authority and stability. For Russia it would be a disaster of colossal proportions and far-reaching consequences.

Britain and France lay siege to the port city and naval base at Sebastopol on the Crimean peninsula in the Black Sea. Sebastopol was protected from attack by sea, so an ill-fated land siege was launched. The war was waged as a shadow of the campaigns against Napoleon forty years earlier. The British commander was a veteran of Waterloo, and the British officer corps was drawn from aristocrats appointed for their family connections rather than their training. The conditions around Crimea were pestilential, and more men died of disease than battle wounds. The British poet Alfred, Lord Tennyson (1809–1892) immortalized the bravery of British soldiers in his stirring "Charge of the Light Brigade" (1864), but the actual conduct of war evoked a grim rather than romantic heroism.

For Russian troops things were even worse. The Russian military was surprised to discover that the army at its disposal was ill prepared to take the field. Overconfidence based on decades-old experience and lack of industrial development in armaments and transportation turned Sebastopol into the site of a devastating defeat. Blame lay in many areas, all of which would be dissected when the war ended, but first of all soldiers were sent into the field with weapons that not only were outmoded, but had been made inoperable by decades of parade ground drills so beloved by the tsar. The guns that looked smart when tossed in the air or smacked from hand to hand performed dismally when required to shoot. The lack of railroad tracks was equally disastrous. No trains were available to bring troops or supplies to the front. Nicholas himself was so distraught at what he perceived to be his own personal failure of duty that he died in the middle of the war, in 1855. His son, Alexander II (r. 1855–1881), would assess the damage with a cold eye toward preventing the repetition of such a national humiliation and would lead Russia on a campaign of unprecedented and promising reforms.

Perhaps the greatest heroes of the Crimean War were women. Independently of each other and for different reasons, both Britain and Russia grudgingly allowed medical aid to be given soldiers by women nurses. Florence Nightingale (1820–1910), a determined and gifted woman, had entered nursing against her parents' wishes. Nursing was considered a disreputable profession associated with suspiciously intimate attentions to the unclothed body. Nightingale almost single-handedly changed that. She volunteered for duty in Istanbul when she heard how horrendously the wounded were being treated there. Her reports back to London were unsparing in their criticism and unrelenting in their demands for better supplies and treatment. She won many of her battles, raised the prestige of nursing, and made herself famous in the process.

Russian nursing was, if possible, even more courageous. While Nightingale and her sisters were confined to the base hospital in Scutari, Russian women were ministering to the wounded right on the battlefront. Organized by Nicholas Pirogov (1810–1881), a physician who believed women could and should be doctors, the corps of nurses impressed even the meanest skeptics with their professionalism and medical expertise, and their courage under fire. Alexandra Krupskaia described the abuse heaped on the nurses by their critics and showed that the soldiers preferred the nurturing women nurses to the cold male medics they were used to. After the war the women who served in Crimea were decorated for valor and publicly thanked by the tsar. British and Russian nurses opened the way for women to receive professional medical training.

The demoralizing war ended finally with the capitulation of Sebastopol in September 1855. The Treaty of Paris in 1856 confirmed Britain's preeminence in Europe and underlined Russia's fall. Moldavia and Wallachia were placed in conditions that allowed the establishment within the decade of an autonomous state of Romania within the Ottoman Empire. The Concert of Europe had been severely shaken by the Crimean War, and during the next two decades the building of individual nation-states would take place independently of and often in conflict with international agreements. Though the nation-states would take a variety of forms, many followed a pattern laid out by the surprisingly dynamic new emperor of the French.

France: The Second Empire

The plebiscites Napoleon III used to confirm himself in power were accompanied by skillful propaganda. Many opponents of the new emperor simply did not vote, and a substantial majority of French men over 21 were apparently willing to accept authoritarian rule after years of unrest. For nearly three decades the full force of popular and fashionable French literature had been at work embellishing the Napoleonic legend and identifying the name of Napoleon with French patriotism. Many voted yes, not to Louis-Napoleon, or to authoritarianism in the abstract, but to the music of the "Marseillaise," the cannon of Austerlitz, the growing cult of Joan of Arc—to all the intangible glories of France.

The new constitution approved by the two plebiscites set up a lightly veiled dictatorship very much like that of Napoleon I. The emperor, who was responsible only to "the nation," governed through ministers, judges, and bureaucrats—whom he appointed. The popularly elected assembly, the Corps Législatif, was filled with candidates whose success at the polls was assured by the emperor's loyal prefects, who could be counted on to pressure voters to cast their ballots as the emperor desired. The assembly had little power to initiate or amend legislation, and public debate of government policy was prohibited. But in the aftermath of revolution there were popular demands, economic demands, and administrative demands that required the attention of government. Napoleon III would try a variety of approaches to meet them. During the 1850s he combined a political system that was a conservative reaction against revolution with relatively liberal social programs. He courted the support of businessmen and the middle classes with policies that stimulated the economy (and hence their own prosperity). He made a number of efforts to organize state resources along scientific lines, provided

A Closer Look

THE RESTORATION OF ABSOLUTISM

The constitution issued by Louis-Napoleon in January 1852 was a repudiation of revolutionary liberalism. Its publication was accompanied by the soon-to-be emperor's lengthy explanation of his political principles. How did he justify his restoration of absolutism?

Frenchmen—

In my proclamation of the 2nd December when I loyally explained to you what, according to my ideas, were the vital conditions of government in France, I had not the pretension, so common in these days, of substituting a personal theory for the experience of centuries. . . . On the contrary, I sought in the past the examples that might best be followed, . . .

I have thought it reasonable to prefer the precepts of genius to the specious doctrines of men of abstract ideas. I have taken as models the political institutions which already at the commencement of the century under analogous circumstance have strengthened tottering society and raised France to a lofty degree of prosperity and grandeur. . . .

It may then be affirmed that the frame of our social edifice is the work of the Emperor [Napoleon Bonaparte] which has stood firm—resisting his fall and the shocks of three revolutions.

The present constitution, . . . proclaims that the chief whom you have elected is responsible to you. That he has the right of appeal to your sovereign judgment, in order that in grave circumstances you may always be able to continue your confidence in him, or to withdraw it. Being responsible, his actions must be free and without hindrance. . . .

Documents in the Political History of the European Continent, ed. G. A. Kertesz (Oxford, 1968), pp. 162–63.

state financial support for building railroads and modernizing the harbors, and expanded credit through state-sponsored banks.

Urban France still bears the stamp of the Second Empire, especially in Paris, where the emperor's prefect of the Seine, Baron Georges-Eugène Haussmann (1809–1891) engaged in a major rebuilding campaign. The main emphasis of this campaign was on streets: old neighborhoods of narrow, winding medieval streets were demolished and replaced with wide avenues, broad boulevards, and circular plazas. Ports and railroad stations were connected with the center of the city by extending and widening avenues. Working-class suburbs were connected with the center as well. Parks were built and fountains constructed in those new plazas to bring fresh air and water to the polluted city scape. In this way, Haussmann (and his followers in cities all over Europe) would seek to replace overcrowded slums, with their disease and radicalism, with more sanitary streets and housing.

Seeberger Brothers, the Place du Châtelet after the work of Haussmann. (Archives Photographiques, Paris)

Haussmann's projects also included improving the public water supply, updating and expanding the underground sewage system, bringing gas street lights to much more of the city, providing a multitude of public buildings and a new central market, Les Halles, and developing new public parks, including the Bois de Boulogne. Haussmann's city planning transformed Paris in the 1850s and 1860s and influenced city planning the world over in the decades that followed. The emperor himself was the catalyst behind many of the most important projects and the particular style they assumed. The massive street projects, the central market, and the Bois de Boulogne were all his ideas. That the market, Les Halles, be built in the most up-to-date style, with an open, light structure of iron and glass was Napoleon III's as well.

Critics then and now believed that the government's main purpose in slum clearance was to prevent further radical unrest. The destruction of narrow streets in working-class quarters would make it impossible to build barricades. But Napoleon's goals were more complicated than this suggests. In his youth, the emperor had been drawn to utopian socialism and in his economic policies employed a former Saint-Simonian adviser. In November 1851 he told the National Assembly that the best means to forestall the revolution was to meet the real needs of the public by offering steady employment through public works. This aim was only partly met. Jobs were indeed created, but neither jobs nor housing could keep up with the rapidly increasing population in Paris. The demolition of working-class neighborhoods and the shift of the workers to the suburbs left many stranded and served only to transfer the locus of working-class radicalism to the outskirts. Haussmann's program, however, served another goal: to turn central Paris into a symbol of imperial power and clear the stage for the ascendance of bourgeois business and leisure. The grand boulevards linked the sites of great economic and political power: railway station, stock market, police station, city hall. Haussmann's model modern city asserted its imperial power, cleaned its streets and its water, and displayed its mastery of nature, not by building over it, but by rationalizing and taming it, making nature fit for city life.

Parisians themselves were deeply conflicted about the transformation of their beloved city, and their conflicts illustrate some of the fundamental tensions inherent in the making of modernity. One of Haussmann's most vocal critics wrote of the new working-class suburbs, that "Artisans and workers are shut up in veritable Siberias, criss-crossed with winding, unpaved paths, without lights, without shops, with no water. . . . We have sewn rags onto the purple robe of a queen; we have built within Paris two cities, quite different and hostile: the city of luxury, surrounded, besieged by the city of misery." Bourgeois prosperity, whose pleasures were on conspicuous display in the new public spaces along Haussmann's broad new boulevards, expelled the people whose labor made prosperity possible.

Other critics recoiled from the new imperial aesthetic—with its too regular avenues and homogeneous new facades—as cold and impersonal in contrast with the cozy, eccentric, romanticized medieval city that Haussmann tore down. The splendor of Haussmann's bourgeois Paris was celebrated in the glorious colors of impressionist paintings but was also seen by some contemporaries as alienating. The poet Charles Valette wrote in 1856, "Cruel demolisher, what have you done with the past? I search in vain for Paris; I search for myself."

During the 1850s France was ruled from Paris, indeed from the office of the emperor. Centralization extended to the appointment of minor local officials; the legislature was muzzled and powerless; newspapers and clubs were closed down or placed under careful state surveillance. Then in 1860 Napoleon began a gradual process of liberalization. First the legislative bodies were given the right to public debate, censorship was relaxed, freedom of speech was widened, the Corps Législatif was given power over budgets. Educational reform followed and soon after the legalization of trade unions gave workers the right to strike.

Historians have not adequately explained why Napoleon III shifted course so suddenly. He may have been responding to increasing opposition and trying to make up for embarrassing foreign policy blunders. Napoleon III always embodied a fundamental conflict between genuine sympathy for workers (and nationalists) and his commitment to preserve stability above all. Ultimately the emperor may have been motivated by his foremost wish to maintain order. His ideological positions had always been eclectic to the point of incomprehensibility; but if his main goal was in fact stability, it is not hard to imagine him subordinating ideology to order, prosperity, and what he hoped would be national glory. When working-class and liberal opposition increased under the repressive measures of the immediate postrevolutionary period, he may have believed that a lifting of restrictions would serve stability better than continuing repression.

Napoleon III believed that the July Monarchy had fallen because Louis Philippe had done nothing to revive France's international position. True or not, foreign policy would be the downfall of Napoleon III. At first, the Crimean War did place France in a powerful position; and Paris became the diplomatic center of Europe, but entanglements in Italy began to change that.

Unification of Italy and Germany

Until the middle of the nineteenth century the center of Europe was a collection of small city-states and principalities. The first efforts to create nation-states—in 1848—failed, but both Italy and Germany were formed in the decades that followed. When Italy and Germany became single, politically unified nations, the balance of power in Europe changed significantly. An industrial and educational powerhouse, Germany came to dominate central Europe in place of a weakened Austria. Italy's unification further weakened Austria's power in the region by taking two important states, Lombardy and Venetia. The non-German peoples of the Austrian Empire would be inspired by these models of nation building to press their own claims to national sovereignty, further weakening the Habsburg dominance of central Europe.

Italy

Italian national unity seemed remote after Piedmont's two decisive defeats by Austria in 1848 and 1849, yet it was accomplished by 1870. The democratic reforms of the 1848 revolutions raised the hopes of Italian nationalists who longed for a resurgence, or Risorgimento, of the power and glory of the ancient Roman Empire. Three of the movement's leaders in its years of triumph were the Romantic nationalist adventurer Giuseppe Garibaldi; Vittorio Emanuele II of the house of Savoy, king of Piedmont-Sardinia (and later of a united Italy: r. 1849–1878); and, above all, Piedmont's prime minister, Count Camillo di Cavour. A man of great energy and enterprise, Cavour was a successful businessman, statesman, and diplomat. Though of aristocratic origin and trained for the army, Cavour enthusiastically supported the economic revolutions and the aspirations of the business classes. He applied the newest agricultural methods to his family estates and promoted the introduction of steamboats, railroads, industries, and banks to prepare Piedmont for leadership in a unified Italy. He arose as a leader of the Risorgimento as cabinet minister in the 1850s, when he transformed nationalist unification from an outlaw movement or a movement simply for liberation from Austria. In Cavour's hands, unification was designed to promote economic and polit-

The Unification of Italy, 1859–1870

ical reform that would bring liberty and prosperity to Italy. He told the conservative Piedmont parliament in 1850, "You will see, gentlemen, how reforms carried out in time, instead of weakening authority, reinforce it; instead of precipitating revolution, they prevent it." Cavour was a pragmatist. He was opposed to the radical tactics and republican goals of the most important nationalist who had preceded him, the passionate, and dogmatic, Mazzini.

Cavour was a superlatively adept practitioner of the brand of diplomacy often called *realpolitik*, or the politics of realism and power. As prime minister of Piedmont-Sardinia, he cultivated French and English support, bringing Piedmont into the Crimean War on their side against Russia. He received no immediate reward, but won a place at the Paris peace conference, where he made it known that Piedmont had as much right to intervene in Lombardy and Venetia as Austria did. He finally persuaded Napoleon III that for Austria to hold power in northern Italy was a denial of the principle of nationality. Napoleon had great sympathy for Italy, but unification would both create another Great Power on France's border, which was dangerous, and destroy the pope's power in the Papal States, which would be unpopular in Catholic France. His goal was an enlarged Piedmont in the north, the weakening of Austria, and a federal system in Italy under the pope.

Thus in 1859 France joined Piedmont in war against Austria. Rapid victories at Magenta and Solferino boded well for the allies, but then Napoleon suddenly pulled out. He had discovered that Cavour was secretly negotiating to annex part of the Papal States and that Prussia was planning to intervene. Angering almost everyone involved, Napoleon worked out a compromise and signed a separate peace with Franz Josef, the Austrian emperor, in July 1859, which gave Lombardy to Piedmont, but left Venetia in Austrian hands. Cavour resigned in bitter protest.

He had however, already won. Cavour's liberal realpolitik was joined by a wave of popular protest against Austrian domination. Popular agitation rose higher in northern and central Italy: in Parma, Modena, Tuscany, and the Romagna (the northernmost province of the Papal States), bloodless revolutions and plebiscites demanded annexation to Piedmont. Early in 1860 Cavour returned to office to manage the annexations and also to pay off Napoleon III (who was opposed to the dismantling of the Papal States) by ceding Savoy and Nice to France.

He turned next to the rapidly developing situation in the southern and Papal States. Unlike the Romantic Mazzini, the pragmatist Cavour had not believed that the unity of all Italy was a real possibility; "silly nonsense" he had called it not long before. But in 1860, under Giuseppe Garibaldi, a leader every bit as Romantic, charismatic, and unorthodox as Mazzini had been, unification of the whole peninsula took place. Garibaldi was immensely popular for his simplicity and honesty, and for his disinterested, passionate commitment to Italy and its people. He was able to raise huge armies and imbue them with the same passion. A republican as well as a nationalist agitator, Garibaldi had defended Mazzini's Roman republic against the French siege. Utilizing the same deceptively contradictory ideology found among peasants in 1848 all over Europe, he called himself a republican and a socialist, and he was ready to take up arms against elite oppressors; but he was devoutly loyal to the monarchy (to Mazzini's disgust), and rallied people around the new king of Italy, Vittorio Emanuele of Piedmont-Sardinia.

In May an expedition outfitted in Piedmontese ports, but not formally acknowledged by Cavour's government, set out for Naples and Sicily under Garibaldi. Cavour deeply distrusted Garibaldi, who he feared might make Italy a republic. Garibaldi's expedition met with resounding victory. With a thousand followers, mostly students and other young men dressed in flamboyant red shirts, Garibaldi defeated twenty thousand troops. He marched across Sicily, promising relief from poverty to peasants and freedom from

Giuseppe Garibaldi was frequently shown on horseback or in a horse-drawn carriage, leading the "war for Italian independence" to the applause of the multitudes. Here he is seen triumphantly entering Naples on September 7, 1860. (Scala/Art Resource)

Naples to landowners. Most Sicilians had never heard of "Italy." Recruits swarmed to his flag, but the underlying, some would say deceptive, nationalist goal of the campaign would lead to bitterness later on.

Garibaldi crossed the Straits of Messina to continue his victorious march on the mainland territories of Naples. He had the support of the British prime minister, with the implication that British naval forces might act to block outside intervention against his movement. Cavour, terrified that Garibaldi would bring on a new crisis by marching north to take Rome from the pope, which would have the added disadvantage of offending France, or worse yet, turning Italy into a republic, sent Piedmontese troops to fight for all the remaining papal territories except Rome and its environs. Cavour told Napoleon that he had to invade the Papal States before Garibaldi got there, but the French were not appeased, and Napoleon was deeply humiliated. Vittorio Emanuele soon joined forces with Garibaldi near Naples and assured the triumph of Cavour's policy. In plebiscites in the autumn of 1860, Sicily, Naples, and the papal domains of Umbria and the Marches voted for union with Piedmont.

The result was the proclamation in March 1861 of the kingdom of Italy—essentially a much-enlarged Piedmont-Sardinia, but with Florence as its capital and Vittorio Emanuele as its monarch. Territorially, the work of the Risorgimento was almost complete. Only two more major areas were needed—Austrian Venetia and papal Rome. The pope protested vehemently against the unification under Piedmont, and Rome was protected by a French garrison. Prussian unification would make Italy's final victory possible. Rome was captured when France was bogged down in its own war against Prussia. On September 20, 1870, Rome became the capital of Italy and the pope was forced to retreat behind the walls of the Vatican, papal recognition of the country would not come for another half-century. Italy received Venetia as a reward for having sided with Prussia in the brief war of 1866, in which Prussia defeated Austria.

To the rest of the peninsula, there was little to prevent the impression that Italy was merely an expanded Piedmont, with its king, its constitutions, and its businessmen. Naples and Sicily resented the northerners, and that resentment was not offset by economic benefits. Free trade did great damage to the southern economy, already deeply impoverished. There was also a great deal of hostility between Catholics and anticlericals. Catholics were embittered by the annexation of the Papal States without papal consent and were enraged by the wholesale closure of religious institutions and the sale of 250,000 acres of church property. The result was semi–civil war and explosive insurrection. Between 1861 and 1865 approximately two-thirds of the Italian army was engaged in trying to maintain order in the south.

The government of Cavour and his followers was devoted to enlarging the middle class and promoting a modern economy, a policy that had its costs and its benefits. The new kingdom made some economic and political progress. A new merchant marine and an army and navy gave Italy some standing as a power. Even the national finances seemed for a time to be sound. The economic development of the industrial north was achieved, however, at the expense of a south both exploited and neglected, which increased regional differentiation and divisive resentments.

The average life expectancy in Italy in the 1870s was just over 30 years; one in four children died in infancy. And the poverty of the southern peasantry was equal to the worst poverty in Europe. Three-quarters of peasant expenditures went to food, the rest to clothing and shelter, so there was nothing left for manufactured goods, by the sale of which the northern liberals had hoped to jump-start Italian industrialization. Even cash was scarce in the countryside, where payment in kind was the norm. In north and south alike migrant field workers often lived in dugouts, and many settled peasants lived in caves, grottos, or one-room huts with dirt floors.

The tragedy of the success of the Risorgimento was that the liberals who accomplished it had no real understanding of the country they were working so hard to unite or of the need, once unification was achieved, to bring the majority of the people into civic life. The questionable legitimacy and lack of qualified personnel in the first Italian governments undermined the stability of the political system and encouraged bribery and patronage in place of bureaucracy and merit. Compounding the tragedy, Cavour fell ill and died in 1861, depriving the country of its most astute and committed leader. After pacifying the opposition to northern dominance in the 1860s and discovering the difficulties involved in real unification and governance of a modern

Prince Otto von Bismarck, the pragmatic German chancellor. (New York Public Library Picture Collection)

nation-state, the Italian government suffered a period of uncertainty, opportunism, and drift.

Germany

The creation of a united Germany was above all the work of Prince Otto von Bismarck (1815–1898). Brilliant, unscrupulous, ruthless, a genius at maneuvering and at concealing his real intentions, Bismarck sometimes pursued two apparently contradictory policies at the same time, until the moment came when he had to make a final decision. His loyalty to the Prussian Crown, even when he manipulated it to his own purposes, did not falter during his long years in office. Influential before 1862, he towered over Prussia from 1862 to 1871, and over the German Empire thereafter until 1890. Yet his efforts could not have succeeded had they not met with general approval from the German people, who had long hungered for unity and came increasingly to favor his brand of pragmatic, forceful *realpolitik* over Romantic concepts of liberty.

In the 1850s German politics was primarily concerned with reestablishing a conservative political order and, despite having become a constitutional monarchy, destroying all vestiges of revolution. Most German state governments combined the "stick" of the harsh political repression with a "carrot" of economic development. In 1851 the German Confederation were reconstituted, but in many states constitutions were withdrawn or revised to limit the power of parliaments and to restrict voting rights. University professors were fired for political beliefs, and police surveillance was introduced to watch those revolutionaries who had not emigrated. The nobility regained some of its privileges, though serfdom was not reinstated. Everywhere bureaucracies grew and became more active and efficient; police power grew as well. The timing and intensity of these policies varied from state to state, but the patterns were similar. On the other hand, an effort was made to use the press to build consensus and win support for the government, a necessity after the challenges of the late 1840s. Peasants were given a land bank, which offered loans for farmers to win their support of the government and to encourage their belief that the government would protect them from the nobility. Public services were improved. In Berlin, a new police chief, Carl von Hinckeldey, epitomized the "carrot and stick" of the day. He created a spy system and used surveillance, identity checks, press seizures, and deportations, to stifle political unrest. He introduced fire departments, public baths, tree planting, street cleaning, and improvements in the water supply as well. In general, governments hoped to use economic development to shift liberal middle class energies away from opposition politics.

Bismarck spent the 1850s as Prussia's representative in Frankfurt at the Diet of the German Confederation, and then as ambassador to St. Petersburg and Paris. Though he remained conservative to the core, these experiences had given him broader ambitions for Prussia. He believed that Prussia should take the lead in unifying Germany and that a break with Austria would be needed to accomplish this. Bismarck also believed that while that there would be a leading role in Germany for the traditional noble and military elite, there would also have to be a key role for the middle classes, who were more energetic, educated, and industrious, and more sympathetic to unification.

By espousing increasingly conservative policies, the Frankfurt Diet had long since lost the support of artisans and industrial workers. The major foreign policy question in the whole region was the competition between Austria and Prussia for dominance in the German-speaking world. At the Diet, Bismarck took every occasion to thwart Austrian designs. Bismarck favored Prussian neutrality in the Crimean War, while Austria harassed rather than helped the Russians. Realizing that Austrian behavior was alienating Russia, and that Russian friendship would be valuable later when Prussia would have to challenge Austria, Bismarck frustrated those Prussians who hoped they would enter the war against Russia and thus line up with the West. Counting on a military showdown with Austria, Bismarck also wooed the French emperor Napoleon III.

These diplomatic and military concerns led directly to the events that made Bismarck the undisputed leader of Prussian policy making. In 1858 Friedrich Wilhelm IV, who had been ill for years, stepped aside; his 61-year-old brother became regent and then, three years later, came to power as Wilhelm I (r. 1861–1888). Though conservative, Wilhelm was committed to ruling as a constitutional monarch; he swore an oath to the constitution and had the parliament validate his regency. Wilhelm was above all a soldier, and he was easily persuaded by his minister of war that an army reorganization was necessary: a conscript army took time to mobilize, but a professional army (like Britain's) did not. Wilhelm proposed to parliament to increase the number of conscripts drafted each year from 40,000 to 63,000, and to lengthen the term of their service from two to three years; he also requested funding to carry out the reforms. The liberal majority in parliament was adamantly opposed to funding an increase in troops, especially since Prussia was following no independent foreign policy at the time. A prolonged political crisis over the budget produced a dangerous stalemate. The government could not function without a budget, and neither side would back down. At the height of the crisis, the king, convinced that Bismarck could outwit the parliament, called the veteran diplomat back from Paris, where he was serving as ambassador, and appointed him to the key posts of minister president and minister of foreign affairs.

Bismarck's approach to the crisis showed his ability to deal with complex issues in imaginative, manipulative, and forceful ways of questionable legality. On the grounds that the constitution permitted the government to use taxes collected for other purposes even when the budget had not yet been approved by parliament, Bismarck told the bureaucracy to continue doing their jobs (including enacting the military reforms) and they would be funded with taxes collected and without an official budget. Over the next years, he again and again dissolved parliament, called new elections, faced another hostile house, and then repeated the process. He suppressed opposition newspapers in defiance of a constitutional provision that the press should be free. Yet despite four years of this illegal behavior (1862–1866), Bismarck got away with everything in the end because of the glittering success he scored by his unorthodox and daring foreign policy. In 1866 an admiring parliament voted retroactive approval of his unauthorized military expenditures, rendering them legal.

Bismarck's plan to win the German public over with foreign policy successes began by consolidating his good relations with Russia and by taking advantage of the unsuccessful Polish uprising of 1863. The people of Congress Poland, observing the success of national movements in Romania and Italy, as well as the relaxation of Russia's authoritarian rule after the death of Nicholas I, and feeling certain of the sympathy of Napoleon III, decided it was a propitious time to press again for their liberation from Russia. This was a terrible miscalculation. Nicholas's son Alexander II was busy preparing major reform legislation at home and required stability. He offered Poland social reforms and land reform, but the Poles viewed these concessions as a sign of weakness in St. Petersburg. They rose up against the tsar in January 1863 and despite the odds were still fighting more than a year later. During the uprising Bismarck offered an agreement that allowed the Russians to pursue fleeing Poles onto Prussian territory. This agreement cemented an alliance that would last twenty-seven years; it also effectively ended Russian–French cooperation and forced Russia into a more antagonistic relationship with Austria, which would raise tensions another notch in disputed Ottoman and post-Ottoman territories. But it benefited Bismarck by providing a critical counterweight for Prussia against France and Austria.

In less than a decade, between 1863 and 1871, Bismarck maneuvered Prussia into three military engagements to win support for unification and neutralize the Austrian and French forces that opposed it:

Schleswig-Holstein (Denmark)	1864
Austria	1866
France	1870

When the king of Denmark died in late 1863, a controversy over Schleswig-Holstein gave Bismarck an opportunity to further undermine Austria's leadership in the German Confederation. In brief, the duchies of Schleswig and Holstein at the southern base of the Danish peninsula had been ruled by the king of Denmark, but as personal properties, not as part of Denmark. A fifteenth-century guarantee assured the duchies that they could never be separated from each other. Yet Holstein to the south was a member of the German Confederation; Schleswig to the north was not. Holstein was mostly German in population; Schleswig was mixed German and Danish.

In 1863 Bismarck moved to win the duchies for Prussia. First, he maneuvered Austria into joining Prussia in a victorious war against Denmark in 1864. This was a key test for Prussia's reformed army, which it passed with flying colors. Each military victory had the added benefit of chipping away at liberal opposition to military force and winning support for the government. After the war with Denmark, Bismarck spent the next two years arguing with Austria about the territories they had won. At the Convention of Gastein in 1865 it was decided that Prussia was to administer Schleswig and Austria was to administer Holstein. Bismarck found a number of ways to disagree with Austria about the policies of administration until, in 1866, Austria thought war was inevitable. In retrospect, it seems clear that the leadership of a united Germany could be decided only by force of arms; but while Austria did little to prevent it. Bismarck did a great deal to prepare for it.

First the Prussian statesman worked to prevent the other Great Powers from intervening. Great Britain and Russia were both preoccupied with domestic reforms and so were unlikely to intrude. France, however, needed to be persuaded into neutrality, and Italy was induced to sign an alliance with Prussia to join in a war against Austria and receive the province of Venetia in return. Bismarck also prepared public opinion for war by suddenly proposing to reform the constitution of the German Confederation along much more democratic lines, including the establishment of a national assembly elected by universal male suffrage. Austria was sure to reject such a proposal, but it impressed German liberals.

When Austria brought the Schleswig-Holstein conflict before the Diet of the Confederation, Bismarck declared the move tantamount to a declaration of war and ordered Prussian troops into Holstein, provoking war with Austria. The result was a German civil war, since Bavaria, Württemberg, Saxony,

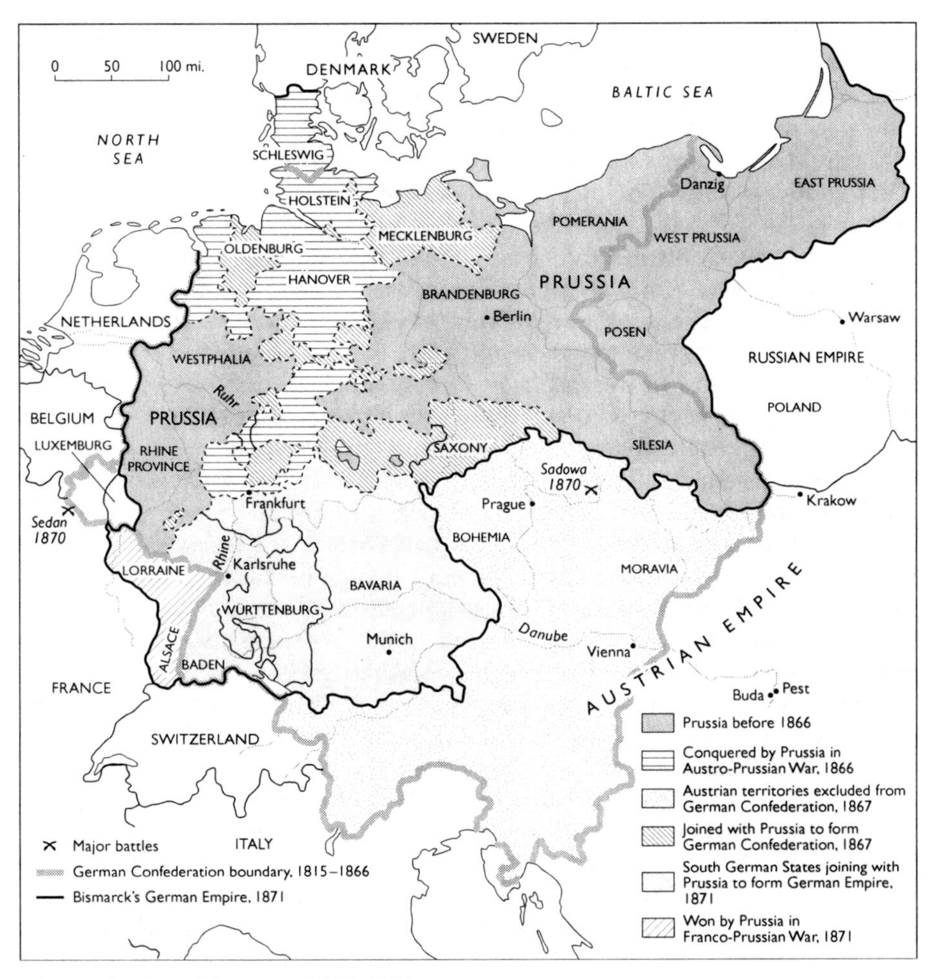

The Unification of Germany, 1866–1871

Hanover (the other four German kingdoms), and most of the lesser German states sided with Austria.

The war lasted only seven weeks and was decided in three. The Austrians, fighting on two fronts, had to commit a substantial part of their forces against Italy. Italy was quickly defeated, but Austria could not quickly transport its forces back to the Prussian front. Prussia, on the other hand, skillfully using its railway network, the telegraph, and superior armaments, overran the northern German states, invaded Bohemia and defeated the Austrians at Sadowa (near Könnigrätz), defeated the Bavarians, and entered Frankfurt, seat of the German Confederation. Here Bismarck came into conflict with his military leadership (they never forgave him), who wanted to press their advantage and go all the way to Vienna. Bismarck, however, saw nothing to be gained from prolonging the war and humiliating Austria and ordered a halt to the hostilities. At the Peace of Prague in August, Hanover, Hesse-Cassel, and Nassau were annexed to Prussia and their dynasties expelled, and Schleswig and the free city of Frankfurt were taken over. The terms of peace were generous, Austria had to pay a small indemnity and lost Venetia to Italy in the Peace of Vienna in October, but suffered no other territorial losses. Most important from Bismarck's point of view, Austria had to withdraw forever from the German Confederation, which now ceased to exist.

In 1867 an assembly elected by universal male suffrage adopted a constitution for the new North German Confederation, which placed enormous power in the hands of the Prussian king, as president. The future parliament (*Reichstag*) was to have no power over the budget, and the ministers were not to be responsible to it. Instead, a Federal Council (*Bundesrat*) of delegates from the member states, who voted according to instructions from their sovereigns, would reach all key policy decisions in secret and would have veto power over any enactment of the Reichstag. A chancellor would preside over the Bundesrat but would not have to defend its decisions before the Reichstag. Since Prussia now had not only its own votes in the Bundesrat but also those of the newly annexed states, Bismarck's plan in effect made it possible for the king of Prussia to run the North German confederation.

The success of the war against Austria further weakened the hands of the liberal majority, who lost seats to conservatives in Prussian elections held during the war. Many liberals in Germany were now increasingly anxious to prove themselves as practical politicians, which in Gordon Craig's words, showed "how effective Bismarck [had] been in debauching the values of his opponents so that they could now forget their former desire for freedom in face of the seductive attractions of force." The war against Austria and consolidation of the North German Confederation also left open the status of Bavaria, Baden, and Württemberg in the south. They were not eager to submit to Prussia, and joining with Austria, which had been evicted from the defunct German Confederation, was out of the question. Going it alone as independent states did not seem favorable to them, and France was opposed to any further expansion of Germany into the south. Bismarck was content at first to move slowly, manipulating an aging and ill Napoleon III and watching him stumble into various foreign policy gaffes.

In 1861 Napoleon used the Mexican government's default on payments of its foreign debt as the pretext for what proved to be a foolish imperialist venture. A French expedition installed the Austrian archduke Maximilian as emperor of Mexico, and French arms and men continued to assist him. The Europeanized Mexican upper classes were in part willing to support this venture, but from the start most other Mexicans resented foreign intruders, and Maximilian had to rely heavily on French support to reach Mexico City, where he was formally proclaimed emperor in June 1863. The United States, preoccupied by a crippling civil war, could do nothing at the time against what Americans regarded as an infraction of the Monroe Doctrine. But after peace had been restored in the United States, the American government protested strongly. The able Mexican republican leader Benito Juarez (1806–1872) had no difficulty prevailing, especially after American pressure forced Napoleon to abandon Maximilian and his Mexican supporters. Maximilian fell before a firing squad in 1867.

As long as Bismarck needed the benevolent neutrality of Napoleon III, he had hinted that he might not object if Napoleon took Belgium. Now the gullible Napoleon found that Bismarck no longer remembered the matter. Hoping to be compensated for his assistance in making peace between Prussia and Austria, Napoleon III tried to acquire Luxembourg by purchase from the king of Holland. Again he was frustrated by Bismarck. Napoleon III tried to obtain an alliance with Austria and Italy to thwart further Prussian expansion, but the Austrians shied away from a commitment, and the Italians were unable to reach an agreement with the French because of the Roman question, which was still undecided in 1866. By 1870 Bismarck saw that the time for decisive action had come. He baited the weakened French emperor, who was hungry for a foreign policy success.

Led by a war party eager to stop German expansion, France declared war on July 19, 1870. The French found no international support. Bismarck also hoped that a war with France would inflame nationalist sentiment, which would support his designs for completing German unification under the supremacy of Prussia. He got this wish too: as soon as France declared war, the southern states committed their troops to fight with the North Germans.

Sluggish mobilization and French overconfidence, together with Prussian superiority in arms, gave the Prussians a decisive head start. Within six weeks the Germans had advanced into France, bottled up one French army inside the fortress of Metz, and defeated another at Sedan near the Belgian border, where a hundred thousand men and Napoleon III himself were humiliatingly captured. The French government promptly collapsed and a new government, the Third Republic, was proclaimed. Napoleon III went into captivity in Germany and then exile in England, where he died in 1873.

The new republic tried to continue the war with Prussia, but within a month a second large French force surrendered at Metz, and a protracted siege of Paris followed. Parisians were brought to the brink of utter despair under the German siege but resisted heroically, surviving on sewer rats and even the zoo animals for food, until starvation brought surrender in January 1871. France was now deeply divided between those who supported the new government and those on all sides who did not. Radical opposition ignited revolts in a number of cities including Paris. While still under the siege, Parisian workers and socialists had tried to seize power and revive the City of Paris Commune of 1792. Bismarck, however, insisted on negotiating with a legitimate government, so elections were held that brought Adolphe Thiers to power as chief executive of the National Assembly. In the elections to the National Assembly the Parisians' stubborn radicalism helped turn provincial voters toward more conservative candidates who were pledged not only to make peace but also to restore the old monarchy.

The Written Record

"The Balance of Power Has Been Entirely Destroyed"

The unification of Germany and the realpolitik with which Bismarck achieved it were widely viewed with alarm. Benjamin Disraeli had this to say about the new state of affairs in an address to the House of Commons, in 1871.

Now let me impress upon the attention of the House the character of this war. It is no common war. . . . This war represents the German Revolution, a greater political event than the French Revolution last century—I don't say a greater, or as great, social event. What its social consequences may be are in the future. Not a single principle in the management of our foreign affairs, accepted by all statesmen for guidance up to six months ago, any longer exists, there is not a diplomatic tradition which has not been swept away. You have a new world, new influences at work, new and unknown objects and dangers with which to cope, at present involved in that obscurity incident to novelty in such affairs. We used to have discussions in this House about the balance of power. . . . The balance of power has been entirely destroyed.

In *Bismarck and German Unification: Documents and Debates,* ed. David Hargreaves (Houndmills, Basingstoke, U.K., 1991), p. 110.

One of the new French government's first acts was to sign the humiliating Treaty of Frankfurt. Bismarck forced the French to pay a massive indemnity, to cede Alsace and much of Lorraine, and to support German occupying forces until the indemnity had been paid. The French defeat and this degrading treaty created an enduring legacy of bitterness in France. The Third Republic never quite shook off the shame of its origins.

In January 1871, even before the peace had been imposed, King Wilhelm of Prussia was proclaimed emperor of Germany. The southern German states that had sent their troops against France now formalized their unification with the north. When a constitution for the new empire was adopted, it was simply an extension of the constitution of the North German Confederation of 1867. Despite a long tradition of regional independence, the federalism of the new system was largely a fiction. The German Empire was dominated by Prussian autocracy, by Prussian nobles and military, and by the Prussian Bismarck. As chancellor of the German Empire from 1871 to 1890, Bismarck became the leading statesman in Europe. As a diplomat, he worked for the preservation of Germany's gains against threats from abroad. As a politician, he worked for the preservation of the Prussian system against all opposing currents. Unification of all German states (except Austria) ultimately made Germany the most powerful country in Europe.

The Paris Commune

The radicals in Paris could not accept the capitulation for which the rest of the country was prepared, especially after they had suffered so heroically during the siege to protect the capital from the Germans. On March 18, after the peace was signed, Thiers sought to suppress the Parisian radicals with the National Guard, but the Guardsmen were billeted in Paris, many of them survivors of the siege, and they went over to the side of the radicals. Angry at the prospect of Germans marching into Paris, the Guard viewed the peace as both a betrayal and a reactionary trap. They seized weapons and ammunition and together with artisans, workers, part of the Parisian middle class, and socialist intellectuals, joined in what became the largest urban uprising of the nineteenth century. The revolutionary revolt sent Thiers and his government fleeing to the royal palace at Versailles. There they gathered new forces (with the help of Prussia), mostly provincial peasants, who were able to retake the city on May 28. But in the intervening 72 days, one of the nineteenth-century's great democratic experiments unfolded.

The Paris Commune was the first government to be made up of workers and to be seriously committed to improving the living and working conditions of the poor. Many of the communards called themselves socialists, but most of them wanted a democratic society of small independent shopkeepers and artisans, and they opposed the abolition of private property. There was not much time to pass legislation, but trade unions were permitted to operate factories that were not already in use (with provisions for compensating their owners when they returned to Paris), and there were schools established for girls as well as boys. There were to be provisions to "improve the social welfare of the citizens," but this was not class warfare, for the "hard working bourgeoisie, honest and robust" was the "sister of the proletariat," if the former could only be induced to return to Paris.

Many people were struck by the celebratory atmosphere that prevailed in Paris during the weeks of the Commune, even though the gunfire of Thiers's troops trying to get into the city could be heard more or less continually. A symbolist poet who wrote for a Commune newspaper, *The Tribune of the People,* exclaimed: "Would you believe it? Paris is fighting and singing! Paris is about to be attacked by a ruthless and furious army and she laughs! . . . The clash of cymbals can be heard in the dreadful silence between rounds of firing and merry dance tunes mingle with the rattle of American machine guns." The Commune did not last long enough for disillusionment to set in or factional political fighting to break down the joy of the workers' victory and it was the last French revolution, so the Commune has acquired the luster of myth. It was remembered as the last good-natured dream of the left, the "Festival of the Oppressed."

On May 21 government troops broke into the city, and the week that followed—Bloody Week—recorded the worst case of civil bloodshed in the nineteenth century. It is not clear why the government felt the need to massacre the communards to suppress the revolution, but twenty-five thousand communards died in the fighting. People were shot on sight and slaughtered en masse. The Third Republic, born in the trauma of defeat and civil war, at once came into a heritage of strife.

Germany: The Nation-State

The new German Empire was more consensual and integrated than was Italy after unification. As a result, political unification was much less controversial. The imperial parliament, or Reichstag, was chosen by universal male suffrage in direct elections with secret ballots. Next to the emperor it was the most important institution in Germany, but it had limited political influence on government policy. The chancellor was responsible to the emperor and not parliament. Some have described the system as a "chancellor dictatorship." Bismarck decided policy outlines and controlled the appointment of the officials who carried them out. However, even "dictatorship" must be understood in a limited sense: Germany had a constitution, the rule of law, and a guarantee of civil rights. Neither the emperor nor the chancellor could rule by ignoring parliament.

During the 1870s and 1880s, Bismarck, as chancellor of the new state, developed German unity in several ways. First, he created a number of national bureaucratic and administrative institutions, which some consider among his greatest achievements. In most cases these were liberal programs that Bismarck appropriated and supported: currency was unified, the railway system centralized, and central agencies were set up for statistics, health care, postal service, and patents. He created a unified and powerful military, though he had to struggle continually with parliament's unwillingness to allocate funds for military development (the Reichstag had no budgetary control, but it had to right to stipulate the size of the army). In 1874 Bismarck, by threatening to resign, forced the Reichstag to fix the size of the army at 401,000 men until 1881; in 1880 he forced an increase to 427,000 until 1888. The privileged position of the army made a military career ever more attractive and served as a constant spur to German militarism. A new Department of Justice and a central Supreme Court also centralized political practices. Together these institutions helped create the sense of nationhood. Bismarck also sought to solidify the sense of a German nation by identifying "outsiders" and alienating them. This tactic usually backfired.

A year after the founding of the German Empire, Bismarck launched the Kulturkampf—a systematic attack on the Catholic minority (about one-third of the population). Genuine worries about the loyalty of Catholics on the eastern and southern frontiers followed Pope's issuance of his *Syllabus Of Errors* (1864). Pius IX was responding to the unification of Italy, which reduced the Papal States and relieved him of political authority. He pronounced Catholicism incompatible with liberalism, and denounced toleration of other religions, secular education, and state participation in church affairs. In 1870 the Vatican Council adopted the dogma of papal infallibility, which asserted that the Pope's judgments on questions of faith and morals were incapable of error. To many non-Catholics, this suggested that no state could count on the loyalty of its Catholic citizens. In Germany, since liberals tended to be both Protestant and anticlerical, Bismarck banked on a lack of opposition to anti-Catholic policies. In 1872 the Jesuits were expelled from the country; in 1873 the May Laws established state control over the Catholic church. Priests were forbidden to use sermons to criticize the government. Church property was seized, clergy were imprisoned, and military force was used against crowds of Catholics protesting their persecution. In response, Catholics formed the Catholic Center party and, in part as a result of the discrimination, it quickly became the second strongest party in Germany, winning a quarter of the seats in the Reichstag in 1874.

The pope declared the Kulturkampf laws null and void and instructed Catholics to disobey them. The Catholic Center party defended papal infallibility and hoped to restore the pope's temporal power, which had been ended by the unification of Italy. Catholic peasants, workers, priests, and nobles opposed the largely Protestant urban middle class and the Prussian military predominance in the state. Bismarck identified his clerical opponents with Catholic France and Austria, two nations he had defeated in forging the new Germany. But the Kulturkampf failed. Instead of suppressing Catholicism, it only undermined Catholic Germans' sense of belonging to the new nation. Ultimately Bismarck had to abandon the policy.

By contrast, these were years of Jewish assimilation and emancipation. There were about a half-million Jews in Germany in 1871, or 1.25 percent of the population. They had won equal legal rights in 1848 and civil equality in 1869. The assimilation of Jews was highly visible, especially in cities and towns, as they were overrepresented in higher education and moved into the middle-class professions. Emancipation was linked with liberal nationalism, so many middle-class Jews who benefited from industrialization and urbanization embraced ideas of progress and individual freedom, central to middle-class liberalism.

This was a period of secularization for many Christians as well as Jews. But for Jews secularization meant a sharp break with a whole way of life: switching from Yiddish to German, and breaking with laws concerning diet, hair, and dress that had distinguished Jews for generations. Even so assimilation in Germany had limits. Jews were still excluded from many public places: certain cafes, schools, and resorts. In numerous professions, while they had jobs, they were not entirely accepted. And there were the costs: Jewish middle-class success would be held against them in times of economic downturn. Generally speaking however, the midcentury was a period of remarkable toleration in central Europe. The playwright Arthur Schnitzler remembered growing up in Vienna in the 1860s and 1870s without knowing any anti-Semitism, a situation that changed noticeably in the next two decades.

The first period of nation-state building in imperial Germany under Wilhelm I, Bismarck, and the Reichstag was a period of some contradictions. There is no denying the hand of Prussian authoritarianism, intolerance, and elitism, and repression of those identified as outsiders. But one should not

A Closer Look

Nationalism in the Era of the Nation-State

Heinrich von Treitschke, a legendary history professor at the University of Berlin, put Germany history at the service of the state. He helped articulate late nineteenth-century German nationalism in lectures and widely read publications. How does his view of the nation published in the 1890s differ from early nineteenth-century liberal romantic nationalism?

On the German Character

Depth of thought, idealism, cosmopolitan views;— . . . familiarity with every human thought and feeling, the desire to traverse the world-wide realm of ideas in common with the foremost intellects of all nations and all times. . . . The simple loyalty of the German contrasts remarkably with the unchivalrousness of the English character. This seems to be due to the fact that in England physical culture is sought, not in the exercise of noble arms, but in sports like boxing, swimming, and rowing, . . . which tend to encourage a brutal and purely athletic point of view, and the single and superficial ambition of getting a first prize.

On the State

The state is a moral community, which is called upon to educate the human race by positive achievement. Its ultimate object is that a nation should develop in it, a nation distinguished by a real national character. To achieve this state is the highest moral duty for nation and individual alike. . . .

The most important possession of a state . . . is power. He who is not man enough to look this truth in the face should not meddle in politics. The state is not physical power as an end in itself, it is power to protect and promote the higher interests. Power must justify itself by being applied for the greatest good of mankind. It is the highest moral duty of the state to increase its power. . . .

The individual has no right to regard the state as a means for attaining his own ambitions in life. Every extension of the activities of the state is beneficial and wise if it arouses, promotes, and purifies the independence of free and reasoning men; it is evil when it kills and stunts the independence of free men. . . .

Only the truly great and powerful states ought to exist. Small states are unable to protect their subjects against external enemies; moreover, they are incapable of producing genuine patriotism or national pride. . . . Weimar produced a Goethe and a Schiller—still these poets would have been greater had they been citizens of a German national state.

Documents of German History, ed. Louis L. Snyder, (New Brunswick, NJ, 1958), pp. 260–61.

overlook the rule of law, the liberal commercial code and encouragement of economic growth, the rise of the middle classes, civil freedoms, and the fact that while many groups (Catholics, Jews, workers, national minorities) were discriminated against, they could still elect representatives to parliament. In this period liberals dominated society and electoral politics, and even the emperor and chancellor could not rule without them.

The Austrian Empire in the Era of the Nation-State

Austria's history during the rise of nation-states was inextricably tied up with nationalism. Italy and Germany united around claims to sovereignty for a single people and nation. Their success raised hopes of the peoples of the Austrian Empire for their own political independence as nations, but under quite different—and much more divisive—conditions. The notion of nationhood easily led to the assumption that humanity was divided into nations—whether by divine intent, nature, or the material force of history—and that therefore the course of history was flowing toward national self-determination. By the mid-nineteenth century most people in western Europe appear to have assumed that the only legitimate type of government was one that carried a society toward national sovereignty.

Nationalism would severely challenge the Austrian Empire and cause it to crumble after the First World War; but it is a mistake to see only decline there in the late nineteenth century. Centrifugal forces that would fragment the empire in the twentieth century were still balanced in the nineteenth by powerful centralizing forces—social, political, and symbolic. Nationalism did not yet undermine the power of the Habsburg Crown to inspire supranational and supraclass loyalty among people of all classes and nations, as we saw in 1848. The dynasty's strong ties to the pope and the Catholic church were unifying forces in the empire where (with significant exceptions) the population was primarily Catholic. The central army and the bureaucracy offered jobs and advancement to people from all regions, both of which served as important sources of homogenization. Finally, the very diversity of the empire's peoples worked in Vienna's favor: the emperor was able to play one against the other to maintain the subordination of all.

The glittering capital of Vienna itself acted as a powerful centralizing symbol. Many people who might otherwise have felt attached to their own capital cities also took pride in the beauty and culture of Vienna and were drawn to live there. Vienna may have exerted an even more compelling attraction after German unification moved the center of specifically German cultural life from Vienna to Berlin. There is a paradox here: Vienna was a source of attraction and pride to non-Germans in the empire who went there for social and cultural career advancement; but the culture Vienna celebrated was predominantly German. Members of national minorities who entered Austrian educational institutions, or the Austrian bureaucracy or the army, learned to converse in German. German middle-class prosperity together with imperial and aristocratic wealth built theaters and opera houses and supplied their audiences, opened cafes, published newspapers, and rebuilt the central artery of the city, the Ringstrasse. In other words, aspiration toward national sovereignty was often combined with loyalty to the supranational empire. Among German-speaking Austrians, living in Austria itself, many people held a concept of nation and empire as overlapping entities, nor was this uncommon among non-Germans.

For over sixty years, from 1848 to 1916, the German-speaking emperor Franz Josef sat on the Habsburg throne. Immensely conscientious, he worked hard reading and signing state papers for hours every day. But he was without imagination, inflexibly old-fashioned and conservative. He was intensely pious, and his mere longevity inspired loyalty and indifference. His decisions usually came too late and conceded too little. And Franz Josef had no statesmen with Metternich's commitment, or the will to stand up to Bismarck's ruthless *realpolitik.*

In 1849 all parts of the empire were for the first time unified and directly ruled from Vienna by German-speaking officials. In 1855 the state signed a concordat with the Catholic church giving clerics a greater influence in education and other fields than they had enjoyed since the reforms of Josef II in the late eighteenth century. After the suppression of the revolution of 1848, there was a decade of repression usually called the Bach system, from the name of the minister of the interior, Alexander Bach (1813–1893). Under the Bach system, ministers and officials committed to constitutional rule resigned or were fired, or changed their tune. Censorship reappeared and political opponents were harassed.

Austria's history during this period is also inextricably linked to Prussia's. Here foreign policy missteps seriously undermined Austria's international standing. A key background to foreign policy is the Austrian economy. The repressive domestic policies of the Bach period required an expanded bureaucracy, expensive armies, and an expanded police system. Instead of investing in railroads and industry to develop a modern economy and produce new sources of revenue for the state, Austria went into debt to protect the central imperial government, to expand bureaucracy, and to spread Germanization. These expenditures left it at a disadvantage compared with Prussia. During the Crimean War, Austria angered its longtime ally Russia and suffered a humiliating defeat at the hands of the French and Italians in Lombardy, which brought about the end of the Bach system.

War continued to threaten, and Austrian leaders realized that if the nationalities inside the empire, especially the Hungarians, were left in a state of perpetual discontent, their troops would be unreliable. Several solutions were tried in an effort to create a structure that would withstand the domestic and foreign strains but would not jeopardize the emperor's position. Franz Josef listened first to the nobles, who favored loose federalism, and then to the bureaucrats, who favored tight centralism. In 1860 he issued the October Diploma to set up a central legislature to deal with economic and military problems, made up of delegates from provincial assemblies (diets) throughout the empire. All the other problems were left to the provincial diets, elected by a system that functionally disfranchised the peasants. This solution did not satisfy the Magyar nobility of Hungary, and it is not hard to see why.

When issuing the October Diploma, Franz Josef said: "We shall have a little parliamentarianism, but power shall remain in my hands and the whole thing will be adapted to Austrian realities." Even so, Austrian liberals and bureaucrats felt that the October Diploma gave the Hungarians too much. It seemed to them that the empire was being dismembered on behalf of the nobility, who dominated the provincial assemblies. Therefore, in 1861 the February Patent reinterpreted the Diploma, creating an even less democratic scheme. A bicameral imperial legislature took over most of the powers that the October Diploma had reserved for the provincial assemblies or diets. Naturally, the Hungarians objected to this second solution even more than to the first, and they flatly refused to participate. To the applause of the Germans in Vienna, including the liberals, Hungary was returned to authoritarian rule. Czechs and Poles also eventually withdrew from the central parliaments leaving only a German rump. Disturbed by this turn of events, the emperor suspended the February Patent and began to listen to the Hungarians, who were represented by the intelligent and moderate Ferenc Deák (1803–1876).

The war with Prussia in 1866 changed everything. The Austrian defeat at Sadowa (Könnigrätz), the expulsion of Austria from Germany, and the loss of Venetia to Italy threatened the entire Habsburg system. Clearly Austria could not risk war with any combination of Prussia, France, or Russia, and some solution to nationalist dissatisfaction had to be found. Franz Josef proposed a series of reforms that lifted censorship, and guaranteed freedoms of speech, press, and property. All were to be equal before the law. At the same time, the emperor controlled all associations and assemblies, had complete control over the armed forces, and had the right to veto all legislation and dissolve parliament. Most important, Franz Josef resumed negotiations with the most powerful of the non-Germans, the Hungarians. In 1867 a formula was found that was to govern and preserve the Habsburg domain down to 1914.

Compromise and The Dual Monarchy

The *Ausgleich,* or "compromise," of 1867 created a unique dual monarchy, the Austro-Hungarian Empire. The Hungarian constitution of 1848 was restored, and the entire empire was reorganized as a strict partnership. Austria and Hungary were united in the person of the emperor, who was always to be a Catholic and a legitimate Habsburg, and who was to be crowned king of Hungary in Budapest. For foreign policy, military affairs, and finance the two states had common ministers appointed by the emperor. A customs union, subject to renewal every ten years, united them. Every ten years the quota of common expenditure to be borne by each partner was to be renegotiated. A unique body, the "delegations," made up of sixty members from the Austrian parliament and sixty members from the Hungarian parliament, meeting alternately in Vienna and in Budapest, was to decide on the common budget, which had to be ratified by the full parliaments of both countries. The delegations also had supervisory authority over the three joint ministers and might summon them to account for their activities. In practice, however, the delegations seldom met and were almost never consulted on questions of policy. The system favored Hungary, which had 40 percent of the population but never paid more than a third of the expenses. Every ten years, therefore, when the quota of expenses and the customs union needed joint consideration, a new crisis arose. Unlike any other nationality in the empire, Hungarians had won respect for their nation and had achieved something approaching very close to sovereignty.

One overwhelming problem remained common to both halves of the monarchy: when Hungarians attained autonomy, every other nationality wanted it too. The constitution of 1867 provided that all nationalities should enjoy equal rights and guaranteed that each might use its own language in education, administration, and public life. And in 1868 the Hungarians passed a law that allowed the ethnic minorities to conduct local government in their own language, to hold the chief posts in the countries where they predominated, and to have their own schools. But in practice the non-German and non-Magyar nationalities suffered discrimination and persecution. Germanization in Austria and Magyarization in Hungary angered the subject peoples. These nationalities experienced varying levels of national self-consciousness. Some were subject to pressures and manipulation from fellow nationals living outside the dual monarchy. All had some leaders who urged compromise and conciliation with the dominant Austrians and Hungarians, as well as those who advocated resistance and even revolution. The result was chronic and often unpredictable instability in the dual monarchy. The conflicting national aspirations of the peoples of the empire could not be satisfied without precluding the national aspirations of some.

The Nationality Question Under the Dual Monarchy: Austria

The Czechs were the largest nationality in the Austrian portion of the empire. After 1867, the "Old Czechs" political party argued that the lands of the Crown of St. Wenceslaus (a martyred prince of Bohemia, d. 929), possessed rights comparable to those the Hungarians had successfully claimed for the lands of the Crown of St. Stephen (c. 975–1038), who had been crowned as first king of Hungary in 1001. Of all the nationalities in the dual monarchy, the Czechs were in the best position to exercise independence. They had the most productive industrial economy in the country, with a high percentage of artisans skilled in the production of porcelain, glassware, lace, Pilsen beer, and sugar beets, and with a thriving tourist trade that gave them access to the broader world.

But the Czechs were unable to bring pressure on Vienna as successfully as Hungary. Czech deputies boycotted the Austrian parliament in the hope that Franz Josef would consent to become king of Bohemia in Prague, as he had

Nationalities in the Austrian Empire

become king of Hungary in Budapest, but this did not happen. The Old Czechs in the Bohemian Diet, from which all Germans had withdrawn, drew up proposals that would have produced a triple instead of a dual monarchy and in 1871 the emperor offered to be crowned as king of Bohemia. Franz Josef was forced to change his mind, however, by the rage of Austrian and Bohemian Germans and the opposition of Hungarian politicians. While the emperor was willing to give Hungarians authority over Slavic and other peoples, he could not give Czechs authority over Germans against the will of the latter. Deeply disappointed, the Czech nationalist leaders turned to passive resistance. Tension increased between the defeated Old Czechs and a rising group of Young Czechs, who advocated more aggressive methods.

Of all the minorities in Austria, the Poles (18 percent of the population) were the least overtly discontented. Most of them lived in Galicia, one of the least industrial provinces, where they formed the landlord class. Like the Czechs, the Galician Poles asked for provincial self-government on the Hungarian model and were denied. But they already had their own schools, and Polish was the language of administration and the courts. The Poles enjoyed favorable financial arrangements, and after 1871 they obtained a special ministry for Galicia in Vienna.

The contrast between the relatively nondiscriminatory treatment of Poles in Austria and the brutality suffered by Poles living in Prussian and Russian Poland led Poles everywhere to look to Austrian Galicia as the center of national life and culture. Polish refugees fled to the cities of Krakow and Lemberg (Lviv), with their splendid Polish universities and opportunities to serve the Habsburg Crown in the provincial administration. The universities trained generations of Poles who would later become leaders of independent Poland. Polish literature and the study of Polish history flourished. But, typically, this haven for Poles was anything but a secure home for other minorities. Polish support for the Habsburg government in Vienna brought the Galician Poles authority over both the Ruthenians (as Ukrainians were then called) and Jews, who suffered Polonization, systematic discrimination, and economic hardship.

The Nationality Question Under the Dual Monarchy: Hungary

In Hungary minority problems were more pressing. The Slovaks, the Romanians, and the Serbs and Croats living in Hungary were the worst victims of a deliberate policy of Magyarization to destroy the national identity of the minorities and to transform them into Hungarians. The weapon used was language. The Hungarians, who made up only 55 percent of the population in their own country (exclusive of Croatia), had an intense devotion to their language—a tongue unrelated to the German, Slavic, or Romanian languages of the other nationalities. They tried to force Hungarian upon the subject peoples, particularly in education. All state-supported schools, from kindergartens to universities, wherever located, had to give instruction in

Hungarian, and the state postal, telegraph, and railroad services used only Hungarian.

The Slovaks, numbering about 11 percent of the population of Hungary, were perhaps the most Magyarized. Poor peasants for the most part, the more ambitious of them often became Hungarians simply by adopting the Hungarian language as their own. As time passed, a few Slovaks came to feel a sense of unity with the closely related Czechs across the border in Austria. The pro-Czechs among the Slovaks were usually liberals and Protestants, while Catholic and conservative Slovaks were more likely to advocate Slovak autonomy.

In the southern reaches of Hungary, complicated religious and class differences among Serbs, Croats, and the people of Bosnia-Herzegovina were exacerbated by imperial political policies. In addition to their relations with the Hungarian or Austria Crown, this region was divided over issues of national sovereignty: some wanted autonomy for each of the major national groups here—a separate Serbia, Croatia, and Bosnia-Herzegovina. Others wanted a united entity for all the South Slavs. Some Serbs and Croats lived in Hungary proper and others in Croatia. After the Compromise, in 1869, many Serbs had been transferred to Hungarian rule, which they disliked, hoping to be united with the independent kingdom of Serbia to the south.

A greater menace to Hungarian unity was provided by the existence of Croatia itself. The Croats, though connected since the eleventh century with the Crown of Hungary, had become strongly nationalistic under the impact of the Napoleonic occupation and had fought on the side of the Austrian monarch against the Hungarian revolutionaries of 1848. Nonetheless, Franz Josef, as part of the Compromise settlement, handed Croatia back to the Hungarians. Croatian nationalists were deeply disappointed. Led by a Catholic bishop, Josef Strossmayer (1815–1905), they had hoped for an autonomous Croatia and Dalmatia (the coastal strip along the Adriatic inhabited largely by Croats but governed by Vienna), which would serve as a nucleus to attract all southern Slavs. Instead, in 1868 the Hungarian moderates, led by Ferenc Deák, worked out a compromise of their own between Hungary and Croatia. All military and economic affairs were to be handled in Budapest by a special cabinet minister for Croatian affairs. Representatives from the Croatian parliament in Zagreb would sit in Budapest whenever Croatian affairs were under discussion. Croatian delegates would be part of the Hungarian "delegation" to the dual monarchy. The Croatian language would be spoken by Croat representatives at the sessions of any body they attended, and the language of command in the Croatian territorial army would be Croatian. The Croats would control their own educational system, their church, their courts, and police; however, taxes would be levied and collected by Budapest.

This compromise did not solve everything. The Hungarian-appointed governor received the support only of those Croats who had become Hungarian speaking, usually great landowners or government officials. The Croat Party of Rights wanted a completely autonomous Croatia for Croatians and

Southeastern Europe

scorned as inferior the Serbs and other non-Catholic South Slavs, whom Strossmayer had hoped to attract. Further problems were created in Catholic Croatia by the existence of a Serb Orthodox minority (more than a quarter of the population), which spoke the same language as the Croats. But the Serbs, as Orthodox Christians, were subject to discrimination.

The region of Bosnia-Herzegovina was the focus of much of the tension over nationalism in the region. By the 1870s these two provinces had been part of the Ottoman Empire for about four centuries. Although solidly South Slavic, the population in 1879 included about a half-million Muslims, another half-million Eastern Orthodox, and perhaps 150,000 Catholics. Most of the Orthodox Christians were peasants, working on the estates of Muslim landlords. In 1875 an uprising against the Ottoman rulers precipitated a general Balkan Slavic uprising against Ottoman rule which led to a larger Great Power conflict and the Russo-Turkish War. In 1876 the Bulgarians rebelled. Serbia and Montenegro came to the aid of their fellow Slavs.

In 1875–1876 Russian tsar Alexander II was committed to finding a diplomatic solution through the League of the Three Emperors, an alliance of the autocratic powers that reunited Germany, Austria, and Russia. Since the Crimean War, Russian foreign policy in Europe had been one of restraint. Domestic issues required the lion's share of the tsar's attention, together with expansion and security on Russia's eastern and southern frontiers. Britain under Disraeli, however, hindered negotiations and encouraged Ottoman resistance in an effort to undermine the Three Emperors League. But reports of Turkish atrocities carried out in repressing the rebellions and the crushing defeat of Serbia in 1876 aroused nationalist Russian public opinion, which screamed for a war of retribution to avenge their fellow Slavs. The government was more cautious, and it tried to resist Pan-Slav agitation, understanding that any Russian incursion in the Balkans could involve Russia in a war with Austria. After receiving assurances that Austria would remain on the sidelines, Russia declared war on the Ottoman Empire. The ensuing Russo-Turkish War of 1877–1878 was fiercely fought, with large-scale massacres on both sides. Inept Russian commanders prolonged what should have been a rapid and easy victory, but the ailing Ottoman Empire was still no match for the Russian army.

Then Russia got greedy. The Treaty of San Stefano that ended the Russo-Turkish War forced the sultan to give up nearly all his European territory, granted independence to Serbia, Romania, and Montenegro, and gave Russia domination over a large autonomous Bulgaria. Even Russia understood it had overplayed its hand, threatening to destabilize southeastern Europe, and acquiesced to a new treaty, signed in Berlin later in 1878. (The choice of city showed the authority Bismarck had already acquired in European power politics.) The Treaty of Berlin retained the independence of Serbia, Montenegro, and Romania. Bulgaria, however, had to give Macedonia back, and Austria obtained the right to occupy the provinces of Bosnia-Herzegovina, two results that were greeted with bitter resentment by the Slavic peoples in the Balkans. Russia's relations with Austria were further damaged. And the situation in Bosnia-Herzegovina was highly unstable: Austria's role was left deliberately ambiguous in the most ethnically complex country in the region with the fastest growing economy.

Given the multiple conflicting loyalties and the interspersion of the national populations, it was rather easy for Hungary to maintain political control of this region—at least temporarily. But national aspirations grew and no easy solution, indeed, no possible solution, presented itself.

New States in Ottoman Europe

A combination of Russian and Austrian diplomatic pressures and military superiority alongside local nationalist aspirations forced the Ottoman Empire to withdraw from southeast Europe in the second half of the nineteenth century. Moldavia and Wallachia (which had been a united Russian protectorate since 1856) was declared to be the independent state of Romania in 1878. Bulgaria was made an autonomous principality; it officially achieved independence in 1911. Albania won independence in 1913.

Romania's experience in state-building was typical of the region (though of course there were significant variations). In 1866 Romanians elected a constituent assembly and adopted a constitution based on the Belgian constitution of 1831, with protection of civil liberties, freedom of association, and freedom of the press. The fledgling democracy, however, had severe limitations. Peasants received few of these rights. Elections were based on universal male suffrage but votes were counted proportionally, with the wealthiest 1.5 percent of the population electing 40 percent of the delegates and 95 percent of the population electing 21 percent of the delegates. Parliament did not form the government as in Britain; rather, the king appointed his own ministers. Budgets and other policy decisions were highly centralized; the judiciary was subordinate to the executive. Jews were excluded from citizenship altogether.

Under these circumstances, corruption flourished. Only a king deeply devoted to democratic principles could have constructed a responsive nation-state in these conditions, and Prince (later King) Carol (r. 1866–1914) did not pretend to be such a man. Power depended entirely on his favor; he dominated both political parties, rewarding those who supported him personally. The press in Romania had some success in limiting excesses, but Carol ruled as an autocrat. Similar conditions prevailed in the other new southeastern states. In these conditions, maintaining power took precedence over establishing civil rights or encouraging economic growth.

After 1848 western nation-states recognized (in varying degrees and forms) the need to provide services to their populations in return for the taxes they collected and the soldiers they drafted to maintain stability and increase the nation's wealth. Loyalty to the Crown could no longer be assumed or coerced, and yet loyalty was increasingly necessary for effective nation-state competition and expansion overseas. To provide services or repay their populations, the new nation-states in the southeast had few of the resources available to the older wealthier nation-states. In most cases, the new entities had come into being primarily for the purpose of coming into being, of drawing a borderline between their "nation" and the neighbors. Yet, despite these disabilities, even the most autocratic regimes in southeastern Europe provided the rudiments of a national administration and presided over the first significant economic growth and industrialization in the region.

Poles of Reform

In Great Britain and the Russian Empire, the form of government and basic boundaries remained unchanged after 1848, but significant reform programs were undertaken in both countries. The reforms occurred more peacefully than in the rest of Europe, but they further established Britain and Russia as contrasting models of the modern imperial nation-state.

The Russian Empire and the Great Reforms

The reform process in Russia begins with the Crimean War. Nicholas I died brokenhearted and defeated in 1855, bringing to the throne his energetic but enigmatic son Alexander II (r. 1855–1881). Alexander would preside over the most far-reaching social reforms any country in Europe had yet seen. Intellectuals had been calling for an end to serfdom and some limits on autocratic power for half a century (as serfs had for much longer). Professional, specialized bureaucrats in the tsar's civil service had also long recognized that reform was necessary, but it was only when Russia was crushed on the battlefield that the autocracy and the noble elite could be convinced that change was inescapable. Within a decade, the entire social structure of Europe's largest, most authoritarian, and most rural country would be dramatically transformed. At first these changes and the tsar's role in initiating them would win the approval and support of the country's young idealistic radicals and revolutionaries. But disillusionment would very quickly set in, resulting in even more radical opposition on the one hand and a more stubborn defense of autocracy on the other.

The ongoing conflict between state and society was based on a fundamental difference in understanding of the purpose of reform. Liberals and radicals in society wanted reform to give to the peasants freedom from serfdom and to give responsible members of society a voice in governing. Most Russians did not wish to slavishly follow western models of development; but they did see that Russian society was for the most part unschooled and impoverished, and the government seemed uninterested in changing that. Members of educated society entered into reform with enthusiasm because they believed that reforms would bring economic and social modernity. They idealistically believed that freedom from serfdom and education of the peasantry would erase differences among the Russian people and create a more harmonious nation. The intelligentsia had confidence in its own leadership abilities and believed that only through constitutional government could

Russians throw off mass poverty and unite as a nation. The autocracy on the other hand had no such interest in reform. Though it was not at all clear at the time, Alexander II did not engage in the arduous process of reform out of humanitarian motives or democratic politics. His interests were purely pragmatic, and political reform was not on his agenda. The Crimean War had exposed Russian security as dangerously vulnerable, and Russian military technology and strategy had been surpassed; nor could Russia's economy in its present state sustain a modern military. Above all, an army of enserfed, uneducated peasants could not win a modern war or support a modern competitive economy. The serfs would be freed to maintain Russia's position in Europe as a Great Power. Those who believed that emancipation was the first step toward political liberalization would be bitterly disappointed.

The Russian nobility was deeply and stubbornly opposed to any serf emancipation. Thus Alexander's personal commitment to abolition was critical in getting the legislation past numerous noble roadblocks. The tsar's commitment to a "landed settlement" in which peasants received a portion of land was also critical to the form emancipation finally took. (When slaves in the United States were emancipated in 1863, they received no land.) There were approximately 100 million peasants in Russia in the 1850s, about half of whom served individual noble landowners. The emancipation promulgated in 1861 (details of which were worked out over the next two years) gave peasants land but made them pay for it, which they deeply resented because they thought the land had been stolen from them in the first place. The Russian serf-owning nobility lived in great luxury but were often deep in debt to the state. The tsar wiped out the nobles' debts and paid them in advance for the land they ceded to the peasants. Then the former serfs were to pay the government back over the next 49 years. The peasants' land was to be controlled by the commune, which was given new functions and spread to new regions, to provide some framework for government surveillance and control. In many cases, this was acceptable to the peasants, since they had farmed communally for generations. In other regions the commune was an artificial imposition. Further, the nobility was able to control the initial allotment of land, retaining as often as possible their best fields, forests, and pastures.

Emancipation represented a compromise that required great diplomacy and patience on the part of the tsar in particular but, as often happens with compromises, no one was happy with the settlement. The peasants resented paying for the land and they were unhappy with the size of their allotments and in fact often received less than was necessary to survive, much less prosper. Most former serfs survived only by returning to work for their former and much detested owners. The nobility resented the loss of income, prestige, land, and unpaid labor. Many noble families sold out altogether and left for new lives in Russia's growing cities and towns. Peasants would follow them, but not until the 1890s when there would be massive migration to cities.

Emancipation deprived the nobility of their right to control their serfs' social lives, so new institutions were created to replace those functions. A limited form of local self-government, the *zemstvo* (from the word for "land") was created. Elected officials were put in charge of building roads, schools, hospitals, and so on. They also hired specialists in statistics, agronomy, medicine, and veterinary medicine to try to improve farming methods and healthcare. The zemstvos achieved some successes in bringing medicine and education to the countryside, but they were hampered by a central state suspicious of their autonomy. Over the next few decades increasing restrictions would be placed on zemstvo activity, especially on its funding. Zemstvo leaders became a major source of Russian liberal constitutionalism. The more the government tried to hinder zemstvo efforts to improve rural life, the more zemstvo leaders became convinced that they needed more political power and a written, constitutional guarantee of civil and political rights.

Judicial reforms (1864) were devised to replace noble police and judicial functions, and these measures introduced a genuinely liberal judicial system: there was equality of all before the law and trial by jury; judges could not be arbitrarily replaced when a higher official disliked a decision. The new judicial system was an anomaly in the autocracy, where the tsar was above the law, but it functioned relatively well until the revolutions of 1917, and it gave millions of ordinary people experience with a modern legal system. Most peasants were segregated outside the judicial system and were subject to courts based on local customary law, but even there, peasants developed a modern legal culture.

Military reform followed, in 1874, the work of some of Russia's most enlightened, even liberal, bureaucrats. It not only removed some of the most brutal aspects of service and introduced universal conscription (with exemptions, of course), and new training regimens, but it included provision of basic education for all recruits. Other improvements included police reform, a relaxation of censorship, and municipal councils with functions much like those of the zemstvos.

On the whole, the Era of the Great Reforms as it was called, was a period of extraordinary promise. To engage the educated population in dialog and in support of government policy, Alexander had encouraged both public discussion of reform and the founding of new journals and newspapers. Educational opportunities increased as the reforms required people to staff new agencies. Women received some opportunities for higher education earlier than in most western countries, in part because of this broad need for educated experts in so many new fields. But the hopes that accompanied the Great Reforms turned quickly sour for two main reasons. First, the government had waited too long to reform, then raised hopes sky-high only to dash them on the reality of political compromise. In the 1850s Alexander Herzen had used his radical journal, *The Bell,* to praise the autocracy for its work toward serf emancipation, but when the emancipation was issued, he immediately condemned it as a fraud and a new form of serfdom, with which the tsar hoped to persuade the people that "black is not black and that two plus two does not equal four."

One can fault the radical intelligentsia for its impatience and unreasonable expectations, but the government's unwillingness to make any concessions to those clamoring for political reform was the empire's second fatal mistake. When it became clear that the Great Reforms would end with social engineering and military priorities, educated society as a whole felt betrayed, disillusioned, and alienated. A friend of Herzen's, writing in *The Bell* after emancipation, spoke for many when he said, "The people need land, freedom, and education. . . . It is impossible to live this way any longer, but things cannot get any better so long as power remains in the hands of a Tsar."

The Great Reforms had the potential to create a genuine public sphere in Russia, and the reforms, politically truncated and compromised as they were, laid the groundwork for the eventual development of a more democratic polity. There was nothing inevitable about the continuation of authoritarianism in Russia, but the tsar's political intransigence and the government's unwillingness to allow private initiative in economic and social development certainly had a hand in alienating successive generations of young idealists and radicalizing the Russian opposition.

In the 1850s and 1860s young radicals emerged from their underground circles, encouraged by the open debates of the period to express new views about self and society. The Russian intelligentsia, like intellectuals elsewhere in Europe, reacted against the Romanticism of their predecessors, turning to a narrowly utilitarian view of art and society. All art must have a social purpose, and the bonds holding the individual tightly to the traditions of society must be smashed: parental authority, the marriage tie, and the tyranny of custom. For these people, the name *nihilist* quickly became fashionable.

Turgenev's *Fathers and Children* explores the mentality of the nihilists and their relationship with their parents' generation. Men and women began to study medicine and the sciences in hopes of offering practical aid to the emerging peasantry. Russian nihilism, however, was a short-lived phenomenon. It preached a radical form of self-improvement that tended to isolate individuals rather than involving them in improving society as well. In the context of the Great Reforms and especially the serf emancipation, a more energetic ideology was needed. Young people idealized the peasantry and placed great hopes in their new freedom. Thousands of women as well as men sought ways to aid them more aggressively.

In the 1860s many young Russian intellectuals went to Switzerland. Among these was a small but highly influential group of women attracted to Switzerland for its unique access to higher education for women. Vera Figner (1852–1943), Sophia Perovskaia (1854–1881), and others were motivated by an almost religious sense of calling to aid the Russian people through practical good works.

Also present in Switzerland were two important Russian revolutionary thinkers, Peter Lavrov (1823–1900) and Peter Tkachev (1844–1886). Lavrov taught his followers that as intellectuals they owed a great debt to the Russian peasant, whose labor had enabled their ancestors to enjoy leisure and had made their own education possible. Lavrov advised the nihilist students to complete their education and then return to Russia and go among the peasants, educating them and spreading propaganda for an eventual revolution of the masses. In contrast, Tkachev taught that revolution would have to come from a tightly controlled revolutionary elite, a small knot of conspirators who would seize power. Mikhail Bakunin pushed these ideas to an extreme. He was a tactician of violence who advocated "anarchism, collectivism, and atheism as the only hope for ridding Russia of autocracy." He looked forward to a great revolution, spreading perhaps from Prague to Moscow and then to the rest of Europe, followed by a tight dictatorship; beyond this he was vague about the future. In his long career, Bakunin was to exert from exile abroad a considerable influence on Russian radicals.

Figner, Perovskaia, and some of their friends came to believe that the tsar's stubborn refusal to share political power with educated society or to offer an emancipation that favored peasant development indicated that autocracy would never reform from within, and that education and health care for peasants were mere palliative measures that would not fundamentally transform their lives. These women and men were moved to give up medicine altogether and fight to transform Russia through revolution. In many cases this meant giving up the comforts of noble privilege and living precariously in hiding. For women the choice of a revolutionary's life was a permanent one. Men might change their mind, and if uncaught, return to a career and a family, but when a woman opted out of the marriage market, there was no return.

Under the influence of teachers such as Bakunin and Lavrov, Russian nihilists turned to a new kind of movement, called *populism*. Young educated men and women decided to return to Russia and live among the peasants. When a government decree in 1872 actually summoned them back, they found that a parallel movement had already begun at home. About three thousand young people now took posts as teachers, innkeepers, or store managers in the villages. Their Romantic views of the peasantry were soon dispelled, however. In any event, the populists were conspicuous and easily traced by the police. Suspicious of the newcomers' motives, the peasants often betrayed them (not unlike the Galician peasants who turned the Polish noble revolutionaries over to the police). Those populists who remained at large decided that they needed a determined revolutionary organization. With the formation of the first organized revolutionary party, Land and Freedom, in 1876, the childhood of the Russian revolutionary movement was over.

The movement became more and more radical, and in 1879 those who believed in the use of conspiracy and terror founded a new party, the People's Will. In 1879, in the belief that the tsar's assassination would spark a general peasant revolution, the members of the People's Will sentenced Alexander II to death. The terrorists shot at the tsar and he crawled to safety on the ground. They mined the tracks on which his train was traveling, and blew up the baggage car instead. They smuggled dynamite into the imperial residence in the Winter Palace, but when they detonated it, the tsar was out of the room and eleven other people, including servants, were killed. Finally, the terrorists organized an attack on the tsar's carriage during its regularly scheduled ride through the capital. In March 1881, a volunteer suicide bomber succeeded in assassinating Alexander by hurling a homemade grenade at him on a busy St. Petersburg street.

With Alexander's death, hopes for reform also died. While the terrorists had been hunting the tsar, liberals had been pressuring him to issue a constitution and establish a national assembly of elected representatives. The night before Alexander took his last carriage ride, he had signed a document promising to create just such an assembly. His son Alexander III would have no patience whatsoever for political reform.

Great Britain and the Cult of Progress

The 1850s and 1860s were decades of active liberal reformism in Great Britain. In domestic policy, the British government had more flexibility and a lighter hand than its Russian counterpart, so while the traditional elites did not give up their monopoly on power easily, they repeatedly chose reform over violence and strife.

After the Crimean War, a short period of political drift set in. Until the mid-nineteenth century the British parliament had been more like a gentlemen's club than a modern arena for political debate and legislation. Laissez-faire ideas dominated government, which meant that Parliament did not seek out opportunities to make legislation but rather allowed the "invisible hand" to create wealth. Social engineering was only undertaken when the government was prodded into action by crisis or powerful interest. In the 1860s modern parties began to coalesce around coherent liberal and conservative platforms (descendants of the Whig and Tory parties). The industrial economy and urbanization created problems that required some refereeing, however, and gradually *laissez-faire* began to seem untenable.

Social changes that had occured in connection with the relatively long history of industrialization in Britain had an impact on British politics. Scientific studies and popular exposés of working-class life convinced a significant number of people that the government ought to get involved in preventing disease and feeding and housing the poor. This sort of active liberalism was partly based on a religious conviction of the need for charity, but there were pragmatic reasons as well. The British middle classes came to believe that their own lives would be more secure if the lower classes who shared their cities were well fed, peaceful, schooled, and respectable.

For their part, a significant minority of workers also aimed for and succeeded in achieving their own version of respectability. A century of industrialization in England had made it possible for a number of workers—skilled and relatively well-paid men, primarily—to aspire to a working-class version of middle-class comfort and respectability. They believed in individual self-improvement and collective self-help. The "worker aristocracy," as they were sometimes called, sought out educational opportunities, dressed well, and behaved with more restraint than the mass of unskilled workers, and they made an effort to distance themselves from people they had begun to consider culturally inferior. Marx had predicted that workers would develop "class consciousness." He thought that all workers with common experiences, values, goals, and enemies would develop similar political ideals and struggle together to achieve them. But in England, worker solidarity did not exist to the same extent that it did in northern France, Belgium, and Germany, where the same kinds of growing cultural differences paled in comparison to political and economic similarities among workers.

Britain's workers in this period came to believe they had more to gain from peaceful collective action through trade unions or cooperative societies than through militant street action or violence. When in the 1850s workers began agitating to win the right to vote, they pressed their claims with legal tactics like those the Chartists and liberals had used in the two preceding decades. Some claimed the right to vote on the basis of a democratic ideology that promised universal rights. Most used arguments middle-class liberals had advanced earlier: workers had a stake in society as patriotic and wage-earning citizens. The workers were joined in their appeals by non-Anglican Protestants known as Dissenters. The Protestant Dissenters resented paying taxes that supported the Church of England and railed against the laws that kept them from attending the best universities or attaining prestigious jobs in civil service. Catholics in England, who were primarily Irish immigrants, faced even stiffer restrictions. Together, working-class leaders and religious dissenters fought to extend the franchise.

In the 1850s and 1860s, after the first Reform Bill brought a preponderance of liberals into Parliament, the Whigs governed Britain. Henry John Temple, Viscount Palmerston (1784–1865), led a coalition that came to be called the Liberal party, composed of religious dissenters and others devoted to *laissez-faire* policies. In the 1860s William Gladstone (1809–1898), together with John Bright (1811–1889) transformed the Liberal party into an active reformist party with modern political tactics. The son of a merchant who made a killing in trade with India, Gladstone espoused a liberalism based on deep moral and religious outrage at the conditions in which the poor lived under capitalism (in Europe) and the indifference of the aristocracy and *laissez-faire* liberals to the poor.

Bright was the son of a cotton manufacturer and a veteran of the campaign to repeal the Corn Laws in the 1840s. During that campaign, Bright developed tactics that would prove useful again in fighting to expand the franchise in the 1860s. He organized banquets and public appearances at which political issues were debated and followers actively sought. Bright was a passionate speaker and a popular one. He stood for free trade, lower taxes, and extension of suffrage to the urban population. He and Gladstone both opposed overseas colonization because it cost money that could be spent to improve lives at home.

Gladstone became the political leader of the Liberal party and remained in that position until the end of the century. As talented a public speaker as Bright, he sounded more reliable and less extreme. Gladstone was also aware of the need to win the support of the public in this new age of modern mass politics. Like Bright, Gladstone was a new style of politician whose popularity was first based on his campaign for tax reforms (which incidentally made newspaper and books less expensive, further extending mass politics). As prime minister, he would create a postal system and insurance system that benefited workers. He argued in Parliament that the vote was inevitable, "You cannot fight against the future. . . . The great social forces . . . are marshaled on our side." But he supported only a partial extension of voting rights, to the artisans and skilled workers.

The Conservative party was largely the work of Benjamin Disraeli (1804–1881), whose mark on party organization was made by forging a party that appealed to conservatives in both the cities and the countryside. He actively sought public support for the conservative cause. As a Jew who received baptism as an Anglican, he was a surprising leader for a party of rural British aristocrats, and always something of an enigma. But he was a powerful speaker and a pragmatic and forceful politician who understood the role of compromise in modern democratic politics. Earlier in his career, like the majority of conservatives who feared that government reform would weaken their economic and political standing, Disraeli had been deeply opposed to letting workers vote. But in the 1860s Disraeli came to believe that lower-class voting was inevitable and might even help the conservative party. He argued that supporting the Reform Bill would win his party the loyalty of at least some workers. He was wrong about that, but his position on the issue got him elected prime minister.

Disraeli and Gladstone and their political parties came to loggerheads over the extension of the franchise. For years reform bills came to Parliament, only to be defeated. Older parliamentary leaders feared that democracy would bring "mob rule," which would be hard to control and would be accompanied by demands for reform that would drain the treasury. When political passions reached the point of violence, though, even conservatives would chose reform over anarchy. In 1866 the defeat of yet another voting rights bill provoked massive public disorders. In July 1866 a crowd tore down the iron railing around Hyde Park in London. In 1867 the conservative Disraeli engineered a far-reaching suffrage bill, the second Reform Bill. The number of voting workers doubled, and representation in Parliament shifted toward the industrial north at the expense of the rural south. But conservatives did not benefit from extending the vote as Disraeli had hoped, and he resigned as prime minister.

Still, the Reform Bill of 1867 did not introduce universal male suffrage. Like the first Reform Bill, it resulted in piecemeal change that brought the electoral districts into greater uniformity and equality but left them divided into boroughs and shires, as in the Middle Ages. The new law nearly doubled the number of voters in Britain by giving the vote to householders—that is, settled men owning or paying rent on their dwellings—in the boroughs. But the new Reform Bill did not give the vote to men in rural areas who lacked the "stake in society" of property. Those who did not own a piece of real estate or a bank account were regarded by many upper-class Victorians as irresponsible and likely to vote away the property of others. Women went unmentioned in the second Reform Bill, an omission that launched the women's suffrage movement. Women could neither vote nor own property with any security, for the Married Women's Property Act of 1870, despite its title, only assured women of the right to keep money they personally earned, so they were generally unable to acquire the theoretical "stake in society" on which the franchise had been based. Only by means of two acts, in 1882 and 1893, did women gain the right to separate ownership of property, the first act applying to married women, and the second to single women.

The Conservative and Liberal parties differed from their ancestors, the oligarchical eighteenth-century factions of Tories and Whigs. The Conservatives kept their old electoral following among country gentlemen, army and navy officers, and Anglican clergymen, but they added many new supporters among agricultural laborers, tradespeople, and even some of the urban working and white-collar classes. The Liberals found many new supporters among businessmen, the religious nonconformists, white-collar radicals, and the more politically conscious workers. Both parties frankly appealed to the "people." The Conservatives, with their Primrose League in honor of Disraeli's favorite flower, their appeal to love of queen and country, their record of social legislation against the worst evils of the new factory system, did at least as good a job as the Liberals of building a party machine and getting out the vote. The two-party system was almost wholly confined to the English-speaking lands: Britain, the United States, and the British dominions. On the Continent, a multiparty or coalition system usually prevailed—not only in France, Italy, and Germany but also in the smaller parliamentary systems in Scandinavia, Switzerland, Holland, and Belgium, as well as in Spain, which had established a bicameral legislature in 1876.

The first elections based on the new suffrage brought a liberal leadership back to Parliament in 1868, which ushered in a period of active social reform. The vote was extended to rural male workers, and the secret ballot was instituted. The state bureaucracy grew and professionalized as Parliament established institutions for aiding the poor and supervising industrial cities. Within the bureaucracy, promotion was to be based on merit. Competitive examinations determined one's career success, and the old days of government based on aristocratic privilege were on the wane. It was still impossible to break into the civil service without an elite education; but within the bureaucracy, work rather than rank got one promoted.

Support among the industrial middle classes for *laissez-faire* social policy remained strong, but deplorable public health and extreme cases of exploitation of child labor led the government to attempt to limit the worst abuses. The Public Health Act of 1866 gave local government some control over water supply. In 1871 workplaces were subject to government inspection. The Education Act of 1870 made schooling mandatory for all children under the age of 13. Under pressure from almost the entire population of Ireland, the liberal Parliament ended the supremacy of the Protestant Church of Ireland.

Reform in this period was less effective than many had hoped, but the process was in place for further efforts to succeed later on. However, the decades of relatively peaceful reformism soon came to an end. Negotiations made possible because parties on both sides shared assumptions about the need for change and the value of compromise broke down entirely.

* * *

British labor historians argue that during the midcentury period, when liberal reformism and legal, parliamentary procedures enjoyed broad support, a shared conception of the nation produced a common language of public discourse and activity. In other words, political opponents shared not just a faith in parliamentary practice or legal procedures, but a belief that progressive and compromise-oriented parliamentary practice was central to their common national identity. This sort of modern national identity papered over serious divisions and differences, which were more visible in other countries in the 1850s and 1860s and would come to the fore soon enough in Great Britain. But it was exactly this kind of national identity that reformers in other European countries sought to generate: a supraclass, suprapolitical, and in the case of the empires, even supranation, national identity. The rise of nation-states in this period rested on the belief that the construction of a single, unified national identity could resolve class and other differences to provide a foundation for powerful, prosperous, modern societies.

EIGHT

Reason, Realism, and Respectability

In 1851 London's Great Exhibition seemed the very symbol of European modernity. After Britain avoided the revolutionary turmoil of 1848, the exhibition represented stability amidst anarchy and productivity amidst destruction, the epitome of industry. It represented Britain's position as the greatest of the Great Powers. Thirteen thousand exhibits from Britain, other European countries, and their colonies around the world displayed machinery and manufactured goods, raw materials, decorative household items, and large guns. The exhibition was displayed in a huge, modern, glass and iron structure known as the Crystal Palace: 1,800 feet long and 450 feet wide, it was tall enough to contain elm trees growing on the site. In addition to exhibiting British ingenuity, the Great Exhibition offered a public space for people to display modern reason and respectability. It was stupendously popular with Britons of all classes, and the people from around the world who came to London to see it or sat at home reading about it. The exhibition embodied British self-confidence in its industry, rationality, ingenuity, and national unity and as such was widely seen in Europe as representing the highest point yet reached by any civilization on earth.

The specific social and cultural context in which the exhibition occurred contributed to its reputation. The "first" British industrial revolution was being joined by the industrialization of other parts of the world, which were now tied in one way or another with the British economy. The exhibition displayed Britain's economic supremacy, while also showing the ways it depended on economic underdevelopment in the rest of the world. From the 1870s through the 1910s, a "second" industrial revolution followed the first, as new technologies and newly industrializing parts of the world changed the nature of industrialization. Artists and writers of the age commented on every aspect of the new social world created by the spread of industry in the new nation-state. Complex and rapid change confronted people with perplexing social and moral conflicts and new ideas about individual and collective identity. These issues were examined in one of the great cultural inno-

The Great Exhibition of the Works of Industry of All Nations, London, 1851. The Crystal Palace was demolished and reconstructed at Sydenham Hill in south London, where it remained a popular tourist attraction until it burned down in 1936. (Picture Collection, The Brance Libraries, The New York Public Library, Astor, Lenox, and Tilden Foundations)

vations of the nineteenth century: the realistic social novel. The social life of ordinary people was also becoming an acceptable subject of paintings and plays alike. And of course modern human dilemmas were examined in the new popular culture as well. Together, modern industry and culture would cast doubt on the very self-confidence and certainty projected by the Great Exhibition and its promoters.

The Economic Boom and Second Industrial Revolution

Between 1848 and the early 1870s, industrialization transformed continental Europe, and the entire world was drawn into the capitalist economy. The second industrial revolution was really two processes in one. First, continental governments and entrepreneurs built railroads and spread mechanized production, often beginning with textiles. Second, new technological innovations and scientific discoveries accelerated and transformed industrialization as it spread. Production of everything—from metals to textiles to luxury items—soared. Trade increased just as dramatically. Investment capital was plentiful, and rising profits created even deeper stores of capital to be invested in new endeavors. Employment in manufacturing and industry also surged. One mark of the boom is that when grain prices rose sharply in the mid-1850s—triggering a rise in the price of bread—hunger and riots did not follow. The economic boom was due in part to the enormous expansion of industry and trade, not only to continental Europe but to the world at large. In the first half of the nineteenth century, world trade had almost doubled; in half that time, between 1850 and 1870, world trade increased by another 260 percent. The discovery of gold in California in 1849 probably helped increase the money available for purchasing manufactured goods and investing in new manufacturing in Europe and Europe's colonies.

Coal and steel still powered the industrial revolution, and the railroad train and steamship brought its products and its momentum to new markets. Railroads fueled and spread mechanized production and stimulated demand for manufactured products; trains brought workers to cities and middle-class travelers on vacation. But the second industrial revolution introduced new sources of energy and new technologies. Electricity became a practical source of power around 1870. Unlike coal and gas, electricity could be transported relatively easily. When Thomas Edison (1847–1931) perfected the incandescent lightbulb, indoor and outdoor lighting became affordable. Machines of many kinds were invented to improve processes of manufacturing. Electricity made possible the production of lightweight, durable aluminum, as well as the telegraph and the telephone. Sewing machines entered homes in the 1850s as one of the first mass-produced and mass-marketed consumer products. Isaac Singer (1811–1875) promoted his sewing machine as a device that would free women from hand stitching and factory work (and even Marx thought the sewing machine would be "revolutionary"). Singer's invention had the opposite effect, however, ensnaring women in old webs of low-wage piecework and new, long-term financial schemes to pay for their "modern" machines.

Advances in chemistry had widespread pragmatic effects. New chemicals and chemical processes found uses in everything from fertilizers, which increased food production, to pharmaceuticals, which eased pain and cured diseases (sometimes). Efficient production of alkali and sulfuric acid made it possible to mass-produce paper, soaps, textiles, and fertilizers. Ideas about respectability and increasing knowledge about the spread of diseases created a new international market for soap and cleaning products. In 1867 the Swedish inventor Alfred Nobel (1833–1896) produced dynamite, a relatively safe explosive. He built a small empire of factories across Europe to manufacture dynamite, which could be used to blast through natural obstacles for the construction of roads, railroad track beds, and canals. Nobel amassed a fortune on dynamite (and 350 other patents). A restless intellect, interested in all the sciences as well as literature, but an intensely private man, Nobel left his entire fortune to fund the international prizes for science, literature, and peace that bear his name.

New fuels and construction materials contributed to mass production and an unprecedented building boom. Oil-fueled internal combustion engines were more efficient than the older steam engines. Oil remained a relatively scarce commodity, however, until the discovery at the turn of the century of new oil fields in Russian-dominated Caucasus, as well as Borneo, Persia, and Texas. After Haussmann transformed Paris, other medieval cities of Europe were similarly renovated. New factory towns appeared, and buildings could be taller and sturdier. Iron and glass buildings (solid and fireproof), pioneered in the early nineteenth century in Britain, were used widely in the construction of new city centers in Europe: London's Crystal Palace of 1851 inspired

Les Halles, Haussmann's new market in Paris (1853–1870), glass houses built in Brussels (1868–1876), and railroad stations everywhere. Before he built the Eiffel Tower, Alexandre-Gustave Eiffel together with Louis-Auguste Boileau designed a new home for the department store Bon Marché (1876).

Scientific discoveries were also responsible for the cure of diseases and improved health and life span. Louis Pasteur (1822–1895) in France and Robert Koch (1843–1910) in Berlin discovered that diseases were often caused by tiny microorganisms. They and others identified the bacteria that caused a great number of diseases including anthrax, malaria, tuberculosis, cholera, bubonic plague, and typhoid. Ronald Ross (1857–1932) discovered that malaria was spread by mosquito bite.

The inventions that had fueled the first industrial revolution were based on relatively simple scientific principles or technological discoveries. The chemistry, physics, and engineering of the second industrial revolution required far more sophisticated laboratories for carrying out more complex experimentation. The new labs tended to be associated with universities and were occasionally industry sponsored (especially in the United States). Education became necessary, practical, and profitable. Governments everywhere tried to educate more people and diminish religious strictures on education. Literacy rates rose, though more slowly in eastern Europe. Girls received primary education, and young women fought their way into universities and medical schools.

Some countries industrialized more quickly than others, with social and political consequences at the time and down the road. The second industrial revolution was most visible most rapidly in Germany, northern France, Sweden, and Belgium. The first and second industrial revolutions arrived together in Russia in the 1890s. Austria-Hungary saw steady aggregate growth throughout the second half of the century, but great regional disparities. After 1900, most regions of eastern Europe began the process of transforming agrarian economies into industrial ones.

France and Germany

Between 1850 and 1870, the German Federation easily overtook France economically, providing the military advantage necessary to bring about German unification and contributing to Germany's defeat of France in 1870–1871. Although industrialization in France was still quite extensive in comparison to the rest of Europe, the French responded to the Great Exhibition of 1851 with self-satisfaction. Many French manufacturers viewed British mass production as inferior to their own small-scale production of stylish luxury goods of high quality. Until the 1860s the French economy had successfully combined some large-scale mechanized production with traditional, small-scale handicraft production and putting-out work. The slower increase in the population and the high productivity of existing manufacturing and agriculture sustained France's relative economic strength. The French system was nearing obsolescence in the 1860s, however, owing to the combination of increasing industrialization in Germany and elsewhere and the low cost of grain coming from Russia and the Americas. In the 1870s and 1880s the luxury trades collapsed as changes in fashion coincided with an upsurge in the demand for inexpensive mass-produced clothing and other goods. In the 1890s France rebounded with capital investment in heavier mechanized industries, resulting in rapid economic growth. The French invested in "second industrial revolution" products: electricity, aluminum, motor vehicles, aircraft. But some of the traditional weaknesses remained: small-scale production, relatively low wages, overdependence on luxury goods, and a large uncompetitive agrarian sector.

German unification, on the other hand, was followed by a remarkable economic boom, accomplishing in twenty years what Britain had taken a century to do. Production of iron, coal, steel, textiles, and chemicals all soared. In the 1880s Germany produced half as much steel as Great Britain. By the late 1890s, however, Germany was producing more steel than any other country in Europe, and by 1913, its production rate was double that of Britain. Over one million new buildings were constructed in Prussia alone between 1852 and 1867, in country and city. As everywhere, railroads spurred production. One of the things that differentiated German industrialization, and indeed all industrialization after Britain's, was a higher level of government investment. In Germany, the government built canals and highways and ran important coal mines in Saar and Silesia. New banks also played an important role in Germany's rapid economic growth. German banks during this period were willing to lend large amounts of money for long periods of time, with the faith that profitable returns were to be had down the line.

The second industrial revolution and the new imperialist global economy made the momentum of industry seem limitless. But that was an illusion. A severe depression in 1873 shook the European and the global economy, stimulated aggressive, new imperialist ventures, and undermined the liberalism that seemed to have triumphed almost everywhere. Europeans were used to economic slumps. They had experienced, and surmounted, trade-cycle slumps in 1826, 1837, and the 1840s and had known traditional weather-related agricultural downturns for centuries. No one, however, was prepared for the Great Depression of 1873 because few realized how significant international economic linkages had become. The boom of the 1860s was marked by highly speculative and risky investments yielding artificially high profits from unsound companies. The industrial economy had not completely overtaken the agricultural economy: grain prices still mattered. In the early 1870s cheaper grain from Russia and Latin American flooded the European market, disrupting local markets in every grain-producing country. As confidence in the economy soured, a bank crisis in Vienna spread to financial capitals around the world with lightning speed, in part owing to recent advances in communications and transportation. Bankruptcies multiplied, stock markets crashed, production halted. The depression would last until well into the

1890s, affecting not only the economy but social, political, and cultural life as well. Although the economy recovered, a sense of economic crisis was pervasive until the 1890s, when a new period of economic growth began.

British productivity doubled; in France it tripled; and in Germany, productive capacity increased eightfold during the 1890s. The heavy industry of the "first industrial revolution" was again the core of the German economy: coal, iron, steel all surged in productivity. In the Ruhr Valley the number of miners increased from 100,000 to 400,000; coal output tripled to the point where Germany extracted one-fourth of all the world's coal. Urbanization also increased, which tripled the number of jobs available in construction. "Second industrial revolution" industries, however, were equally impressive and led the world. German chemicals, electricity, engineering, precision instruments, and optics were all the best to be had anywhere. And consumer goods, such as food and drink, were widely mechanized during this period.

One of the reasons for Germany's success was the appearance of business cartels. German businessmen organized into business associations to control a cutthroat competitive growth market. In a cartel, decisions were made according to a new kind of division of labor. Market decisions were made by commercial specialists at cartel headquarters, production decisions by a shop-level production staff, and financial policy was controlled by the cartel's bankers. These business arrangements were more cautious than individual entrepreneurship, but what they lacked in risk-taking innovations they made up for in ability to apply new technologies and respond to market changes quickly and efficiently. Thus, for example, when Germany's AEG and Siemens, two giants in the "second industrial revolution" sector, agreed on prices, the costs to consumers went up but there were no corresponding raises in wages. So although German workers' wages rose in the aggregate during this period, prices rose too resulting in a loss in "real wages."

Along with cartels, there was an emphasis on "rational" production: division of labor and strategic planning were new elements of production. Such specialization and planning led to a large increase in the number of white-collar employees: statisticians, managers, accountants, and draftsmen, increasing further the size of the middle classes.

Russia and Italy

Although Russia would always suffer economic disadvantages in relation to its western neighbors, once its industrialization campaign began, in the 1890s, it proceeded at a phenomenal pace. Even though the population remained 80 percent rural on the eve of World War I, its industrial output was at the same time competitive with and even exceeded that of the other Great Powers by the 1910s.

The main obstacle to industrialization in Russia had been the lack of investment capital: Russia was land rich and cash poor. The ministers of finance, Ivan Vyshnegradsky and his successor Sergei Witte (1849–1915), realized that they needed to find investment capital in the rural economy. Vyshnegradsky bluntly said, "We may starve, but we will export grain." And in fact peasants

Allgemeine Elektrizitäts-Gesellschaft (AEG) advertisement, Berlin. In this ad, modern technology is endowed with the symbolism of mythic national history; and the human invention, the lightbulb, is shown as able to improve upon nature and conquer the entire globe.
(Deutsches Historisches Museum)

starved. In 1890–1891 there was widespread crop failure, and the government's prior forced selling of grain meant that peasants had no reserves to fall back on. Four hundred thousand people died during the winter of 1891–1892, Vyshnegradsky lost his job and Witte searched for capital elsewhere. He still forced peasants to sell grain to the foreign market, but more slowly, while he aggressively recruited foreign investment, especially in France.

In the 1890s the rates of industrial growth in Russia were exceptional, about 8 percent per year. Witte also embarked on a massive railroad-building campaign and used government funds for direct investment. Russia, like Germany, enjoyed the "advantages of backwardness." Having started late, Russia could import the latest technology. Central planning allowed for the building of huge plants and large-scale industries. Government involvement meant that developments were greatest in weapons and armaments industries. The state-owned railroad network doubled in length between 1894 and 1904, and millions of peasants flooded the cities in search of wage-paying jobs. Russian industrialization was rapid and successful in keeping Russia politically and militarily competitive.

Italy presented yet another variation on the pattern of industrial revolution, with industrial development in one region, primarily in the north, and slow growth in other areas, primarily the south. Even in the north, industrialization proceeded by fits and starts. In 1850 spinning was mechanized, but weaving remained a handcraft until 1900. An iron production industry got started, but development was hampered by the scarcity of coal. Then in the 1880s and 1890s government expenditure moved away from industry to deal with the social problems resulting from the great disparity between north and south, the agricultural depression, and the rise of socialist and anarchist unrest; enhancement of national pride was another goal. Investment in housing, public works, and urban development and beautification slowed industrial growth but may not have hurt social stability.

Nevertheless, the north–south disparity was hard to break down. By 1900 southern Italy, with 41 percent of Italian land had only 17 percent of the industrial workers; it had 26 percent of the population and only 12 percent of the taxable property. In England and France, regional differences provided specialization of production and consumption that stimulated economic growth. But in Italy the discrepancy between north and south was far greater. The south was too deeply impoverished to supply a market for northern Italian goods, while the north could not find work for all the surplus labor of the south. The result was widespread emigration, exceeded in Europe only by that of the Irish.

By 1914 the northern industrial triangle of Genoa, Milan, and Turin had modern steel, armaments, and automobile industries, spurred in large part by defensive military considerations. Railway and automobile builders subsidized their consumer production with armaments contracts. And Italy was a major producer of that all-important commodity of the second industrial revolution: electricity. In Italy electricity rather than railroads spurred forward and backward linkages. The energy allowed for the mechanization of small-scale production even in tiny workshops and fledgling southern manufacturing concerns. It could tap the massive amount of cheap water power available in the Alps by running mountain streams through hydroelectrical plants. Electricity was cheap to transport, so the energy could be spread inexpensively and used to power new consumer industries: bicycle and automobile engineering, food processing, and the making of rayon and cement. Eventually, at the turn of the century, Italy found a way to industrialize that did not resemble the paths chosen by any of its European neighbors.

Austria-Hungary

The Czech economy continued to grow in the second half of the nineteenth century, and increasingly ethnic Czechs dominated. Czechs came to outnumber Germans in the Czech lands at midcentury and continued to increase that ratio to about 3:2 in Bohemia and 7:3 in Moravia. Jews also settled in relatively large numbers in Prague and tended to benefit from assimilationist policies and possibilities, as in Budapest. Hungarian industrialization began later but experienced significant growth after 1867. Industrialized agriculture was a major catalyst and Hungary became the second largest exporter of milled flour in the world. Coal output increased 14 times between 1867 and 1914, iron output increased fivefold, and steel doubled between 1898 and 1914. The number of workers in industry increased from 110,000 to 620,000 between 1880 and 1913. Railroad growth was also extensive. The Hungarian nobility looked down on industrial occupations, so foreign investment was the main catalyst for mining, coal, steel, and railroad building. The new industrial middle class in Hungary was composed primarily of Germans and Jews. Legal restrictions against Jews were lifted in 1867 and 1896; and 300 Jewish families received noble rank. Almost a quarter of the population of Budapest was Jewish. Most urban Jews were culturally assimilated, which pleased the Hungarian political rulers and may have kept prewar anti-Semitism in check in comparison with Vienna, Paris, and Berlin.

Prussian Poland saw a rise in agricultural productivity; Galicia was still primarily agricultural, with a Polish nobility and an impoverished Polish and Ukrainian peasantry. Congress Poland (under Russian control) experienced significant industrial development after the 1850s. Sugar refining, textile production, and in the 1890s coal and steel led the way. But on the whole, until Russia began its major industrial development in the 1890s, Russian Poland was still dominated by its nobility and its rural society.

Urbanization and Migration

Industrialization combined with agricultural crisis and the mechanization of agriculture produced a new upsurge in European urban growth. Except in Russia, rural industry virtually disappeared, and manufacturing concentrated in cities. By 1900 the population of nine European cities had surpassed the one-million mark. Some workers had improved their living conditions, but large neighborhoods of horrific, dangerous, and disease-ridden slums still housed most of Europe's working classes. Nonetheless, demographic trends begun earlier in the century accelerated: people were living longer, and more children were surviving infancy. Better sanitation and medicine extended life expectancy, and more infants were surviving. Births outnumbered deaths, even as more families sought to limit conception and control family size. Between 1870 and 1914 the population of Europe increased from 290 million to 435 million.

The population would have increased even more dramatically but for the high rates of migration from Europe to the Americas. Economic depression and ethnic or religious discrimination sent millions of people to the New World in search of better lives. Ireland, Britain, and Germany were the first to send emigrants in mass numbers, but Russia and eastern Europe were not far behind. While much of this movement, especially after 1880, was from south-

Emigrants on the wharf in Naples, 1908. Economic disparity in Italy continued into the twentieth century, causing more than 3 million people, overwhelmingly from the south, to leave Italy. (Archivo Touring Club Italiano)

ern and eastern Europe, more of it was from the United Kingdom. Nearly 23 million emigrants left Europe between 1850 and 1900; 10 million of these were from Britain. Between 1871 and 1914, Jewish emigration from Russia totaled 1.5 million Jews left Russia. Over a million people left Europe each year between 1900 and 1910 from Italy, Ireland, Poland, Germany, and Scandinavia combined. Mass migration from Europe was an important social safety valve. The restless, ambitious, and impoverished people who left to seek a better life elsewhere were similar to the kinds of people drawn to social and political protest. Historians argue that the presence in Europe of millions more such people could have seriously destabilized social life at the end of the century.

Respectability

The second industrial revolution raised the prestige of scientists and science. Bourgeois Europe was proud of its accomplishments, and the bourgeoisie associated prosperity with science, hard work, and self-improvement. In contrast to the culture of Romantic excess, midcentury Europe saw the increase in cultural forms and behavioral norms that emphasized reason, restraint,

Emigration from Europe (in Thousands)

Country of origin	1860s	1880s	1900s
Austro-Hungarian Empire	40	248	1,111
Belgium	2	21	30
Denmark	8	82	73
Finland	—	26	159
France	36	119	53
Germany	779	1,342	274
Italy	27	992	3,615
Netherlands	20	52	28
Norway	98	187	191
Portugal	79	185	324
Russian Empire	—	288	911
Spain	7	572	1,091
Sweden	122	327	324
Switzerland	15	85	37
United Kingdom	1,572	3,259	3,150

Source: Raymond Pearson, *European Nationalism, 1789–1920* (New York, 1994). p. 243

and responsibility. This culture of "respectability" encompassed public and private behaviors that emphasized self-help and education, deference and respect in public, sobriety, demure entertainment, and an avoidance of all emotional extremes. Members of the middle classes all over Europe, believed that respectability was what distinguished them from the unkempt and unruly lower classes. But elements of respectability were available to all who could afford them. For many workers and peasants who chose to avoid drink, dress well, and educate themselves, respectability was a mark of achievement.

Respectability was also connected with a trend toward secularization, but this needs to be understood carefully. Secular education was on the increase, and church attendance dropped, especially among the poor and especially among urban workers. Church building had been dwarfed by the construction of civic structures (museums, libraries, municipal halls), and theology gave way to history, economics, sociology, and, of course, science. Secularization was the creed of Europe's most prosperous Jews as well as Christians. For some Jews, it seemed as if Christian secularization had opened doors to their acceptance in society. While many Jews (especially in rural areas) continued traditional religious observance, many did not, and church congregations came into being that welcomed acculturated Jews who wanted to blend into Europe's new middle classes at work and in public, while practicing Judaism at home. As one successful doctor put it in the 1880s, "A physician's religion is humaneness—that is, love of humanity without regard to wealth or poverty, without distinction of nationality or confession."

Liberals and socialists like Mill and Marx believed that the critique of contemporary society must begin with a critique of religion, and in 1843 Marx

A Closer Look

SELF-HELP

One of the key concepts of nineteenth-century middle class culture was *self-help,* that is, reason applied to daily life to improve one's self; a kind of progress of the soul. The Scottish reformer and popular writer Samuel Smiles (1812–1904) extolled the concept and practice of self-help in a book first published in 1859. In what ways does *Self Help* represent the culture of the era of nation-state building?

"Heaven helps those who help themselves" is a well-tried maxim, embodying in a small compass the results of vast human experience. The spirit of self-help is the root of all genuine growth in the individual; and, exhibited in the lives of many, it constitutes the true source of national vigour and strength. Help from without is often enfeebling in its effects, but help from within invariably invigorates. Whatever is done for men or classes, to a certain extent takes away the stimulus and necessity of doing for themselves; and where men are subjected to over-guidance and over-government, the inevitable tendency is to render them comparatively helpless.

National progress is the sum of individual industry, energy, and uprightness, as national decay is of individual idleness, selfishness, and vice. . . . If this view be correct, then it follows that the highest patriotism and philanthropy consist, not so much in altering laws and modifying institutions, as in helping and stimulating men to elevate and improve themselves by their own free and independent individual action. . . .

The spirit of self-help, as exhibited in the energetic action of individuals, has in all times been a marked feature in the English character, and furnishes the true measure of our power as a nation. Rising above the heads of the mass, there were always to be found a series of individuals distinguished beyond others, who commanded the public homage. But our progress has also been owing to multitudes of smaller and less known men. Though only the generals' names may be remembered in the history of any great campaign, it has been in a great measure through the individual valour and heroism of the privates that victories have been won.

Samuel Smiles, *Self-Help*, rev. ed, (London, 1882), pp. v, 1–3, 5–7, 294.

predicted that in Germany, "the criticism of religion has been largely completed." In 1851 a survey of British church attendance taken on a single Sunday revealed that more than half the Christians in the country had failed to attend services. However, churches were still powerful institutions and continued to play an important role in life for most Europeans. In Britain a surge of church building followed signs of flagging attendance. The government also lifted some of the most onerous laws of religious discrimination. Dissenters, or Protestants of churches other than the Church of England were allowed to hold office and to attend the colleges of Cambridge and Oxford. Dissenters were far more active in work among the poor than the Church of England, which was most closely associated with the English elite and the state. Catholics in England, most of whom were Irish, still faced considerable prejudice.

Outside England, the Roman Catholic Church remained a powerhouse and a staunch supporter of traditional aspects of culture against the tide of new political ideologies, nationalism, secular education and science. Pope Leo XIII, was just as determined to bolster papal authority as his predecessor Pius IX but he understood that Catholicism was tarnished by its support of the most reactionary movements of the day. Leo called for cooperation with liberal, representative governments and tried to encourage the church to take an active role in ameliorating the miseries workers suffered from industrial capitalism. The greatest strength of Catholic and Protestant churches in this period may have been abroad. Missionary activity drew Christians of all faiths to Asia and Africa.

There is no doubt that religious practice was changing during the nineteenth century and that many people explored alternatives in mysticism, spiritualism, or agnosticism and atheism. But, even in this secular age, most people continued to seek some comfortable coexistence for belief in God and faith in science and self. The uneasy truce would be sorely tested by Charles Darwin (1809–1882), arguably the most important scientist of the nineteenth century.

Darwin and Darwinism

In 1859 Charles Darwin published *On the Origin of Species by Means of Natural Selection,* based on extensive study of natural history, the physical record of hundreds of thousands of years of organic life on earth. Already well established by geologists and paleontologists, this record told of the rise, the development, and sometimes the disappearance of thousands of different forms of plant and animal organisms or species. The record appeared to contradict the biblical book of Genesis, which describes all forms of life as having been made by divine creator in the space of a single week about six thousand years ago.

Darwin found one clue to the past in Malthus's *Essay on Population,* which maintained that organisms tended to multiply to a point where there was not sufficient food for them all. In the intense competition for food, some organisms did not get enough and died. This was the *struggle for existence.* Darwin next asked himself what determined that certain individuals would survive and that others would die. Obviously, the surviving ones got more food, better shelter, better living conditions of all sorts. If they were all identical organisms, the only explanation would have to be some accidental variation in the environment. But it was clear from observation that individual organisms of a given species were not identical. Variations appear even at birth. Thus in a single litter of pigs there may be sturdy, aggressive piglets and also a runt, who is likely to be shoved aside in suckling and starve. In the struggle for existence, the runt is proved "unfit."

This was the second of Darwin's key phrases—the *survival of the fittest*. The organism best endowed to get food and shelter lives to procreate young that will tend to inherit these favorable variations. The variations may be slight indeed, but over generations they are cumulative; finally an organism is produced that is so different from the long-distant ancestor that it can be considered to be a new species. This new species has *evolved* by the working of *natural selection*. Plant and animal breeders had long made use of this process and had even directed it by breeding only the most desirable strains.

Darwin held that in individuals of the same species, variations at birth are accidental and are generally transmitted to later generations through inheritance. Darwin's theory was modified as scientists concluded that the important variations in the evolutionary process were not so much the numerous tiny ones Darwin emphasized but rather bigger and much rarer ones known as mutations. The actual mechanism of heredity we know much better than Darwin did, thanks to the Austrian monk Gregor Mendel (1822–1884), whose experiments with cross-breeding garden peas laid the scientific basis of modern genetics and its study of genes and chromosomes.

The Origin of Species became a best seller, reviewed all over the world. The major reason for this attention was almost certainly the challenge that Christians felt they found in the book. Darwin received such wide attention because he seemed to provide for the secularist a process (evolution) and a causal agent (natural selection), where before there had been only vague "materialistic" notions that emphasized accident rather than order. He also seemed to have struck a final blow against the argument, very popular in Victorian times, that the organic world was full of evidence of God, the great designer. Finally, Darwin gained notoriety because of the frequent, though quite wrong, accusation that he made the monkey the brother of man. Later, in *The Descent of Man* (1871), Darwin carefully argued that *Homo sapiens* was descended not from any existing ape or monkey but from a very remote primate ancestor.

The Origin of Species stirred up a most heated theological controversy. Fundamentalists, both Protestant and Catholic, damned Darwin and much of science itself. But the Catholic church and many Protestant bodies eventually viewed Darwinism as a scientific biological hypothesis, neither necessarily correct nor necessarily incorrect. Most Christians already accepted sufficient modification of the Genesis account of creation to accommodate the scientists' time scale, and they adjusted the classic theological arguments to propose a God who worked through organic evolution. Moreover, it was clear to reflective individuals that nothing any scientist could produce could give the ultimate answers to the kind of problem posed by the concept of God; it was no contradiction to believe that just as God's eye is on the sparrow, it must have also been on the dinosaur.

If Darwin seemed to be writing about events that none could see, August Comte (1798–1857) wrote about "the scientific age" in a way that was much more consoling to the urban middle class. It was Comte who coined the term *positivism*. His recommendations for bettering the human conditions retained some of the utopian and messianic qualities of Saint-Simonian teachings. Comte applied the term *positivist* to the third stage of humanity's attitude toward the world. First, in the infant period of history, humanity was in the theological age, standing in awe and fear of nature and seeking to placate the gods that controlled it. Second, in the adolescence of human history, metaphysical concepts replaced divinities as perceived controlling forces of the world. Finally, science would enable people to understand nature without recourse to theological or metaphysical intermediaries, so that they might take positive action to manipulate the world to their advantage.

In many ways Comte was simply restating the Enlightenment's optimistic faith in the miracle-working potential of science. Yet he also realized that the attempt of the French revolutionaries to build a new society from the blueprints of eighteenth-century intellectuals had ended in terror and dictatorship. Accordingly, Comte concluded, utopia must be achieved peacefully through dedicated teaching, so that the masses could free themselves from their old dependence on theology and metaphysics. Comte envisaged these liberators as preachers of a new "religion of humanity," but his critics argued that they were propagandists of a new positivist dogma that might be more intolerant than old religious dogmas.

The attraction of Comte's positivism lay in assembling diverse beliefs and arranging them with new emphasis. Social problems were growing more urgent every day, he felt, and humanity required a sweeping intellectual system if it was to avoid destroying itself. Comte scorned metaphysical philosophy in favor of systematized common sense, as he called his views. By using this term, he hoped to appeal to women, to the working class, and to those who were generally but wrongly thought to be unable to perform abstract reasoning.

Positivism found clear expression in public issues. In Britain, Comte's arguments were used to formulate debates on the "condition of England" question and also on whether the British ought to intervene directly in their colonies to effect social change. In France those who rejected both the Revolution and the restoration of the monarchy found in positivism a way to enjoy bourgeois comforts while rejecting bourgeois values. The movement was solidly middle class, generally professional and academic. In an age acutely aware of history, the positivists believed that they could bring to history and society the predictive abilities of science. This was a comforting doctrine that formed an ethical bridge between science and religion.

Realism in the Arts

Just as modern science, technology, and industry appeared in new social and cultural conditions, nineteenth-century art was produced in a new context created by urbanization, industrialization, and invention. Education and rising literacy rates increased the size of audiences and the number of readers.

Bourgeois prosperity increased time for leisure activities, especially for middle-class women, who for the first time in history were free from work outside the home. Mechanization of printing and new cheap paper processing decreased costs. Rail and steam shipping further enlarged audiences, further decreased costs, and sped the communication of ideas. As a result, the production of literature and the performing arts became commercial operations. Previously, artists either were independently wealthy or worked for royal or other wealthy patrons. In the nineteenth century, writers sold their works to publishers.

Similar changes affected the ways music, painting, and theater were produced and consumed. Music had been composed for royal, clerical, or wealthy patrons and performed for closed audiences in specific settings, usually in connection with a court gathering or religious occasion. In contrast, in the nineteenth century, the fate of a new composition by Beethoven, Chopin, or Franz Liszt depended on the number of ticket buyers and their pleasure or displeasure with the new piece and its public performance. Paintings, like operas, might still be commissioned, but artists were free to create for a broader audience with more diverse and less predictable tastes. As royal patrons withdrew, new and ambitious municipal governments and individual wealthy bourgeois entered the cultural arena. But even under civic patronage, whether privately or publicly funded, the new museums, opera houses, and theaters were built for public attendance. And civic patronage built libraries, schools, and universities, where those audiences could prepare themselves to appreciate the robust proliferation of literary, visual, and performing arts.

Public consumption of art gave Europe's bourgeoisie additional reasons for satisfaction. The inscription at the entrance to the Birmingham, England, art museum proudly read "By the gains of industry we promote art." The newly wealthy aspired to being "cultured." They despised the ignorance of the masses, and they disapproved of the frivolous decadence of the aristocracy (while aspiring to aristocratic ease amid the pleasures of high culture). Bourgeois progress included a dose of cultural self-improvement, both for its own sake and to attain a "cultured" status that would clearly distinguish the bourgeoisie from the "uncivilized" masses. Opera halls, museums, exhibitions, and world's fairs combined private individual improvement with public displays of status and sociability. One listened to a new symphony sitting quietly in a new recital hall, while displaying one's attentiveness, one's admirable self-improvement, and one's new dress.

These experiences also created new norms for measuring what Europeans increasingly called "civilization." European society would use the norms they created out of their own experiences as standards for evaluating the people they considered savages: the lower classes of their own countries and the natives of countries they colonized. The new conditions for producing and consuming art in Europe allowed for the emergence of a great profusion of artists creating highly diverse works for diverse audiences in multiple markets. This diversity was not viewed with approval at the time. Many of the

Continent's greatest thinkers dismissed nineteenth-century art as lacking a single, great, original unifying idea. But this very diversity was the essential creative contribution of nineteenth-century art. Unifying ideas would return with a vengeance in the twentieth century as fascism and Soviet communism, both of which sought to destroy the chaotic unpredictability of modern artistic innovation.

Literature

The nineteenth century saw the rise of two critical instruments for shaping modern culture and modern state building: the novel and the newspaper. New printing technologies allowed for the appearance of the mass circulation press. For the first time, printed literature was cheap enough for new kinds of popular reading fare to emerge. Novels and magazines, newspapers and broadsheets, as well as sheet music (and affordable musical instruments) changed everyday entertainment for the middle and lower classes. In a famous explanation for the rise of nationalism, Benedict Anderson has argued that the spread of communication through newspapers helped homogenize multiple dialects into single national languages and provided information about and a link to all the people reading the same language, which made it possible for readers to imagine themselves as members of nation with recognizable shared characteristics.

As news became more widely and more uniformly available, responses to the news had a profound impact on the formation of subgroups within the nation as well. People collected around common responses to current events, and they could learn more about people in similar situations on another side of the country or the world. Newspapers with specialized readerships appeared in every European country. Railroad trains brought the news to more remote rural spots as workers traveled to and from their native villages. Newspapers provided the public marketplace of ideas that Voltaire imagined, influencing the evolution of political ideas into ideologies and parties. They also had "norm-setting" functions in the modern city. Middle-class popular newspapers in particular commented regularly on every possible form of public behavior, defining civilization and respectability for a reading public anxious to be considered both civilized and respectable.

Social and cultural life was profoundly affected by the proliferation of fiction in the nineteenth century as well. The realistic novels that we can buy in chain bookstores and airports were originally published in serialized installments in newspapers and weekly journals. The English realist novelists Charles Dickens (1812–1870), and William Makepeace Thackeray (1811–1863), the Russian Fyodor Dostoevsky (1821–1881), the French Stendhal (Marie Henri Beyle, 1783–1842) and Honoré de Balzac (1799–1850) all raced to meet deadlines and stay out of debt.

These writers rejected the dreamy, otherworldliness of Romanticism and chose the role of social critic. The realists were thoroughly immersed in the world of their time. Thackeray's *Vanity Fair* was a condemnation of the false values of a money-mad, power-hungry society. The novels that constituted what Balzac called "the human comedy"—*La Père Goriot, Eugènie Grandez, La Cousine Bette,* and many others—were savage exposés of the crassness and corruption of bourgeois society under the July Monarchy.

The leading French realist of the next generation, Gustave Flaubert (1821–1880), hated the bourgeois world he satirized in his masterpiece, *Madame Bovary,* though at the same time he acknowledged both his universalism and his kinship when he said, "Mme Bovary—that's me." Flaubert's great novel, about a petty provincial woman in a soul-deadening marriage, casts a merciless eye on every bourgeois convention and cliché. The heroine's Romantic sense of herself shows her superficiality rather than her emotional depth; her efforts at self-improvement are a farce; her husband's amateur attempt at scientific experiment ends in disaster; and after yearning for escape to a more glamorous and more authentic life in Paris, Mme Bovary finds nothing but artifice and heartbreak there as well.

Charles Dickens's many novels exposed the cruelty and suffering experienced by the poor, especially poor children, in mid-nineteenth century England. He attacked the workhouse, the boarding school, the factory, and the shop with wild plots and colorful, unforgettable characters reflecting his minute observation of almost every corner of the life of his day. Dickens' novels were immensely popular during his lifetime; they were read by everyone who could read, including the queen.

In Russia, the didactic and critical aspect of the nineteenth-century social novel was both taken to an extreme and rejected by writers considered realists. While in prison for engaging in revolutionary activities, Nikolai Chernyshevsky (1828–1889) wrote the most popular (now almost forgotten) novel of the Russian nineteenth century, *What Is to Be Done?* (1863). The novel followed the fates of a circle of idealistic young men and women as they engaged in fictitious marriages to liberate women, as they set up utopian working communities to establish social justice and save prostitutes, and as they dreamed of revolution based on rational self-interest that would transform society. The novel was Romantic, revolutionary, realistic, and didactic at once. It offered models of behavior eagerly taken up by idealistic young men and women for several generations, but its extreme utilitarianism inspired literary attacks by some of Russia's greatest writers. Turgenev's controversial *Fathers and Children* (1862) explores the conflict between the generation of enlightened, liberal aristocrats and their children, rationalist, hard-nosed reformers.

Dostoevsky, who had himself already spent years in prison for revolutionary activity in the 1850s, wrote *Notes from Underground* (1864) and *Crime and Punishment* (1866), both complex psychological studies, in part as a rebuttal to Chernyshevsky. In *Notes,* Dostoevsky uses a protagonist who defiantly rails against the laws of nature to expose and celebrate the irrational in human nature and the folly of social engineering based on reason. "Underground Man" inveighs against London's Crystal Palace as the symbol of heartless reason and western bourgeois materialism. *Crime and Punishment* takes this theme further by exploring the tragically immoral consequences of following a rational argument to its logical conclusion and the search for a higher, supernatural standard of morality: an impoverished young man murders a cruel old woman and spends the rest of the novel searching, against his rational will, for forgiveness and salvation. Like other Russian writers of his day Dostoevsky's mature novels, *The Devils* (1871) and *The Brothers Karamazov* (1880), are Romantic *and* realistic, works of social criticism and spiritual searching, which show compassion for all humanity, an almost frenzied desire to remake society in all its complexity and an attack on all intellectual systems.

The other giant of Russian literature in this period, Leo Tolstoy (1828–1910) was a member of an old aristocratic family, who lived a dissolute life as a young man and army officer, settled down, and wrote ninety volumes of literature and criticism. His great novels seem to realistically recreate whole worlds of Russian society. *War and Peace* (1863–1869) is not only the story of the Napoleonic Wars and the aristocrats who fought in them but a disquisition on history, time, and the role of individuals in great events. In 1876, while writing *Anna Karenina,* a masterpiece of moral tragedy, Tolstoy underwent what he called a conversion to a belief of Christian love and nonresistance to evil. He shared the populists' Romantic view that the Russian future lay with the peasants, for urban society had become inevitably corrupt and violent. He thus became a spokesman for pastoral simplicity and Christian anarchism.

Women's writing occupied a paradoxical position during the midcentury given the idealization of "separate spheres" and the commercialization of culture. Much of the melodramatic and other popular fiction of the period, published in large numbers in books and journals, was written by and for women. And some of the most enduring masterpieces of the nineteenth-century novel were written by women, but these works often had to be published under pseudonyms or by women who were especially courageous and willing to live outside society's accepted boundaries. Like some of their Romantic predecessors, the novelists admired traditional women's roles and values but paradoxically could express such views artistically only by taking on the unconventional (and despised) role of a serious professional.

George Eliot (Mary Ann Evans, 1819–1880) was a prolific and influential novelist whose works do not shy away from detailed observations of the poverty, immorality, and petty-mindedness of provincial life. Yet unlike for example, Flaubert, she created sympathetic characters who were mired in a mercenary world. Her masterpiece, *Middlemarch* (1871–1872), is a study of individuals struggling to live up to their ideals in a society dominated by money and the people who control it. Like all the great realist novels, it teems with details of everyday life in towns and villages where the action takes place. The heroine of *Middlemarch* longs to become a social reformer and make some impact, but she is thwarted first by her own marriage and then by the constraints of marriage on the idealistic young doctor she tries to help. The novel was criticized at the time it appeared as too depressing, especially coming from a woman writer.

Many social novelists, especially in eastern Europe, took up the cause of Romantic nationalism. *Grandma* (1855) by Czech writer Božena Nemcová (1820–1862) unites the cause of preserving rural Czech culture with the desire for a modern Czech state.

By the end of the century, the commitment to portray society realistically was taken a step further by writers who sought an almost scientific accuracy of observation in their novels, giving attention (and a sense of power) to minutely observed physical details and social nuances. Turgenev, Eliot, and above all, Émile Zola (1840–1902) showed clearly the influence of the scientific revolution inspired by Darwin. Zola sought to arrive at laws of human development, much as the biologist seeks laws of organic development. He called his twenty-volume series of novels the "natural history" of a family. Each novel focused on some problem: *La Terre* (The Earth) on the land and peasantry; *L'Assommoir* (The Drunkard) on alcoholism; *La Débâcle* on the trauma of the war of 1870. Zola's *Germinal* (1885) provides an encyclopedia of misery, dehumanization, and smoldering resentment in a mining village in northern France. Danger and injury are ever present in the mines, starvation and humiliation lurk around the corner: the bourgeois mine owner forces the village women to trade sex for food to feed their hungry children. A prolonged strike ignites this explosive tinder, and an orgy of violence ensues. In the end, everyone goes back to work as if nothing had changed.

The pessimists among the social novelists reacted against the eighteenth-century doctrine of the natural goodness of humanity. By the close of the Victorian era, nature apparently had made people greedy, selfish, combative, and addicted to sexual irregularities. Some writers, like the English novelist Thomas Hardy (1840–1928), built this pessimism from a series of incidents in private lives into a grand, cosmic irony. Hardy's characters were often the victims of coincidence, accident, and other unforeseen circumstances; they could hardly be held responsible for their own misfortunes. Anton Chekhov (1860–1904) in Russia used the prose drama and the short story to show how life harasses everyone, but his stories retain a profound empathy and understanding for even his most superficial characters.

Henrik Ibsen (1828–1906) in Norway and George Bernard Shaw (1856–1950) in England helped to develop the "problem play," a form of drama characteristic of the late nineteenth century. The problems were often of wide moral and political concern, as in Shaw's *Man and Superman* or Ibsen's *Enemy of the People*. Ibsen shocked his contemporaries with *A Doll's House,* a portrait of marriage as unbearably stultifying for women, in which his heroine rebelled by leaving her husband and their children.

The cultivated middle classes were not the only ones to enjoy the proliferation of fiction in the nineteenth century. Mechanized printing and rising literacy also accounted for new literary forms marketed to people with fundamental reading skills and a minimum of free time. Dime novels and pennydreadfuls, together with serialized melodramas, mysteries, and adventure stories printed in the mass circulation press, were devoured by their target audience, the young urban workers and deplored by those who considered themselves civilized. Dickens and Dostoevsky were also avid readers of the "boulevard" press, for both the thrills the stories offered and the information they provided. This popular fiction adapted its style and structures from the theatrical melodramas of the early part of the century. Exotic locales, incredible plot twists, and sagas of villainous princes taking advantage of innocent girls combined the realistic detail of urban working-class life (the defenseless girls were now often working girls) with fantastic settings including the Wild (U.S.) West and the underground dens of urban criminals and bandits; detective stories and historical romances were also popular. With titles like "The Wild Boys of London," "Ned Kelley, the Ironclad Australian Bushranger," "The Mother's Grief and Her Favorite Daughter," and "The Bandit Churkin," cheap fiction racked up enormous sales figures everywhere in Europe. Less obsessed with social observation or psychological exploration than the realist social novel, the pennydreadfuls nonetheless offered fast-moving stories about characters more complex than the heros and villains of the early melodramas. In stories that were serialized for months or even years, readers became attached to their bandit's or detective's or domestic servant's fluctuating fates. Like more serious novels, the popular adventures offered parameters of thought and behavior on everything from the tension between community and individual to the national character, gender relations, and conflicts between city and village life. As such, they brought lower-class voices into the public sphere, where they contributed to the construction of national identities, ideas about science and technology, community, and individualism.

Fiction written for many audiences captured previously unexplored corners of life in nineteenth-century Europe. The realist novel explored social and moral dilemmas and modeled new behaviors for individuals in the growing and changing industrial cities they depicted. The collective function of the realist novel was to catalog, examine, and analyze every detail of modern social life. These novels give us a sense of the issues that animated writers and readers in the mid-nineteenth century and the ways those issues might have been treated or resolved; the worlds they depict, however, should not be taken for exact replicas of the age. Balzac's Paris, Dickens's London, Dostoevsky's Petersburg were all depictions shaped by the hand of a particular writer. When we see Russian society through the eyes of the adulterous heroine of Tolstoy's *Anna Karenina,* we see a tragedy of misguided Romantic individualism, in which self-fulfillment is construed as immoral self-indulgence and leads to suicide. However, Anna is a projection of Tolstoy's own prejudices about gender, family, marriage, class, and nation; not a snapshot of reality. Readers of novels with such persuasively real worlds can be entirely drawn in, whereupon they are tempted to think they have discovered something more objective or detached. But, ironically, it was the realist writers' claim to "realism" that made the next generation of writers at the end of the nineteenth century begin to question the limits of realistic representation.

Music

Perhaps the least immediate response to the interests and new capacities of the industrial society was to be found in music. Here, too, there was emphasis on monumentality and education—in the founding of many great modern symphony orchestras and opera companies, in the creation of touring groups that brought the oratorios of Handel and Bach to country towns, and pianos to thousands of private homes. But in musical taste, most people remained firmly rooted in the era of the Romantics.

One ambitious composer of the age did attempt to break with tradition. Richard Wagner (1813–1883) called opera "music drama" and set out to make it the supreme synthesis of the arts, with drama, music, costumes, and scenery all fused into one. His characteristic device was the *leitmotif,* a recurring melodic theme associated with a given character or symbolizing an element in the drama. Wagner chose subjects from the Arthurian legends or the heroic epics of medieval Germany. These subjects showed his awareness of the human need for archetypes and myths, the demigods and supermen of the past who still haunt the memory.

The French composer Claude Debussy (1862–1918) holds the now-conventional title of founder of modern music. Debussy developed new rhythms, harmonies, and dissonance that were a radical departure from conventional composition. In reaction against Wagnerian gigantism, he attempted to convey subtle, sensuous moods in *The Afternoon of a Faun* or the sounds of the sea in *La Mer*. Debussy's style is often called impressionistic, for he sought to convey the sounds and emotions of a transitory moment, much as the impressionist painters sought to capture light and color.

Painting

Painters began questioning the value of realistic representation earlier than writers. While novelists were perfecting realist description and psychological exploration at midcentury, painters were also examining the real world they lived in, but they were doing so with experimental methods of representation based on pioneering work by Goya, Delacroix, Turner, and other Romantics. By exploring the artifice of the two-dimensional canvas along with the artifices of bourgeois social life, painters sought to convey a reality more authentic than mere representation.

The rebellion against academic painting, begun by Delacroix, continued in the mid-nineteenth century with the French artists Honoré Daumier (1808–1879) and Gustave Courbet (1819–1877), who also protested against the values of laissez-faire capitalism and the social mores of the middle class. Daumier exploited to the full the new technological developments that made it

Eduard Manet, Le Déjeuner sur L'Herbe *(Lunch on the Grass, 1863). (Réunion des Musées Nationaux/Art Resource, NY)*

possible to mass-produce inexpensive copies of his lithographs. With moral indignation and savage bite, Daumier exposed the evils of French society. Courbet upset the academic painters by portraying commonplace subjects—wrestlers, stonecutters, nudes who bore no resemblance to classical nymphs—without any attempt to prettify them.

The hostility of the academics reached a peak in 1863, when canvases by followers of Courbet were refused a showing in the annual exhibition known as the Paris Salon. The rejected artists countered by organizing their own Salon des Refusés, which gained the backing of Emperor Napoleon III. Other painters objected to the academy's restrictions of subject matter: only historical or mythological themes were acceptable. Young painters wanted to depict the contemporary world of cafés, city streets, workers, prostitutes, and card players, circus and cabaret performers. Edouard Manet (1832–1883) followed Delacroix's experiments with composition and color, but he forged ahead artistically, startling the viewer into seeing painting in new ways. Where Delacroix used a classical figure to give dignity and pathos to his symbol of the French people, Manet, in *Le Déjeuner sur l'Herbe* (Lunch on the Grass, 1863) contrasts a classical female bather with a startling female nude, who stares frankly out at the viewer in the foreground of a conventional picnic with two fully dressed male companions. The nude's gaze arrests the viewer, eliminating the neutrality and objectivity of classicism and realism. She forces us to acknowledge her and take her seriously.

That science might encourage as well as impede artistic revolution was evident in the case of the impressionists, whose name was invented by hostile critics after viewing a painting entitled *Impression: Sunrise* by Clande Monet. The impressionists followed Constable's admonition to view painting as an "inquiry into the laws of nature." They learned from physics that color was a complex phenomenon put together by the human eye from the prismatic reflections of natural light. They proposed to break both light and shadow into their component colors and then allow the viewer's eye to reassemble them. They painted landscapes and seascapes for the most part, using thousands of little dabs of color; the result, when seen from up close, is hardly more than a formless mesh of color, but, when viewed from the proper distance, it is magically transformed into a recognizable scene flooded with light.

Two more inventions gave the impressionists their newly vibrant palette. In 1841, an American invented collapsible metal tubes for oil paint; their studios thus made portable, artists were quick to take painting outdoors. Second, new chemical dyes, derived from discoveries connected with the second industrial revolution, made a much broader range of pigments available to painters. In the 1860s Monet, along with Camille Pisarro and Pierre-Auguste Renoir began painting a new kind of landscape. Less interested in showing real fields, rivers, and gardens, the impressionists wanted to compose on canvas the colors and shapes of objects in natural light and shadow. Their landscapes captured sites of exquisite ephemeral beauty, like the flower gardens at Giverny.

Ironically, the impressionists were also the first artists to celebrate the aesthetics of industry, especially the train and the railway station. Monet's paintings of the Gare St-Lazare from the 1870s show his fascination with the qualities of light in the industrial city. The train and its station provide a laboratory for examining light in its industrial settings: in steam, through glass, with rain, all in an outdoor interior landscape. Monet's is an ambivalent take on the effect of the railroad on modern life; almost painfully busy and yet, the architecture and the way the steam catches and dissolves the light and the color of buildings in the background offer a statement of a new kind of urban industrial beauty.

All these experiments focused attention on the act of viewing, on the human ability to see and perceive, drawing attention away from the subject matter itself, which became an ephemeral unstable object, changing its form with every change of light or brushstroke. The object of avant-garde art was no longer the realistic depiction of the world. By the 1880s impressionism as a movement would dissolve, but its experiments with perception and picture plane effected a genuine revolution in painting and set the stage for more radical treatments of color and composition by the postimpressionists at the end of the century.

Some painters experimented with radically altered perspective to invest their cityscapes with all the tensions of modernity. Gustave Caillebotte's *Paris Street, Rainy Day* (1877) is composed with such acutely plunging lines of perspective, as to give its sturdy Haussmann plaza and surrounding architecture a nightmarish fragility. That tension between solidity and illusion is reinforced by the anonymity and isolation of the individual bourgeois figures, clad in uniform black and carrying uniform umbrellas. Caillebotte's other masterpiece, *Les Raboteurs de parquet* (The Floor Scrapers, 1875), is a remarkable commentary on Paris in the 1870s as the quintessential modern nation-state capital, recovering from enemy siege and civil war. Belying its photographic realism and its deceptive simplicity, this painting articulates many of the tensions of modern, Parisian life. The making of modernity depended not only on the rational city planning of imperial officials or on bourgeois financial success and taste, but on the sheer physical labor of hungry men. *Les Raboteurs de Parquet* caused a scandal when it was exhibited for its display of the half-naked bodies of men at work—both their nakedness and their everyday labor were considered inappropriate subjects for painting. Ordinary laborers and the labor they perform, however, are given great dignity here, conveyed by the physical exertion of the floor scraping—backs bent, sinewy, muscular arms outstretched—and the deep, unspoken connection among the men. The unusually high horizon line of the composition and the sharply plunging perspective of the floor make work itself the central focus of the painting. This working-class camaraderie is in sharp distinction to Caillebotte's paintings of bourgeois Paris. The three men in this painting are joined by an invisible language of collective labor, depicted by minute gestures: the tilted head of the figure on the right, the rhyming arms, and single, possibly shared glass. Each of the men is engaged in a different stage of the construction of a new floor, a precinematic montage of one man in three successive poses, each task essential to the construction of the new floor. The simplicity of color and line, the absence of all but the barest decoration, highlights the labor itself as an act that paradoxically exudes stillness and serenity, with no hint of subservience.

Other tiny details hint at a possible political reading of this painting as well. The artist's choice of skilled craftsmen as a subject reminds us of the continuing importance of artisans in the age of modern factory industry. But one must also remember that artisans formed the main corps of working-class participants in every French revolution of the nineteenth-century, especially the recent Commune of 1871. The few interior details mark the building's style as Haussman's and from what we know of Caillebotte's other paintings from this period, the building probably stood in precisely the part of Paris most damaged during the bloody suppression of the Commune just a few years earlier. The reconstruction of the city and nation, the equally realistic and romantic depiction of labor, the camaraderie of the workers in the barren bourgeois flat, and the dizzying experimental perspective of the deceptively spare composition combine to offer an exquisite image of the complexity of modernity.

Realist painting was already on the wane in western Europe while it was flourishing in the Russian social–cultural context in the mid-nineteenth century. The Russian realists would employ some of the formal techniques developed by the impressionists, but their goal was the depiction of Russian reality: its unique natural beauty, its native (national) culture, and its deplorable social life.

As elsewhere in Europe, painting had been dominated by a single authoritarian Academy of Fine Arts until the 1860s when a group of artists broke with the academy to form their own "Society of Traveling Exhibitions of the Works of Russian Artists," known in English as the Wanderers. The Wanderers sponsored traveling exhibitions to take their work out of the academy and the studio directly to people. These painters depicted peasants, workers, local government officials, women of all classes, villages and towns, rivers and open roads. They tended to be liberal reformers who exposed the poverty and often the dignity or at least the humanity of the impoverished. Their work was very popular with viewers, critics, and a new class of gifted bourgeois art collectors. The greatest painters of this period all began as Wanderers.

Ilya Repin (1844–1930) painted the widest variety of subjects with great emotional power and social sensitivity. Repin captured and defined a national visual imagination in *The Barge-haulers* (1870), which shows the terrible labor of the Volga boatmen without a trace of sentimentality; his portraits of the ruling State Council depict men of dignity and power; his historical depiction of Ivan the Terrible moments after killing his son captures the tsar's terrifying violence and even more penetrating remorse, and his *Easter Procession* shows a remarkably complex cross section of images representing religious piety and the subtle brutality of state power. Valentin Serov (1865–1911), Russia's greatest portraitist, studied with Repin but combined realistic portrait painting with modern composition rather than social critique. Serov painted portraits of unusually powerful women, and almost every serious artist, writer, and composer, as well as the tsar, Nicholas II. Several accomplished painters combined realism with elements of Russian folk art or Orthodox iconography. Isaak Levitan (1860–1900), a rare Jew allowed to study at the Academy, became Russia's greatest landscape painter. Together these and other painters created a visual store of images for the construction of Russian nationalism. The Russian bourgeoisie and intelligentsia developed a sense of themselves as the cultured leaders of a humane reformism in a country endowed with great natural beauty, extraordinary strength of character, and a unique spirituality, which together could solve the problems of economic backwardness, autocratic indifference, and the legacy of serfdom.

Impressionism and realism in painting engaged in formal experimentation, playing with notions of *how* we see, while at the same time celebrating the achievements of modern bourgeois culture and the pleasures of nature, science, and social life.

Sculpture, Monument, and Architecture

An age that mastered the industrial arts so well produced memorable monumental statues, of which the most famous was *Liberty Enlightening the World* in New York Harbor, the work of the French sculptor Frédéric-Auguste Bartholdi (1834–1904), a gift from the Third French Republic to the American republic. But the statues of statesmen and warriors that came to adorn public places everywhere in the West were conventionally realistic, designed for formal display to honor the subject rather than the artist. Toward the end of the century the French sculptor August Rodin (1840–1917) began to simplify, strengthen, and, to a degree, exaggerate the contours of men and women, treating his subjects with less academic convention and more power. Inexpensive, small-scale copies of the great sculpture of antiquity and of the Renaissance also became common. Museums could all afford large plaster casts of classical works, so some exposure to the great artistic achievements of the past was now possible for a very wide general public. In particular, the middle class saw the museum and the art gallery as educational institutions.

In architecture, structural steel freed construction from the restrictions that had limited Gothic builders. Structures could now go almost as high as architects pleased. Thus the first "skyscrapers" were put up in Chicago in the 1880s. The general tendency imposed by the materials was toward simplicity of line. This taste for simplicity began to spread, and by the twentieth century the way was open for modern "functional" architecture. Often the architect was also an engineer, and perhaps the finest and most aesthetic structures of the industrial societies were the great railway bridges, the complex Brooklyn Bridge begun in 1869 by John Roebling (1806–1869) and not completed until 1883, and the massive work of Gustave Eiffel (1832–1923) in France.

Photography

It makes sense to end a survey of mid-nineteenth-century arts with photography because photography is the emblematic art form of the nineteenth century. Technological developments made it possible, and it combines artistic vision with technical prowess. The mechanical nature and apparent fidelity of the camera's record of reality was seen at the time as ultrascientific. When Louis J. M. Daguerre (1789–1851) exhibited his "daguerreotypes" for the first time in 1839, people marveled at the level of detail they captured. Though some art critics dismissed photography as too automatic to be art, it was also praised as a shortcut to realistic depiction. Nothing could be more realistic, or so it seemed, than a photograph, which automatically recorded reality, almost without intervention of the photographer. As such, photography embodied human progress in art and science. The nineteenth-century faith in science produced a machine that could render the authenticity of real modern life, artfully and perfectly. But that fidelity to reality was an illusion. And as soon as people began to make photographs and praise their realism, others began to notice that the very perfection of the photographic image was framed and cropped by the photographer, removed from a larger context that might complicate its meanings. Everyone who looked at a photograph saw something different in it. Some of Daumier's lithographs from 1840, merely one year after Daguerre's sensational exhibit of photographs, caricatured the illusion of photographic realism by depicting nearly empty frames with figures departing the pictorial space: in one, *Ascencion de Jésus-Christ*, Christ's feet are all we see of his resurrection. The photograph, it turns out, was real in only a very limited sense: a fragment of reality, shaped by the hand of the photographer and the eye of the viewer. Photography became a metaphor for both faith in realistic depiction and doubt about the very idea faithful representation.

* * *

Science, industry, and art at midcentury all revealed great problems in European society and yet expressed confidence that human beings could understand and improve the world or at the very least coexist peacefully in it. Communications created "imagined communities" of class, gender, and nation, and artists sought to depict the universal in their own particular communities. Invention, massive production, and prosperity, together with liberal reforms and improvements, all made the industrial middle classes proud and self-confident. Literacy was spreading, and novels helped everyone in literate society find themselves by exploring change, behavior, feelings, and events. Music and art sponsorship allowed people to feel that they were improving society while entertaining and enlightening themselves. Cultural consumption of literature, painting, music, and newspapers gave to many a sense of their place in the world and a connection with people of their own class and nation.

One major ingredient in the midcentury economy and culture has been missing from this discussion. The money for industrialization, as well as the markets, and raw materials for its products increasingly came from outside Europe. At the same time that Europeans were reaching new heights of scientific invention, cultural imagination, and economic prosperity, they were living in and imagining themselves as a part of, an international world, a world of European imperialism, which they dominated.

NINE

The Age of Imperialism, 1870–1914

In the late nineteenth century, European nation-states decided to complete the conquest of the world—politically, economically, and culturally. European imperialism was not a new phenomenon, but it took new forms at the end of the nineteenth century. Imperialist policy was a central, if problematic, feature of state policy and Great Power relations. Conscious decisions on the part of businessmen, statesmen, engineers, and missionaries shaped nineteenth-century imperialism, and conquest was greeted with great enthusiasm in the popular press and popular culture in most European countries. Colonial domination took on a new intensity: more land came under European dominion, by more advanced armed force, and with more brutality and more publicity than in earlier eras. Eleven percent of Africa was under European domination in 1875. By 1902 that portion had grown to 90 percent. Some 70 percent of the land surface of the planet was under the control of Europe and the United States by 1914. Great Britain alone ruled over one-fourth of the land and one-third of the world's population. The effects of European imperialism were profound, complicated, and long lasting, continuing to the present. Imperialism at the end of the nineteenth century changed the ways Europeans thought of themselves and their nations as modern.

Imperialism in this period entailed the use of military strength and industrial technology to impose control over the territory, resources, and population of large regions of Africa and Asia. Europeans had, of course, explored, charted, profited from, and dominated peoples in other parts of the globe for centuries. What some historians have called the "new imperialism" differed from earlier eras of expansion and colonization in that it did not involve settling large numbers of Europeans in the lands under control and it usually occurred without direct annexation. More often European powers trained local leaders to carry out European directives in political organization and economic extraction. Commonly, "informal imperialism" took the form of one-sided trade agreements or the exchange of advanced technology for control of the profits issuing from that technology. Informal imperialism was often negotiated with a threat or show of military force. The hallmarks of this period of imperialism were first, an extreme inequality between the power of the European "metropole" and the non-European colony, and second, the marked subordination of the indigenous people to the European economic and political administrators who supervised their lives.

In some parts of Europe the early nineteenth century had seen something of an imperial retreat. Spain and Portugal lost their colonies in the New World, as one after another won its independence (following in part from Spanish and Portuguese humiliation at the hands of Napoleon). The Dutch lost their edge for the same reason; then London replaced Amsterdam as the financial center of Europe. Even the British lost important colonies in the New World, when the United States broke free. But Britain rebounded from this loss to acquire new territories and advantageous trade agreements throughout the century and around the world, including Burma, Hong Kong, Lagos, Borneo, and Ceylon. Modern French and Russian imperialism began early in the nineteenth century as well. But the process of European domination accelerated beyond all previous experience after 1870. Europeans forced their way into the Chinese and Japanese markets and cultures (and Japan embarked on its own imperial adventure), and Britain tightened its hold on India. Russia finally secured its grip on the northern Caucasus and drove further into Central Asia. Europeans spread through massive waves of migration into North America and across the northern American continent. And seven small European states divided up the African continent as if it were an empty lot.

Imperialism in this period is intimately linked with the other major historical developments of nineteenth-century European history: industrialization, liberal politics and economics, democratic revolutions, technological advance, racism, and mass nationalism. The process of extending European power around the globe made major contributions to nineteenth-century ideas about social welfare, human culture, the nature of civilization, and modernity itself. But imperialism was not only a story of European power over other peoples. Domination certainly transformed the places that Europeans colonized, but the practice of colonization and contact with indigenous cultures transformed European culture and political culture at least as profoundly. Categories of race, state, religion, democracy, civilization, and modernity were contested concepts when they sailed out of European ports, and they were continually redefined in the course of contact with indigenous cultures and the experience of conquest, foreign rule, and indigenous resistance.

Motives

The reasons for this extraordinary expansion and domination are complicated. No single cause explains the frenzy of acquisition in the late nineteenth century. Everywhere one looks, similar sets of circumstances cohere in different patterns (not unlike the results of efforts to explain the origins of industrialism or the rise of the nation-state). But the main difficulty with explaining imperialism during this period is that each of the individual causes was and looked different at the time than in historical retrospect. Self-delusion was a large part of the imperial age.

Money

The earliest explanations for the acceleration of European imperialism at the end of the nineteenth century come from the age of imperialism itself. J. A. Hobson (1858–1904), a reformer and social critic, and Vladimir Lenin (1870–1924), the Russian revolutionary leader, wrote influential works, each with an emphasis on economics. Hobson's *Imperialism: A Study* (1902) argued that Europeans had exhausted their own demand for goods and warned that unless new markets for European products and investment could be found, profits would be kept low at home. Governments were forced to seek new colonies as an outlet for their surpluses. In *Imperialism: The Highest Stage of Capitalism* (1917) Lenin agreed with Hobson that European nations sought new colonies for their potential markets, but he viewed expansion as a sign of a systemic crisis in capitalism. The only way to increase markets at home was to pay workers more so that they could consume more; but that would lower profits. Capitalists thus were forced to seek out new markets to make high profits and keep workers from developing class and revolutionary consciousness. Only the overthrow of capitalism would halt this vicious cycle. In fact, according to Lenin, competition among the Great Powers in overseas expansion disrupted the balance of power in Europe and led directly to world war.

In part, Lenin and Hobson emphasized economics because they correctly observed businessmen to be among the first Europeans to expand overseas, and to call for support from their governments. The British East India Company administered large sections of India before the British government asserted direct rule. In the 1860s Prussian businessmen began lobbying their government to buy seaports in Africa and settle them with German colonists. They pressed harder after German unification and after the Treaty of Berlin had begun to establish German prestige. Through imperialism, one nationalist lawyer and explorer wrote, "a country exhibits before the world its strength and weakness as a nation." But business alone was not enough. Before the end of the century most statesmen considered colonies unacceptably difficult to administer hence more expensive than they were worth.

Power

Political imperatives gathered force through a process of competition. Once one power began to acquire new colonies, the least powerful countries saw the need to acquire colonies of their own to remain competitive. In 1870–1871 the French government was so uninterested in its small colonies in Africa that they offered them all to Bismarck in the hope that Germany would return Alsace-Lorraine. Bismarck was even less interested. African colonization was unnecessary at that time, he said, adding tactlessly "it would be just like the silken sables of Polish noble families who have no shirts." But competition is addictive. In France, the great economic historian Anatole Leroy-Beaulieu argued that "colonization is for France a question of life and death; either France will become a great African power or in a century or two she will be no more than a secondary European power." In England, Liberal leader Gladstone hesitated, and in Germany Bismarck hesitated, but the Conservative Disraeli and French prime minister Jules Ferry did not. In the early 1880s, Ferry countered his parliament's doubts with all the arguments made by the businessmen and nationalists: France as an industrial nation needs new markets; if Frenchmen did not colonize Africa, France would drop "from the first rank to the third or fourth." By the mid-1880s even Bismarck had changed his tune and was arguing to his Reichstag that the German economy needed colonies and that imperialism would provide "a new field for German activity, civilization, and capital."

The European state system had been molded at the Congress of Vienna around the concept of a balance of power. While this balance of power rested largely within Europe until the mid-nineteenth century, after 1870 the growing importance of overseas trade appeared to shift the balance toward nations with colonial possessions. International competition magnified the rationale and increased the pace of conquest.

Security

A related motive for the acquisition of territory was strategic. Islands, river mouths, and peninsulas that dominated trade routes and where forts might be built were coveted because they could protect economic and political positions. Often colonies were little more than adjuncts to some larger area of an empire; for example, after the completion of the Suez Canal in 1869, Britain took Perim, Aden, and Socotra solely to protect the new route to India. Strategic considerations were transformed by new technologies—the telegraph, the steamship, and the airplane. Even so, an area was of strategic importance only in relation to the prevailing economic and political theories of the powers, and thus the strategic motive may largely be subsumed under the other explanations. This was especially true in the acquisition by Britain, France, Germany, and Italy of territories in East Africa after 1880. Britain wished to maintain control of Egypt, although without formal annexation; conquest of the Nile to its headwaters seemed a strategic necessity. To stabilize the Nile holdings, the highlands and parts of Kenya were therefore taken by Britain, while Germany acquired the vast land from Lake Tanganyika to the coast.

As strategic needs changed, the tenacity with which a nation held to an area might also have been expected to change and to some extent such changes did occur. Yet imperialism was not a wholly rational system of world organization, so for the most part empires continued to grow in defiance of economic wisdom and strategic planning.

Ideology

A number of ideologies were enlisted to stimulate and shape imperial acquisition and rule: nationalism, racism, religion, the "civilizing mission." Two underlying intellectual projects unite these diverse ways of explaining and justifying imperialism: all attempt to construct and explain *difference* between people, and all attempt to construct and justify *hierarchies* of those different peoples.

Though on the surface, imperial justifications seem to be based on a simple idea about the difference between Europe and its colonies—civilization and barbarism—examination of any particular case quickly shows that this simple dichotomy was repeatedly enlisted to cloak anxieties about the difficulties in making such distinctions. Europeans were relatively certain that their world was more civilized than the colonial world, but even in Europe there were enough signs of barbarism to cast grave doubts on that distinction. Slums, illiteracy, state and popular violence, differences between modern urban bourgeois life and rural peasant life created underlying anxiety about the state of European civilization that blurred the distinction Europeans wanted to make between themselves and the "savages" of Africa and Asia.

Other normative boundaries and categories were being challenged in European society. The ideology of the separate spheres was being tested, and previously accepted gender roles were changing, becoming more muddy by the day. The increasing presence of women in the public sphere, anxieties about masculinity in a bourgeois industrial society that required little physical exertion, a fear that physical degeneration was a by-product of modernity—all produced unarticulated fears about declining masculinity and threatening, too-powerful women. Secularization in European thought, dilution of religious observance, and uneasiness about the assimilation of Jews and other religious minorities blurred religious boundaries as well. Progress itself was increasingly dubious in the late nineteenth century, as hopes for a more harmonious and prosperous society were dashed on the rocks of continued poverty and increasing discontent. Nationalism, which began as a search for unique and special cultural characteristics of a people, had produced competition with and exclusion of outsiders alongside celebration of the nation.

Imperialism seemed to be an antidote to some of these uncertainties. Conquest was a masculine activity and was repeatedly represented as such: as one professor at the University of Berlin lectured his students: "Every virile people has established colonial power." Optimists saw imperialism as an instrument for erasing all differences, boundaries, and categories, and unifying all the peoples of the world under the banner of one culture: "The authority of the British Crown," said Earl Grey in 1853, "is at this moment . . . diffusing amongst millions of the human race the blessings of Christianity and civilization." Educated Russians believed that "raising the cultural and intellectual level" of Russian peasants and of the people in their colonies would create a harmonious, civilized society in the image of the intelligentsia.

The civilizing project of imperialism, with its attempt to create clear-cut gender, cultural, and racial hierarchies, was in part an attempt to clarify the distinctions people wanted to feel between Europeans, Asians, and Africans, as among Europeans.

The problems with such racial, gender, and cultural dichotomies is that they did not hold any better in Africa and Asia than they did at home. British colonial agents in Lagos, Nigeria, complained to their superiors that while they sympathized with official desires to introduce the "law and order of civilized life," they expected that the results would be superficial compliance and enduring hostility toward the same elements of civilization. There would be no simple path from indigenous culture to civilization, no linear route to enlightenment. The French in West Africa and the Sudan realized that to bring European civilization to Africans they would have to wipe out an existing culture: not only slavery and violent customary laws but local languages and entrenched political institutions. European norms of masculinity proved to be even less simple when transplanted to the colonies, where colonial administrators faced resistance to their authority as robust in its own ways as peasant and labor unrest at home. And sex complicated everything. European men saw imperialism as an opportunity to experience intimacy with foreign "exoticism" through sexual liaisons with indigenous women, but these relationships were usually hidden, winked at, or forbidden outright by both laws and conventions against "going native."

Encounters with such new ambiguities produced a vicious cycle. Challenges to ideal categories created desire for new clearer dichotomies and hierarchies, while colonial administrators tried to cope with the real complexities of rule: administration, economic organization, passive and violent resistance. In some places, complexity would be resolved with force: new technologies of suppression in the form of machine guns, new laws, and sanctions against intermarriage. In other cases, the ideologies became more rigid. The popular press in Europe trumpeted imperial ventures with increasing stridency. People sought to impose even sharper distinctions between races, genders, classes, religions, and nations. Mass nationalism and racism escalated at home in Europe as a result.

And overarching all these issues stood the question of what it meant to be a European. As Ann Stoler writes, "What did it mean to be 'European' for colonials who had never set foot in the Netherlands, England or France? How could children identify with a Dutch homeland when many spoke Dutch less often and with less ease than they spoke Malay or Javanese? How fixed was the notion of being 'European' if a Dutch woman who chose to marry a native man could lose her Dutch citizenry rights because of that desire?" In an era of increasingly rigorous efforts to define nationality as the basis for creating modern nation-states, the imperial project challenged such notions as often as it clarified them.

British Rule in India

Great Britain was the premier imperial power. Long before the "new imperialism" of the late nineteenth century, the British had established informal and settled colonies with integral ties to Britain's society and economy. The advantage of early industrial and technological innovation, followed by strong financial resources, allowed Britain to occupy imperial outposts on every continent and in every sea by 1914. The colonies settled by Britons were originally rather thinly inhabited lands, but the settlers displaced resident populations. Though the settlers saw themselves as "civilized" and the indigenous population as "savages," these were relative terms. Scholars disagree over the size of the native population of the Americas; earlier estimates that suggested 1 million have been scaled upward to 10 million to 12 million north of the Rio Grande and 80 million to 100 million south of that line. There is general agreement that the effects of "the Columbian exchange"—the importation of Europe's diseases, firearms, and disruptive practices in exchange for the New World's diseases, foods, and land—reduced the aboriginal population of the New World by 90 percent within a century of European contact, primarily under Spanish and Portuguese rule.

In Tasmania, a large island to the south of the Australian mainland, the aborigines were totally wiped out. In Australia, they came close to meeting the same fate. On the north island of New Zealand, the Maoris fought guerrilla wars in the 1840s and 1860s in a vain attempt to exclude white settlers from their lands; their numbers shrank from 250,000 to 40,000 during the nineteenth century. By 1815 the British recognized that colonies occupied largely by settlers from the British Isles would most likely move toward independence, and therefore they sought to control the pace and nature of this movement in order to assure continued loyalty to the concept of Greater Britain.

India was the richest of Britain's overseas possessions, the center and symbol of empire, the "Jewel in the Crown." In 1763 India was not a single nation but a vast collection of identities and religions. As the nineteenth century began, two main methods of British imperial control were in effect: indirect rule and direct annexation which developed as the British coped with changing economic, social, and political conditions. In the early nineteenth century, the British East India Company, an independent organization with close ties to the British government, was the de facto colonial administrator. The company had the right to collect taxes from Indian peasants and use its own military to enforce those and other rights over the local population. In its heyday, the East India Company had taken over enormous territories and made treaties like a sovereign power. There was no clear line here between economic and political authority, but the company developed a number of ways to assert its power in different contexts. Some areas it governed directly, in others it co-opted local elites, and in others it controlled the economy with trade monopolies granted by the government back in London.

Even where the East India Company enlisted local elites with offers of military or civil service posts and economic advantages, however, its rule was repressive and deeply resented. In 1857 the company's army of native recruits rebelled. The Indian soldiers, known as sepoys, had come to hate the British customs being imposed on them, to the destruction of their own ways. "The Mutiny," as the British called it, spread beyond the sepoys to become what Indian historians call a "war of liberation." Indian peasants attacked

European Imperialism in Asia and the Pacific

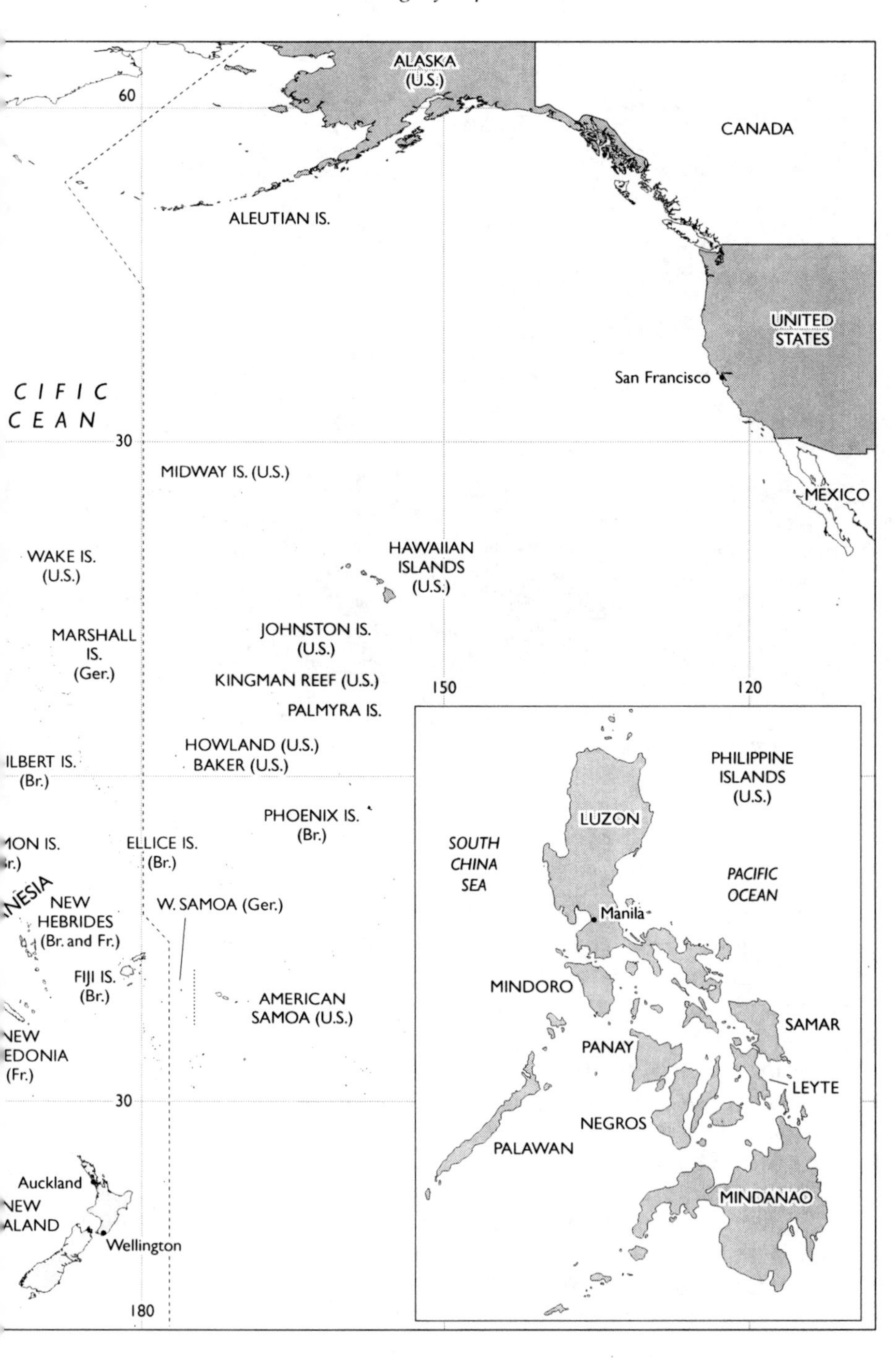
ALASKA (U.S.)
CANADA
ALEUTIAN IS.
UNITED STATES
San Francisco
CIFIC
CEAN
MIDWAY IS. (U.S.)
MEXICO
WAKE IS. (U.S.)
HAWAIIAN ISLANDS (U.S.)
MARSHALL IS. (Ger.)
JOHNSTON IS. (U.S.)
KINGMAN REEF (U.S.)
PALMYRA IS.
HOWLAND (U.S.)
BAKER (U.S.)
ILBERT IS. (Br.)
PHOENIX IS. (Br.)
ION IS.
ELLICE IS. (Br.)
NESIA
NEW HEBRIDES (Br. and Fr.)
W. SAMOA (Ger.)
FIJI IS. (Br.)
AMERICAN SAMOA (U.S.)
NEW
EDONIA (Fr.)
Auckland
NEW
ALAND
Wellington
PHILIPPINE ISLANDS (U.S.)
LUZON
SOUTH CHINA SEA
PACIFIC OCEAN
Manila
MINDORO
SAMAR
PANAY
LEYTE
NEGROS
PALAWAN
MINDANAO

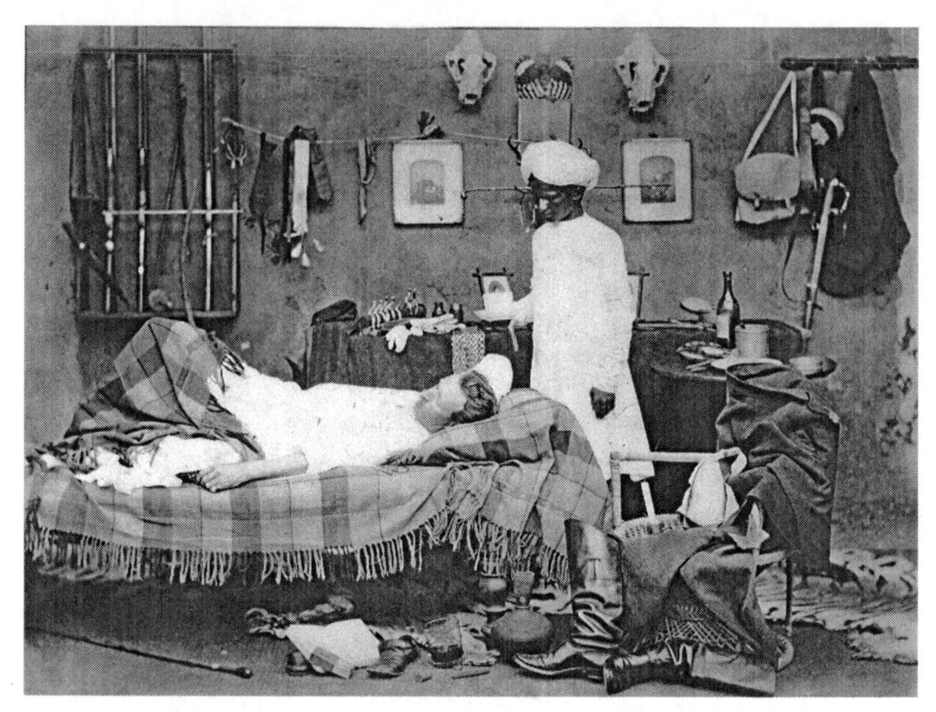

"Englishman Being Served Coffee in Bed," 1870. This photograph shows all the accoutrements of empire at its most informal. (British Library)

law courts protesting corruption and economic subjugation that left them in debt. In some regions rebels defended local leaders who had been displaced by the British. Indian army officers resented the way they were treated by the British. Hindu and Muslim leaders denounced British Christian missionaries for undermining native beliefs and practices. Cruel violence occurred on both sides during a year of fighting. The Sepoy Rebellion was put down, but not before massacres of Europeans had occurred, followed by harsh military reprisals by the British, which ended in brutally cruel punishment and the execution of some of the rebels.

The mutiny spelled the end of the East India Company. In 1858 the British Crown took over the company's lands and obligations. The richest and most densely populated regions, centering on the cities of Calcutta, Madras, Bombay and on the Punjab, were maintained under direct British rule. Direct rule still did not mean massive emigration and settlement. The British sought to improve their system of elevating indigenous leaders from the Indian upper classes. The British "civilizing mission" to India also shifted. Missionary activity was discouraged in favor of the secular benefits of railroads, irrigation, and economic development. Territories not under direct rule, the so-called feudal or native states, were left nominally under the rule of their own princes, who might be fabulously rich sultans, as in Hyderabad, or merely local leaders. The "native" states were governed through a system of British resident advisers, but the India Office in London never hesitated to interfere. One consequence of this institutionalized meddling, perhaps unintended, was to allow Britain to "divide and rule" the diverse continent.

In the 1880s the British extended their rule in India. French expansion into neighboring Southeast Asia and Russian expansion near India's northern borders motivated British consolidation. The viceroy of India from 1899 to 1905, George Nathaniel Curzon (1859–1925), was deeply committed to maintaining the centrality of India to British power and self-image. Curzon's accomplishments prior to sailing for India included authorship of books on the strategic necessity of maintaining a strong British presence in India to counter French and Russian aims in the region. His outlook once in India, however, was distinctly economic—access to trade and industrial development, not superior military force, would provide power in the future. Curzon's administrative and economic reforms were extensive. He contributed significantly to both the modernization of the Indian economy and the modern intervention of British government in every realm of public life. This contradiction is at the heart of the imperial enterprise. Curzon did not believe that Indians were advanced enough to take full responsibility for their own development; rather, he thought the British could improve India more efficiently. And indeed, his reforms brought enough improvements to convince some contemporaries and historians that British rule in India was largely beneficial.

Material growth under British rule is readily measurable. In 1864 the population of India was about 136 million; in 1904 it was close to 300 million. Although the latter figure includes additional territories in Burma and elsewhere, it is clear that nineteenth-century India experienced a significant increase in total population. In 1901 one male in ten could read and write—a high rate of literacy for the time in Asia; only one in 150 women could read and write. On the eve of World War I, India had thousands of miles of railroads and telegraph lines, as well as universities (where classes were conducted in English), hospitals, factories, and busy seaports. Statistics show a native ruling class sometimes fantastically rich, and an immense peasant class for the most part living at subsistence level. A middle class was just beginning to form, and it had proportionately far more aspirants to white-collar posts in law, medicine, and other liberal professions than to posts in international trade, engineering, and industry.

The total wealth of India increased under British rule and was spread more widely among the Indian populations in 1914 than it had been in 1763. Proportionately more wealth was invested in India than was going into the pockets of British agents. Anglo-Indian economic relations typically took the form of trade between a developed industrial and financial society (Britain) and a society geared to the production of raw materials (India). Indians took an increasing part in this trade, and toward the end of the century local industries, notably textile manufacturing, began to reappear in India.

These benefits pale in comparison with the costs. India's consumer market provided Britain with its largest export market on the eve of World War I. In other words, Indian trade was dominated by British manufactured goods, hindering the development of local manufacturing. Ten percent of the trade of the whole British Empire passed through Indian port cities. India provided human resources in the form of cheap labor to British industrialists as workers on tea plantations, and as railroad and construction workers in Egypt and southern Africa, increasing British profits and keeping wages low. More than a million indentured servants left India to work elsewhere in the British Empire, and the British army used Indian soldiers to maintain order in other imperial outposts (they sent Irish and Scots troops to do some of the most brutal fighting to put down the Sepoy Rebellion). While the British created institutions of higher learning and job opportunities for a small Indian elite, the vast majority of Indians were peasants living in terrible poverty, improved not at all by sectors of modern development.

The contradictions of imperialism and the possibility of delayed benefits that reveal themselves only over time make evaluating British impact on India difficult. The first generation of Indian nationalists believed that the consequences of British rule were negative. They argued that imperialism crushed the precolonial economy and then drained whatever new wealth was created into British coffers. Both these accusations are difficult to prove, but the ideas influenced Indian public opinion. It is more certain that British authorities were never sufficiently committed to raising the standard of living for all India to make investments or improvements substantial enough to produce the industrial momentum necessary to stimulate growth from within. The British in India were always more concerned with security and control than with development. These priorities allowed the elevation of a tiny elite able to serve British interests, but displaced local mechanisms of economic stimulation that might have spread the benefits of modern industry more widely.

Imperialism in East Asia

Formal and informal imperialism in East Asia also predates the "new imperialism." European powers strengthened their hold on older colonies and acquired new ones in Southeast Asia: the mainland areas of Burma, Indochina, and the Malay states, and the island groups of Melanesia and Polynesia. The Chinese Empire was never subjected to actual partition and direct annexation. However, China was not sufficiently united politically or advanced industrially to resist European penetration. One of the Chinese leadership's tactics for maintaining domestic stability was to limit and regulate trade with foreigners. The Chinese considered European culture to be inferior to their own so remained isolated by choice. Trading was limited to one city, Canton (Guangzhou). Europeans had a hard time breaking into the Chinese market because they had very little that the Chinese wanted, but in the early nineteenth century, the British were determined to find a way. The British forced their way into China with the use of drugs and violent compulsion that would seem to contradict the basic tenets of the civilized order they celebrated at home.

British anger over the Chinese treatment of the few British subjects living in China and British hunger for economic expansion set the scene for confrontation. The spark would be opium. Opium poppies grew in India, where the drug was also then processed and distributed to markets around the world. Chinese demand for opium was growing in the early nineteenth century, and the British had control of Indian opium production and trade. The Chinese government, alarmed at the spread of the drug into China through Canton, cracked down. In 1839 the Chinese seemed to be on the point of eradicating opium imports when the British decided to use military force. In 1839–1842, in the first of the so-called Opium Wars, Chinese defense forces were no match for British steamships. In 1842 the humiliating Treaty of Nanking forced the Chinese to open up five more cities to British trade and foreign residents and gave Britain Hong Kong "in perpetuity." The French followed soon after, and by the end of the century China was subjected to a de facto partition among Britain, France, Germany, and Russia. Each power operated from certain treaty ports and exercised some control over considerable areas or spheres of influence, as they were called.

French, German, and Russian interests claimed the right to build railroads using cheap Chinese labor and to police communities of Europeans living in Chinese cities. Rivalry among the European powers and the United States, which favored an "Open Door" policy of permitting as much free trade in China as was possible and of preserving Chinese sovereignty, served to counterbalance Chinese weakness and left China an independent nation. But the Chinese experienced the Open Door as a humiliating invasion by people they considered barbarians. The European incursion was a very sudden reversal of roles, which stunned and demoralized the Chinese, helping to undermine the Qing dynasty and leaving a bitter legacy.

In rural China, European missionaries continued to inflame antiforeign feeling. In 1898 the Chinese government began secretly training a militia made up of impoverished young men, ostensibly to fight banditry, but in fact to go up against the "foreign devils." Organized in secret societies, the Fists of Righteous Harmony, better known as the Boxers for their martial arts prowess, began attacking European railway lines and trading posts, killing missionaries and burning down missions. In 1900 in Beijing, the Boxers overran the small garrison protecting the European settlement, but the several thousand foreigners withstood the siege until European troops arrived. Eighteen thousand troops from Britain, France, the United States, Italy, Japan, and Russia (the Germans arrived too late) rescued the European settlement in Beijing and brutally put down the rebellion. Afterward China was forced to accept even greater foreign intrusion.

Japan was also invaded by Western powers in the middle of the nineteenth century, but the smaller Asian empire responded differently to the humiliating challenge. There was a party within Japan that was open to negotiating with the foreigners, in this case the United States, which helped Japan preserve some prerogatives. Whereas Hong Kong was wrested from China, Japan never had to cede territory, and the Japanese were not forced to tolerate Christianity. Japan was a less tempting morsel for Europeans, so it was less integrated into the world imperialist economy in the nineteenth century. Still the treaties of the 1850s with U.S. and European powers were not popular and led to the downfall of the Tokugawa government in 1868–1869. The new rulers realized that they could not withstand both foreign imperialist incursions and popular antiforeign demonstrations unless they had military power to back them. So, very much as Russia had done after the devastating loss in the Crimean War, Japan embarked on a series of social and economic reforms intended to make the country militarily and economically competitive with the Great Powers of Europe. By the 1890s, Japan had a modern army and navy, and Japanese steamships played a major role in East Asian trade. In 1894–1895 Japan defeated China in a conflict over Korea, adding Korea and Formosa (Taiwan) to the Japanese sphere of influence and embarking on its own imperialist campaign. In the same year Japan was able to force the British to give up their unequal trade clauses, freeing Japan to trade on equal terms with the European powers by 1899. Then in 1904–1905 the world was stunned by Japan's victory over a seemingly formidable Russia. The Russo-Japanese War allowed Japan to tighten its grip on Manchuria and Korea. The western Europeans saw Japan's rise as a counterbalance to Russia's power in the East and to Germany's growing naval threat. Britain signed an alliance with Japan in 1902, as a result of which Japan fought against Germany in World War I.

The Partition of Africa

Between about 1876 and 1894 all of Africa was divided among seven European powers. Two small exceptions were Abyssinia in present-day Ethiopia, which Italy failed to subdue, and Liberia, a state established on the continent's west coast by freed slaves from the United States. Otherwise, during this period, the European states carved up the continent without regard for the more than 700 existing indigenous societies, their distinctive political structures, or ancient cultural histories. Africa was divided by Europeans according to their own priorities and according to conflicts among themselves. As a result, the "nations" that were created were highly artificial.

Before the 1870s, Europeans were not very interested in Africa and lacked the technology to get far beyond its port cities. Only a few ports were required to take care of the European slave trade and provide fueling stops for European trading ships. At first, when the technology finally began to make it possible to move beyond the coastline into the interior of the continent, only missionaries and explorers from Europe cared about Africa. In the

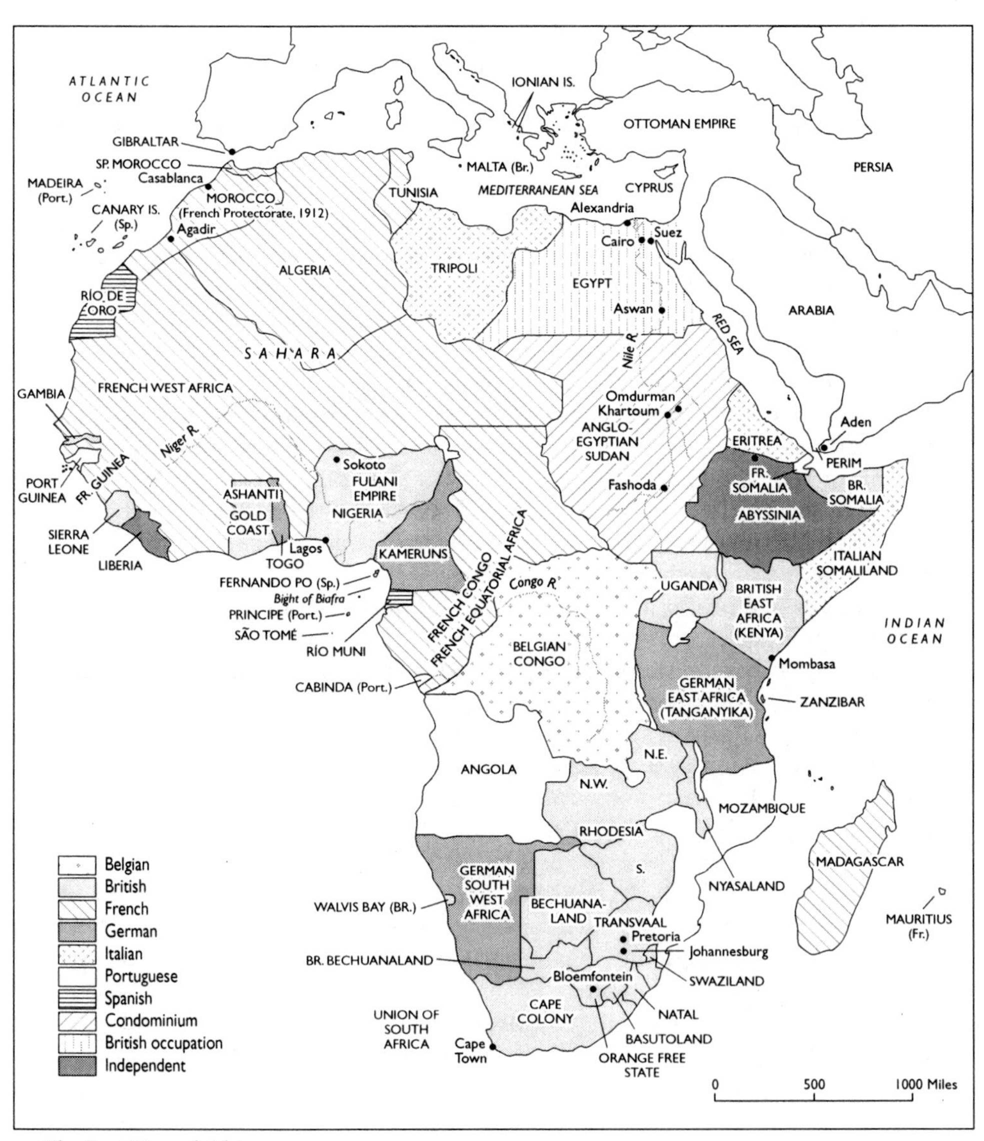

The Partition of Africa

mid-nineteenth century missionaries intending to convert the indigenous people to Christianity were the forerunners of European political expansion. They represented a cultural advance guard. Missionaries believed that they were bringing civilization, of which Christianity was only one part, to "the heathen." But they also wanted to teach European working skills and impose a work ethic designed for industrial nations. The cultivation of plantations and markets was considered essential to the making of a modern people. "Christianity, commerce, and civilization" was a slogan of missionary pioneers and the capitalist entrepreneurs who followed them. Missionaries brought European values and customs, but they did not intend to bring political imperialism.

Scientific exploration was also a popular pastime for adventurous Europeans. Darwin had made such expeditions seem possible and exciting, and Africa offered an open field to ethnographers, cartographers, and natural scientists. In 1861 the French-American zoologist Du Chaillu reported his discovery of the gorilla. Later, he published studies about a society of pygmies and other discoveries. Similar expeditions took place in Siberia and Central Asia, India, and elsewhere in Africa. They were reported widely in popular newspapers in Europe, fueling the mass nationalism that would celebrate imperial conquest.

A single catalyst initiated the competitive frenzy that partitioned Africa: the ruthless greed of Leopold II, King of the Belgians. In 1876 Leopold read that the Congo Basin was "a country of unspeakable richness." Frustrated with his small kingdom in Europe, Leopold, acting as a private investor, established the International African Association in 1876, with the purported goals of suppressing the illegal slave trade and gathering scientific information. He hired Henry Morton Stanley (1841–1904) to negotiate Leopold's rights in the region of the Congo. Stanley, already famous as an explorer and adventurer, had previously been hired by the *New York Herald* to find the Scot explorer David Livingstone. His reports of this adventure and other explorations became popular books.

Between 1879 and 1884 Stanley negotiated with local leaders and established river landings and trading stations on the Congo under the auspices of the association, while Leopold lobbied European rulers for sole access to Congo's riches. The British, Germans, French, and Portuguese feared this expansion and eventually called a meeting in Berlin to settle the issue. The European statesmen created the Congo Free State with Leopold as its head and made the Congo Basin a free trade zone, opening the way for destructive exploitation. This meeting was also important because it set down the ground rules for African partition. Henceforth, a European imperial power would have to establish its intention to provide for the welfare of the local population before claiming territory and planting a flag.

Though many Europeans went to Africa and Asia with a mission to bring civilization to backward peoples, Leopold went to get rich. His rule in the Congo is notorious for the horrific conditions he created there. African slave laborers worked under pervasive threat of violence, under the watch of guards with guns, their wives taken hostage to force the men to maximize the harvest of rubber. The Africans worked without sufficient food, clothing, or shelter. Starvation was common; disease and overwork alone killed millions of Congolese workers. Mutilation was the punishment for minor offenses. European administrators who complained or criticized were blackmailed and silenced; many found escape routes blocked if they tried to leave before their contracts expired. Rumors of atrocities that reached Europe were hushed up, while Leopold claimed that he had eliminated slavery and was "civilizing" the Congo. Only in 1908 after dozens of authenticated reports of atrocities, including Joseph Conrad's novel *Heart of Darkness* (1902), was Congo taken over by the Belgian government and an attempt made to curb the brutality.

The promise of wealth in Congo combined with accumulated lobbying during the 1860s and 1870s brought politics, business, and nationalist ideas together to pressure other European powers to establish colonies in Africa before all the territory was taken.

France acquired new territories in west Africa and attempted to shore up its control of French settlements in Algeria and along the Mediterranean coast. During the nineteenth century France acquired a colonial empire second in area only to that of the British. Despite frequent revolutionary changes in government, France maintained an imperialist policy that added some 50 million people and close to 3.5 million square miles to the lands under the French flag. This empire was concentrated in North, West, and Equatorial Africa, and Indochina.

Little of this colonial empire was thought suitable for settlement by Europeans, especially since a third of it was taken up by the Sahara Desert. A major exception was French North Africa: Tunisia, Algeria, and Morocco. These lands, with a typically Mediterranean climate, were inhabited chiefly by Muslim Berbers and Arabs. Though the total indigenous population increased greatly under French rule, more than a million European colonists moved in. Mostly French, but including sizable groups of Italians and Spaniards, these *colons* took land from the indigenous people. Though they added to the total arable acreage by initiating irrigation projects and other improvements, they were hated by the native population.

The French spent forty years "pacifying" the hinterland of Algiers in the face of stubborn local resistance. Undaunted, the French added protectorates over Tunisia to the east (1881) and over Morocco to the west (1912). In 1904 Britain gave the French a free hand in Morocco as compensation for their exclusion from Egypt. In Algeria and Tunisia the French hoped to assimilate Africans into French civilization. They hoped to create an empire of "one hundred million Frenchmen," more than half of them overseas, and to draw on abundant local manpower to fill up the ranks of the republic's armies.

In the main, assimilation proved difficult and was only partly achieved. Militarily, the policy worked out pretty much as the French had hoped; black troops from Senegal and *goums* (Moroccan cavalry serving under French or Algerian Muslim officers) gained a reputation as tough fighters. The French

A Closer Look

EUROPEANS IN AFRICA: JOSEPH CONRAD AND HENRY MORGAN STANLEY

Two accounts of a voyage up the Congo River. One by a foe of imperialism, the other by one of its leading practitioners. What do they share? How do they differ?

Joseph Conrad, *Heart of Darkness* (1902)

I watched the coast. Watching a coast as it slips by the ship is like thinking about an enigma. There it is before you—smiling, frowning, inviting, grand, mean, insipid, or savage, and always mute with an air of whispering, Come and find out. This one was almost featureless, as if still in the making, with an aspect of monotonous grimness. The edge of a colossal jungle, so dark-green as to be almost black, fringed with white surf, ran straight, like a ruled line, far, far away along a blue sea whose glitter was blurred by a creeping mist. The sun was fierce, the land seemed to glisten and drip with steam. . . . The voice of the surf heard now and then was a positive pleasure, like the speech of a brother. It was something natural, that had its reason, that had a meaning. Now and then a boat from the shore gave one a momentary contact with reality. It was paddled by black fellows. You could see from afar the white of their eyeballs glistening. They shouted, sang; their bodies streamed with perspiration; they had faces like grotesque masks—these chaps; but they had bone, muscle, a wild vitality, an intense energy of movement, that was as natural and true as the surf along their coast. They wanted no excuse for being there. They were a great comfort to look at. For a time I would feel I belonged still to a world of straightforward facts; but the feeling would not last long. . . .

Going up that river was like traveling back to the earliest beginnings of the world, when vegetation rioted on earth and the big trees were kings. An empty stream, a great silence, an impenetrable forest. The air was warm, thick, heavy, sluggish. There was no joy in the brilliance of the sunshine. . . . We penetrated deeper and deeper into the heart of darkness. It was very quiet there. At night sometimes the roll of drums behind the curtain of trees would run up the river and remain sustained faintly, as if hovering in the air high over our heads. . . . Whether it meant war, peace, or prayer we could not tell. . . .

The earth seemed unearthly. We are accustomed to look upon the shackled form of a conquered monster, but there—there you could look at a thing monstrous and free. It was unearthly and the men were—No, they were not inhuman. Well, you know that was the worst of it—this suspicion of their not being inhuman. It would come slowly to one. They howled and leaped, and spun and made horrid faces; but what thrilled you was just the thought of their humanity—like yours—the thought of your remote kinship with this wild and passionate uproar. Ugly. Yes, it was ugly enough: but if you were man enough you would admit to yourself that there was in you just the faintest trace of a response to the terrible frankness of that noise, a dim suspicion of there being a meaning in it which you—you so remote from the night of first ages—could comprehend.

Penguin Classics (1986), pp. 39–40, 66, 68–69.

Henry Morton Stanley, *The Congo and the Founding of Its Free State* (1885)

Taken as a whole, the scenery of the Upper Congo is uninteresting; perhaps the very slow rate of ascent has left that impression. . . . We sighed for change . . . we are menaced with . . . ennui. . . . As for your own fancies, during this day trance, created mainly by what you see as the banks glide steadily past, who will dare to fathom them? They come in rapid succession on the mind, in various shapes, rank after rank. Unsteadfast as the grey clouds which you see to the westward, they pile into cities, and towns, and mountains, growing ever larger, more intense, but still ever wavering and undergoing quick transitions of form. . . . all suggest some new thought, some fancy which cannot be long pursued, since it is constantly supplanted by other ideas suggested by something new, which itself is but a momentary flash. . . .

Meantime, at dusk, each steamer's crew of white officers and passengers will be found around their dinner-tables on deck or on the bank, if the camp has permitted it. . . . Of food there is abundance, but not much variety. It may comprise soup of beans or vegetables, followed by toasted chikwanga (cassava-bread), fried or stewed fowl, a roast fowl, or a roast leg of goat meat, a dish of desiccated potatoes, or yams, roast bananas, boiled beans, rice and curry, or rice with honey, or rice and milk, finishing with tea or coffee, or palm-wine. . . . A few months of this diet makes the European sigh for his petit verre, Astrachan caviar, mock-turtle, salmon—with sauce Hollandaise—filet de boeuf, with perhaps a pastete and poularde mit compôte und salat. . . .

As we anticipated, the natives soon came up, and fowls, goats, ripe and green plantains and bananas, cassava rolls, cassava flour, sweet potatoes, yams, eggs, and palm oil were bartered so speedily that by sunset we had sufficient to last two or three days. . . . At sunrise the following day canoe after canoe appeared, and the barter was so successfully conducted that we had soon secured three dozen fowls, four goats, a sheep, and eight days' rations for each member of the coloured force. The fear the natives entertained of the strange steamer was now changed for liveliest admiration. We were no longer supposed to be laden with mischief, but full of "good things."

(New York, 1885), vol. 2, pp. 5–7, 10–11, 15–16, 281–82.

bequeathed their language and laws to part of the indigenous elite. Under the Third Republic they made Algeria a part of France itself, organizing it into three departments each with representatives to the Chamber of Deputies; the franchise was open to the relatively small group of Europeanized Algerians as well as to the *colons.* By 1914 France had nearly as many inhabitants in Africa as in the home territories (about 39 million). Yet outside North Africa and certain coastal towns where their administration and business enterprises were concentrated, the French had not achieved much progress toward assimilating or Westernizing their vast districts.

The primary benefit of colonial development in France was cultural: the imperial idea was popular at home. Conquest made the French feel that they were both powerful and beneficent. The French imperialists put special emphasis on the "civilizing mission." The assertion of power over colonies, however, conflicted with cherished concepts of national sovereignty which the French had pioneered. This conflict created painful contradictions when imperial missions encountered various forms of resistance. The French tried to assert control by developing the economy and introducing institutions of liberal European rule in combination with traditional, native institutions. At the same time that urban design was being modernized in Paris, the French brought modern urban design to West Africa: improved sanitation, water systems, roads, economic infrastructure, and schools. But development ran into problems. For example, indigenous peasants refused to work in mines and on railroads, so the French had to resort to slave labor. The costs were enormous and profits very low.

The British steadily added to their African possessions throughout the century. At its end they had nearly half the continent: 4 million square miles out of more than 11 million, with control of 61 million people out of some 100 million. The most significant areas were in West Africa.

The most important was the colony and protectorate of Nigeria. Centering on the great river Niger, Nigeria was formally put together from earlier West African colonies in 1914. Northern Nigeria was ruled by Muslim emirs of the Fulani people; southern Nigeria was inhabited by divided groups that had long been harassed by slave raids. The region over which the British asserted control comprised the lands of the Hausa, Yoruba, and Ibo peoples—the first Muslim, the others increasingly converted by Christian missionaries, and all three in conflict.

In the British partition of Africa one man played an extraordinarily large role. Cecil Rhodes (1853–1902) was one of the original adventurer explorers. As a sickly boy he was sent to a brother's farm in Africa to improve his health. Arriving just when diamonds were being discovered, by industriousness and luck he made a fortune and was simultaneously cured of his ill health. Rhodes was instrumental in establishing British rule in a long swath of southern Africa. He had no doubts about the superiority of English culture and his right to use cheap African labor to gain huge profits from his diamond and gold mines. The country he named after himself, Rhodesia, (now Zambia and Zimbabwe), was ostensibly a British protectorate but was more like a private company whose profits Rhodes himself reaped.

Italy got very little out of the partition of Africa. Tunis, which Italy had coveted, went instead to France. Italy's major effort centered on the lands at the southern end of the Red Sea, but after the defeat by the Abyssinians in 1896, Italy had to be content with a few thousand square miles, most of it desert, in Eritrea and Somaliland. Italian efforts to add to this insignificant empire by taking Tripoli from its nominal Turkish ruler succeeded in 1912. The Italians also secured Rhodes and other islands off the southwestern corner of Anatolia, known collectively as the Dodecanese (the twelve). These acquisitions were the fruit of the Italo-Turkish War of 1911–1912.

Even as an undergraduate, Cecil Rhodes had in mind a grand plan for the British Empire in Africa. While at Oxford he wrote his "Confession of Faith," which asked, "Why should we not form a secret society with but one object, the furtherance of the British Empire and the bringing of the whole uncivilized world under British rule for the recovery of the United States, for the making the Anglo-Saxon race but one Empire? What a dream, but yet it is probable, it is possible." (The Granger Collection)

Until the 1880s, Bismarck had resisted calls for imperial expansion, for he felt that domestic unity and military strength on the European continent were paramount. In 1882 a German Colonial League was founded by northern merchants who feared that without overseas expansion, Germany would not keep pace with Britain. Two years later Germany signed treaties creating a German protectorate in Southwest Africa, largely as a strategic challenge to Britain, and acquired Togoland and the Cameroons. In 1885 Germany declared an official protectorate over East Africa, but only Tanganyika and Zanzibar had any potential economic significance, and the latter was traded to Britain in 1890 for the tiny British-held island of Heligoland, in the North Sea. In the Pacific, the Germans picked up some small islands and a large territory on the island of New Guinea. Germany also took part in the attempted partition of China, taking a ninety-nine-year lease on Kiachow Bay, on the north China coast. The Portuguese had sought to extend their trading activities into the interior of both Angola and Mozambique, and they continued to control the strategic island of São Tomé in the Bight of Biafra.

Conflicts in Africa After Partition

Direct conflicts between imperial European powers in Africa at the turn the century contributed to overall instability in Europe.

Fashoda

The first major crisis came about at the intersection of British and French imperial aims in Egyptian Sudan as a direct result of European competition, which had undermined traditional African authority structures in the region without replacing them. In the late nineteenth century French prospects in Egypt seemed particularly bright. Between 1859 and 1869 the private French company headed by Ferdinand de Lesseps built the Suez Canal, which united the Mediterranean with the Red Sea and shortened the sea trip from Europe to India and the Far East by thousands of miles. The British had opposed the building of this canal under French patronage; but now that it was finished, the canal came to be considered an essential part of the lifeline of the British Empire.

The British secured a partial hold over this lifeline in 1875, when Disraeli arranged the purchase of 176,000 shares of stock in the canal company from the financially pressed khedive Ismail (r. 1863–1879). The shares gave Britain a 44 percent interest in the company. Despite the sale of the stock, Ismail's fiscal difficulties increased. The Egyptian national debt, which was perhaps £3.3 million at Ismail's accession, rose to £91 million by 1876. That year, the European powers (from whose private banks Ismail had borrowed large sums at high interest) obliged Egypt to accept the financial guidance of a debt commission that they set up.

Two years later Ismail had to sacrifice still more sovereignty when he was forced to appoint an Englishman as his minister of finance and a Frenchman as his minister of public works to ensure that foreign creditors had first claim to the Egyptian government's revenues. In 1879 Ismail himself was deposed. Egyptian nationalists, led by army officers whose pay had been drastically cut by the new khedive as an economy move, revolted against foreign control and against the government that had made this control possible. Using the slogan "Egypt for the Egyptians!" the officers established a military regime that the European powers feared would repudiate Egyptian debts or seize the Suez Canal. In 1882 the British and French sent a naval squadron to Alexandria, ostensibly to protect their nationals. A riot there killed fifty Europeans. The Egyptian military commander began to strengthen the fortifications at Alexandria, but the British naval squadron destroyed the forts and landed British troops, declaring that they were present in the name of the khedive to put an end to the disorders. The khedive gave the British authority to occupy Port Said and points along the Suez Canal to ensure freedom of transit. Thus Britain acquired the upper hand in Egypt, taking the canal and occupying Cairo. Dual French–British control was over, but stability was still elusive as resistance to European rule did not abate.

Egyptian nationalists were also offended by British policy toward the Sudan. This vast region to the south of Egypt had been partially conquered by Muhammad Ali and Ismail, then lost in the 1880s as a result of a revolt by an Islamic leader, Muhammad Ahmad (c. 1844–1884), who called himself the *mahadi* (messiah). Fears that France or some other power might gain control over the Nile headwaters prompted Britain to reconquer the Sudan. The reconquest at first went very badly for the British. An Egyptian army under British leadership was annihilated. The British press trumpeted for revenge, and General Charles George Gordon (1833–1885) was dispatched to Khartoum, the Sudanese capital. But Gordon was surrounded in Khartoum. A relief expedition to rescue Gordon was too late, and after passing most of 1884 under siege, Khartoum fell to the Mahdists on January 26, 1885, sixty hours before relieving steamers arrived. Gordon died in this final battle of the siege.

National pride, an increasingly important factor in the New Imperialism, required the avenging of Gordon and the reconquest of the Sudan. This was achieved by Lord Kitchener (1850–1916) in an overwhelming victory against the Mahdists at Omdurman in 1898. Between the defeat of Gordon and the battle of Omdurman the British brought their technological superiority to bear. They had also shown ruthless cruelty. Their new machine guns made it possible to kill 11,000 Sudanese, while only 20 Britons and 20 of their Egyptian allies were killed. Winston Churchill described the scene, in which "The infantry fired steadily and stolidly, without hurry or excitement, for the enemy were far away and the officers careful. . . . And all the time out on the plain . . . bullets were shearing through flesh, smashing and splintering bone . . . valiant men were struggling through a hell of whistling metal, exploding shells and spurting dust." Against the new British Maxim machine guns the Mahdists were armed with muzzle-loading muskets and spears.

Kitchener's victory raised French concerns, leading to a major showdown. A week later news reached Kitchener that French troops had reached Fashoda, within the Sudan and on the upper Nile, having made an arduous crossing from the Atlantic coast. Fearing that the French intended to dam the Nile and block new irrigation for Egypt, Kitchener pressed on toward Fashoda. In 1898 for a few weeks the French and British squared off against one another there. But fearing the outbreak of war with Britain, the French withdrew and renounced all claim to the Nile Valley. The British made the Sudan an Anglo-Egyptian *condominium* (joint rule), of which they were the senior partner. This assured clear British dominance in Egypt, since Britain now controlled the source of the water supply, and it assuaged public opinion at home, which had clamored for war. But it enraged Egyptian nationalists, who believed they had lost a province that rightfully belonging to Egypt alone.

A Closer Look

Technology and Empire

The industrial revolution in Europe had given the West an immense advantage throughout the world in weaponry, shipping, invention, and health. One British writer, Hilaire Belloc (1870–1953), wrote satirically of how technology—in the form of the machine gun—gave the British led by a Colonel Blood, victory over the Boers in the South African war:

I never shall forget the way
That Blood upon this awful day
Preserved us all from death.
He stood upon a little mound,
Cast his lethargic eyes around,
And said beneath this breath:
"Whatever happens we have got
The Maxim gun,
*and they have not."**

Technological superiority was not, of course, to be measured only or even primarily in terms of instruments of war. Quinine, which helped to control malaria; the development of efficient steamships; the laying of submarine cables—the English Channel was first crossed by cable in 1850—and the explosion in information and communications; the building of railroads; these and many other technological developments gave Western nations more and more power. In 1837 Macgregor Laird (1808–1861), an explorer, early expert on steamboats, and co-owner of one of the most famous Scottish shipyards, described a voiyage by steam vessel up the Niger River in West Africa:

We have the power in our hands, moral, physical, and mechanical; the first, based on the Bible; the second, upon the wonderful adaptation of the Anglo-Saxon race to all climates, situations, and circumstances, . . . the third, bequeathed to us by the immortal James Watt. By his invention every river is laid open to us, time and distance are shortened. If his spirit is allowed to witness the success of his invention here on earth, I can conceive no application of it that would meet his approbation more than seeing the mighty streams of the Mississippi and the Amazon, the Niger and the Nile, the Indus and the Ganges, stemmed by hundreds of steam-vessels, carrying the glad tidings of "peace and good will towards men" into the dark places of the earth which are now filled with cruelty.**

---

* Hilaire Belloc, "Colonel Blood," in *The Age of Imperialism,* ed. Robin W. Winks (Englewood Cliffs, NJ: 1969), p. 59. Reprinted by permission of Gerald Duckworth & Co., Ltd., and Random House, Inc.

** Macgregor Laird and R. A. K. Oldfield, *Narrative of an Expedition into the Interior of Africa, by the River Niger, in the Steam-Vessels Quorra and Alburkah, in 1832, 1833, and 1834* (London, 1837), Vol. II, pp. 397–98.

The Boer War

The legacy of empire was particularly complex in South Africa, where there were not one, but two, white settlement groups. Britain acquired the Cape Colony from the Netherlands in 1815. Because the Southern tip of Africa was strategically important and the climate appealed to European settlers, Britons arrived and soon began to compete for land with the European colonists already there, the Dutch *Boers* (Dutch for "farmer"). The adoption of English as the sole official language, the abolition of slavery throughout the empire, and the attempts by London to protect the aboriginal population went against the grain of the patriarchal Boers, fundamentalist Christians who believed the Bible told them that slavery was ordained by God. Between 1835 and 1837 some ten thousand Boers moved north into sparsely settled country in the Great Trek. Needing more land to support their custom that each farmhouse should be an hour's walk from any other house (making the average farm six thousand acres in size), and refusing to acknowledge any African rights to the land they were occupying, the Boers pressed against the Bantu and other groups. After some confused three-cornered fighting among Boers, British, and Zulus, the Boers established two virtually independent states—the Transvaal and the Orange Free State. The British settled another province, known as Natal, to the east along the Indian Ocean. Cape Colony and Natal, which both had African populations heavily outnumbering the British and remaining Boer residents combined, acquired self-governing rights.

The British Empire at the southern end of the African continent grew slowly, but in 1877 Britain reversed course and annexed the Transvaal as a step toward the federation of all South Africa under the British Crown. The Boers revolted in 1880, and in 1881 the Liberal Gladstone lived up to his principles by making a treaty with the Boers at Pretoria that reestablished the Transvaal as independent, though under the "suzerainty" of Great Britain.

The British were already filtering up through the arid country to the west of the Boer republics when the discovery of gold and the development of a diamond industry in these republics undid Gladstone's work. The Transvaal was no longer a poor and isolated grazing country; it offered a great source of wealth that tempted settlers of a different kind. The region about Johannesburg, the Rand, filled up with adventurers and entrepreneurs of a dozen nations, all looking to Britain to protect them from the conservative Boers, to whom they were undesirable *Uitlanders* (outlanders).

The simmering conflict came to a head with the Jameson raid of December 29, 1895. The British in South Africa were now under the leadership of Cecil Rhodes, the prime minister of Cape Colony and a determined imperialist who, as noted, had made a fortune in the chaotic diamond industry. The raid itself, under Dr. Leander Jameson (1853–1917), was an invasion of the Transvaal from British territory and was planned to coincide with an uprising of Uitlanders in Johannesburg. But the uprising did not take place, and the president of the Transvaal, Paul Kruger (1825–1904), had no trouble defeating Jameson's handful of invaders. Boer resistance to the Uitlanders hardened with alien expulsion and immigration restriction acts, and controls were placed over the right of assembly and freedom of the press. The two Boer republics renewed a defensive alliance and presented an ultimatum to the British government. The ultimatum was rejected, and the Boer War began on October 11, 1899.

The British did not have enough troops available immediately to put down determined Boer fighters, who were on their own ground and were accustomed to the rigors of outdoor life. Western opinion generally sided with the underdog Boers, and even in Britain many Liberals strongly opposed the war. The indigenous African population were the real losers in that the fighting ravaged their farmland, disrupted their commerce, and brought famine and disease.

The British determination to win the Boer War at all costs led to the brutal treatment of Boer prisoners and the invention of the "concentration camp." Boer civilians and prisoners of war were rounded up and forced to live in enclosed camps to prevent them from supporting the guerrilla fighters. Such treatment and the deaths of tens of thousands as a result of disease and terrible conditions provoked international outcry against the British. In the long run the overwhelming strength of the British forces and technology prevailed, despite popular opinion. By the middle of 1900 the British had won in the field, but it took another eighteen months to subdue the determined guerrillas. In 1902, by the Treaty of Vereeniging, the Boers accepted British rule, with the promise of ultimate self-government. In 1910 the British created the Union of South Africa, linking Cape Colony, the Transvaal, the Orange Free State, and Natal.

Thus, on the eve of the First World War, South Africa was among the self-governing British dominions. Briton and Boer seemed to be ready to collaborate in developing an increasingly important European outpost. But there were ominous signs even then. The Boers resisted being Anglicized, and the foundations of an intensely divisive policy of racial segregation had been laid. Since racial barriers were applied to freedom of movement, the very notion of a "frontier" of opportunity failed to arise, and South Africa created for itself a major problem relating to migrant labor. The two European elements together were in a minority of one to four compared with the non-Europeans. Enmity between Afrikaners and the British was a factor in Afrikaner support for the system of racial segregation called apartheid.

Russia: Between Nation and Empire

Russian imperialism differed in some ways from the expansion and colonialism of the west European powers. Russia's colonies were all located along its land borders. Expansion on the western frontier, which had begun in the sixteenth century, had wrapped up in 1815, at which point Russia turned to the south and east. Expanding throughout the nineteenth century, Russians first annexed Georgia in the Transcaucasus in 1801, then asserted domination over ever larger regions in Siberia, and next moved into the Amur Valley and Manchuria. After gaining control of the steppe (or prairie) north of the Black and Caspian seas, the Russians moved into the Kazakh steppe and the deserts and oases of central Asia. Russia's expansion into central Asia challenged British dominion in India and twice threatened to bring the two countries to war.

Russia's conquest of the Caucasus did not go smoothly. The imperial army met fierce resistance in the mountains there, resulting in a long, bloody guerrilla war that lasted more than three decades. When the Russians finally settled the fighting and captured the region's main city in the mountains, they burned it to the ground and renamed it Grozny, the Russian word for "terrible and awesome power."

Russian expansion on its borders was based at least partly on genuine security concerns to protect its borders against invasion. But by the mid-nineteenth century, imperialism took forms that more closely resembled the "new imperialism" in the west. Strategic and political motives still probably outweighed economic issues, but new raw materials and markets were sought in the colonial borderlands. Central Asia was attractive for establishing a cotton growing industry; the Transcaucasus had lucrative oil fields.

In midcentury at the time of the Great Reforms, the Russian government's "civilizing mission" to non-Russians was not very different from its Enlightenment mission to its own Russian peasantry. To "raise the cultural and intellectual level of the people" was a common cry in Russia, based on the belief that free and educated Russian peasants would become more or less like the Russian intelligentsia, and a modern civilized society would result. Peasant culture was idealized for its naturalness, its authentic communalism, its elemental religious faith; but it was also disparaged for its savagery, its stifling of individual initiative, and its superstitions. Likewise, Russians viewed the imperial project as an enlightening one. During the Great Reform period, there were some pragmatic efforts to integrate native institutions and elites into Russian colonial rule. The attempt to integrate peasant customary law with modern Western statute law in the 1860s was paralleled by attempts to integrate Muslim legal traditions (sharia) with statute law in Tatar and Turkic regions. This combination of pragmatism and idealism was not unlike the French "civilizing mission." Complex cultural interactions involved delicate negotiations and a great deal of attention by sympathetic elites, for both sides had something to gain. When a more reactionary and Russian nationalist government came to power in the 1880s, such negotiations were replaced by greater centralization, Russification, and less tolerance for cultural differences.

Economic development of these areas was, as elsewhere, increasingly for the benefit of the Russian metropole or individual Russian entrepreneurs. The oil fields in Baku, Azerbaijan, were worked by Azerbaijani Turks and by Iranian, Russian, and Armenian workers, but the profits were siphoned off by the Nobel and Rothschild families who owned the oil. In 1883 Nobel's market share of exported oil was 55 percent. Central Asian cotton fields displaced traditional nomadic herders, mountain peoples, and hunters, providing both raw materials to manufacturing centers and markets for finished goods. But

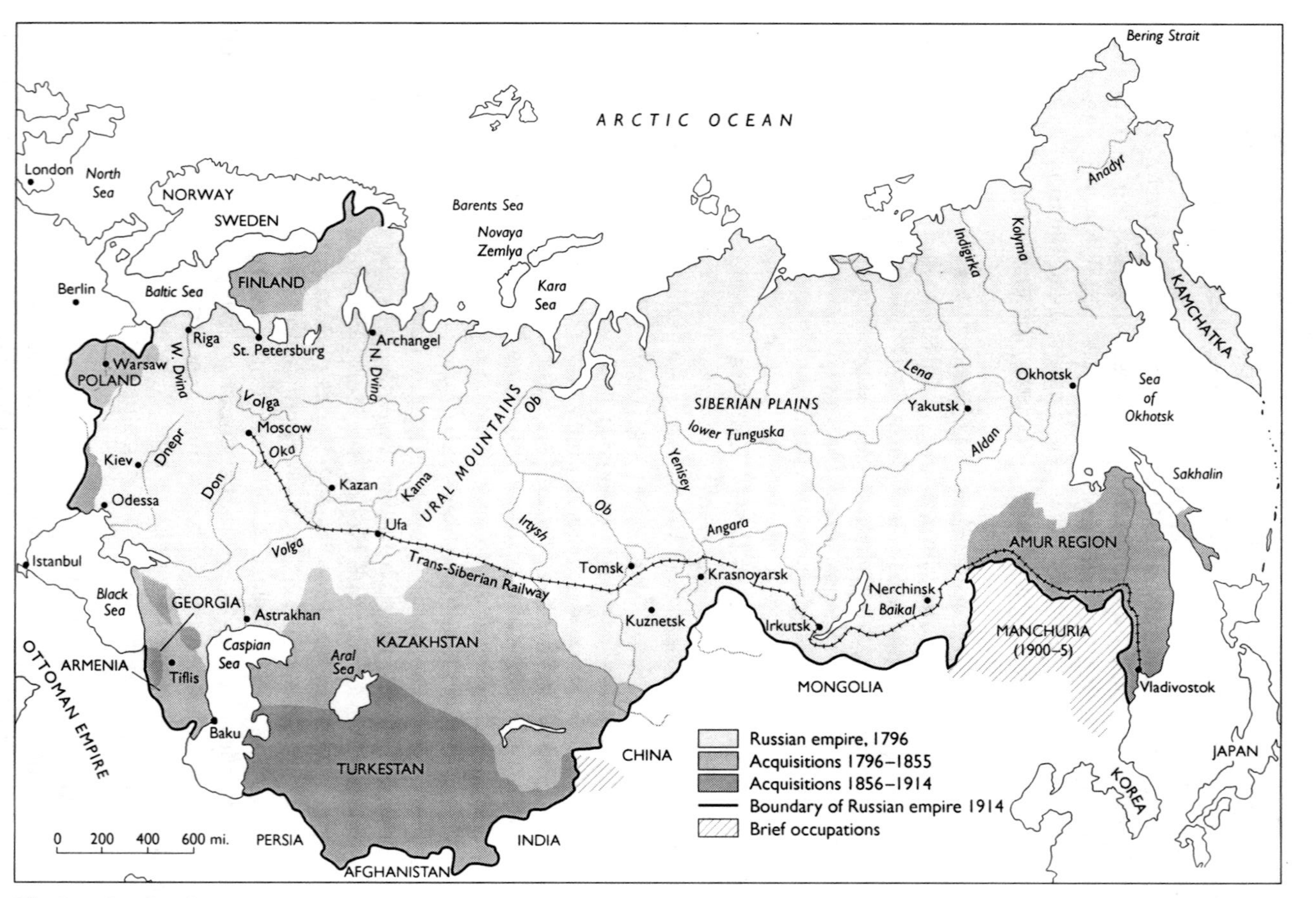

The Russian Empire

local development was not a priority beyond what was necessary for extraction and exploitation.

Still the pattern of cost and benefit is more complex than meets the eye. In the Caucasus, while oil profits were drained away, traditional local elites, especially the Armenian middle classes and a small Azeri elite, grew and benefited from increased investment in the region. Ukraine was a Russian colony in that it was under the political control of St. Petersburg and provided heavy industry for the military needs of the center; but every index of social, educational, and economic achievement places Ukrainians at higher levels than Russians by the end of the nineteenth century. Evaluating Russian imperialism is complicated further because in the 1890s Russia was itself dependent on France and other west European countries for investment, technology, management know-how, and entrepreneurs.

The Russian case is interesting for its tension between such forces of integration and diversification, characteristic of its experience of modernity. On the one hand, imperial acquisitions and the Great Reforms made the Russian Empire more diverse and dynamic. Non-Russians were integrated into the empire's civil and military administrations in relatively high numbers and even more into its burgeoning public sphere. At the same time, modern bureaucratization and industrialization increased central desires for homogeneity and standardization to contain the growing diversity of public life. This tension existed in one form or another in all the European metropoles, intensified by the appearance of complex relationships with foreign cultures now under European dominion. Another element was added in Russia, where the tsarist government worked to counteract the diversity and standardization of modernity by clinging to an archaic ideology of autocratic rule, dynastic government, and a rigid social order.

Russian nationalism in this period reflected these contradictions and reinforced social and economic conflicts. Russian nationalism was never a single ideology but rather a series of alternatives. There was great Russian nationalism, based on Russian ethnicity, language, and Orthodoxy. But that sense of nation was always countered by a supranational imperial "nationalism" based on Russia's role as the center of a multiethnic state and society. These were complicated by Russians' sense of themselves as straddling Europe and Asia. Though Russians almost exclusively thought of themselves as Europeans, that identity was never entirely secure, so the acquisition of an Asian empire had the added benefit of reinforcing Russians' sense of their European identity. As Dostoevsky put it in 1881, "In Europe we were only poor recipients of charity and slaves, but we come to Asia as masters. In Europe we were Tatars, but in Asia we are also Europeans."

Imperialism at Home

The impact of imperialism on European domestic politics and culture was complex and ultimately contributed to tensions generating racial hostilities and international conflicts.

Mass Nationalism and Racism

Imperial conquest was immensely popular in most European countries. It took determined opponents of imperialism nearly twenty years to evoke government and public outrage at the terrible atrocities of Leopold's Congo. Newspapers celebrated conquests, highlighted cultural differences, and generally offered simplistic and consoling answers to complex questions. The popularity of imperialism was seen in everyday life. Advertisers used imperial imagery to sell products. Museums and world's fairs exhibited the stuff of imperial production. Cultural artifacts, like masks, carvings, and mud paintings, were exhibited as fascinating evidence of native primitivism. Imperialist songs were popular in music halls; serialized newspaper and magazine reports of exploration and colonial cultures were eagerly read. People collected bits of empires as souvenirs: porcelain figures representing native peoples, decks of cards decorated with ethnographic drawings, and postcards of veiled women appeared in polite society as well as in pornography.

Imperialism shaped Europeans' evolving ideas about nation and modernity, fueled by the rise of mass nationalism. Mass nationalism was politically conservative. Where early nineteenth-century nationalism favored sovereignty and suffrage based on belief in universal individualism and equality, mass nationalism was based on belief in the superiority of one people over another. When nationalism became a mass phenomenon, it tended to support conservative parties that called for national aggrandizement through military power, territorial acquisition, and imperial conquest.

Imperialism also gave new influence to theories of race. Joseph Arthur de Gobineau's (1816–1882) book *The Inequality of Races* had little impact when it was published during the heyday of liberalism in 1853, but his work won a new lease on life at the end of the century. Civilizations fell, Gobineau argued, because of racial mixing. He and many others considered the ultimate degradation of civilization to be inevitable: society was not progressing, it was in danger of degenerating. The "lower races" were breeding faster and less selectively, and democratic egalitarianism was leveling down the best while encouraging the worst. Consequently, evolution was sliding downward rather than heading upward. Racist ideology held that inherent, biological differences among the various races determined cultural and individual achievement, so that one race might be considered superior to another in a given context. When combined with social Darwinism, this sort of racism could be applied to explain the superiority of Europeans over other peoples. For people like the English imperialist Cecil Rhodes, "natural selection" explained the preeminence of the English people. Rhodes held that a world wholly and exclusively peopled with Anglo-Saxons would be the best possible world. The easy conquest of Africa and Asia, the "primitive" artifacts displayed in museums, the exotic customs and images circulated in the mass press all served to convince at least some Europeans that they were a superior race.

This sort of racist nationalism fed conflicts within Europe as the search for evidence of national uniqueness became a search for evidence of superiority.

Racialism intensified the damaged pride of the French after defeat by Germany. It also contributed to the context in which anti-Semitism revived. Nationalism that posited the superiority of Europeans over Africans and Asians flowed easily into superiority over Jews. Anti-Semitism had for centuries been based on religious and cultural difference. But the rise of racial theories based on biological differences hardened attitudes toward Jews. Conversion had always been possible in the past; but at the turn of the century, when Jews came to be seen by some as defined less by religious practice than by biology, conversion was correspondingly regarded by anti-Semites as deception rather than assimilation.

Economic and Political Consequences of Imperialism

Economic motives spurred imperialism, but did imperialism pay for itself? Clearly some individuals made fortunes, but on the whole taxpayers bore the costs of attempts to develop economies in Africa and Asia. Some historians have argued that midcentury industrial progress in Britain was financed largely from the cheap labor of India. Such judgments are at best guesses, although revenues from the colonies undoubtedly were drained to serve imperial interests. The Dutch drew 18 million guilders a year from the Dutch East Indies (Indonesia) from 1831 until 1877, at a time when the entire Dutch budget was only 60 million guilders. In 1890, when Britain's entire defense budget was 38 percent of its revenue, 42 percent of Indian revenues went to finance the Indian Army, under British officers, and serving primarily imperial purposes.

Against such financial gains from empire must be set the heavy costs of the colonies, which originally faced deficit budgets that had to be met by the imperial power, involved many small wars of great expense, and were also costly to administer in terms of health. French expenses in Morocco more than wiped out any profits from trade. Italy's colonies cost the country 1,300 million lire, more than was produced by all Italian colonial trade between 1913 and 1932. Germany's external trade with its colonies was 972 million marks between 1894 and 1913, while the expenses of the colonies were 1,002 million marks. For Britain the colonies were more important; but there, too, the balance was generally unfavorable: in 1850 the empire took 28 percent of Britain's overseas trade and 40 percent in 1934. Of the 1934 figure, however, well over half was with the dominions (i.e., Canada, Australia, New Zealand, Newfoundland, South Africa); 7 percent was with India; and only 9 percent was with the remainder of the empire. In short, for Britain the chief economic advantage lay in the former settlement colonies and in India, while the new African possessions were of little importance in economic terms.

In political terms, late nineteenth-century imperialism was an even greater disaster than in economics. The peoples of Africa and Asia were given a taste of European civilization that left more than a bitter residue. Where desire for industrialization and modernization was created, Europeans offered none of the means to achieve satisfying levels of economic development. Indigenous political institutions and cultural traditions were destroyed and replaced with half-hearted attempts to recreate European institutions. Boundaries were drawn in ways that exacerbated existing rivalries and created new tensions. European rulers tended to support leaders who served European interests no matter how corrupt or destructive locally. In regard to European power politics, imperialism created new sources of competition and hostility, new motivations for arms buildup, and new impetus toward war. The politics and economics of imperialism together drained resources and diverted attention from social and economic conflicts at home. In Russia it is hard to avoid the conclusion that imperialism contributed to Russian economic underdevelopment, which led to the social–political unrest that soon escalated into revolution.

* * *

Imperialism brought to the surface many of the contradictions of modern European life and helped undermine bourgeois certainties about liberal democracy, Enlightenment rationalism, and progress. If for many people imperialism proved the superiority of European civilization, it also planted the seeds of cultural doubt and relativism. Criticism of imperialism, no matter how flawed, incomplete, or ineffective it may have been, was based on universal concepts of human nature and human rights. Critics of imperialism denounced it as a racist, arrogant, and greedy. Contradictions between imperialist repression and French ideals of republicanism or English liberalism may have led to ever more convoluted justifications for the civilizing mission, but the very existence of these discrepancies raised moral and political objections. Movements to inform European publics about the atrocities of imperial rule were small before the First World War, but they established networks that would later grow. The Pan-African Conference of 1900 drew delegates from around the world to unite in condemning international racism and imperialism.

Imperialism brought people together in ways that made both Europeans and indigenous peoples nervous. Both cultures were transformed by interactions with each other. Hybrid cultures were intellectually exciting but also culturally threatening. Just as Russians had wondered how they could introduce Western culture and institutions and still remain Russians, the people of China and India and elsewhere wondered how to retain their own cultural identity while introducing the benefits of industry and modernization. Imperialism raised some fundamental questions about the nature of European modernity. The difficulties of transferring bourgeois progress to the colonies, intractable cultural differences, the attraction, fear, and exoticism of cultural differences all made modernity seem increasingly complex and contradictory.

TEN

The Challenges of Modernity

Many Europeans greeted the twentieth century in the confidence that the past hundred years had solved most of humanity's material and spiritual problems. They defined modernity as progress: it was historically inevitable that individual freedoms would expand, along with prosperity, civilization, and peace. Yet underneath that heady confidence lay an equally powerful sense of unease. Since the mid-1870s and accelerating in the 1890s, critiques that had long been implicit or limited to small groups of the skeptical and disenfranchised were more often voiced as grave doubts about progress and modernity. Advances in science and industry brought new wealth and comfort to an unprecedented number of people, but society was still unable to relieve the dreadful living conditions of the people who labored to produce capitalism's plenty. The same science, technology, and medicine that extended and improved life produced weapons that made it easier for modern armies to annihilate each other. The control of nature weakened faith in God and in a natural, divine order of things. Traditions of order and hierarchy were crumbling in the face of women's assertions that they could do men's work and deserved man's rights. While global capitalism and imperial conquest extended the reach of European power and culture, contact with different cultures raised questions about the uniformity of human nature and inevitability of a progress defined as European. Finally, while peace had so far reigned among the Great Powers, colonial competition had already brought them to the brink of war and would do so with increasing regularity after the turn of the century. While some claimed that economic interdependence and the terrifying power of new weaponry would keep nations from going to war, others felt that a modern apocalypse was inevitable and imminent.

At the end of the nineteenth century and through the years that led to world war, the contradictions of the preceding hundred years came to the surface. The depression of the 1870s, together with the authoritarian unification of Germany led people to question the liberal principles at the heart of economic progress. Industrialization and nation-state building brought not harmony and universal human improvement but crude materialism and class war. The Paris Commune seemed to embody the "spectre haunting Europe," that Marx and Engels had promised in 1848. Even those who defined change positively as progress began to see and articulate thoughts about the dark sides of change. Mass transport, regular baths, and telephones were cheered by those who benefited from their use and denounced by those who feared that making life easier made people weaker, set their clean bodies in cities filthied by pollution, and invaded their privacy with jangling telephones and immediate communication. Because this occurred in the 1880s and 1890s, at century's end, many people in Europe associated moral and physical decline with the sense of an ending. Since the contradiction between material progress and moral decline was expressed most widely in France, which lagged economically and led culturally, we label this phenomenon with its French appellation, the *fin de siècle.*

Feelings of malaise, dangerous political conflicts, a cultural probing of human irrationality and passions all continued up until the outbreak of war in 1914. But social and international conflicts were accompanied by economic revival in the 1890s and by the spread of industrialization to yet new markets in eastern and southeastern Europe, a movement that accelerated in the 1910s. Dramatic improvements in everyday life, shared by increasing numbers of people, brought an equally dramatic increase in time and money for leisure. Looking backward nostalgically, across the horrific mass carnage of the First World War, the period at the turn of the century would also be identified as the *Belle Époque,* the good times. Fin de siècle anxiety would last and spread in the 1900s and 1910s amidst the Belle Époque's pleasures, a contradiction that contributed to a remarkable, unprecedented explosion of artistic creativity known today as modernism.

City Life: Fin de Siècle and Belle Époque

By the end of the nineteenth century cities dominated national cultures even in countries where most people lived in the countryside. With the general rise in European population, the urban population grew rapidly in the second half of the nineteenth century. Between 1850 and 1911 the percentage of the French population living in cities nearly doubled, from 25 percent to 44 percent, and, while still remaining under half the population, Paris set standards in art, fashion, and popular culture for all of Europe. In Germany the urban population rose from 30 percent to 60 percent, and by the turn of the century Berlin was a major cultural mecca for Germans and traveling Europeans. The poverty of the village and the pull of factory work drew millions of peasants to cities in every country, so each elegant cultural center was also part peasant village. At the turn of the century Moscow boasted the most exciting avant-garde art scene in Europe in theater, painting, poetry, and ballet, but some people kept cows and raised chickens in their courtyards.

Growth of Urban Population (in Thousands)

City	1850	1900
London	2,685	7,488
Paris	1,053	2,714
Berlin	419	1,889
Vienna	444	1,675
St. Petersburg	485	1,400
Glasgow	357	1,052
Moscow	300	1,000
Istanbul	600	1,000
Budapest	156	732
Madrid	270	540
Barcelona	175	533
Warsaw	114	423
Lisbon	240	356
Prague	118	202
Belgrade	25	69

Source: Raymond Pearson, *European Nationalism, 1789–1920* (New York, 1994). pp. 240–41

As the depression waned, a new period of material productivity and cultural creativity began. From the 1890s to 1914, the middle classes grew, and more people—including more laborers, working for fewer hours for higher pay—had time and money for leisure. New inventions like street lighting, cars, typewriters, elevators, and telephones, along with better sanitation, again held out promise for continued growth and improvement. Mass-produced clothing was available even to poor people; mass transport allowed workers to ride to work, electricity lighted businesses, streets, and music halls; and some of the poor could afford a bicycle ride on a day off.

The telephone, invented by Alexander Graham Bell (1847–1922) in 1876, began to appear in private businesses and homes. Cinema, invented simultaneously in 1895 in the United States by Edison and in France by the Lumière brothers, was immediately popular with audiences all over the world, whether local entrepreneurs built elegant "palaces" or strung up white sheets in tents and town halls to project moving pictures. In the 1890s the horse-drawn tram gave way to electric trolleys, lowering prices and speeding transport through cities. London had had an underground railway since 1863, and at the turn of the century underground railway systems were carrying passengers in Paris and Budapest. In 1903 Orville and Wilbur Wright managed to get a flying machine to fly. The first automobile was built in 1896, and assembly-line production for automobiles was brought back to France from the United States by Louis Renault (1877–1944); cars became almost commonplace, if still unreliable, in European cities. Their production, like the production of railroads before them, spurred growth in related industries: rubber tires, glass windows, steel, aluminum, petroleum. Oil had been

Women workers in a Spanish cotton mill, early 1900s. *(© Corbis)*

flowing in Baku, Azerbaijan, since the 1870s, but huge new oil fields were discovered in Texas in 1901 and Persia in 1908.

The spread of technology, universal education, and the expansion of professions and bureaucracies increased the number of people who could live middle-class lives. In Britain the number of people who considered themselves lower-middle-class rose from 7 percent of the population in 1850 to 20 percent in 1900. Bank clerks, retail store clerks, bookkeepers, accountants, postal workers, government inspectors and records keepers, stenographers, schoolteachers, telegraph and telephone operators, nurses, waiters, all made more money than factory workers, did not do physical labor, and sought cultural markers to distinguish themselves from the working class.

The doctrine of "separate spheres" would be powerfully challenged at the end of the century, but it still defined most middle-class lives. A wife who did not work for wages remained a central facet of middle-class respectability. Disposable income to care for children, decorate the home, and hire servants was available in middle-class families, but even at the end of the century, running a household in European cities was hard work. To cook food and heat the home, wood or coal still had to be hauled up from a basement or courtyard. Fireplaces and stoves needed to be cleaned and blacked, ashes needed to be removed, soot needed to be cleaned from draperies, carpets, windows, mirrors, lamps, bed linens, and furniture. In poor and rural homes, the soot remained.

Middle-class British family enjoying their new gramophone, 1908. *(© Corbis)*

Lighting was complicated. One of the first questions a mistress would ask a potential servant was whether she could make a fire. Kerosene lamps replaced candles, which were weak and dangerous. But lamps required tinder to be prepared from old silk stockings, then steel and flint struck together to make a spark; when the tinder had caught, a wick could be lit and placed in the glass lamp, which had of course been washed, polished, and filled with kerosene. By century's end electric lighting was growing more common, but indoor plumbing was a rarity for all classes everywhere in Europe until after the First World War or, in the case of Russia, after World War II.

In Paris at the turn of the century most homes had at least one room lighted by electricity, but water, which was hard to get and harder still to dispose of, was a major preoccupation for all European women or their servants. Rivers in towns were polluted with factory and human waste; wells were too. In 1872 Haussmann gave Paris a hundred fountains with clean drinking water, but clean running water was rare elsewhere. By 1900 the sewer system Haussmann had rebuilt was serving an additional one million people. Manufactured soap was one of the biggest growth industries in the consumer market, but full-fledged baths were still rare and even aristocratic mansions lacked separate bathrooms.

Everything had to be washed by hand: fancy clothes, underwear, sheets, menstrual rags. Laundry required hauling large amounts of water and boiling clothes, stirring, scrubbing, twisting dry, ironing. Washing was nasty, hard work, so people who could afford it sent their clothes and linens to laundresses. Immortalized in so many fin de siècle paintings, the laundress came to symbolize the trials of poor female labor. The poor simply avoiding washing their clothes, but so too did many in the middle classes. Ready-made clothes were widely available at the end of the century, and even many workers could afford them, freeing women from yet another laborious task, sewing.

Still women and girls hemmed and embroidered sheets and towels, made nightshirts and underwear, knitted outer woolen garments. In many cases, sewing and cleaning occupied middle-class girls while their brothers were at school. Middle-class girls were expected to bring a storehouse of clothing and linens with them when they married. A typical bourgeois "trousseau" in France in the 1880s included 42 chemises, 30 nightgowns, 43 pairs of stockings, 60 handkerchiefs, 72 aprons, 96 dishtowels, 72 towels, 24 antimacassars (coverings for the backs of sofas and chairs), all handmade and often embroidered. Even in families with a servant or two, girls and women worked hard. The servants, of course, worked harder.

Technology simplified some tasks. In 1890 electric street cars cut travel time and the cost of tickets in half, allowing workers to ride to work and making it easier for shoppers to carry their packages home. Women also managed their families' budgets because they were the main consumer of the great variety of things now available to ease and entertain the middle classes. Advertising was directed toward women, and women learned to shop.

Department stores made their appearance in mid-century, but they became central to city life in the fin de siècle. The *Bon Marché* in Paris, Harrods in London, the *Gostinnyi Dvor* and *Passazh* arcades in St. Petersburg were only the most glamorous of the many stores for middle-class women to shop, socialize, display themselves, and dream of purchases they could not afford. The department stores were arranged to celebrate the products of material progress with the added benefit of being available to take home. The shopping arcades attracted the cities' best architects of the new iron and glass style. Bon Marché was copied in other cities the way the palace at Versailles had been copied by absolute monarchs in the seventeenth century. Spectacular public consumption and display were more than economic activities. By 1900 enclosed shops and departments stores replaced open-air markets for most purchases.

By the late nineteenth century, the rise of the middle classes and the enormous profits they realized from working-class labor made consumption a higher social value than production. Buying and having things were publicly celebrated as leisure activities, while the hard work of producing things was hidden behind the brick walls of factories on the outskirts of Europe's great cities.

The conflict between *laissez-faire* and social reform continued in this period, though the extreme liberal self-interest of the early part of the century took new forms. A conservative political interpretation (or misinterpretation) of Darwin's theory of natural selection took the place of *laissez-faire* for those who did not wish to spend state or private finances on providing sanitation, housing, or transportation to the poor. Here was scientific validation of the middle-class conviction that the universe was designed to reward hard work, attention to duty, thrift, intelligence, and self-help, and to punish laziness, waste, stupidity, sexual promiscuity, and reliance on charity. Above all, Darwin's ideas seemed to vindicate the notions that the poor were poor because they were unfit, badly prepared by nature for living a competitive life, and that efforts by private charity or by state action to take from the well-to-do and give to the poor were useless attempts to reverse the course of evolution. Herbert Spencer (1820–1903) summing up this view, wrote that, "among adults the individuals best adapted to the conditions of their existence shall prosper the most, and the individuals least adapted to the conditions of their existence shall prosper the least." The original social Darwinists thought that people should be left to their own devices to fend for themselves.

Not everyone agreed, however, and many favored social engineering through urban design. Municipal authorities in Paris, Vienna, Berlin, St. Petersburg, and elsewhere rearranged streets, constructed sanitation, lighting, and transportation systems, and built housing. Urban transportation, elevators, and the possibility of a large leisured middle class changed the geography of European cities. Elevators raised the middle class to top floors of houses, where in earlier decades the poor had been left to climb by foot. Increasingly, workers and factories were removed from city cores to city peripheries. Isolated and segregated, it became even easier for late nineteenth-century elites to believe that the poor were responsible for their own poverty.

At the same time, strike activity and revolutionary movements motivated city authorities to improve conditions for the working poor. Their records of social reform were spotty, but in the 1880s and 1890s in western Europe the deplorable conditions in which the poor were housed became an issue of public policy. At the turn of the century in Glasgow one-third of families lived in one room, while in St. Petersburg, an average of sixteen people in working-class neighborhoods shared a single room. Often day- and night-shift workers used a single bed. Some large corporations built housing for their workers, particularly in Germany and Moscow, where a paternalistic view toward workers was common. In England in 1885 and France in 1894, legislation encouraged the construction of public housing. In Russia, decent housing made it onto local governments' agendas, but scarce funds and lukewarm commitment prevented significant action. In St. Petersburg, Moscow, Riga, Tiflis, and Baku, municipal authorities used scarce resources to improve middle-class neighborhoods and city centers, while leaving vast rings of slums more or less untouched.

Fears of disease emanating from working-class quarters continued through the century. Many bourgeois and aristocratic women became involved in public health initiatives but did little to address the fundamental causes of epidemics among the poor. As long as overcrowding, overwork, and lack of plumbing defined the lives of the working poor, public health could not be significantly improved.

Crime was on the rise everywhere at the turn of the twentieth century, but nowhere is it clear whether more crimes were committed or more were simply being prosecuted and reported in mass newspapers as lurid entertainment. As before, crime was associated with the poor in official and middle-class conceptions of the city. The difference from the 1890s on is that lower-class crime was now seen as an unavoidable fact of modern city life and a permanent, biological characteristic of criminal individuals. Science was replacing morality in explanations of social behavior. Whole professional specializations appeared to explain the criminal character, the criminal mind, and the criminal brain. Historians have conclusively shown that in fact crime rates in the nineteenth century follow directly upon economic downturn and fluctuations in food prices, suggesting that the criminal "class," which nineteenth-century moralists and scientists purported to study, did not exist. Yet at the end of the century, physicians, anthropologists, statisticians, criminologists, and psychologists found new ways to turn a recurring social problem into an inescapable physical fact. Criminal, moral, and health concerns opened the way to greater interference in the everyday life of the poor by government officials. New legislation in Germany, France, England, and Russia allowed medical officers, judicial authorities, building inspectors, and policemen to enter homes, inspect bodies, and regulate daily life.

Disease and crime came together in middle-class fears of prostitution. The numbers of prostitutes continued to grow in the nineteenth century, as tens of thousands of women plied their trade on streets, in back alleys, and in brothels for every taste and price. Like criminality, prostitution came to be seen as a chronic problem in the second half of the century. When syphilis became epidemic, the state got involved. Already by midcentury laws were passed in many European countries that gave medical and police authorities the right to regulate prostitution. Prostitutes were forced to register with the police and were required to submit to regular physical inspection by the same policeman, or sometimes a police doctor. The customers of prostitutes were never subjected to the same regulations. An act passed in 1864 required the registration of prostitutes in military and port towns in England; any woman frequenting a public place alone was interpreted by local authorities as a prostitute. A second act gave the police the power to pick up any woman suspected of being a prostitute; a magistrate could order a medical examination and registration. A special police force was created to enforce the law, a clear invitation to abuse. Josephine Butler (1828–1906), the wife of an ordained Anglican minister and founder of the feminist group the Ladies National Association, took the lead in protesting the discriminatory acts in the 1870s. In 1886 the contagious disease acts were repealed. In Austria, Sweden, Russia, Germany, and elsewhere, middle-class women motivated by the belief that poverty rather than immorality turned girls to prostitution and angry about working conditions for women also formed protest groups.

The lives of the poor were subject to society's gaze in new cultural forms as well. Newspapers of a great variety increasingly published reports of visitations to city working-class quarters, taverns, tenements, and slums. Excursions to poor neighborhoods were reported with increasing sensationalism in the popular press as if they were dangerous forays into foreign cultures. The poor spoke different languages and regarded outsiders with hostility. Their houses smelled, and they engaged in strange customs, like ragpicking, smoking and drinking openly, and fighting on the streets. Such reports tended to cause more alarm about the city than insight. But they also served a cultural function: by identifying the qualities that distinguished middle- from lower-class culture, they reassured those who clung to the bottom rung of the middle-class ladder that they had made it safely to respectability. Middle-class newspapers, music halls, and variety shows resounded with jokes about the differences between the poor and the rest of society.

The actual world of workers' life and work was as diverse as it had been during the first industrial revolution, but by the turn of the century more workers were more deeply rooted in the city and the factory. In Marxist terms, they were more proletarianized. They had less contact with their villages of origin, or if they did, they returned for holidays as "city folk," bringing with them urban culture, dress, newspapers, and vices. Proletarian families expected their children to be workers, and they tended more often to take pride in their identity as workers. Unlike the bosses, in their view, they did an honest day's labor and deserved to be treated with respect. From St. Petersburg to London, striking workers' grievances included demands to be treated with dignity. But for every proletarian worker, there were scores or in some places hundreds of new recruits from the peasant village to the factory world. Within the labor force there were cultural hierarchies and political differences. Skilled workers who adopted a culture of respectability looked down upon the illiterate, drunken, or unskilled. And with the rise of popular nationalism, many workers (skilled and unskilled) rejected socialist labor politics for conservative and often racist nationalism, which placed loyalty to the monarchy or state above class consciousness.

Women faced additional hardships on the factory floor. Most women worked in small workshops or did sewing and made crafts by piecework at home. But a growing number found jobs in factories, where the routines of factory life conflicted with their roles as women and gender politics generally. Women's wages were always lower than men's even for similar work, and most women accepted this as natural. Women were usually less militant than men, often because they had primary responsibility for feeding their children and could not afford to be arrested or fired. On the rare occasions when they did try to enter labor politics they often found their way barred by male workers who excluded them from unions and refused to include in their strike demands women's grievances, such as time off to give birth or nurse infants.

The majority of workers in every country lived in poverty, especially the further east one traveled in Europe, but it seems clear now that standards of living improved at least marginally for some workers and considerably for others. In Britain real wages rose by a third between 1850 and 1875 and

Doing History

What did people eat?

In the very poorest countries during the hardest times, diet was simple:

Peasants in southern Italy survived on polenta (cornmeal porridge) or black barley bread.

Russian peasants consumed kasha and shchi (buckwheat porridge and cabbage soup). However, even the poorest Russian peasants in all but the worst famines gathered mushrooms, nuts, berries, and honey in the forests, and baked rye flour into bread. In the summer, they had fruit, cabbage, cucumbers, beets, and other root vegetables; abundant rivers and lakes provided fish. Everything was preserved for winter: pickled, brined, salted, and dried. Russian peasants ate relatively well in good years. About one in ten years, however, crop failures meant severe winter and spring shortages when peasants made "bread" from straw, flax seeds, acorns, or pine cones; or in desperation, they ate leaves and bark.

English agricultural workers surveyed in the 1890s in villages near Oxford University reported a family budget spent on bread, bacon, butter, sugar, tea, soap, oil and candles, tobacco, wood and coal, and rent. As in Russia, people worked hard and ate well in the summer and went hungry and idle in winter. A pig and some chickens slaughtered in the fall were important to make it through the winter, and preserves were as important here as for Russian peasants: onions, cauliflower, beans, fig-jam, berries and pickles.

Working-class Londoners' diet improved significantly between 1850 and 1900 but hunger was still common, food was still simple, and poor people worried constantly about it. One child remembered that his mother rattled plates at dinner time for the neighbors to hear when there was nothing to eat. A child from a relatively well-off family remembered her mother making dinner for 12 people: "She would buy half a pound of leg of beef, a ha'porth worth of suet, and three ha'porth of potatoes, and for this sixpence there was a dinner for all. I suppose the young ones had gravy and dumplings." That bought less than an ounce of meat per person. The majority of poor families in London survived on bread and butter or bread and jam during the week, so that they could afford meat for Sunday dinner, a ritual as important to workers as to the middle classes. Many poor families either had no stoves or could only afford gas once a week to cook the Sunday roast. There was a thriving market in cooked take-out meals like fish-and-chips at the turn of the century.

For the middle classes, the most influential household advice book in Europe was Mrs. Isabella Beeton's *Book of Household Management,* first published serially in 1859–1861. It was read all over the world and copied in every country. Included were hundreds of sample weekly menus.

Here is a sample November menu for middle-class families in England.

Sunday: 1. Crimped cod and oyster sauce. 2. Roast fowls, small boiled ham, vegetables; rump-steak pie. 3. Baked apple pudding, open jam tart.

Monday: 1. The remainder of cod warmed in maître d'hôtel sauce. 2. Boiled aitchbone of beef, carrots, parsnips, suet dumplings. 3. Baked bread-and-butter pudding.

Tuesday: 1. Pea-soup, made from liquor in which beef was boiled. 2. Cold beef, mashed potatoes, mutton cutlets and tomato sauce. 3. Carrot pudding.

Wednesday: 1. Fried soles and melted butter. 2. Roast leg of pork, applesauce, vegetables. 3. Macaroni with Parmesan cheese.

Thursday: 1. Bubble-and-squeak from remains of cold beef; curried pork. 2. Baked Semolina pudding.

Friday: 1. Roast leg of mutton, stewed Spanish onions, potatoes. 2. Apple tart.

Saturday: 1. Hashed mutton; boiled rabbit and onion sauce; vegetables. 2. Damson pudding made with bottled fruit.

---

http://etext.library.adelaide.edu.au/b/beeton/household/index.html

increased by half again by 1900. The price of food fell with increased grain production, importation, and better transportation. In the second half of the century, in France, consumption of bread, potatoes, and wine increased by 50 percent; consumption of meat, beer, and cider doubled. Bread fell from 20 percent of the diet in 1850 to 9 percent in 1900. Germans consumed almost twice as much meat in 1912 as in 1873. Working-class families were spending a smaller percentage of their income on food, so there was more money for clothes, simple appliances and utensils, and entertainment. Such aggregate figures mask the disparities between better- and worse-off families, however, and almost all workers were undernourished and more likely to die at an earlier age than the bourgeois and the aristocrat. And these gains took place in societies where bosses, managers, and owners of factories and shops made huge profits. Uneven progress contributed to lower-class discontent.

The Workers' Challenge

In the last third of the nineteenth century workers began to organize effectively to press their claims for improved living and working conditions. All over Europe, workers and socialist intellectuals organized parties and other associations based on socialist and anarchosyndicalist ideas. The rise of working-class movements coincided with a loss of faith in *laissez-faire*, the rise of the nation-state, and the financial crisis and depression of 1873. It was during the last third of the century that Marxist socialism spread its influence.

In 1864, three years before the first volume of *Capital* was published, Marx joined in the formation of the First International Workingman's Association. This was an ambitious attempt to organize workers of every country and variety of radical belief. A loose federation rather than a coherent political party, the First International terrified government officials and social observers but soon began to disintegrate, expiring in 1876. Increasing persecution by hostile governments helped to bring on its end, but so, too, did the factional quarrels that repeatedly divided its members.

In countries where government figures began to see the value of legislation for social welfare, workers tended to want to cooperate with legal institutions. In countries where workers' movements were repressed and their grievances ignored, workers often embraced more radical tactics. Socialist organizations were often split between those who sought peaceful change and those who called for revolution. All the socialist movements and parties included both workers and intellectuals who sympathized with their plight, saw capitalism as the source of their misery, and believed governments had the power to improve the lives of the poor but resisted doing so. In many cases movements were led by intellectuals who expected the uneducated and overworked workers to follow their lead. Socialist parties tended to experience tensions between workers and their intellectual leaders over tactics and direction. Among other issues, socialists disagreed about whether to cooperate with bourgeois and aristocratic governments for incremental reforms such as unemployment insurance or a minimum wage or whether they should work toward the destruction of the bourgeois state altogether. But despite these and similar problems, working-class politics achieved some successes in winning concessions from employers to raise wages, cut hours, and increase safety and economic security. Labor activism had mixed effects in that it both frightened the public and established the legitimacy of workers' grievances.

The Second International, organized in 1889, lasted until the First World War and the Bolshevik Revolution in Russia. The Second International represented the Marxian Socialist or Social Democratic parties, which were becoming important forces in the major countries of continental Europe. Among its leaders were men and women more politically adept than Marx himself. Yet factionalism continued to weaken the International. Some of its leaders tenaciously defended Marx's ideas and forbade any cooperation between socialists and the bourgeois political parties. Other leaders of the Second International revised Marxist doctrines in the direction of moderation. These socialists were branded "revisionists" by those who believed that workers would never benefit under bourgeois political systems, that only the revolutionary overthrow of the bourgeois state would bring social justice. Revisionists put their faith in parliamentary practice rather than in a struggle to the death, and they hoped that human decency and intelligence, working through the machinery of democratic government, could avert outright class war. These were the ideas that attracted the voters of the German Social Democratic Party, the French Section Française de l'Internationale Ouvrière, and the British Labour party. These parties attracted radical, republican, oppositional members of the middle classes as well as workers.

Socialist parties with the aim of overthrowing existing states were formed after 1875 in Germany, Belgium, France, Austria, Italy, and Russia. All the socialist parties combined Marxist ideas and other theories about social change, local political realities, and the influence of Marx himself and other political leaders. The conflict between the radical opposition to all governments and the willingness of some socialists to work through government to achieve economic improvements fragmented socialists all over Europe, but labor militancy continued to coexist with parliamentary reform activity.

Governments' responses to labor activism were inconsistent. From the 1890s until the outbreak of war in 1914, labor militancy, trade union activity, and strikes were on the rise. The most strike-prone and violent workers were not necessarily the most "proletarian." In France the most active workers were artisans finally forced into industrial factories by the demise of luxury craft production, together with agricultural wage laborers. The strongest trade unions (miners and printers) tended to vote for reformist parliamentary parties. Though this contradicts Marxist theory, it makes sense: workers in industries with the longest histories of opposition and organization had the most hope of gaining improvements through recognized legal actions; those in transition or in mobile jobs or in occupations that were harder to organize expected little from organized political action. Workers became increasingly frustrated and militant in the 1910s, with England, France, Italy, and Russia experiencing a major surge of strike activity on the very eve of the war. At that point neither Europe's liberal parliaments nor its autocratic monarchies could accommodate workers' demands or resolve conflicts with socialist parties.

Even more frightening than the rise of workers' activism and socialism (and often lumped together with them) was the growth of anarchism. Anarchism was a small movement, most popular in Russia, Italy, and Spain; but its use of bombings and assassinations made it more frightening than its numbers. It was popular with those who felt the most disenfranchised and frustrated by both bourgeois society and socialist parties. Anarchists believed that all government should be destroyed, and at the turn of the century they began using "direct action" to make that happen sooner rather than later. At first many anarchists put their hopes in a general rising of the peasantry. Similar to Russian populists of the 1870s, Italian anarchist followers of Bakunin tried to organize peasant uprisings but failed miserably. Decades of poverty and frustration with corrupt or autocratic governments, which seemed helpless or indifferent in the face of mass suffering, made anarchists turn to terrorism. In a wave of assassinations during the 1890s King Umberto of Italy and President William McKinley of the United States were murdered. In Russia dozens of high tsarist officials were killed by anarchists and the "fighting detachments" of the Socialist Revolutionary party, including two ministers of interior and a grand duke.

In the face of such stark conflicts, nation-states were most active during this period in reviving or inventing symbols and rituals to create a unified sense of popular nationalism. Even in France nation building was an ongoing project. Universal conscription was instituted in 1889 in part for military reasons and in part to create a uniform sense of patriotism; universal education spread "standard" French at the same time, although local dialects were eliminated only when Paris and urban, commercial, literate culture became widely desirable. Similar projects had similar effects in other European countries. In the 1880s and 1890s commemorations of historical events and victorious battles became national holidays, with parades, fireworks, church services, and dancing. All over Europe commemorative monuments were built as symbols of shared history and memory.

New laws defined citizenship in the nation-state—and made it easier to exclude Jews, Muslims, and other nonnationals. Classifying inclusion and exclusion, whether based on ethnicity or religion, helped create a coherent sense of the nation. These ideas took on new meanings in the context of imperialism and attempts to redefine European civilization as a national rather than a universal phenomenon. Both these local and international elements of nation-building contributed to the rise of an anti-Semitism that was racial as much as religious. Sometimes national identities provided cohesion across classes, but just as nations adopted more public and visible signs, so did socialists and other parties identify themselves with visual symbols. Workers in France adopted red flags and the "Internationale" against the tricolor and the "*Marseillaise.*"

Neither class conflict nor international competition was new in the late nineteenth century, but more people were invested in identifying themselves visibly and publicly with a nation or a class, which increased the tension involved in defining differences and helped undermine the Enlightenment faith in universal human ideals.

The Women's Challenge

The visibility of women in new public roles further challenged accepted cultural beliefs and the ways that people identified themselves. The modern industrial economy welcomed women as workers and active participants in the face of widespread ideas about women as passive, domestic creatures inferior to men and in need of protection. Poor women worked in factories and workshops; middle-class women worked as journalists, clerks, teachers, and social workers; elite women engaged in philanthropy and artistic patronage. The notion of "separate spheres" was being seriously undermined at the end of the century by the women stepping out of the domestic sphere into the public—unapologetically. The spread of education, the need for an income, and the aspirations of individuals brought women out into the world of work in increasingly visible and powerful positions. Since the beginning of the nineteenth century, women who did not need to work for wages were involved in public causes: poor relief, the antislavery campaign, missionary work, writing, and journalism. But when they took such work it was usually in accepted female roles as nurturers, an extension of motherhood. At the end of the century women redefined womanhood by legitimizing independence, wage earning, public achievement, and physical strength.

The fin de siècle saw the appearance of a new social type: the New Woman, who defied passive roles and rejected the cult of domesticity. New Women used birth control, smoked cigarettes in public, rode bicycles, and postponed marriage. They had political opinions and were politically active. In the 1890s and 1910s a multitude of novels, journal articles and illustrations, plays, and even films depicted New Women—celebrating as well as abhorring them.

Restrictions on women's education began breaking down in the second half of the century as growing bureaucracies needed educated employees, universal education called for more teachers, and women demanded access to higher education. Swiss universities and medical schools admitted women in the 1860s, attracting students from all over Europe. Oxford and Cambridge established women's colleges in the 1870s and 1880s. In Germany in 1914, 80 percent of retail employees were women. In 1911 in France, women made up 40 percent of workers in banking, insurance, and retail. Nursing and teaching were female occupations. Sturdy gender hierarchies kept women from becoming bank managers, physicians, or supervisors except in the most unusual cases. And when women did move into occupations such as teaching, the salaries and status of those jobs fell. Women became well-known stars of stage and screen, writers and subjects of a vast artistic and popular literature; a few became painters, professors (in women's colleges), and even athletes. Eventually, in the last quarter-century, women won legal rights to divorce and more control over their own property.

But despite growing acceptance, or at least toleration, of women's work and personal independence, political rights came only after protracted, bitter conflict. It is important to remember that in the nineteenth century (and later) many women accepted their position as politically subordinate to men even as they asserted their moral superiority. Many women saw their public activities not as a first step toward equality, but as an extension of their domestic and specifically feminine qualities as nurturers and educators. It is also important to remember that when exceptional women, like Mary Wollstonecraft in 1792 or Louise Otto and Harriet Taylor Mill in the 1850s, began calling for women's political rights, most men could not vote. But in the latter part of the century when suffrage was extended to men of all classes, disenfranchisement came to be based entirely on gender. Many women participated in liberal nationalist movements in 1848 to win full civil rights and national sovereignty, only to find that when the battle was over, gender hierarchies were reestablished and they were not allowed to participate in the new nation-states as full-fledged citizens.

By the end of the century, women were active in all spheres of public life except state politics, so the right to vote took on extraordinary significance. Women had been active in calling for political reform since at least the 1840s, culminating in the revolutions of 1848. In the disillusioned and repressive environment after the revolutions, women organized for social and legal reforms in everyday life. Women petitioned parliaments and autocrats alike for laws ensuring custody of their children and control over their property. In Ireland, women were active in independence movements. In Germany, Frieda Dünsing (1864–1933), entered the field of child welfare services and helped to put female social workers at the heart of Germany's growing juvenile court system. In France women were actively involved in placing women's issues at the forefront of the Commune's agenda, and they were massacred along with the men.

In the 1860s political issues again became paramount, beginning in England, where women began calling for the right to vote. In 1867, the year Parliament extended suffrage to most men, a bill legalizing women's suffrage was voted down. Suffrage groups were organized all over Europe; though they were smaller and less influential in countries where few men could vote. In Italy, Anna Mozzoni (1837–1920) argued that women should enjoy full rights of citizenship because they contributed as much to the nation as men: "For [the woman] taxes but not an education, for her sacrifices but not employment, for her strict virtue but not honor; for her the struggle to maintain a family but not even control of her own person; for her the capacity to be punished but not the right to be independent; strong enough to be laden with an array of painful duties, but sufficiently weak not to be allowed to govern herself."

In the 1890s the term "feminist" was commonly applied to these diverse movements. At the same time, women's suffrage became a cause that united women across political borders. By 1900 middle-class women had formed associations to win political and other rights in all of western Europe, Scandinavia, Russia, and the Austro-Hungarian Empire. In Austria-Hungary hundreds of public rallies were held in the 1910s to publicize women's demand for the right to vote. As in western Europe, Czech and Slovak women organized suffrage societies, fought for education, and founded women's journals. Women sought the vote not only for the right of individual citizenship but because they believed that men's legislative priorities created unbalanced and ultimately ineffective laws. Suffragists calling for the right to vote were criticizing fundamental government policies on the basis of women's exclusion from citizenship. Suffrage societies were large, visible organizations that were threatening to the existing order in ways that are hard to imagine today.

Suffragists, or as their detractors called them, suffragettes, were most militant in England. Under the leadership of Emmeline Pankhurst (1858–1928), women took to the streets in spectacular displays of unexpected, shocking violence. In addition to making public speeches, women destroyed golf courses, broke shop windows, torched theaters, slashed paintings in museums, interrupted political meetings, and even bombed the house of David Lloyd George. Pankhurst said, "We have tried to be womanly . . . and we have seen that it is of no use." When arrested, the suffragists went on hunger strikes in prison and were force-fed. German, French, and Russian suffragists condemned the use of violence, not as unwomanly but as counterproductive. In 1913 the International Women's Suffrage Association met in Budapest, in full expectation of imminent success. By 1918 women could vote in most European countries, though French and Italian women would have to wait until after another world war.

The failures of liberal societies to provide universal rights to women led some women to embrace socialism. The Germans Clara Zetkin (1857–1933) and Lily Braun (1865–1916), and the Russian Alexandra Kollontai (1872–1952), were Marxists who believed that only by overthrowing bourgeois capitalism, with its entrenched ideology of male superiority, would women finally achieve equality. Socialist women were active in trying to improve conditions for women workers both as women and as workers.

"A Suffragette's Home," published by the National League for Opposing Woman Suffrage, 1912. A great deal of antisuffrage literature was aimed at working-class men; it not only raised the specter of family life neglected and destroyed but argued that votes for women would result in "turning the order of nature upside-down." (Bodleian Library, John Johnson Collection: Posters: Women's Suffrage)

They understood that women often had grievances that differed from those of male workers.

Many male socialist leaders had a theoretical commitment to women's equality, but in practice socialist feminists ran into trouble. Male party leaders were opposed to separate organizations for women because they believed that workers had to be liberated as a class. Male leaders objected to separate organizations for part of the working class (whether for women or Jews or ethnic minorities) because they thought such divisions would dilute the class struggle. Or so they said. Male socialist activists had little sympathy in fact for the specific grievances of women workers, and they viewed women workers as inherently conservative. Where women were able to establish separate women's organizations, as in Germany, socialist feminists had the most success reaching women workers and helping them organize to voice their own grievances about living and working conditions.

Changes in women's employment and changes in public life made women more active and visible at the end of the nineteenth century than their grandmothers had dreamed possible (or even desirable). But breaking down the line that divided the separation of spheres and the cult of domesticity was threatening to men (and to many women). Some historians have argued that there was a "crisis of masculinity" in response to the appearance of the New Woman. The results of the new gender roles were complex. On the one hand, in art and popular culture, powerful women were sometimes portrayed as monstrous and larger than life, while at the same time traditional gender hierarchies were being reaffirmed in popular cinema and literature as fragile women were repeatedly saved from dastardly villains. The health and sports movements sought to revitalize the male body. And for many in 1914, war would seem an enticing proving ground for European masculinity.

Leisure and Mass Culture

By the end of the century every major city in Europe had museums and galleries, as well as opera houses, concert halls and theaters, musical societies, literary salons, elegant restaurants, and cafés. The vast majority of people, however, never set foot in any of these. They went to amusement parks, circuses, dance halls, variety shows in music halls, wrestling and soccer matches, bicycle races, and taverns. For people of every social stratum there was more public entertainment in greater variety than ever before. While many of these activities were segregated by class, some simply transformed themselves to conform to taste: aristocratic opera became middlebrow operetta and working-class song and dance. The aristocratic "traveler" became the middle-class "tourist"; workers with a free afternoon could journey by electric street car to a park at the end of the line (and their newspapers made jokes about the differences in destination). In England the elite played rugby, golf, polo, and cricket while workers played soccer (football) and boxed. After 1910 everyone went to the motion pictures, though even in cities where they patronized the same film "palaces" they were often segregated by section.

Leisure activities contributed to the making of modern society in a number of ways. Mass education and mass production made mass culture modern. Literacy rates rose higher in western Europe and among men generally than in Russia and eastern Europe. Even in Russia, however, popular newspapers in St. Petersburg had subscription rates in the tens of thousands and street sales of ten times those numbers. Activities that had been spontaneously or popularly organized in earlier times were rationalized, institutionalized, commercialized, and hierarchicalized by the end of the nineteenth century. Popular street fairs that grew up around neighborhood markets were enclosed, regulated, and accessible by ticket only. Fist-fighting matches or games played spontaneously with balls and sticks were organized into wrestling and soccer teams. Sports teams developed organized competition, official rules, newspapers devoted to their whole sport, and histories in the form of statistics and records. Such organizations created new communities as well as new loyalties and rivalries. Elites liked to think that organized sports would keep workers from organizing unions or developing militant class politics; but there is no evidence that this was the case. Some sports teams and clubs were organized at factories. Sports loyalties could be extremely disruptive. A match between Catholic and Protestant teams in Glasgow at the turn of the century ended with the stadium burned to the ground.

National sports teams participating in international competitions fed mass nationalism. In 1896 the first modern Olympic games were organized in Athens, home of the ancient games. The Frenchman Pierre de Coubertin (1863–1937) led the revival. Like many advocates of physical fitness, he believed that people were becoming weak as industry and materialism spoiled them. Some people hoped that the Olympic movement would prevent international warfare by encouraging men to exhaust their aggressive drives on the playing fields. Others hoped that physical conditioning and strengthening of men would help counter fears of a growing modern gender imbalance as women became stronger and more active and men seemed weaker.

The popularity of sport was part of a broader health and hygiene movement meant to counter the physical weakening of the middle classes and prevalence of disease among the poor. Exercise and fresh air were encouraged. Sports clubs of all kinds and for both sexes were formed: for hiking, hunting, tennis, bodybuilding, soccer. Some philanthropists formed sports clubs to keep juvenile criminals off the streets and direct them toward activities healthier than smoking, billiards, and pickpocketing. The popularity of the clubs for rich and poor members alike drew individuals into new social organizations, which in turn multiplied the sources of modern cultural identities (beyond family, work, church, and nation). The organization of leisure helped make structure, rationalization, and physical discipline a part of the modern identity.

Bicycle riding became extremely popular both as a spectator sport and as a leisure activity. Bicycles gave people a sense of individual velocity and freedom not possible before. Men and women both rode bicycles, which figured in the changing gender roles developing at the end of the century. The New Woman not only worked and demanded the vote, but she could transport her individual self without assistance. Bicycle-riding women aroused additional fears that women would become sterile from the pain of too many jolts or debauched from the alleged pleasure of those jolts. Bicycles also frightened some into thinking that crime would increase as thieves could get away more quickly from the scene of the crime. Bicycles provided entertainment for those who could afford them and for those who could not. The first Tour de France was held in 1903 and covered fifteen hundred miles. The English daredevil Robert Jefferson rode his bicycle along an even more arduous route from Irkutsk (in Siberia) to Moscow in 1896. His trip was reported in the Russian national cycling magazine and local cyclists rode along the route with him as he passed through their towns.

Team and national sports contributed to the new phenomenon of modern celebrity. Like film and stage stars, athletes attracted fans and cults. They were portrayed in newspapers and magazines. Their behavior and appearance modeled behavior and appearance for their fans. But the gender messages sent by celebrities were mixed. Women film and stage stars made acting into a reputable profession. The high fees they earned and the legions of fans who adored them legitimized public roles for women even when they played conventional wives and mothers. At the same time the New Woman was also portrayed as a malevolent, deceptive, greedy, all-consuming vampire in some popular fiction, art, and films. Gender roles, seemingly so stable, are in constant flux and negotiation. Nowhere were the new gender conflicts played out with greater authority and ambiguity than in the new, wildly popular medium of cinema.

It took about ten years from the invention of the motion picture camera and projector for filmmakers to realize that they could tell stories with a film camera, but when idea took hold, around 1908–1910, narrative cinema became the most popular entertainment of all. For the first decade, motion pictures were exhibited in nightclubs and brothels, cafes and cabarets as short bits of entertainment. A stationary camera filmed a play or a contrived scene, or a documentary scene of people in everyday action. A few stop-action animated films were made, but nothing sustained for more than about ten minutes. Responses to the first moving pictures ranged from delighted surprise (it looks so real!) to existential alarm (such eerie shadows, bled pale of all color and sound!)

By the 1910s, feature films were developing their own innovative cinematic conventions for telling stories, but the people who made them always had an eye on the commercial market. All the classic genres of entertainment were represented: melodrama, historical drama, psychological thrillers, horror, animation, adventure; and adaptations of classic novels and plays were recast in film. As the quintessential mix of technology, art, and mass consumption, cinema helped shaped conceptualizations of modernity. Moving pictures projected in a dark space established an intimate, psychologically penetrating, and novel connection with the viewer. By arranging images to both shock the viewer's existing notions of space and time and force the viewer to make meaning from fragmented soundless images, early cinema engaged its audiences in new ways that proved addictive. Once filmmakers started to move the camera around, they could tell new kinds of stories by both relying on and subverting the viewer's conventional expectations. To tell stories with silent images, filmmakers had to find visual ways to give spectators insight into characters' motivations and effects. Cinematic narratives had the effect of intensifying the viewer's capacity to identify with people and events on the screen, as films were able to manipulate perception and touch audiences more profoundly than ever before.

The cinema was so established in the 1910s that in France, for example, documentary, scientific and historical films were used by the government in its national school network and even by the Catholic Church in its diocesan schools. French writers on the right thought films could be used to create a patriotic national identity and even control people in French colonies; on the left (not just in France), cinema was seen as a universal language that could foster international understanding.

Everyone went to movies, but women went more than men. And since cinema was from the first a thoroughly consumer-oriented industry, filmmakers sought to appeal to their greatest market. As a result, they cared less about reinforcing standard gender roles than about pleasing their audiences as consumers. Women's lives became the central subject matter, stories about women multiplied, and fashion came to be almost as important an element of a film as the plot. Female stars, who lived in that ambiguous zone between their roles as active professional, public women and constantly changing characters of someone else's invention, were adored by audiences as both. Because films could be and were transported all over Europe (and across the ocean), the amount of exposure film stars received was unprecedented. Gossip about their personal lives became a consumer object as well.

Typically modern, cinema had an ambivalent affect on public construction of gender roles. On the one hand, the publicity and professionalization of roles for women empowered and reinforced the increasingly public roles women were seizing for themselves. On the other hand, film narratives, with their fragile women, manipulative male villains, male adventure fantasies, and conventional female melodramas and fashion pageants, reinforced traditional gender roles. Modernity at the movies was as fragmented and conflicted as in the rest of European culture on the eve of the First World War.

The Cultural Challenge: Modernism

Sometime around the 1890s a fundamental shift took place in the way artists, scientists, and other intellectuals viewed the world around them. There were precursors earlier in the century, and it would be decades until their views would be widely shared. But in the two decades before the outbreak of war, a dramatic and comprehensive cultural transformation took place that produced a profusion of creative works in all the arts.

Confusingly, *modernism,* as that movement was called, began as a rejection of what the artists and thinkers thought of as *modernity.* Modernism was born in a radical critique of bourgeois capitalism and the culture of respectability, which were seen as artificial, banal, superficial, materialistic, crass, and spiritually exhausted. Modernism was motivated in part by the desire to shake up complacent bourgeois society, to "throw a bombshell into the joyless, provincial street of the generally joyless existence," as one Russian modernist put it, or in the words of another: to "Slap the Face of Public Taste." The distaste for bourgeois banality and hypocrisy was not entirely new; the poet Charles Baudelaire had described French society in 1859–1860 as "wholly worn-out—worse than worn out, brutalized and greedy, . . . adoring only material possession." At the end of the century, antibourgeois sentiment was transformed into a far-reaching critique of European artistic traditions and a search for a new modern language of expression and a new role for art.

Modernist artists sensed that bourgeois respectability and materialism masked a more satisfying, more authentic experience of life. They rejected the art forms that corresponded to bourgeois materialism: the realist novel as catalog of modern society, realist painting and photography as objective representations of reality, architecture that embodied the rational, scientific achievements of capitalism. The Austrian composer Arnold Schoenberg declared that "one must express oneself . . . *directly!* Not one's taste or upbringing, or one's intelligence, knowledge or skill. Not all these *acquired* characteristics, but that which is *inborn, instinctive.*" The artists who recoiled from bourgeois superficiality rejected the claims of previous generations of artists to have portrayed reality objectively. Like Schoenberg, they wanted to replace a false depiction of the surface of reality with something more deeply real. They sought to depict a new kind of realism, situated in the subjective rather than the objective realm.

Culture had a new function for the modernists: not to represent, explore, analyze, or catalog objective reality, but to turn inward and explore under the surface of things, to express the subjective experience unique to each individual, including contradictory feelings, drives, energies at the very heart of human life. Going further than the Romantics who had also idealized individual expression, the modernists developed whole new languages, codes, and aesthetic principles for representing the complexity of subjective human experience in each of the arts. Music, painting, poetry, dance, theater, and eventually cinema, all developed new systems of artistic representation to express inner states, the variability of perception, and the unstable truths of reality.

Modernism also shifted the focus in artistic creativity from the artist to the audience. Starting from the impressionists' play with perception, the modernists went on to draw particular attention to the difficulty of knowing reality with any certainty. They recognized that it was impossible to analyze reality without addressing the infinite variation in the ways each individual perceives reality.

These ideas developed gradually and through intellectual projects of great diversity. There was an unusual amount of interplay among the artistic genres during this period as well: painting influenced and was influenced by music, poetry, and fiction. Almost all the modernists were inspired in one way or another by works written decades earlier by Friedrich Nietzsche (1844–1900). Nietzsche is perhaps best known for saying "God is dead." But this was not a simple statement of modern secularization. He meant that in place of a universe organized by a central all-powerful being and knowable as the creation of a single divine vision, we live in a world that has no preordained purpose, no fixed perspective. There is no preexistent reality waiting for us to discover its natural and scientific laws, but rather a random arrangement, governed by chance, and knowable only, as he put it in *Thus Spake*

Zarathustra (1883) by "your reason, your image, your will, your love." Nietzsche believed that there was no single identifiable truth that could be considered true in all situations and from every point of view. On the contrary, there was only perspective and interpretation—and truths in conflict with one another. For Nietzsche, there was no meaning in life other than the meanings we give it through the exercise of our will. Nietzsche also explored the conflicts that divided the modern sense of self. Moral values, he argued in *On the Genealogy of Morals* (1887) are not absolutes but always appear in particular historical circumstances and change to meet the needs of the context. People in power will always justify themselves morally, disguising disreputable drives of some kind. Universal ideas about good and evil and other values are a form of deception and to the extent that they are internalized, self-deception, as well. Tension between deception and secret acknowledgment divides the self. This understanding of the world was both artistically exciting and profoundly alarming.

Painting

Painting was the quintessential art form of modernism. In painting there is a clear progression from the postimpressionists' experiments with the use of color and form, through the cubists' breaking down of realistic perspective into multiple points of view, to abstraction in its most relative, expressive, transcendent and antirationalist forms. In the 1890s Vincent Van Gogh and Paul Gauguin used colors expressively and extravagantly. Van Gogh used color allegorically to express the torment of violent mood swings to which he was hostage and which seemed to represent the passionate extremes unavailable to placid bourgeois respectability. He meticulously mixed colors to achieve a red and a green that could express "the terrible passions of humanity" and show *The Night Café* (1888) as "a place where one can ruin oneself, go mad or commit crime. . . . in an atmosphere like a devil's furnace, of pale sulfur." Gauguin, considered a mediocre painter by his contemporaries, gave up his comfortable life in bourgeois finance for repeated trips to the island of Tahiti. His paintings of Tahitian women brought the exotic colors and primitive sensuality back to a Europe that never looked more dreary by comparison, but his exquisite paintings were based less on the reality that he found in the French colony than on his fantasy of a primitive energy that could be used to revive the exhausted culture of bourgeois materialism. The Norwegian Edvard Munch (1863–1944) used vibrant color to express states of mind and suffering; his subjects are modern individual (especially male) alienation, sexual obsession, and a deep enmity between women and men. Swirling forms convey the dreamlike states of irrationality associated with psychosis or hallucination as in *The Scream* (1893), while two-dimensional forms in his woodcuts strip feelings down to their most painful and moving as in *The Kiss* (1897–1898).

The most radical and influential of the postimpressionists is Paul Cézanne (1839–1906). Cézanne rejected the works of impressionism as paintings of shallow, surface effects. He broke down the three-dimensionality of the image further than anyone had yet to emphasize both the painter's hand and the disorienting absence of any single "true" perspective. Cézanne often painted the same subject over and over again—still lifes, for example, and the landscape at Mont Sainte-Victoire—undermining in yet another way the concept of the one "true" representation. Somewhere between Van Gogh's highly colored expressionism and Cézanne's flat multiperspectivism stands the Viennese painter Gustav Klimt (1862–1918). Like Munch, Klimt sought to bring the unconscious to the canvas but without sacrificing the aesthetic pleasure of decorative forms. His paintings of women are subtle psychological studies, some are frankly sexual, and all are decorated in vibrant, flat, fabriclike patterns of colors and shapes. His women are beautiful, alluring, frightening, but not alienated. Klimt painted modern fairy tales that mix psychoanalysis with pure aesthetics.

Henri Matisse (1869–1954) took further the flattening of the pictoral space found in Cézanne and Klimt; in his *Harmony in Red* (1908) the flowers on a tablecloth flow musically into the flowers on the wall paper and seem at least as alive as the trees in the garden outside. Matisse was after a musical harmony with its own integrity independent of the subject matter it represented: "I cannot copy nature in a servile way, I must interpret nature . . . in all the tones there must result a living harmony of colors, . . . analogous to that of a musical composition." His deceptively simple paintings of dancers were meant to convey the transcendent pleasures of musical harmony, rhythm, and melody.

Pablo Picasso (1881–1973) took Cézanne's experiment with form to radical new heights in *Les Demoiselles d'Avignon* (1907), the painting that many people consider the essential modernist painting. Flat two-dimensional planes of color intersect with one another at impossibly tilted angles to just barely represent five naked women, a few bits of drapery, and a small table with some fruit. The figures are portrayed from various angles at the same time; one has her back to the viewer but her face forward. A sensation when it was first exhibited, *Les Demoiselles* shows that Picasso rejected conventions of form and composition just as radically as he rejected conventions of beauty. The women are frightening in ugliness and angularity, and in their masklike primitivist faces, their staring lidless eyes are dehumanized. The painting is as horrifyingly misogynistic as it is intellectually exciting: neither truth nor beauty, only fractured perception and dehumanization. Cubism made explicit what Nietzsche had suggested, that if painting need not be organized around a single point of view, neither did stories need to be told by a single voice.

Two Russian painters would take these experiments with form to their logical conclusion. Vasily Kandinsky (1866–1944) liked the musical analogy in Matisse's dancers, but for him musical harmony in painting was not just a source of aesthetic pleasure but a path to spiritual transcendence. In 1910 Kandinsky did away with the most basic requirement of the visual arts, a recognizable subject, in painting the first nonrepresentational, abstract, painting. His abstractions of pure color and form were meant to convey a pure aesthetic experience and gain access to the "spiritual in art" as his theoretical work on the subject was called, *On the Spiritual in Art* (1911). His abstract forms were not meant to be meaningless—all forms and colors had meaning—but no artist could predetermine that meaning for the viewer.

Before Kandinsky gave up representation for abstract forms he had incorporated images from folk art, Russian Orthodoxy, and popular culture in his paintings. This eclecticism was common in modernist art of all genres and was especially pronounced in Russian modernism. Early work by Kazimir Malevich (1878–1935) combined cubist elements with stylizations suggesting folk embroidery and Orthodox iconography. But he also abandoned representation and in the 1910s was painting geometrical forms, like *Black Square on a White Ground* (1913) and the ultimate, *White on White* (1918). Malevich called his painting "suprematism" to convey the supremacy of feeling in art: pure forms, not the imperfect representations of reality, offer visual analogs of consciousness. *White on White* is oddly affecting in its purity and minute variation in color.

Another route of escape from the harsh iron and steel world of capitalist materialism was the rediscovery of forms taken from nature and the dreamy subconscious images of *art nouveau* as it was called in France, *Jugendstil* in Germany and *art moderne* elsewhere in Europe. Art nouveau influenced painting, interior design, decorative arts, architecture, and fashion. It is characterized by flowing "organic" forms, sinuous design elements, or softened geometrical patterning that suggest plants and animals. The lilies and lettering of the Paris Metro, Fyodor Shektel's Moscow mansion with its waterfall marble staircase sprouting turtles and mushroom caps as lamps and railings and its cascades of roses carved into doorways, the stylized geometric organicism of Charles Rennie Mackintosh's Glasgow furnture and designs, all began as a retreat from capitalist materialism, but ended up becoming a favored style of the urban wealthy bourgeoisie.

Music

While painters aspired to musical harmony, modernist musicians shunned harmony for dissonance and an assault on the senses. The late-Romantic composer, Richard Wagner had already departed from classical harmonic structures to write music of personal expression. Arnold Schoenberg (1874–1951) liberated classical music from melody; Igor Stravinsky (1882–1971) liberated it from rhythm. Schoenberg was Austrian and Stravinsky was Russian, but like most of the modernist artists, they traveled widely and worked in a variety of European capitals. In 1908 Schoenberg wrote his first "atonal" composition, breaking away from the traditional musical referents that had always structured music and given it meaning. He did not see himself as rejecting the traditions and historical developments of classical music; on the contrary, he believed that atonality was a continuation of musical history. Schoenberg was guided by his unconscious in expressing dissonance where "the individual parts proceed regardless of whether or not their meeting results in codified harmonies." His music was emotionally disturbing both because it did not provide melodic or harmonic referents and because the dissonance was never resolved in the ways that listeners expect based on conventions. Schoenberg forces us to hear in an entirely new way. He began with tonalities that would then disappear, leaving the listener in a state of modernist anxiety or awash in the unmediated unconscious.

Stravinsky used different tactics to shock the viewer. Abandoning the sentimental music that usually accompanied ballet, Stravinsky's *Rite of Spring* (1913) used wild, jarring tones and unfamiliar jazz rhythms to match the modern choreography by Vaslav Nijinsky (1888–1950). The search for the elemental in the human psyche led many modernists to embrace "primitivism" either of earlier European cultures or based in objects collected from colonies in Asia and Africa. Stravinsky and Nijinsky were both striving for modernist "primitive" effects in the *Rite of Spring*—the story was based on a spring ritual sacrifice of a young girl. The dancing is nonballetic and bluntly physical but also highly stylized, nonnatural as well. We are meant to be shocked by the violence of the music, the movement, and the events depicted. Stravinsky claimed to have written it in a kind of unconscious dream state: "I had only my ear to help me. I heard and wrote what I heard. I was the vessel through which *Le Sacre* passed." He used extremely complex techniques of composition to express what was supposed to be "primitive" and elemental.

The Other Arts

Novels, poetry, drama, and dance all followed suit by exploring the unconscious and opening up the possibilities of multiple perspectives. Early experiments in French poetry lay the groundwork for some of the fundamental ideas of modernism. Stéphane Mallarmé (1842–1898) and Arthur Rimbaud (1854–1891) invented free verse, with its visually suggestive typographical arrangements, juxtaposition, and collage of ideas. They believed that poetic language should transcend the conventions of everyday speech to escape from bourgeois conformity. Their poems were not random but carefully constructed with symbolic language that suggested other spheres of consciousness. The literary historian George Steiner has called French symbolist poetry a "revolt of literature against language." This revolt was felt in all the arts, as one after another invented new languages to challenge prior conventions and explore deeper recesses of human experience.

The modernist novel came into its own after World War I in the work of James Joyce (1882–1941) and Virginia Woolf (1882–1941). The main modernist writer in Europe before the war was Marcel Proust (1871–1922), whose seven-volume novel *In Search of Time Past* (1913–1927) pioneered the use of "stream of consciousness." Proust would chose a single object or sensation and allow his mind to freely come up with various things associated with its memory. In dance, classical ballet was joined by modern dance when the expatriate American Isadora Duncan (1878–1927) challenged the conventions of ballet by introducing natural body movements by barefoot dancers in flowing robes.

In sculpture, Auguste Rodin (1840–1917) challenged monumental forms of traditional sculpture as an impressionist in the 1870s and 1880. By the 1890s and 1900s Rodin was attempting to express the "human soul in the face of nature." This work culminated in *Balzac* (1898), a portrait of formal complexity that suggests the modernist multiplicity of perspectives and emotional expressivity. The sculpture represents the writer Balzac as an embodiment of his enormous creative energy. Cubist sculpture used convex and concave forms as well as empty spaces to expand on the notion of multiple perspectives, unknowability, and emotional expressiveness of form. Much sculpture of this genre, including that of Picasso, is also playful and whimsical.

The Scientific Challenge: Discontinuity, Randomness, and Relativity

At the same time that artists were rediscovering Nietzsche, disturbing conclusions about the natural world were finding their way into general understanding. In 1895 Wilhelm Röntgen (1845–1923) publicized his findings on X-rays. The ability to see bones through skin would be considered eerily alarming when it became common knowledge and complemented the modernists' sense that there was an unseen reality to be discovered beneath the surface. Scientists were also coming to the conclusion that we cannot analyze reality without thinking about the ways we perceive reality. By painstaking observation of the cells operating inside a bird's brain, Ramon y Cajal, a Spanish scientist, discovered in 1889 that brains function by sending messages across minute spaces, later named synapses. In 1896 a Polish physicist living in France, Marie Curie (1867–1934), discovered radium, a radioactive element. She earned not one but two Nobel prizes, though she was excluded from the French Academy of Sciences for being a woman.

In number theory, mathematicians stopped thinking in terms of continuities and seamlessness and embraced discontinuity and rupture. In 1872 Ludwig Boltzmann (1844–1906) founded modern physics with his "H-theorem," which stated that atoms behave unpredictably, so physics is not based on iron laws but mathematical probabilities. In 1900 his student Max Planck (1858–1947) discovered that energy flows in the universe not in continuous emissions as was earlier believed but in separate and discontinuous units he called quanta.

Unpredictability and randomness appeared everywhere in the sciences where the previous century had found order and measure. In 1900 biologists rediscovered Gregor Mendel's experiments in genetics written 35 years earlier and were able to build on his theory of reproduction through genetic variation and mutation. Then in 1905 Albert Einstein (1879–1955) published the first of his revolutionary papers extending Planck's work on quantum physics, proposing the special theory of relativity, which argued that reality is four-dimensional, that the fourth dimension is time; that time and space exist in a continuum. The only constant in the universe, said Einstein, is the speed of light; all other measurements of time and space depend on the placement of the observer. He also argued that energy and mass are equivalent in a way that would later allow scientists to control the extraordinary amounts of energy released when an atom was split, producing the "atom bomb." In 1915 Einstein published his general theory of relativity. Einstein, however, was never comfortable with the randomness his work suggested. "God does not play dice with the universe," he said. But his theories and the popularization of them after the First World War would help spread the uncertainties and relativity of the culture of modernism.

Social Sciences

Attempts to apply scientific laws to the study of human society and personality had paradoxical results at the turn of the century. Imperialism had stimulated interest in people of non-European cultures. Social Darwinism supported some forms of racism by suggesting that whole classes of people could compete in the "survival of the fittest." It became common to classify people according to "races."

Other studies of African and Asian peoples resulted in the modern fields of ethnography and anthropology. At the turn of the century, some thinkers were beginning to see "culture" in neutral terms. The word *culture* came to be associated with the attributes of a given people in a given context, neither inherently good nor bad. Cultural relativism was first explored in *The Golden Bough* (1890), the monumental study by James Frazer (1854–1941). Frazer studied the customs, beliefs, and living arrangements of ancient and present-day peoples in Europe as well as Africa and Asia. He argued that all modern peoples evolved from a culturally "primitive" stage. Though less disparaging than earlier studies of foreign cultures, Frazer's theories were essentially Eurocentric. He argued that people still living in primitive states would also evolve into cultures that resembled European culture, which seemed to explain the "backwardness" and even "childishness" of other cultures.

The modern field of sociology was founded during this period in studies by Max Weber (1864–1920) and Émile Durkheim (1858–1917). Both were interested in the forces that create conflict and cohesion in society. Each was a firm believer in his ability to apply scientific principles to the study of society, but each nonetheless contributed to modern notions about the emotional, irrational, or uncontrollable drives that influence social life. Weber studied the origins of Europeans' economic success, which he located in Protestant religious values applied to social behavior. He also studied bureaucracies, which he saw as the proof of human capacity for rational organization, but worried that bureaucracies would develop their own impersonal rationales and become distanced from humane values. Durkheim was interested in the apparently dramatic rise in crime rates. He theorized that modern impersonal urban life was dehumanizing because it broke down traditional religious and community ties and freed people's baser instincts. Durkheim was the first to apply scientific principles to the study of suicide, which he blamed on increasing *anomie*, or alienation of urban life.

Scientific methods were also applied to studies of individual behavior, resulting in the field of psychology. Russian physician Ivan Pavlov (1849–1936) revealed regular behavioral patterns in dogs. By ringing a bell when dogs were fed, he conditioned the animals to associate bell ringing with hunger. They would salivate when the bell was rung, even when there was no food. Pavlov argued that his conclusions applied to human beings as well, which was as disturbing to the public as the notion, a distortion of Darwin's views, that humans descended from apes.

The founder of modern psychoanalysis, Sigmund Freud (1856–1939), began his studies of the brain with biological and mechanistic beliefs much like those of Pavlov. The son of an Austrian Jewish merchant, Freud moved to Vienna as a child, where he benefited from the liberal laws in midcentury Vienna, which allowed him to study physiology and then medicine. He had a medical practice in Vienna from 1886 until he fled the Nazis in 1938. He died the next year in England. His first studies were attempts to understand nervous disorders as medical diseases, which he treated with hypnosis. But then he realized that when patients could consciously identify their symptoms and associate them with earlier traumatic experiences, the symptoms often cleared up. Many of the childhood experiences of Freud's patients were disturbing sexual events or desires, which led to his theory of infantile sexuality.

Such theories were not popular with the medical establishment in Vienna, and they challenged widespread nineteenth-century notions of childhood innocence as well. In 1896 Freud coined the term "psychoanalysis" to describe the science he was developing for studying the mind and its drives. He believed that the mind was an orderly organ and could be studied scientifically and that dreams were the unconscious language of the mind. He believed that apparently irrational dreams had rational meanings, which could be analyzed. In *The Interpretation of Dreams* (1900) he argued that dreams represent the unconscious drives and desires that we repress during our waking hours. Further, he proposed that we all have natural desires that are too strong to be eliminated, but since society considers them sinful or dangerous, they are forced into the unconscious. Mental illnesses, neuroses, inappropriate behavior, even slips of the tongue are signs of the unconscious breaking through the barrier of repression.

Freud established the unconscious and the irrational as intrinsic to human behavior; yet, paradoxically, he was convinced that they could be studied with nineteenth-century rationalist methods. He ushered in an essential element of modernism and twentieth-century culture; yet he remained an Enlightenment thinker in that he had ultimate faith in human reason. When that faith seemed to falter, he saw classical tragedy rather than fin de siècle degeneration. His last great work appeared after World War I and on the eve of World War II. *Civilization and Its Discontents* (1939) argues that the price of civilization is the repression of natural drives toward the expression of sexuality and aggression, a tragic conflict for a healthy society, even more tragic when repression seems to be ceasing to function.

* * *

Though modernists sought to dethrone modernity, they ended up redefining it. Modernity would continue to be associated with progress through rational enterprise, with cities, industry, and bourgeoisies, but after the turn of the century, modernity would also be associated with doubts about the objective, accessible, and positive qualities of modern life. By the end of the century more people were living in more comfort than ever before in human history, but prosperity had not solved the riddle of increasing poverty. More people had more individual freedom than ever before, but their lives were more circumscribed by government interference, routinization, and fears of falling behind. Artists and scientists knew more than ever before about people, cities, and the natural world, but their knowledge was infinitely more destructive, intrusive, and frightening.

ELEVEN

Political Polarization and Conflict

The power and prestige of European nation-states peaked at the turn of the twentieth century, and seemed to have reached a high point of political development and stability as well. Numerous crises beset each of the Great Powers of Europe between 1890 and 1914 that, in hindsight, show how unstable the region really was. Mass politics, in the form of labor, feminist, and nationalist movements, destabilized domestic political arrangements everywhere in Europe in the late nineteenth century. The delicate balance of new industrial wealth with old aristocratic power, of middle-class liberalism with conservatism and nationalism, of liberal reformism with industrial poverty and lower-class discontent: all were challenged by the new factor of public mass politics. Because the Western powers had developed elected institutions in which representatives had by necessity learned to compromise with one another and with the will of the mass of the population, only Russia faced revolutionary upheaval in this period, in 1905. But parliamentary democracy had its own problems.

Three developments made domestic politics and international affairs more contentious at the turn of the century. First, social hierarchy and market injustice became more apparent to more people during the depression of the 1870s–1880s, and the existence of socialism as ideology and political organization gave those with grievances a ready structure for articulating them. Second, after a century of expanding opportunities and rights, when all things seemed possible, late nineteenth-century political conflicts eluded all resolution. In fact, Irish Home Rule, voting rights for women, and Russian autocratic intransigence, and the discontent of nationalists and the poor had existed as intractable problems since the beginning of the century, but by the 1890s more people had lost hope of finding political solutions. Third, overseas conquests created new arenas for international conflicts among European powers, military technological advances and the arms race made new, more deadly, weapons available, and the consensus that had helped deter war throughout the century was breaking down. The result was political polarization. People were increasingly attracted to extreme parties on the left and the right, and they sought scapegoats instead of solutions. Moderate, liberal parties lost what authority they had enjoyed. International conflict distracted rulers from stubborn domestic problems. War came to seem inevitable, even desirable.

Imperial Germany, 1880–1914

After the failure of the Kulturkampf and in response to the financial crisis of the 1870s, Bismarck began a gradual shift in policy, dictated at first by the need for more revenue. To get the Reichstag to vote for higher indirect taxes, he needed to assemble new political alliances. In the 1880s, thinking to win over the Center party against his former allies, the Liberals, Bismarck repealed most of the anti-Catholic measures he had passed in the 1870s. The German chancellor moved away from the Liberals because he found their demands for power exorbitant and because he and many others blamed them for the market crash of 1873. Bismarck used the changed economic climate to his advantage. He turned to justify protectionism and make alliances with conservative parties and to shift the balance of political forces away from liberalism.

Up to this point German tariff policy had basically been one of free trade, with little protection for German goods. But after the financial panic in 1873, the iron and textile industries put pressure on Bismarck to shift to a policy of protection that would help them compete with England. Moreover, an agricultural crisis led conservatives to abandon their support of free trade and to demand protection against cheap grain coming in from eastern Europe. In 1879 Bismarck began moving away from free trade by passing a general protective tariff on all imports. The Catholic Center party favored his protectionist policy, as did German peasants and big landed interests. Bismarck secured the support of both the center and the conservatives and was able to avoid making concessions to the liberal majority in the Reichstag. This was a crucial shift in German politics. Bismarck's new alliance brought into power the most traditional, conservative, antidemocratic forces. Their influence would outlast Bismarck himself. Parliament would have less power and be come more polarized.

To cement this new set of political alliances, Bismarck initiated an attack on the Social Democratic Party. In 1878, using as a pretext two attempts by alleged Social Democrats to assassinate Wilhelm I, Bismarck rammed through the Reichstag a bill making the Social Democratic party illegal, forbidding its meetings, and suppressing its newspapers. The Liberals supported this law, but they would not allow Bismarck to make it a permanent statute; he had to apply to the Reichstag for renewal every two or three years. Right after the bill was passed, the police launched a ruthless attack: socialist leaders were deported, fledgling trade unions and workers' clubs were shut down, ordinary workers were forced to resign from the party to save their jobs. But this policy backfired just as the Kulturkampf had.

The German Social Democrats were moderates, content to fight for improvements in workers' living and working conditions through legal parliamentary means. Two Marxists, Wilhelm Liebknecht (1826–1900) and August Bebel (1840–1913), had founded this small party in 1869; in 1875 they joined another Marxist party organized by Ferdinand Lassalle (1825–1864). The unified German Social Democratic Party, much to the disgust of Karl Marx, was Marxist in its criticism of capitalism but not in its tactics. In works written in the 1890s, Eduard Bernstein (1850–1932) gave a theoretical and practical basis for gradual socialist reform. (Bernstein was among those bitterly denounced as a "revisionist" by revolutionary Marxists.) Ultimately, Bismarck undermined a legal party committed to parliament, thereby encouraging its supporters to become more radical.

The ever-pragmatic Bismarck, however, matched political repression with social-economic welfare: "Give [the worker] work as long as he is healthy. Look after him while he is ill. Take care of him when he is old. If you do this and don't shy away from the sacrifices involved or scream about state socialism the minute someone mentions 'care for the elderly' or when the state shows a bit of Christian charity towards the worker, then I believe the supporters [of the socialists] will play their pied pipes in vain."

As a result, during the 1880s the government put forward bills in favor of the workers: compulsory insurance against illness in 1883 and against accidents in 1884. In 1889 old age and disability insurance followed. This legislation would provide a model for western European "welfare states" for decades to come. Most west European countries passed some legislation protecting workers, legalizing unions, and supervising the workplace. But the program did not have the effect Bismarck planned, as the workers' voting record shows. Under the new law, Social Democrats were still allowed to run for the Reichstag as individuals, and hundreds of thousands of men voted for SD delegates. Their votes increased during the years when they were suffering legal restrictions; from 12 delegates in the Reichstag in 1877 to 110 in 1890, with 1.4 million votes. Bismarck's failure to win over the workers would be spectacularly displayed in a series of violent mass strikes in May 1889.

Bismarck's policies did much to encourage extremist ideologies and strategies and to undermine the legitimacy of the parliamentary politics and the political arts of compromise. And by the late 1880s he had played almost all his cards. In 1888 Wilhelm I died at the age of 90 and his son, Friedrich III, already mortally ill, ruled for only three months. In the "Year of the Three Emperors," Friedrich's son, Wilhelm II (1859–1941), came to power at age 29. Wilhelm II was determined to govern actively, which led directly to conflict with Bismarck.

The emperor and the chancellor came to blows over the antisocialist law. When the antisocialist law came up for renewal, the emperor, who had proclaimed his sympathy for the workers, supported a modified version that would have abolished the power of the police to expel Social Democrats from their homes. Bismarck, while hoping that the Social Democrats would indulge in excesses that would give him the excuse to suppress them by armed force, opposed the measure. He lost, and as a result the antisocialist law was not renewed again after 1890. Other differences arose between the chancellor and the emperor over an international workers' conference, over relations with Russia, and over procedures in reaching policy decisions. Finally, in March 1890, to the great shock of many people, Wilhelm commanded Bismarck to resign.

Bismarck had made Germany the most powerful country in Europe. But the structures he had created were wobblier than they seemed. His contempt for popular government and his own arrogance led him to undermine compromise and reinforce discord in many areas of public life. His greatest achievements may have been in foreign policy. He increased Germany's power exponentially but always kept an eye on European peace and stability. He did not believe in militarism for power's sake, but in power for stability's sake. After Bismarck, Germany appeared to lose sight of these principles.

Wilhelm II was energetic but unsteady, pompous and menacing but without the intention or the courage to back up his threats, Wilhelm was ill suited to govern any country, much less the militaristic, highly industrialized imperial Germany, with its social tensions and its lack of political balance. Tendencies already present under Bismarck soon became more apparent. The Prussian army, and especially the reserve officers, came increasingly to exercise great influence on Wilhelm II. He did follow up Bismarck's social legislation during the 1890s with health regulations, factory safety legislation, protective restrictions on child labor, and a bureau of labor statistics. But workers continued to vote for Social Democrats in ever larger numbers, and soon Wilhelm gave up on the "ungrateful" workers and turned his attention to international issues.

Mass politics was as divided as educated opinion in Germany. During the 1890s and after, more people were drawn into the political processes by the spread of education, literacy, newspapers, which included political coverage even in mass circulation papers, and by politicians who traveled around and spoke directly to people in mass meetings and campaign rallies. The largest mass movement was still socialist, all the way up to 1914. In 1912 the German SD party was the largest in parliament; it won 75 percent of the Berlin vote, three-fifths of the vote in all of Saxony, and half the votes in towns and cities with over ten thousand people. But by the 1890s the rise of conservative nationalist parties and political fragmentation produced a backlash.

It was in this environment of increasing political polarization that public anti-Semitism reappeared. In 1880 Berlin had forty-five thousand Jewish residents (at a time when all of France had only fifty-one thousand). Anti-Semitic attitudes, which had been dormant in Germany since the 1820s, were rekindled by those who identified Jews with the Liberal party, with stock market manipulation in general, and unearned capital in particular. Popular public figures, including Catholic leader and politician Adolf Stoecker (1835–1909) and the most respected historian of the time, Heinrich von Treitschke (1834–1896), along with many less respectable writers and demagogues, made anti-Semitism acceptable again. Treitschke declared in a much-

A Closer Look

German Militarism under Wilhelm II

Wilhelm II's aggressive program of naval shipbuilding contributed to international tensions. Did it increase German security or place the country in greater danger?

Memorandum Appended to German Navy Bill, 1900

The German empire needs peace at sea. For the German empire of today, the security of its economic development, and especially of its world trade, is a life question. For this purpose the German empire needs not only peace at any price, but peace with honor, which satisfies its just requirements. . . .

To protect Germany's sea trade and colonies in the existing circumstance, there is only one means—Germany must have a fleet so strong that even for the adversary with great sea power a war against it would involve such dangers as to imperil his position in the world.

For this purpose it is not absolutely necessary that the German Battle Fleet should be as strong as that of the greatest naval Power, for a great naval Power will not, as a rule, be in a position to concentrate all its striking force against us. But even if it should succeed in meeting us with considerable superiority of strength, the defeat of a strong German Fleet would so substantially weaken the enemy that, in spite of the victory he might have obtained, his own position in the world would no longer be secured by an adequate fleet.

Documents of German History, ed. Louis L. Snyder. (New Brunswick, NJ, 1958), pp. 282–83.

quoted article late in 1879 that "the Jews are our national misfortune." Thereafter, the myth of a Jewish conspiracy was a recurring theme of German politics, and no government figure did much to stop its growth.

Meanwhile, issues of military, colonial, and foreign policy further complicated Germany's tense internal politics. Gordon Craig characterizes German foreign policy in this period as illogical, arrogant, and dangerous. Wilhelm's naval policy was from the first directed as a challenge to Great Britain and so embittered relations between the two countries. In 1897 the emperor and State Secretary of the Imperial Naval Office Admiral Alfred von Tirpitz (1849–1930) planned a high-seas fleet to replace the naval forces that had originally been designed for coastal and commercial defense. But the army and navy were only the most obvious weapons of world power. The Colonial Society, founded to support the case for overseas expansion, grew rapidly in membership as Germany acquired territories in the Far East and in Africa, despite the drain on the budget (for the German colonies were never profitable). Pan-Germans planned a great Berlin–Baghdad railway to the Near East and cried for more adventure and more conquest.

While Bismarck was in control, the British had hoped that Germany would limit its goals to altering the existing order of power in Europe; after 1890 it seemed clear that Germany also intended to alter the world balance of power, and the British felt their interests directly threatened. Foreign policy in both nations was shaped by a complex mixture of social, economic, political, and ideological factors ranging from religious and cultural connections through the changing attitudes of parties, the press, pressure groups, and the bureaucracies. Leaders in business and politics in both countries worked for a harmonious relationship between the nations, but in the end they failed.

Britain had other than diplomatic and military reasons to be apprehensive of German power. By the turn of the century Germany had clearly overtaken Britain industrially. This surging development of Germany made its militarism possible, while its militarism in turn fed industrialism.

Great Britain: Protest on Three Fronts, 1867–1914

Great Britain's preference for compromise over conflict would be sorely tested at the turn of the century. A major transition occurred in British politics in 1901 with the death of Queen Victoria, who had ruled for 64 years. Her son Edward VII came to the throne, replacing the dignified Victoria with a court that was openly pleasure seeking and self-indulgent. But while the monarchy displayed the privileges of national wealth, the economy was much weaker than it seemed to be at the time. Industry was still growing but at a significantly slower pace. Output was still high in the important industries of coal, steel, and iron; but it was in precisely those industries that Britain was being outpaced by Germany and the United States. London was still the financial capital of the world because the advantages of early industrialization allowed the British to invest in European and colonial industry, which brought enormous wealth (in cash and gold) into the country. But that wealth masked the creeping threat of a trade deficit with the decline of exports.

Politically, Britain seemed stable because the new middle classes had entered political life with relatively little conflict. Though political differences could be deep, the conservative aristocracy and the liberal bourgeoisie were very similar by the end of the century. Educated at the same schools, including Oxford and Cambridge, which were imbued with an ethos of public service as the duty of the elite, members of both parties recognized the need to improve the lives of the working poor. Parliament passed laws legalizing trade unions, rebuilding large areas of major cities, and providing elementary education for all children. In 1884 suffrage was widened again, allowing male agricultural workers to vote and bringing the total of voters to 75 percent of the male population. Some striking inequalities continued, however. Workers could scarcely hope to become members of Parliament, for MPs served without pay; voters with business property in one district and a home in another could vote two or more times; and graduates of Oxford and Cambridge could vote a second time for special university representatives.

Despite ameliorative political measures, millions of British workers were still mired in poverty. Wages were stagnant while prices were rising (throughout Europe). The long depression of the 1870s and 1880s hit workers hard. In response the trade unions began to draw in more unskilled workers, especially from the rough iron and steel industries. They were less bourgeois in their attitudes, less inclined to adapt bourgeois culture, and more militant. New unions in the 1880s and 1890s organized the dockworkers, gas workers, and other unskilled groups. Then in a landmark event in 1892 James Keir Hardie (1856–1915) became the first independent worker to win election to Parliament. Several big strikes in the late 1880s impressed Parliament with their seriousness. A dockworkers' strike for a minimum wage lasted five weeks in 1889 and won support from far-off Australian workers as well as from local Catholic leaders.

Parliament tried to undermine growing union power, but failed. The economy recovered in the 1890s but it was once again volatile and unpredictable. As workers became more involved in politics, they expressed their grievances more effectively, but neither parliamentary party seemed to represent workers' interests. In reaction to the new union activism in the 1890s, employers formed anti union associations and lobbied Parliament to limit unions' right to strike. For their part, workers wanted more powerful trade unions, a bigger voice in government, and "worker-control," a socialist concept that meant worker ownership and supervision of factory labor, production, and marketing.

To win more power in the political arena, workers joined with middle-class socialists to form a new party in 1901, the Labour party. Keir Hardie became Labour's main spokesman, and the party quickly won representatives in Parliament. The Labour party was not explicitly socialist, exclusively working class, or revolutionary. British socialists generally believed in democratic parliamentary practice to win concessions legally. The Labour party included a group of well-known socialist intellectuals from the Fabian Society, which had formed in the 1880s. These moderate socialists, George Bernard Shaw (1856–1950), Sidney and Beatrice Webb (1859–1947 and 1858–1943, respectively), and H. G. Wells (1866–1946), favored government programs for housing, welfare benefits, and higher wages, through a peaceful parliamentary strategy of advancing one step at a time. The name comes from Fabius, a Roman republican general who wore down the Carthaginians in the third century, "one step at a time." In 1906 Labour won fifty-three seats in the House of Commons.

In the early 1900s Fabianism seemed to be working as the Liberals, who depended on Labour votes to maintain a majority, put through important legislation in the interest of the worker. In response to socialist pressures, a Liberal government passed legislation like the social welfare laws passed in Germany under Bismarck twenty years earlier: legalization of peaceful picketing, sanctity of trade union funds, and employers' liability to compensate for accidents (all in 1906); modest state-financed old-age pensions (1909); health and unemployment insurance (1911); and minimum wage regulations (1912).

Labour interests passed minimum wages in some industries. Two young Liberal leaders pushed this legislation through against much opposition in their own party: David Lloyd George (1863–1945), a radical lawyer from Wales, and Winston Churchill (1874–1965). To finance these measures, Lloyd George wanted to institute inheritance and progressive income taxes (the more one earns, the more one pays). When wealthy aristocrats in the House of Lords threatened to prevent the new taxes from becoming law, the Liberal prime minister, Herbert Asquith (1852–1928), threatened to create new peers to dilute their power. Eventually, in 1911, Parliament passed a law prohibiting the House of Lords from vetoing measures passed by the House of Commons.

The intensity of the debate over workers' rights, taxes, and the budget were typical of the period in Great Britain and elsewhere. Despite these parliamentary concessions to workers, new militant strikes occurred in 1911 and 1912. Troops were often called to disperse the strikers, and in numerous cases the confrontations took workers' lives. Dockworkers, railwaymen, and miners all went on strike, threatening to paralyze the economy, but the majority of even the most militant trade unionists remained committed to peaceful reform.

Part of the motivation for liberal social legislation was a desire to forestall Labour initiatives. But over the long run the workers on the whole stuck by the Labour party. The Liberal party was beginning a long decline that would be hastened by the effects of World War I and would drive its right wing to Toryism and its left wing to Labour. The imperialist wing of the Liberal party, led originally by Joseph Chamberlain (1836–1914), remained unreconciled to this trend, and in 1901 a union between the Fabians and disaffected Liberals began to hint that a new national party was needed to make national efficiency its goal. As the Liberal party fragmented, declined, and sought to hold onto its followers against the rise of Labour, it became more a coalition than a functioning whole within a two-party system. On one subject it remained reasonably united, however—the significance of the British Empire. As one member of Parliament, Halford John Mackinder (1861–1947), noted after his election in 1910, free trade would protect imperialism. He maintained that Britain must become a nation of "organizers," of workers whose patriotism led them to realize that they existed primarily to serve the national ends of the state.

Even more threatening to public order and political stability than labor unrest were the Irish movement for Home Rule and the movement for women's suffrage.

In the 1860s Irish activists began agitating for autonomy and land reform. The Catholic majority continued to resent the power of the Protestant minority in Ulster, and Irish small farmers who worked the land of absentee English or Irish Protestant owners resented the landlords' ability to control this land. In 1868 Gladstone began working in Parliament to improve conditions for Irish farmers. In 1870 the Irish Land Act began a series of agrarian measures that were designed to protect tenants from "rack renting" (rent gouging) by landlords. The reforms were neither far-reaching nor rapid, intensifying Irish awareness of cultural and national differences and intensifying the desire for Home Rule. In 1875 a brilliant Irish leader, Charles Stewart Parnell (1846–1891), was elected to the British Parliament and he welded the other Irish nationalists in Parliament into a firm, well-disciplined party, which could often swing the balance between Liberals and Conservatives. He also persuaded the Irish Catholic Church to support Home Rule. The critical step came in 1885, when Liberal leader Gladstone was converted to the Irish Home Rule cause. In the next year Gladstone introduced a bill providing for a separate Dublin-based Irish parliament (still, however, under the British monarchy).

But Parnell's fervor, Gladstone's advocacy, and the Conservatives' fierce opposition to Irish independence split the Liberals, severely weakening the party. The cause of Home Rule was further complicated when a more radical minority in Ireland revived the Irish Republican Brotherhood, known as the Fenians, to push for radical land reform and outright independence. In the 1880s, Conservatives argued that talk of Home Rule encouraged violence, and Parnell was imprisoned for a year. When two British officials were murdered in Dublin, and thirty more were assassinated, the British government authorized repression of the Irish Republicans. In 1886 Gladstone's bill establishing Irish Home Rule was defeated, and he was forced to step down because the issue was continuing to divide the Liberal party. Chamberlain led the other Liberal faction (the "Unionists") against Home Rule; he believed that if England "lost" Ireland, British power would be fatally weakened.

Agitation continued in Ireland, however, becoming more and more bitter. An aging Gladstone became prime minister again in 1892, but by then his alliance with Parnell was undercut by a sex scandal that had ended Parnell's political career. In 1893 the House of Commons approved a Home Rule bill, but the proposal failed in the House of Lords and was dropped once more.

Irish Home Rule remained an important political issue and a source of political conflict all the way up to the First World War. In the early twentieth century, Irish cultural nationalism was on the rise as well, with a remarkable literary revival in English and Gaelic writers like the poet W. B. Yeats (1865–1939), the dramatist John Millington Synge (1871–1909), and Lady Augusta Gregory (1859–1932), cofounder of the Abbey Theatre, which staged plays with deeply Irish themes. Writers and politicians encouraged a revival of traditional Irish culture, the Gaelic language, and Gaelic music. Irish men and women everywhere—including Irish-Americans—would be satisfied with nothing less than an independent Irish state.

Cultural nationalism cloaked class differences at times, but conflict between the Catholic majority and the Protestant minority in Northern Ireland helped Parliament drag its feet on Irish independence. Powerful Irish Protestants opposed Home Rule because they did not want to be governed by the Catholic majority. When both sides formed armed paramilitary organizations in the 1910s, Ireland was on the verge of civil war. In London, Home Rule was still deeply controversial, and the issue seemed to be at an impasse. But when the Liberals were back in power after 1905 they tried to work out a bargain. In need of the votes of the Irish nationalists to carry his party's own proposal for ending the veto power of the Lords, Lloyd George tried to draw attention away from the conflict and use the Irish vote to dilute the power of the House of Lords. The Liberals made a deal: they would support Home Rule in return for the Parliament Act of 1911. A Home Rule bill passed in 1912 but never went into force, for just as Home Rule seemed about to become a fact, the predominantly Protestant north of Ireland, the province of Ulster, bitterly opposed to separation from Great Britain, threatened to resist by force of arms. The Home Rule bill carried the rider that it was not to go into effect until the Ulster question was settled. The outbreak of the European war in 1914 put settlement out of the question, and the stage was set for the Irish Revolution of the 1920s and the long extension of the Time of the Troubles well into the twentieth century.

The suffrage question, ultimately more easily solved, was equally divisive, and extremely disruptive in Britain in the 1910s. Most of the suffrage activists were from the middle classes, but there was strong support among textile workers, miners, and other workers, which made the movement that much more ominous in the polarized context of the 1910s. Suffragists were treated with scorn, ridicule, and hostility, but until Emmeline Pankhurst and her daughters began to employ violence and street theater, the hostility remained within the bounds of published and spoken discourse. The Pankhursts' refusal to maintain decorum brought that hostility out into the open. Men grabbed the suffragists and assaulted them in public, and they fought back. Whether violent suffragism helped or hurt, it certainly demonstrated and even fueled the further polarization of public political life. Liberals did not help their own cause by refusing to pass a suffrage bill extending to women the rights that liberals of all parties claimed were universal "natural" rights.

In the 1910s women, workers, and the Irish and their supporters avoided Parliament, which seemed to be ineffective in meeting their needs. Taking their causes to the streets helped undermine the Liberal party altogether, so that it ceased to play a major role after the world war.

France: The Third Republic, 1870–1914

Polarization in France was equally apparent during this period, though after the tragedy of the Paris Commune, it was less based on class and labor conflict. The French political system was the most democratic in Europe, and its population the most homogeneous. An active socialist party kept working-class grievances in the public eye, but as a parliamentary rather than a revolutionary party, as in Germany and Great Britain, it made workers and their representatives amenable to political negotiation and conciliation. Instability, then, was primarily rooted in politics, ideology, and nationalism, rather than social discord, at least until the 1910s.

The Third Republic was born in humiliating defeat, which haunted the French for at least a generation. As late as 1910, a textbook taught students that the treaty ending the war was "a truce, not a peace; which is why since 1871 all Europe lives permanently under arms." That defeat at the hands of the Prussians was augmented by trauma of civil war in the bloody fighting that ended the Paris Commune.

France's disadvantages after 1870 were also economic and demographic. Unlike Germany and the United States, France participated in the second industrial revolution with some reluctance. Unlike anywhere else in Europe, in France population growth declined during this period, feeding a sense that modern life, with its conveniences and conflicts, its pollution and noise, was weakening the French body. In the country that had led the way in demanding modern political liberties, experts in medicine, criminology, and the arts insisted that modernity had brought physical degeneration and required new regimes of supervision and improvement.

In this context of defeat and fear of degeneration, a new government was formed. The lines between monarchists and republicans were etched as sharply as ever. From 1871 to 1879 French politics seesawed between the left and right. Most members of the new National Assembly were monarchists, but they lacked a monarch and could not agree on a new one. About half the monarchist deputies were pledged to the elder legitimate Bourbon line represented by the Count of Chambord. The other half supported the younger Orleanist line, represented by the Count of Paris, grandson of Louis Philippe. When they finally settled on Chambord he stubbornly refused to accept the revolutionary blue, white, and red tricolor flag that Louis Philippe had himself accepted as the flag of France, demanding instead the white flag and gold lilies of the Bourbon dynasty, which for millions would have signified complete repudiation of all that had happened since 1789.

Political stalemate followed the emotional debates over the symbols of legitimacy, monarchy, and nation; in the resulting impasse the republican minority was able to gather strength. Adolphe Thiers, recognized as "president of the Republic," carried through the final settlement with Germany. In 1873, however, he lost a vote of confidence in the Assembly and was succeeded by Marshal MacMahon (1808–1893), a soldier and a monarchist who was chosen to hold the government together until the monarchist majority of the Assembly could appoint a new king. That never occurred, as Chambord continued to insist on the white flag. Ultimately, Thiers's strategy worked, and in 1875 enough Orleanists joined with the republicans for the Assembly to pass a series of constitutional measures formally establishing the Third Republic, with MacMahon as president.

These laws, known collectively as the constitution of 1875, provided for a president elected by an absolute majority of Senate and Chamber of Deputies sitting together as a National Assembly. The Chamber of Deputies was elected by universal male suffrage; the Senate was chosen by elected members of local governmental bodies. The critical point was the responsibility of ministers, which was not spelled out in the laws of 1875. Had the president been able to dismiss them, a new Napoleon III might easily have arisen to destroy the republic. MacMahon attempted to exercise this power on May 16, 1877, when he dismissed an anticlerical premier. But the Chamber was now antimonarchist and voted no confidence in MacMahon's new premier;

MacMahon then dissolved the Chamber and called for a new national election. In the election the republicans retained a majority in the Chamber and could have forced the president to name a republican premier. Disgruntled, MacMahon resigned in 1879 and was succeeded by a conservative republican, whereupon the presidency became a largely ceremonial office.

The real executive in the Third Republic was the ministry, which was in effect a committee responsible to the Chamber of Deputies. The Chamber of Deputies soon became the focus of political action, leaving the Senate little real power. The Chamber was composed of a dozen or more parties, so that any ministry had to be supported by a coalition subject to constant shifting of personalities and principles. The day-to-day task of governing was carried on by a civil service. This permanent bureaucracy, subject only to broad policy control from above, preserved basic continuity in French politics.

Functionally, the system was highly democratic, for it could work only through constant and subtle compromise arrived at by the several parties in open debate and voting in the legislature *after* an election. All men could vote in France, and most did. Bitter antagonisms continued to threaten the Third Republic between 1879 and 1914, but they did not destroy it. The government made efforts to unite the nation around powerful symbols of France: Bastille Day was instituted as national holiday, and the "Marseillaise" as the national anthem in the 1880s. Legislation was passed that promoted civil liberties, the right of assembly, freedom of the press, and legalization of trade unions.

After the accession of Pope Leo XIII in 1878, Catholics were gradually encouraged to accept the freedom of worship that the constitution of the republic guaranteed. But Catholics understandably remained apprehensive about the deeply anticlerical republicans, who passed legislation introducing divorce into the civil code and minimizing the power of the church over education. This last was part of a major education reform in 1882 that made education free and compulsory for all children. An effort was made to restore the Sorbonne to a premier place among universities.

The attack on the power of the Catholic church disturbed many on the right, in the church, in the army, and among the wealthy who still hoped for government by a single strong man, but these groups remained divided over the extent of their monarchism. The political left was also divided, between pro- and anti-Marxist socialists, anarchists, and syndicalists. Party fragmentation remained intense, and outside Paris, sodalities, religious associations, semisecret lodges, and other forms of voluntary association became the focus of both political and social life. Slowly but decisively, communal groups began to be replaced by formal organizations that spoke for special-interest groups, especially for segments of the industrial working class.

In the late 1880s those who feared this shifting, growing fragmentation turned to General Georges Boulanger (1837–1891) in the hope that he might unite France under authoritarian leadership. A radical general, Boulanger represented an unusual combination of outlooks. He helped modernize the army, introducing up-to-date weaponry, and catered to French desires for revenge on Germany. He was relentlessly self-promoting and immensely popular as a leader who might unite people across political and class lines. On the right, people disheartened with parliamentary fragmentation supported the general's strong personality; on the left Boulanger attracted radical nationalists and socialists.

Nationalism played a greater role in politics during this period, increasingly serving conservative rather than liberal aims. Conservative nationalist political leaders wanted revenge against Germany and a return of the lost provinces of Alsace-Lorraine, and they considered the republic too weak to achieve this. Boulanger was a demagogue with no clear positive program, other than order, power, and revenge. Professional politicians hated him and eventually outmaneuvered him. When it became clear that if given power he might rush the country into war, his following threatened to desert him. In January 1889 he swept a by-election in Paris, but instead of seizing power by force of arms, he waited to see if his followers would act. The Chamber of Deputies threatened to try him for treason; Boulanger fled to Brussels, where he committed suicide in 1891. The republic had surmounted its first great crisis.

Three major scandals followed to dog the republic. First, the president's son-in-law was implicated in the selling of posts in the Legion of Honor. Then more fuel was added to the fire in the early 1890s with a scandal in Panama, brought on by the failure of Ferdinand de Lesseps's attempt to duplicate in Central America his success in building the Suez Canal. Ministers and deputies had accepted bribes for backing the shaky Panama company. Anti-Semitic propagandists were able to make much of the fact that several Jewish financiers were implicated. Bad as it was, however, the Panama scandal was to pale before the Dreyfus affair, which divided France and brought the force of modern anti-Semitism to worldwide attention.

Jews made up less than 2 percent of the French population, but they were overwhelmingly concentrated in Paris. As shopkeepers, peddlers, and petty tradesmen they competed for jobs and trade and tried to improve themselves. A few Jews were prominent in banking and publishing, and it was widely believed that Jews dominated the arts, especially the theater. In the 1880s and 1890s, Jews fled by the thousands from eastern Europe and Russia to Paris, where they were despised both by the French and by well-established French Jews. And according to some historians, Jewish immigrants from the east were associated with the hated Germans, and hated all the more for it.

In this context the Dreyfus affair exploded. Captain Alfred Dreyfus (1859–1935), a member of a wealthy Jewish family that had fled to France when Alsace was lost to Germany, was falsely accused of spying for the Germans.

Evidence surfaced that someone in the French army was selling military secrets to the Germans. Dreyfus was railroaded into a trial as a scapegoat on the skimpiest of evidence in a secret court-martial. He consistently maintained his innocence. Convicted of treason in 1894, he was sentenced to life imprisonment at the prison colony on Devil's Island, off the coast of French Guyana. In 1896 Colonel Georges Picquart (1854–1914), an intelligence officer, became convinced that the document on which Dreyfus had been con-

The Traitor, *an anti-Dreyfusard caricature representing Alfred Dreyfus as a dangerous, evil monster, the mythological Seven-Headed Hydra.* *(Musée des Horreurs (1900), The Jewish Museum)*

victed was a forgery and that the real traitor was a disreputable adventurer, Major Ferdinand Esterhazy (1849–1923). Picquart was quietly shipped off to Africa by his superiors, but the Dreyfus family, by independent investigation, also concluded that Esterhazy was the traitor and sought to reopen the case. Esterhazy was tried and acquitted, but the affair was now too public for such a cover-up. In 1898 the renowned novelist Émile Zola brought the crisis to public attention by publishing an inflammatory open letter, under the headline "J'accuse." Zola accused the military leaders, one by one, of deliberately sacrificing an innocent man, because he was a Jew, to save the reputation of the army.

France was now divided into Dreyfusards and anti-Dreyfusards. Dreyfus was retried in the midst of a frenzied campaign in the press. The military court, faced with new evidence brought out by the suicide of the forger of the most incriminating of the original documents used to convict Dreyfus, nonetheless again found Dreyfus guilty of treason. However, Dreyfus was then pardoned by the president of the republic, and in 1906, after the tensions had abated, he was acquitted by a civilian court, restored to the army, and promoted to the rank of major.

The Dreyfus affair divided France as the Paris Commune had done in 1871. But the years of debate brought radicals, socialists, liberals, republicans, anticlericals, and intellectuals—all who were suspicious of the army, of the church, and of anti-Semitism—into a loose alliance. Many on both sides of the question worked themselves into a mass hysteria in which the question of Dreyfus's guilt was wholly submerged in the confrontation between the "two Frances"—the France of the republic, heir to the great revolution and the principles of 1789, and the France of the monarchy, the throne, the altar, and the army, which had never reconciled itself to the revolution.

With the victory of the Dreyfusards, the republic punished the church for supporting the army and the anti-Dreyfusards. In a series of measures between 1901 and 1905 the triumphant republicans destroyed the Concordat of 1801 between Napoleon I and the pope, which had established the Roman Catholic Church in a privileged position in the French state. Catholic teaching orders were forced to dissolve, and some twelve thousand Catholic schools were closed. The state would no longer pay the clergy, and private corporations organized by the faithful would take over the expenses of worship and the ownership and maintenance of the churches. But Catholicism was not outlawed. Indeed, the separation did not radically alter the fundamental social position of the church in France: the upper classes and the peasantry of the north, northeast, and west remained for the most part loyal Catholics; many of the urban middle and working classes and many peasants in parts of the south, southwest, and center remained indifferent Catholics or determined secularists.

The Third Republic had become more republican without moving noticeably toward the welfare state. This was hardly surprising in a country that remained essentially a land of small-farm-owning peasants, conservative in their agricultural methods, and of relatively small family-controlled industries, conservative in their business methods. French business owners preferred internal financing because they wished to maintain their independence, either because the firm was part of family property or because they preferred to maintain substantial emergency reserves to meet sudden drops in the market or unexpected technological changes, mostly from outside France.

The Dreyfus affair permanently polarized French society just at the time new tensions were arising from below. The republicans gained considerably from the affair because they showed courage in supporting Dreyfus against great criticism and at risk of personal danger, because they supported legality against corruption, and because they turned out to be right. The monarchists, especially the military, were tarnished. The socialists gained the most in terms of power and respect because their leader, Jean Jaurès (1859–1914),

A Closer Look

TRADE UNIONS AND LABOR RADICALISM

In countries where trade unions were legal, the workers' organizations often had fractious relationships with socialist parties. The largest French trade union, Confédération Général du Travail (CGT), passed the following resolution at the congress held in Amiens in 1906. How does the CGT assert its independence from the party and take a more radical stance?

. . . The CGT unites, without regard to their political beliefs, all workers who are conscious of the struggle to be carried out for the disappearance of the wage-system and the class of employers.

The congress considers that this declaration is a recognition of the class war which, in the economic field, puts the workers in revolt into opposition to all forms of exploitation and oppression, material and moral, of the working class by the capitalist class.

. . . In its day-to-day activity the trade union movement seeks the co-ordination of workers' effort, the increase the workers' well-being by the achievement of immediate improvements, such as the reduction of the hours of work, raising of wages, etc.

But this task is only one side of the work of the trade union movement: it prepares the total emancipation which can only be achieved by the expropriation of the capitalist class; it commends publicly the general strike as the means [to this end] and it considers that the trade union, which is today the organization of resistance, will in the future become the unit of production and distribution, the basis of social re-organization.

Documents in the Political History of the European Continent, ed. G. A. Kertesz (Oxford, 1968), p. 327.

played an important role in protecting the republican government against military coup. Socialist support allowed the formation of a new republican government, strong enough to resist the military.

But because the Socialist party was parliamentary and conciliatory, many workers lost faith in it and resorted to direct action. Workers would continue to vote for socialists, but they had little faith that political activism would improve their living and working conditions. French, Italian, and Spanish workers tended to embrace syndicalist ideas and tactics. They formed associations to rival the socialist parliamentary parties and used direct action to win concessions. A wave of strikes occurred in the 1910s, coinciding with increased labor activity in England, Germany, and Russia. But instead of concessions the state responded with severity. The government was afraid that concessions would alienate conservatives and destabilize politics just when the international situation was becoming more tense.

Domestic and international conflicts dominated politics in France in the 1900s and 1910s, as governments zigzagged between aggressive nationalism and antimilitarism. Georges Clemenceau (1841–1929, premier 1906–1909) was a nationalist and antisocialist. He used the army to quell labor unrest, which had the effect of further radicalizing workers and increasing their antimilitarism. In 1911 Premier Joseph Caillaux (1863–1944) sought to downplay conflict with Germany. But then a crisis between Germany and France over Morocco pushed the pendulum back toward aggressive nationalism, and Caillaux's government fell. The next premier, Raymond Poincaré (1860–1934), a nationalist subject to spasms of Russian-style paradomania, sympathized with those who wanted to win back Alsace and Lorraine. Looking ahead to possible military action, Poincaré sought alliance with the Russians (also a likely enemy of Germany) and supported Russian action in the Balkan Wars.

The Dreyfus affair had an impact on nationalism and international relations that would not become manifest for many decades. It led some Jews to think that assimilation and integration into European society would never be possible. They came to believe that neither legal rights, self-improvement, nor contributions to economic and cultural life would bring Jews the acceptance they needed to be secure. Theodor Herzl (1860–1904), a Hungarian Jew working in Paris as a journalist, originated the Jewish nationalist movement, Zionism. Combining liberal individual aims with socialist collective aspirations, Zionists called for an independent Jewish homeland in the Holy Lands where Judaism was born. Like many other European nationalists, Herzl became involved in politics in Europe, lobbying for Zionism; but also like many other Europeans, he had little understanding of the situation in the Middle East, where he hoped to establish a Jewish state.

By 1914, the French scene contained political polarization, a loss of faith in moderation and compromise, a leadership eager to win mass support by stirring up memories of loss and desire for revenge, an increasingly dangerous enemy on its eastern border, and a military looking to redeem itself with sensational conquest. The pleasures of the *Belle Époque* had given way to hopes for national revival through war.

Italy After Unification, 1870–1914

Italy became a state more quickly and easily than it became a nation. Like the other Great Powers (a status Italy was only sometimes accorded), the country had a modern bureaucracy, an army and navy, a national police force, and an interlocked economy. Still, for most people, at the end of the century local allegiances prevailed over national identities. Most Italians spoke a dialect of the language unintelligible to other Italians. Unlike France, where mandatory, free, nationwide education made a significant impact on creating a national language and cultural identity, the majority of Italians were illiterate in 1871. And since by 1900 only half the population could read in any language, the creation of Italian as a national language was slow. The Italians, like the French, were divided between Catholics and anticlericals, and ardent Catholics remained bitter about the annexation of Papal States without papal consent.

Economic disparities contributed to the hindering of real unification. Wealthy industrial northerners dominated the political system and treated the south as the Great Powers treated their overseas colonies: as a source of raw materials, cheap labor, and socially inferior people. Southerners were also subject to the criminal organizations of Sicily and Naples, which ruled their regions even without political authority. The state was able to begin to protect the poor from the violence of organized crime, but Mafia and Camorra feuds continued with the same violence as before. There was also deep-seated class antagonism and profound mistrust of governments.

Consequently, united Italy moved very cautiously toward greater democracy. The constitution remained the one granted to Piedmont in 1848 by Carlo Alberto; it put effective checks on the power of the kings by making the ministers responsible to the Chamber of Deputies; but it also put severe limitations on the suffrage. Only 2.5 percent of the population could vote in national elections until 1882, when the franchise was expanded to 20 percent of the adult male population. It was not until 1912 that something close to universal male suffrage was introduced.

The lack of real political leadership in the decades after unification meant that polarization came early to Italy. Parliament fell into disrepute when it appeared that politicians were purely concerned with local or personal interests. Francesco Crispi, who became prime minister in 1887, tried to reinvigorate the political system. He ignored economics for the most part, tried to stir patriotic support for the Italian cause, and restored order to the government. Many people felt that representative government was bound to fail in a country as fragmented as Italy, that a more authoritarian government was necessary to provide direction and to counter corruption and the terrorism of the left and the right. Crispi sought the main source of national unity in popular nationalism, which he tried to inspire with an aggressive foreign policy. In the 1880s and 1890s, Italy developed imperial aspirations. Since France and Britain had empires, and since a Great Power had to have "a place in the sun," some way of territorial expansion had to be found if Italy was to be taken seriously as a Great Power. But since other countries had a head start in empire building, very little territory was left for the Italians to colonize. Nonetheless, Italy acquired two of the poorer parts of Africa in the late nineteenth century: Eritrea on the Red Sea, and Somaliland on the "horn" of Africa, where the Red Sea meets the Indian Ocean.

Next Italy attempted to conquer the independent highland empire of Ethiopia, known then as Abyssinia. The Abyssinian War drained the resources of the Italian government and abruptly ended in 1896 with the disastrous defeat of the Italian expedition by a large Ethiopian army at Adowa. The disaster at Adowa cast a shadow over Italy that has been compared to that cast over France by the Dreyfus case. A bank scandal and the ongoing depression further undermined Crispi's government, and he resigned. When severe bread riots broke out in Milan in May 1898, they were unapologetically crushed by King Umberto. In 1900 King Umberto was assassinated by an anarchist. The accession of a new king, Vittorio Emanuele III (r. 1900–1946), who was believed to have liberal leanings, gave heart to many. The economy picked up in the mid-1890s, though most southern peasants still lived on the brink of starvation. The southern parliamentary delegates wanted only one thing, from unification to the First World War: the status quo, which would leave them in control of the land and peasants who lived there.

The dominant political figure in the prewar years was Giovanni Gioletti (1842–1928). Gioletti did not believe that repression would stamp out socialism; on the contrary, he allowed trade unions to grow and strikes to take their course, and he introduced social reforms. He believed extremism could be bought off with reasonableness. Liberal and conservative business leaders put up with this set of policies as long as the economy continued to grow. When it faltered, Gioletti sought to stabilize his own power and enhance Italy's position with another round of imperialist adventures.

Denied Tunisia by French occupation in 1881 and then forced out of Ethiopia, Italy went to war to secure Libya in 1911. Gioletti did not gain much: an expensive war, an expensive colony, where thousands of men lost their lives resisting Italian rule, and continued polarization at home. The political left advocated further social reforms to achieve social justice and political equality, but accomplished relatively little because of internal dissension. The remnants of the left wing of the Risorgimento split into largely non-Marxist factions, and no successful reform party emerged from the middle class. Italian parliamentary government remained weak, Italian class structure militated against the development of effective multiple parties, and political debate increasingly appeared to be shaped by intellectuals who purported to speak either for a ruling elite or for the Italian masses. In 1914 nationalists discarded the liberals and formed a right-wing nationalist party, which elected six deputies to the Chamber of Deputies. The new party, and nationalists generally, saw war as a proving ground. Rather than fearing it, they looked forward to war as a showcase for Italian courage and glory.

Russian Reaction and Revolution, 1881–1914

Revolutionary events in the Russian Empire had an impact on all of Europe during this period. The terrorists who assassinated Alexander II hoped that they would spark a general peasant rebellion against the landlords and government that kept them impoverished. No revolution occurred however, and Alexander III (r. 1881–1894) came to the throne determined to eradicate the opposition that had taken his father's life. All liberal voices in government and society were silenced. Five of the revolutionaries responsible for the assassination, including women, were hanged; hundreds were arrested and imprisoned. The most promising elements of the Great Reforms were abbreviated or abolished altogether in a series of counterreforms, which restored some noble privileges and state prerogatives.

A special bank extended credit to the impoverished nobility, censorship was reinstituted, and in the countryside land captains were given extraordinary powers over the peasant population. Election procedures for the zemstvos and municipal assemblies were made far less democratic, and the central government placed financial and other obstacles in the way of zemstvo efforts to improve rural infrastructure and education. The decade of the 1880s was known as the "era of small deeds," in which the opposition went underground. A vicious cycle followed, in which government reaction pushed liberals toward radicalism, and radicals toward extremes; then the radicalism of the opposition stimulated new rounds of reaction. Neither Alexander III nor his son Nicholas II (r. 1894–1917) could distinguish between monarchist reformers and radical revolutionaries.

Vigorous persecution of Jews and national minorities took place. The assassination of the tsar in 1881 was followed by a series of *pogroms,* or violent riots directed against Jews and their property, as some people blamed the Jews for revolutionary activity. Other pogroms followed during periods of political upheaval. Rumors circulated that they were organized by the government, but although state officials often stood by without preventing the violence, and many high government officials were openly anti-Semitic, the pogroms were in fact the result of mass anti-Semitism. After 1881, around one million Jews (one in five) left Russia, many for the United States. And while Jews had not dominated the revolutionary movement before 1881, increased persecution drove a large number of them into the various revolutionary movements, including socialism and Zionism.

Alexander III was also responsible for some positive measures, particularly in the economic sphere, though at first these were contradictory and counterproductive. A peasant bank made redemption payments easier for the peasantry, the hated soul tax (levied exclusively on peasants) was abolished, and harsh conditions in early factories were partly ameliorated by labor legislation and a factory inspectorate system. But the first effort to finance industrialization with peasant grain revenues produced the terrible famine of 1891, which was not quickly forgotten. The famine awakened the opposition of a new generation of radical revolutionaries and liberal constitutionalists. Whether the agrarian sector was in economic crisis or experiencing a rise in productivity is disputed, but all agree that peasants still bitterly resented the land settlement of the emancipation.

As industrialization picked up steam under Nicholas II and his finance minister, Sergei Witte, the social transformation unleashed by the Great Reform accelerated. A more open and active society came into conflict with the goals and principles of autocracy. From the late 1890s until 1914, millions of peasants left their ancestral villages for wage labor in Russia's bursting cities, shifting the arena for revolutionary activity from the countryside to the city. As in the West, the government was unwilling spend scarce resources on their basic necessities.

Population of Largest Cities in the Russian Empire (in Thousands)

City	1856	1910
St. Petersburg	491	1,566
Moscow	369	1,481
Warsaw	156	781
Odessa	101	620
Riga	71	370
Kiev	62	527
Saratov	62	217
Vilnius	46	193

Source: Michael Hamm, ed. *The City in Late Imperial Russia* (Bloomington, IN, 1986), p. 3.

Many of the same developments occurred in western and central Europe, but more virulent revolutionary movements resulted in Russia for several reasons. The rapidity of economic change intensified its effects. Because the disruption of industrialization occurred in Russia at the end of the century, a number of well-developed revolutionary political ideologies and organizations already existed and were adopted quickly. The large role of the autocracy as sponsor of industry tied politics directly to the workplace, made the government a natural target for working-class unrest, and drove the government to repress the strike movement harshly when it arose. Cultural conflict compounded class tensions in the ethnically mixed cities such as Tiflis, Baku, Riga, Warsaw, and Odessa on Russia's borderlands and in the Pale of Settlement. Political discontent added to long-standing hostility between Slavs and Jews; between Armenians, Georgians, and Azeris; and between Russian colonial authorities and Poles, Ukrainians, Finns, the Turkic peoples of central Asia, and other non-Russian, non-Orthodox peoples. Official Russification, which forced schools and public offices to replace native languages with Russian, added to the resentments. The government of Nicholas II refused to take any political criticism seriously or to offer any concessions to the opposition. Openly anti-Semitic, Nicholas blamed even the most mild opposition on "wild-eyed radicals and Jews." When reform came, it was too little, too late.

Nicholas's refusal to listen to any voices of society radicalized even the liberal opposition. In the 1890s rural zemstvo leaders joined urban professionals to form the liberal movement, which called for a national assembly, limitation on the powers of the tsar, and some guarantee of civil rights. The heirs of the populism of the 1870s formed the Socialist-Revolutionary party. The SRs, the largest of the radical parties, believed that the peasant commune would allow Russia to avoid capitalism and progress directly to socialism. An extreme SR wing began a terror campaign to assassinate tsarist officials. By the time the minister of interior was murdered in 1904, society was so disenchanted with the autocracy that the news was greeted with indifference and even celebration.

Other radicals believed that capitalism had already made significant inroads in Russia. Marx's view that capitalism was both inevitable and necessary in the road to socialism offered them a more practical strategy for organizing workers. The Russian Social Democratic party formed in 1898. In 1903 the SDs split over tactics. V. I. Lenin, the alias of Vladimir Ilyich Ulyanov (1870–1924), provoked the split, arguing that workers needed the intelligentsia to lead them beyond mere economic grievances to revolutionary consciousness and activism and that only a small, disciplined party would be safe from the secret police. His Bolshevik faction of the party rejected alliances with any other party. The Mensheviks favored a broadly based, open party and sought to train workers to lead their own movement. Though membership in political parties was tiny in the early 1900s, the radicals' educational and agitational activities paid off as the rising mass movement of the 1890s manifested itself in hundreds of organized strikes.

A decade after Nicholas had come to the throne, discontent was felt in every sector of Russian society. Bureaucratic arbitrariness and the tsar's incompetence were widely discussed. Even the conservative rural gentry complained about the urban-oriented policies that had undercut noble prestige and wealth since the emancipation of the serfs in 1861. Students were stirred up by new restrictions on university autonomy. A sharp recession in 1900 left many workers in straitened circumstances, but those hardships produced a wave of strikes in 1903 when the economy picked up again. In 1902–1903 massive peasant uprisings swept through two southern provinces, and on the non-Russian borderlands, discontent with Russian colonialism was ready to ignite.

Russia was ripe for revolution when its imperialist aims in East Asia brought the country into conflict with similar Japanese aims in 1904. Russia's humiliating defeat at the hands of a country most Russians thought to be culturally inferior destroyed what was left of the tsar's authority. The Russian fleet, which had steamed all the way around Europe and across the Indian Ocean into the Pacific, was decisively defeated by the Japanese in the battle of Tsushima Strait (May 27, 1904). To the Russian people, the war was a distant, poorly understood political adventure, of which they wanted no part and by which they were now humiliated. Many intellectuals opposed it, and the SRs and SDs openly hoped for a Russian defeat, which they expected would shake the government's position. Alarmed at the growing unrest at home, the Russian government was persuaded by the president of the United States, Theodore Roosevelt, to accept his mediation, which the Japanese had also actively wished.

Witte, who had opposed the war from the first, was sent to New Hampshire, as Russia's representative to sign the Treaty of Portsmouth (1905). Here he not only secured excellent terms for Russia but also won a favorable verdict from American public opinion, which had thought of Russians as either brutal aristocrats or bomb-throwing revolutionaries. Russian prestige as a Far Eastern power was neither deeply wounded nor permanently impaired by the defeat or by the treaty. Yet the effect of the defeat in Asia was to transfer attention back to European Russia, where a crisis had already begun.

The Revolution of 1905

Frustrated with the tsar's incompetence and his unwillingness to share power with society, liberal professionals adopted the French tactics of 1848 and held banquets, at which they discussed politics and pressed their demand for an elected national assembly of zemstvo representatives. After having once approved the assembly, Nicholas withdrew approval and issued a decree so mild and vague that all hope for reform through legal means evaporated.

Ironically, it was a priest and police agent who struck the fatal spark. Father Georgy Gapon (1870–1906) had been part of a police effort to organize legal assemblies of factory workers to guide them away from revolutionary parties. Many workers also hoped for peaceful reform and believed they could appeal directly to what they saw as the tsar's benevolent paternalism. Father Gapon organized a massive public procession, based on a traditional ritual, to humbly present a petition directly to the tsar requesting an eight-hour day, a national assembly, civil liberties, the right to strike, and other modest demands. On January 9/22, 1905, workers and their families gathered at designated points around the city. Carrying icons and portraits of the tsar and refusing to let radicals unfurl red banners, they began to proceed peaceably to the Winter Palace. Nicholas, however, had fled the city, leaving orders to repel the demonstrators. As the workers converged on the Winter Palace, troops blocked their way and shouted at them to disperse, then opened fire. Hundreds of people were killed and injured, and the people's faith in the tsar was slaughtered along with them. The massacre that came to be known as "Bloody Sunday" outraged Russian workers and society and confirmed international opinion of Russia as a clumsy, brutal dictatorship.

For the next several months workers went on strike in every major city and many smaller cities of the empire. Liberal leaders agitated on their behalf, calling for an elected national assembly and a constitution. The tsar hesitated to concede to the public outcry, further fueling the opposition. Radical parties were taken entirely by surprise. Most of the SD and SR leaders were in exile in western Europe. The leadership of the Revolution of 1905 was provided by liberals; its power by workers and, in the summer, by peasants. Weak concessions from the tsar, along with disastrous news from the war in Asia, only further enraged the populace. Peasant unrest peaked in the summer, as did several strategic mutinies.

The unrest culminated in a railway strike in October that expanded into a general strike, shutting down the entire economy of the Russian Empire for ten days. Workers' councils, or *soviets,* were formed with SD assistance to organize the general strike. The Bolsheviks saw the soviet as an instrument for the establishment of a provisional government, for the proclamation of a democratic republic, and for the summoning of a constituent assembly. This program differed relatively little from the program of the moderate liberals, who originally had hoped to keep the monarchy and obtain their ends by pressure rather than by violence. At the time, the Bolsheviks, like other Marxists, accepted the view that it was necessary for Russia to pass through a stage of bourgeois democracy before the time for the proletarian revolution could come. They were therefore eager to help along the bourgeois revolution.

On October 17/30, bowing to the pressure of his advisers, especially Witte, Nicholas issued the October Manifesto promising full civil rights at once, a constitution, and elections by universal male suffrage to a legislative assembly, the Duma. With liberal demands met, the government hoped the revolution would be over. But even the liberals understood that the tsar's promises could be broken, and they vowed to continue the pressure until the constitution had been written and the Duma met in session.

On the right, a government-sponsored party called the Union of the Russian People demonstrated against the manifesto and proclaimed undying loyalty to the autocracy. The right was understandably dismayed by disrespectful behavior of the opposition during the "Days of Freedom" that followed the October Manifesto, as when demonstrators hung icons and portraits of the tsar around their dogs' necks. The "Days of Freedom" were quickly overwhelmed by days of violence. Peasants retaliating against noble landlords set fire to over 3,000 manor houses, while on the right, the so-called Black Hundreds launched more than 700 pogroms in which 3,000 Jews were killed, raped, or mutilated.

The SDs shifted their tactics to support the development of the soviets into revolutionary fighting organizations. Led by the charismatic Leon Trotsky (1879–1940), SDs in Moscow began to call for the soviets to rise in armed insurrection. Street fighting occurred in a number of cities, including Moscow, in December 1905 but the disturbances were easily quashed by loyal troops. The violence that followed the October Manifesto and the armed uprisings divided the opposition, and the government began its own bloody reprisals. Socialist leaders were arrested or fled back into exile, workers were blackballed or locked out of factories, and punitive expeditions were sent into the countryside to arrest and execute peasant rebels on the spot.

By early 1906, Nicholas had regained enough authority to make a mockery of the legislative process. The Fundamental Laws (as the promised constitution was called) gave the tsar the power to control foreign policy, military matters, and the treasury, as well as the right to dissolve the Duma at will. Nicholas made it clear that he would do everything possible to thwart the Duma's ability to function. Elections to the First Duma brought a liberal majority, the Constitutional Democrats (nicknamed Kadets), largely because the radical parties boycotted the elections. The liberals, however, adopted most of the socialist platform calling for major land redistribution and an eight-hour day. A stalemate ensued.

The First Duma, the "Duma of Popular Indignation," met between May and July of 1906. It addressed a list of grievances to the tsar, including radical land reform that would give the peasants all state and church land and part of the land still in private hands. The government flatly refused, and

Tsar Nicholas II acquired a reputation for indifference to his subjects and incomprehension of their grievances. Here a satirist depicts him reading placidly, under the stern watch of his father, while mice eat away at the feet of his throne and outside on the street police attack demonstrators who are eating away at the foundation of his regime. (© AKG Photo)

after some parliamentary skirmishing the Duma was dissolved. The Kadet membership, maintaining that the dissolution was unconstitutional, crossed the frontier into Finland, and there issued a manifesto urging the Russian people not to pay taxes or report for military service unless the Duma was recalled. Its authors were tried in absentia and declared ineligible for office. Future Dumas were thus deprived of the services of these capable Kadet moderates.

With the dissolution of the First Duma, the highly intelligent and conservative Peter Stolypin (1862–1911) came to power as minister of the interior. Stolypin put through a series of agricultural laws that enabled the peasants to free themselves from the commune and establish family farms. The program accomplished much of what Stolypin had hoped for: about a quarter of the peasant households of European Russia (almost 9 million) emancipated themselves from the communes between 1906 and 1917.

At the same time that his agrarian program was going into effect, Stolypin carried on unremitting war against terrorists and other revolutionaries. He did everything he could to interfere with elections to the Second Duma, but the SRs and SDs were well represented, so the second Duma (March–June 1907) could not work with the government any better than the first.

After the dissolution of the Second Duma, the government illegally altered the election laws, cutting the number of delegates from the peasants and the national minorities and increasing the number from the gentry. By this means the government won a majority, and the Third Duma (1907–1912) and the Fourth (1912–1917) lived out their constitutional terms of five years apiece. Though unrepresentative and limited in their powers, they were still national assemblies. This period was also notable for the rise of mass Russian nationalism, the continuation of Russification, and the revival of labor activism and radicalism. In 1911 after several failed attempts to assassinate him, Stolypin was killed by a revolutionary who was also a police agent.

Under the Fourth Duma, the government tended even more toward reaction. The leftists organized for another revolution, working in unions, cooperatives, evening classes for workers, and a network of other labor organizations. A vast web of police spies challenged them at every turn. Meanwhile, the imperial family drifted into a dangerous situation as the empress fell under the spell of a strange and power-hungry monk from Siberia. Grigory Rasputin (1872–1916) was said to have the mysterious ability, possibly hypnotic, to stop the bleeding of the young heir to the throne, who suffered from hemophilia. Since the empress had enormous influence on her beloved husband, Nicholas II, Rasputin was widely but falsely rumored to be the ruler of Russia, much to the horror of loyal supporters of the imperial house, and greatly to the benefit of those who knew how to manipulate rumor.

After several years of quiescence, the radical labor movement revived with a vengeance in 1912, when government troops killed striking workers at the Lena gold mines in Siberia. Sympathy strikes broke out immediately in protest, culminating in a general strike in St. Petersburg in July 1914, as Europe teetered on the brink of war. When World War I began, Russia was in the throes of a major crisis precipitated by the government's reactionary policies, the scandal of Rasputin's influence, the indignation of the loyal Duma, and the outrage of urban workers.

The Austro-Hungarian Empire, 1867–1914

Politically and economically Austria-Hungary stood somewhere between Russia and western Europe. It was less authoritarian than Russia, but more so than England and France; less agrarian than Russia, but less industrialized than England and Germany. The Dual Monarchy experienced the same social and political pressures faced in Germany, Great Britain, France, and Italy, but always compounded by conflicting nationalisms. Consequently, political polarization contributed to and was usually overshadowed by worsening polarization in conflicts over nationalist aspirations. Nationalist conflicts, however, had a similar effects on parliamentary politics and liberal parties: both lost legitimacy and the faith of their constituents. Through it all Emperor Franz Josef thought of himself as the last "monarch of the old school." He reigned far longer than any other European monarch, loyal to the Habsburg ideal to the end. There is considerable controversy about whether the Habsburg Empire was doomed to destruction even before its defeat in the First World War. In this connection, it should be noted that before the war, while every nationality within the empire was calling for autonomy, almost all their leaders fully expected that autonomy to occur within the structure of the existing empire.

The decade of the 1890s was a period of mass politics, growing opposition, and radicalization along social and national lines throughout the Dual Monarchy. Socialist parties arose and began to win mass followings, as did nationalist parties and parties that tried to combine socialism and nationalism. The central government in Vienna made an attempt to address some of the opposition by expanding the number of voters in 1893 and instituting universal male suffrage in 1907. Since Austria was 90 percent Catholic, it did not experience the German Kulturkampf or French anticlericalism. However, liberals did fight clerical conservatives over religious issues, and they succeeded in passing bills legalizing civil marriages, quasi-secularized schools, and taxes on church property. But liberalism was discredited by the financial crash of 1873, during which it was revealed that some liberal officials had accepted bribes. As in Germany, the working class turned toward socialism after the crash, while the Austrian nobles took little interest in the nation's problems. The peasants' standard of living and level of literacy were extremely low, so that communication and organization for political unity were limited. Furthermore, the Austrian clergy remained loyal to the dynasty and worked on behalf of the nobles against possible peasant uprisings.

The middle class was smaller than in Britain, France, or Germany. Among the bourgeoisie were many Jews, who generally could be neither nobles or bureaucrats. Forced to enter trade, the professions, and the arts, where they prospered, the Jewish minority gave Viennese life much of its charm, its music, its cafés, its image of "the good life" that was so attractive to western European visitors yet so offensive to peasants and nobles in the provinces.

In the late nineteenth century the stresses and strains inherent in this social structure produced two important new political movements among the Germans of Austria: Pan-Germanism and Christian Socialism. In the early 1880s, moderate Austrian Germans wanted to hand over the Slavic lands of Austria to the Hungarians to rule, and then to unite economically with Germany. The Pan-Germans at the turn of the century were more radical. They demanded that Austria become Protestant and agitated for political union with Germany. The Christian Socialists under the leadership of Karl Lueger (1844–1910), became the most important Austrian political party. Strongly Catholic and loyal to the Habsburgs, they appealed to both the peasants and small-business owners by favoring social legislation and opposing big business. A large part of Lueger's appeal (like Stoecker in Berlin) was his scapegoating of Jews, blaming them for Austria's economic problems and political weaknesses. In 1895 when Lueger was elected mayor of Vienna, the government refused to let him take office, but the people of Vienna voted for him again. As mayor of Vienna from 1897 to 1907, Lueger sponsored public ownership of city utilities, parks, playgrounds, free milk for schoolchildren, and other welfare services, while catering to his followers' hatred of Jews, Marxists, and Hungarians. Anti-Semitism grew rapidly among the lower middle classes, often unsuccessful competitors in the world of small shopkeeping.

One response to the reappearance of anti-Semitism in Austria was Zionism. Theodor Herzl, who had reported on the Dreyfus affair as a journalist in Paris, had begun his career working for a liberal newspaper in his hometown of Vienna, where he experienced the new anti-Semitism firsthand and concluded that there would never be a safe place for Jews in Europe.

The Austrian Social Democrats, founded in 1888, responded to the Pan-Germans and the Christian Socialists with a Marxist program calling for government ownership of the means of production and for political action organized by class rather than by nationality. But like their counterparts in western Europe, the Austrian Social Democrats were not revolutionaries; their goals were universal suffrage, fully secular education, and the eight-hour working day. On the nationality question, Social Democratic leaders strongly urged democratic federalism. Each nationality should have control of its own affairs in its own territory; in mixed territories, minorities should be protected; and a central parliament should decide matters of common interest.

In Hungary the situation was rather different. The great landed nobility, loyal to the dynasty and owning half of Hungary in estates of hundreds of thousands of acres apiece, were a small class numerically. Hungary had a much larger class of country gentlemen; their holdings were far smaller and their social position was lower, but their political influence as a group was greater. After the emancipation of the serfs in 1848, many members of the gentry became civil servants or entered the professions. At the bottom of the urban social pyramid was a class of industrial workers in the cities, mostly in the textile and flour-milling industries.

The Jewish population grew rapidly, mostly by immigration. Many Jews were assimilated and became pro-Magyar in sentiment, but, as in Austria, they were disliked, especially among the poorer city population and in the countryside, where they were associated with moneylending and tavern keeping, two professions that kept the peasants in debt. Anti-Semitism in Hungary never became as important a political movement as in Austria or Germany, but it was just as nasty. Political leaders beginning in the 1880s represented the Jews as a serious threat: demagogues argued that unless Hungarians waged a "struggle of life or death" they would find themselves living in a Jewish state as second-class citizens.

The Catholic Church was immensely powerful and rich, but represented only about 60 percent of the population. Clericalism could never become the

Ethnic Composition of the Austro-Hungarian Empire, 1910

Ethnicity	Number (in millions)	Percent of population
Germans	12	23.9
Magyars	10	20.2
Czechs	6.6	12.6
Poles	5.0	10
Ruthenians (Ukrainians)	4.0	7.9
Romanians	3.25	6.4
Croats	2.5	5.3
Slovaks	2.0	3.8
Serbs	2.0	3.8
Slovenes	1.25	2.6
Italians and others	2.9	3.5
Total	50.8	100

Source: Raymond Pearson, *European Nationalism, 1789–1920* (New York, 1994).

dominant force in Hungary that it was in Austria and Hungary did not produce strong parties like the Austrian Social Democrats and Christian Socialists.

Hungary never effectively changed its law of 1874, by which only about 6 percent of the population could vote. The only real source of political differences among Magyars was the question of Hungary's position in the Dual Monarchy. Some, followers of Lajos Kossuth, favored complete independence; others, called the Tigers, wished to improve the position of Hungary within the monarchy by securing Hungarian control over its own army, diplomatic service, and finances, and by limiting the tie with Austria to the person of the monarch. While the Tigers were generally victorious, the Kossuthists were able to disrupt the government of 1902, and in 1905 they won a majority. When Franz Josef refused to meet the demands of the new majority and appointed a loyal general as premier, the Kossuthists urged patriots not to pay taxes or perform military services, and until 1910 they kept their parliament in convulsion.

Conflicts Among Nationalities

The rise of mass parties polarized debates over nationalities.

In the Czech lands cultural nationalism was fostered at the end of the century by an active Czech-language press, by patriotic societies, by Czech schools, and by the *sokols,* physical-training societies with strong nationalist leanings. From about 1890 on, Czech nationalism made it virtually impossible for the parliamentary system to function.

Since the 1880s and the 1890s, each time the Czechs won cultural or political gains, the German extremists bitterly opposed them, strengthening the Czech extremists and weakening the moderates. A law requiring all judges in Czech lands to conduct trials in the language of the petitioner led to the development of an experienced body of Czech civil servants, since many Czechs knew German already, while Germans usually had to learn Czech. In 1890 the government and the Old Czechs tentatively agreed on an administrative division of Bohemia between Germans and Czechs, but the Young Czechs rioted in the Bohemian Diet, and Prague was put under martial law until 1897. When a new law was passed requiring that all civil servants in the Czech lands be bilingual after 1901, the Germans in the Vienna parliament forced out the ministry, while Czech extremists began to talk ominously about a future Russian-led Slavic showdown with the Germans. The disagreement paralyzed the Austrian parliament, and government had to be conducted by decree. In 1913 the Bohemian Diet was dissolved, and in 1914 Czech deputies in the Austrian parliament refused to allow national business to proceed. Thus World War I began with both parliament and the Bohemian Diet dissolved and with the emperor and ministers ruling by themselves.

In this context a remarkable politician and national leader entered the arena. Tomaš Masarýk (1850–1937), professor of philosophy and student of Slavic culture, deeply influenced generations of students and upheld democratic ideals in politics. Masarýk inspired poets and novelists to write of a glorified national past for a popular audience, and from 1907 he formally led the Czech national movement. But instead of national independence, he called for a federalist system of national states within the empire. Cosmopolitan, internationalist, and with a large middle-class following, Masarýk alone in this period linked national sovereignty with democratic and civil rights. In 1918 he would become president of the new nation of Czechoslovakia.

As in earlier periods, problems of ethnic conflict and rising national identity were more acute in the Hungarian portion of the empire. The Hungarians had won autonomy on the basis of a claim to national sovereignty; other minorities saw no reason not to achieve the same autonomy according to the same reasoning. The Hungarian government understood this threat and continued its campaign of Magyarization. The Hungarian (Magyar) language became the official language of education and administration, as well as postal, telegraph, and railroad services, much to the chagrin of the non-Hungarians.

Slovaks were perhaps the most Magyarized. Poor peasants for the most part, the more ambitious of them often became Magyars simply by adopting the language. Romanians, living primarily in Transylvania, had been fighting for centuries to achieve recognition of their Orthodox Christianity. And despite laws designed to eliminate the use of the Romanian language, Romanians fiercely resisted assimilation. Many further hoped that Transylvania might regain the autonomy it had once enjoyed. These hopes were crushed in 1892, when their petition to Vienna on these points was returned unopened and unread. Romanian nationalist leaders were arrested, tried, and imprisoned after circulating their petition and publicizing their cause abroad.

Relations among the South Slavs in Hungary (Serbs, Croats, and the people of Bosnia-Herzegovina) remained as complex and explosive as ever. Since the Congress of Berlin in 1878, Austria had occupied the provinces of Bosnia-

Herzegovina. As the fragile autonomy of the people there was increasingly threatened by Austrian ambition, South Slav nationalists resented the occupation all the more. Many observers in Vienna pressed for some sort of all-South-Slav solution that would join Dalmatia, Croatia, and Bosnia-Herzegovina into one kingdom under Franz Josef, with the same status as Hungary—a Triple rather than Dual Monarchy. However, the advocates of this solution, known as "Trialists," met with opposition from Hungarians who opposed all efforts to offer their special status to another nation, from Germans who opposed any further dilution of the Habsburg monarchy, and from some Serbs who wanted to see the Serbs of the region join together in an independent and separate Serbia. Trialism was, however, supported by the heir to the throne, Franz Ferdinand (1863–1914), which gave hope to the many South Slavs who favored this solution.

The rise of mass politics and the intersection of nationalist and social-political protest were especially important in Congress Poland, that part of Poland under the Russian Empire. After the suppression of the 1863 uprising, Russian authorities tried to use a favorable emancipation settlement both to maintain the peasants' hostility to their landlords and to prevent the unification of nobles and peasants around nationalism. This tactic failed. Russification and anti-Catholic policies drove the peasants to embrace the nation. For several decades Poles in Russia turned away from politics and helped develop Poland into a thriving industrial and agricultural producer. The industrial middle classes offered themselves as spokesmen of the new modern nation, and for several decades there was little challenge to their position from the discredited nobility or the nascent working classes. The decades of the 1870s and 1880s also saw some cooperation between Poles and Jews and a certain amount of Jewish assimilation.

Starting in the 1890s, however, the successes of industrialization produced the same class conflicts seen elsewhere. On the right the National Democratic League, led by Roman Dmowski (1864–1939), promoted a peasant nationalism, based on social Darwinism. The National Democrats did not see themselves as a political movement competing with other political ideologies for votes, but rather as an "organic" representative of the nation. But Dmowski did believe in "struggle" against the nation's enemies, first of all Jews, the 1880s bringing to an end a period of good relations between Poles and Jews. Ukrainians and Lithuanians were considered Poles by Dmowski's party: "Ukraine never did exist, does not exist, and will not exist."

Nationalism was also a component of the Polish Socialist party led by Jósef Pilsudski (1867–1935). Pilsudski believed that the oppression of workers was reinforced by the oppression of the nation and that the liberation of the nation was impossible without the elemental strength of the working class. The socialists were challenged by antinationalist communists led by Rosa Luxemburg, who believed that national liberation and the reconstitution of the nation would do nothing for workers, in fact would make their situation worse. Finally, in 1897, there arose the Bund, a socialist party committed to improving the lives of Jewish workers (and thereby all workers) by overthrowing the Russian autocracy. The Bund combined nationalism (Jewish) with internationalism (proletarian). The 1905 revolution offered a field of activity for all these parties, the result of which was the further polarization of politics between left and right, Pole and non-Pole, and further fragmentation on the left.

Finally, the last decade of the century and the first decade of the next saw the mass activization of peasants in eastern Europe. Rural unrest became epidemic in this period and in some cases led to the appearance of peasant political parties. In Hungary, peasants rose up with economic and political demands throughout the 1890s, culminating in 1897, when fifteen thousand well-organized peasants rose up to demand redistribution of the land. The movement was brutally repressed, but pacification of the countryside took more than a year. In Russia, peasants played an important role in the revolution of 1905. In 1902 major disturbances disrupted the provinces of Poltava and Kharkov in Ukraine and everywhere in the empire in the summers of 1905 and 1906. Hungry peasants demanded grain and plundered manor houses; angrier peasants burned estates and, during the revolution, killed their inhabitants.

For all their differences, mass politics everywhere in Europe pressed political goals with more organization and with greater violence at the turn of the century. Impatience with parliamentary politics undermined processes of compromise and consensus building and brought conflicts of all kinds to the surface. Mass politics gave voice to people who had been historically unrepresented, but in few cases did it bring them relief for their hunger or answers to their demands.

The Road to War

There are many reasons the Great Powers of Europe went to war in 1914 but no clear explanations. When it was over, the victorious allies forced Germany to take the blame for starting the war, but in fact there was plenty of blame to go around. Another popular explanation at the time stressed the instability of eastern Europe and the Balkans: "the tinderbox of Europe." But this too apportions the blame unfairly. Conflicting nationalisms in eastern Europe and the weakness of Ottoman authority in the region were certainly factors in the destabilization of the continent as a whole, but war resulted only because the west European powers turned multiple regional conflicts into a conflict of their own. The Great Powers had their eyes trained on eastern and southeastern Europe throughout the century and were involved in all the conflicts that arose as the Ottoman Empire withdrew and Austria and Russia jockeyed for power.

In the aftermath of the Russo-Turkish War of 1877–1878 the continental powers entered into a series of treaty agreements. First, in 1879, Bismarck signed a treaty with Austria-Hungary forming the Dual Alliance. This alliance had a novel feature, which would profoundly influence later events. It included provision for mutual assistance if one of the partners were attacked by a third country. Bismarck's hoped this innovation would force Russia to repair relations with Germany but it had the opposite effect.

Bismarck, who believed politics to be "the art of the possible" and saw that future conflict was inevitable, favored moderation toward defeated enemies (except France), for they might be needed one day as allies. Since life threw into conflict a shifting kaleidoscope of social classes, political parties, special-interest groups, sectional loyalties, intemperate individuals who had attained positions of power, and entire nations and states, one could not predict with accuracy a nation's future needs in terms of alliances. Therefore, one must always have an alternative course of action ready, a course not too brutally contradicted by any former alliance, so that the middle ground might be credibly taken. Accordingly, in the 1880s Bismarck worked to restore the Russian–German alliance. In 1881 Germany and Russia signed the Reinsurance Treaty, which also contained a mutual assistance guarantee. Both Austria and Russia could expect German support if they fell victim to military aggression; and neither could expect support if they were the aggressor. This was an important deterrent. Next Bismarck took advantage of Italy's desire to protect itself against France and to shore up its imperialist ambitions in North Africa. In 1882 Italy joined Germany and Austria-Hungary in what was now the Triple Alliance. Bismarck was pleased because Germany's long-standing enemy France was isolated and Germany was protected.

After Bismarck was dismissed, however, German policy was not so judicious and careful. Wilhelm II had ambitious plans, and he did not want to be constrained by complex treaty promises. The German emperor, thinking it highly unlikely that republican France would ever ally with autocratic Russia, allowed the Reinsurance Treaty to lapse. This was a serious miscalculation, and it allowed the two powers on either side of Germany to sign their own agreement. In 1891 France and Russian signed a secret pact, and in 1894 they made it public as the Dual Entente.

Thus a highly unstable configuration of alliances replaced the Concert of Europe. Given the acknowledged weakness of Ottoman rule in Europe, any instability in the Balkans had the potential to bring France and Russia into conflict with Austria-Hungary and Germany.

The unlikely French–Russian alliance was enhanced by economic ties in the 1890s. Minister of Finance Sergei Witte went out of his way to attract French investors to Russian industry. In 1914 one-quarter of all French foreign investment was in the Russian economy. Bismarck, however, discouraged German investment in Russia, and German and French economic cooperation was minimal. Needing a powerful ally after its disastrous defeat by Germany, France began to repair its relations with Great Britain, severely damaged by wars of imperialism in Africa and Southeast Asia. Great Britain had long maintained that it needed no military alliances because it could depend on its own navy for protection. But the Boer War (1899–1902), fought by Britain against South Africa, was highly unpopular in Europe and in part convinced Britain that it might need some friends. In 1904 Britain and France signed the Entente Cordiale (friendly agreement) in which they settled old

Europe in 1914

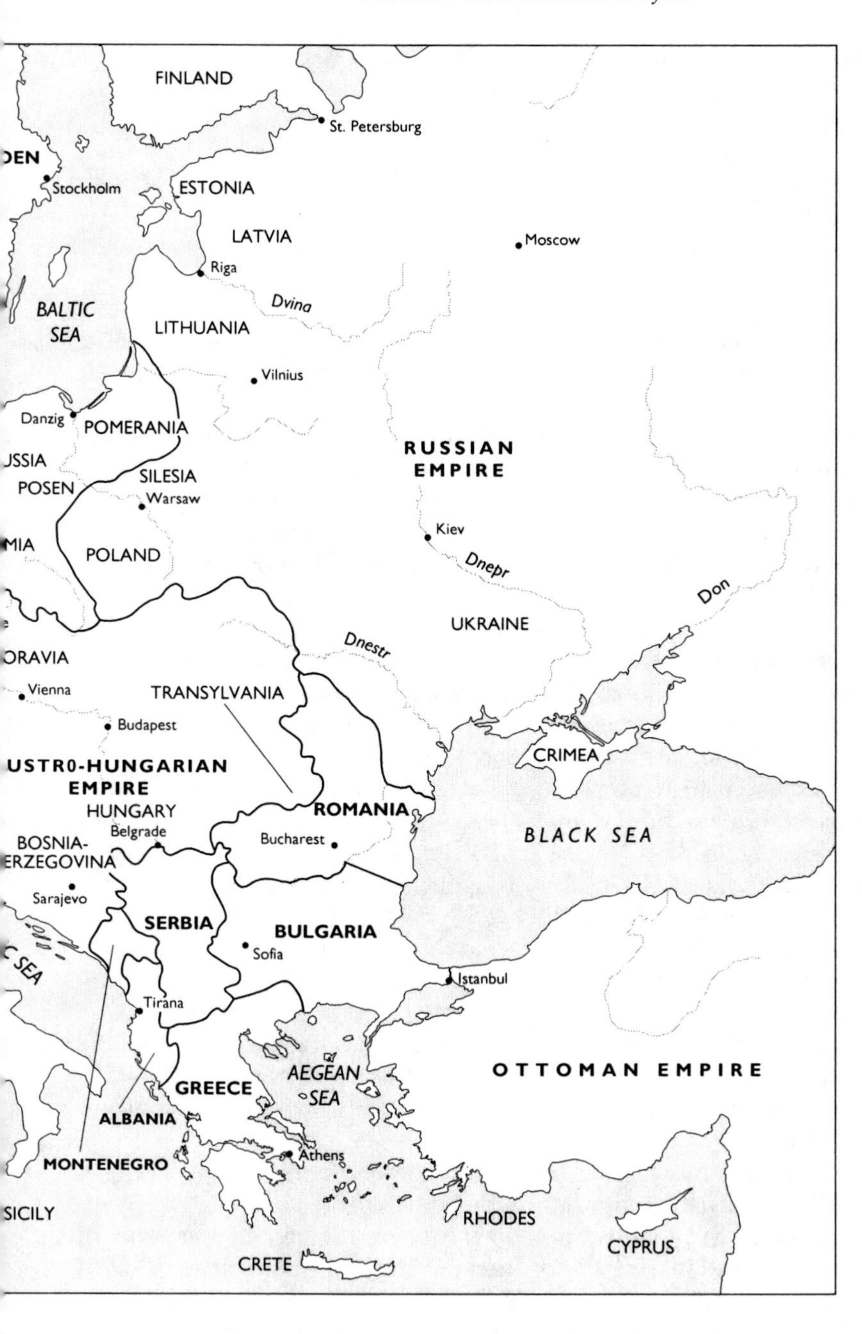
FINLAND
St. Petersburg
DEN
Stockholm
ESTONIA
LATVIA
Moscow
Riga
Dvina
BALTIC SEA
LITHUANIA
Vilnius
Danzig
POMERANIA
RUSSIAN EMPIRE
JSSIA
SILESIA
POSEN
Warsaw
Kiev
MIA
POLAND
Dnepr
Don
UKRAINE
Dnestr
ORAVIA
Vienna
TRANSYLVANIA
Budapest
CRIMEA
USTRO-HUNGARIAN EMPIRE
HUNGARY
ROMANIA
Belgrade
BOSNIA-
ERZEGOVINA
Bucharest
BLACK SEA
Sarajevo
SERBIA
BULGARIA
Sofia
C SEA
Istanbul
Tirana
AEGEAN SEA
OTTOMAN EMPIRE
GREECE
ALBANIA
Athens
MONTENEGRO
SICILY
RHODES
CYPRUS
CRETE

Major Treaty Alliances on the Road to the First World War

1879	Dual Alliance	Germany–Austria-Hungary
1881	Reinsurance Treaty (secret)	Germany–Russia
1882	Triple Alliance	Germany–Austria–Hungary–Italy
1894	Dual Entente	France–Russia
1904	Entente Cordiale	France–Britain
1907	Triple Entente	France–Russia–Britain

colonial disputes over Morocco, Egypt, Indochina, and Newfoundland. And in 1907 Britain entered into alliance with Russia, creating the Triple Entente, to balance Germany's growing power.

Wilhelm's policies, however, were somewhat contradictory. He had broken with Russia in part because he wanted an alliance with Great Britain against Russia. But at the same time, he embarked on a massive naval building campaign, which could only have been perceived by Britain as a direct challenge to its control of the seas. Furthermore, Germany embarked on a much more ambitious and provocative foreign policy generally.

Numerous crises arose, or were provoked, that brought one European power into conflict with another, each one threatening to ignite a European war. The Great Powers all seemed less interested in maintaining peace than in testing one another to establish hierarchies of power in Europe and see who could win a war. In 1905 Germany threatened French interests in Morocco to test the British support for France and possibly isolate France. Both sides backed down, but Germany was humiliated and determined not to let that happen again. And France, Britain, and even the United States were more than ever convinced of Germany's aggressive aims and began solidifying their alliance against the possibility of German belligerence.

Russia and Britain settled some long-standing tensions in Asia when Russia lost the war to Japan. Russia decided that its priorities were in the Balkans, where it conflicted with Austria-Hungary, rather than in Asia, where it came into conflict with Britain. British loans helped in Russia's recovery after the Russo-Japanese war in 1904–1905 and the revolutionary crisis of 1905–1907. The two countries also agreed to respect each other's zones of influence in Persia and central Asia.

If it seems that the Great Powers treated the rest of the world like pawns in a game of global chess, they did. But in the given world context, every pacifying move, such as the Anglo-Russian agreement, threatened someone, in this case Germany. And in the Balkans there was a dangerous combination of nations asserting their claims to independence but no Great Power willing to commit itself to maintain the status quo or able to do so without scaring one of the other powers. Borders and sovereignty seemed to be up for grabs because any move in the region by one Great Power might provoke a general war among the now well-armed nation-states. In the early 1900s national movements were once again assertive, particularly among the South Slavs living in Serbia and under Austro-Hungarian and Ottoman rule. If Germany was acting provocatively among the Great Powers (and historians debate this), the Serbs were acting provocatively in eastern Europe.

Serbia relied on Russia for support of its aspirations, and all the other powers knew this well. Serbia began calling for union with the Serbs living in other countries, first in Macedonia, then in Bosnia-Herzegovina, both of which Serbia wanted to annex. Such statements affected not only relations between Serbia and Austria-Hungary but between Austria-Hungary and Russia, viewed as Serbia's protector. Austria and Serbia entered a war of wills.

First, Austria tried economic sanctions, by blocking the importation of Serbian livestock, resulting in the so-called Pig Wars, and then by building a railroad line to further isolate Serbia. In 1908 a serious crisis occurred following a revolution in Istanbul. A group of reformers, the "Young Turks," took over the army and forced the government to hold elections. This development was very popular and made it appear as if Turkey, the sick man of Europe, might get well after all. The Young Turks had international ambitions to revive the Ottoman Empire, which increased instability in the Balkans by threatening both Russian and Austrian ambitions there. Russia wanted free access for its navy to the Mediterranean Sea through the Straits of Bosporus and the Dardanelles, and Austria wanted to annex Bosnia-Herzegovina to force Serbia to back down from its plans for a Greater Serbia. Both goals were hindered by the reawakening of the Ottoman Empire by the Young Turks, and in secret negotiations Russia and Austria agreed to support each other.

But fuel was thrown on this smoldering fire when Austria went ahead and annexed Bosnia-Herzegovina at a moment when Russia was weakened after the 1905–1907 revolution. Serbia was not alone in being enraged, Austria's action was highly unpopular in Russia too. Russia denied ever supporting Austria. Serbia mobilized its army, assuming it had Russian support. Austria-Hungary readied for war as well. But the Hungarians were opposed to war, as was the heir to the Habsburg throne, Archduke Franz Ferdinand. Russia was not eager either, and Russia's ally France was against it, too. The British worked out a compromise, but then Germany felt the need to support Austria to the fullest extent; anything less, would made Germany appear weak. Germany forced the Russians to accept an ultimatum, and the Serbs had to back down entirely, which allowed the Austrian annexation to stand. The crisis passed in 1908, but enmities hardened.

A second Moroccan crisis occurred in 1911, when Germany threatened France after its old enemy had intervened in disorders in Morocco. Germany sent a gunboat to the Moroccan seaport of Agadir for no clear diplomatic reasons, and then made fantastic demands for compensation that provoked not only France, but Britain as well. All three parties raised the stakes by making inflammatory public speeches about attacks on their national honor, and a combination of Russian and British diplomatic skill had to be summoned to cool temperatures again. This crisis passed too, but only after coming close to war; French–German hostility also hardened.

The danger of these crises leading to general war was increased by the involvement of each of the powers in massive and unprecedented military buildups. Between 1900 and 1910 military spending increased in Germany by 20 percent, in Russia by 60 percent, in Italy by 50 percent, in France by 35 percent, in Austria-Hungary by 25 percent, and in Great Britain by 35 percent. Then in the period between 1910 and 1914, military spending doubled again in Germany and Austria-Hungary and rose significantly everywhere else.

Few people appreciated how industrial weapons technology had transformed such basics as guns and artillery. All the European powers were engaged in producing new high-powered repeating rifles, automatic weapons, and long-range artillery, which would make it possible to fire at the enemy from greater and greater distances. In 1914 the face of modern warfare would be transformed by weapons that could fire twenty times more ammunition twenty times faster and ten times further than had been possible fifty years earlier.

Naval spending was especially dangerous. France (like Japan and the United States) had a powerful navy and Russia contributed to war fears by rebuilding its fleet after the debacle against Japan. Britain watched these developments carefully. But German naval building was particularly worrisome. Wilhelm had numerous reasons for personally launching a naval building campaign: to support heavy industry, to appeal to nationalists of all stripes, and to meet requirements for becoming a modern world empire. Historians, however, generally agree that the massive naval buildup begun in 1898 was directed against Britain specifically. Britain responded with naval buildup of its own at a pace Germany could not match. The temptation to blame Germany alone for the arms race is countered by military expenditures in other nations: Russia, France, and Britain all put a higher percentage of their gross national product into military spending than did Germany. The German military concluded from this that in any armed confrontation, Germany would have to strike first before these discrepancies would count.

The next crisis came in the Balkans. In 1912 Serbia and its neighbors Bulgaria, Montenegro, and Greece took advantage of turmoil in Turkey to join together in the Balkan League to declare war. In less than a month the Ottoman Empire was utterly defeated by this alliance and forced finally to withdraw altogether from Europe. In 1913, however, those allies fell out over the spoils of war. Bulgaria attacked Serbia seeking more land in Macedonia. Again, none of the Great Powers wanted South Slav nationalism to draw them into a war against each other, but the stage was set for general conflict.

The arms race, as well as the international crises in the colonies and in eastern Europe, occurred the context of a growing fatalism about war. Seemingly intractable social and political problems and a sense of impending crisis made many Europeans hope for war to "clear the air" and provide for "a fresh start." Whether the rulers who declared war also chose international conflict to solve domestic problems is more controversial. Nationalist, chauvinist pressures were being placed on all the governments by mass nationalist sentiment in every major country. It is clear, however, that in the face of mounting domestic and international pressures, few politicians had any decisive answers, while military leaders by contrast had energetic and clear plans. By the 1910s people had been talking about war for so long that it came to seem inevitable.

When war did break out in 1914, there was no single cause; the repeated crises, however, had persuaded many Europeans and their leaders that sooner or later they would have to resolve the recurrent problems once and for all with war. Peasants and workers were noticeably less enthusiastic, but opposition to war came from socialists and pacifists (often women) alone. Imperialism, mass politics, reckless nationalism, economic competition, the arms race, and anxieties about modern degeneration certainly pushed Europeans toward war after a century of relative peace. But more important was the erosion of serious deterrents. The will to maintain peace, the memory of war's horrors, the rules and institutions that curbed appetites for aggression and contained disagreements, all of which were in place in the decades after 1815, had gradually eroded.

The final decisions were set in motion on June 28, 1914. The heir to the Austro-Hungarian throne, Franz Ferdinand, and his wife, Sophie, were assassinated while on a state visit to Sarajevo, the capital of Bosnia. The assassin, Gavrilo Princip (1895–1918), was connected to a militant Serbian nationalist group, the Black Hand, and probably received support from the Serbian government itself. Austria-Hungary vowed to punish Serbia and to bring it under Austrian control once and for all. Serbia, which could neither combat Austria militarily nor accept Austria's humiliating conditions, offered an evasive answer to Austria's ultimatum. Austria mobilized for war. Germany offered its unconditional support. Russia could not stand by and watch Serbia crushed. France could not stand down once Russia committed. Frantic British negotiations failed. Socialists' opposition to war failed to convince anyone. Germany attacked France by crossing through neutral Belgium, which brought Great Britain into the war.

People greeted the declaration of war with relief, patriotism, even celebration. Friedrich Meinecke, later a great historian, described the outbreak of war as "one of the great moments of my life, . . . [which] suddenly filled my soul with the deepest confidence in our people and the profoundest joy." No one remembered a major war. Everyone underestimated the changes in warfare that advanced technology would make. People in every country expected a short engagement. But they were all wrong. Only Sir Edward Grey, the British foreign minister, depressed over the failure of diplomacy to stop the war, was able to guess what was coming. He stood in his office on the night of August 3, 1914 and said, "The lights are going out all over Europe, they shall not be lighted again in our lifetimes." With these words, the nineteenth century came to a close.

* * *

Nation, industry, democracy, progress: in the nineteenth century (and much of the twentieth) these stood for the concept of modernity. By the beginning of the twentieth century, most European countries would have constitutions, elected, representative governments, and limits on monarchical power. Even Russia got a constitution of sorts in 1906. Peoples and states all over the Continent seemed to be forming nations, abandoning agriculture for industry, and moving toward more democratic governments. There was pressure everywhere in the world to follow the same path. But from the vantage point of the twenty-first century, it is clear that the democratizing path laid down by England, and perhaps France, Germany, and the United States, was only one alternative among many.

The similarity in political trajectory among European nation-states conceals some significant differences. In parts of Europe and in Russia in particular, the wolf of authoritarianism lay concealed in the sheep's clothing of parliament and constitution. In Spain, Italy, and the Balkans, constitutional politics were a front for traditional forms of conflict and corruption. Even in the most democratic countries, democracy was resisted. Women had to wait until after the First World War (or in France, the next one) to vote in national elections; former slaves and their descendants, despite laws giving them the vote, waited even longer. The most democratic countries often had the most repressive and exploitative control over their overseas colonies, making it clear that "natural rights" and "popular sovereignty" were never absolute truths for universal application. The Europeans' treatment of the people in their colonies and the minorities in their own countries, together with the reemergence of authoritarianism in the twentieth century in forms more violent and repressive than ever, make the resistance to democracy everywhere at least as important to understand as its impressive ideals and hard-won achievements.

During the nineteenth century, increasing control over nature with industrial machines and modern capitalism offered Europeans a growing sense of their own individual power, as well as the technology and prosperity to assert their power over other peoples at home and in colonies abroad. The nineteenth-century head start gave European modernity, especially in western Europe, enormous advantages, and people everywhere were forced to respond to the changes that accompanied modern industrial capitalism and the powerful new nation-states. But the Europeans' use of modern power to dominate, educate, classify, and economically exploit others created new conflicts over cultural identities, over sovereignty, over security, and over the essential components of human nature. These conflicts, beginning with colonial struggles and the First World War, would call into question the very foundation of European power and Europeans' faith in progress and the cultural achievements of the nineteenth century.

Chronology

1762	Rousseau, *Social Contract*
1769	Watt invents steam engine
1772	First partition of Poland (Russia, Prussia, Austria)
1776	Adam Smith, *The Wealth of Nations*
1789	French Revolution begins
1790	Burke, *Reflections on the Revolution in France*
1793	Revolutionaries execute King Louis XVI Reign of Terror begins Second partition of Poland Louvre opened as art museum
1795	Third partition of Poland abolishes Polish state
1796–1801	Paul I (Russia)
1797–1840	Friedrich Wilhelm III (Prussia)
1798	Wordsworth, Coleridge, *Lyrical Ballads* Pixérécourt, *Victor, or the Child of the Forest* Malthus, *Essay on the Principle of Population*
1799	Napoleon overthrows Directory and seizes power
1800	Volta, first electric battery
1801	Act of Union joins Great Britain with Ireland
1801–1825	Alexander I (Russia)
1803	Beethoven, Third Symphony (Eroica)
1804	Napoleon declares himself emperor of the French Proclamation of the Austrian Empire
1804–1835	Franz Josef II (Holy Roman Empire) becomes Emperor of Austria as Franz Josef I
1806	British establish Cape Colony in South Africa
1807	Britain abolishes transatlantic slave trade
1808	Sierra Leone becomes a crown colony Goethe, *Faust*, Part I
1809	Metternich appointed foreign minster (Austria)
1811	Luddite machine-breaking riots (Great Britain)

1812	Napoleon invades Russia, retreats in disarray Goya, *Disasters of War*
1812–1818	Byron, *Childe Harold's Pilgrimage*
1814	Napoleon abdicates, exiled to Elba
1814–1824	Louis XVIII returned to throne
1814–1815	Congress of Vienna
1815	Napoleon tries to reclaim power; the Hundred Days Defeated at Waterloo, Napoleon is exiled to Saint Helena Holy Alliance (Russia, Austria, Prussia) Quadruple Alliance (Great Britain, Austria, Russia, Prussia)
1818	Mary Shelley, *Frankenstein, or the Modern Prometheus* Prado museum opened, Madrid
1819	Peterloo massacre Karlsbad Decrees suppressing German political activity Géricault, *The Raft of the Medusa* Byron, *Don Juan* (first part published)
1820	Revolts in Spain and Portugal Percy Shelley, "Prometheus Unbound"
1820–21	Revolts in Piedmont, Naples, Greece Hegel, *Philosophy of Right*
1822	Liberia founded by former American slaves Greek Declaration of Independence
1823	Monroe Doctrine establishes U.S. hegemony in Western Hemisphere O'Connell, Catholic Association of Ireland Pushkin begins *Evgeny Onegin*
1824	Delacroix, *Massacre at Chios* Beethoven, Ninth Symphony
1824–1830	Charles X (France)
1825	Decembrist revolt (Russia)
1825–1855	Nicholas I (Russia)
1826	Joseph Niépce produces first photograph
1828–1829	Russo-Turkish War
1829	Catholic emancipation (Ireland, Britain)
1830	Revolutions in France, Belgium, Poland, Papal States, parts of Germany French conquest of Algeria begins Dutch conquest of Java complete Hugo, *Hernani* Stendahl, *The Red and the Black*
1830–1837	William IV (Great Britain)

1830–1848	Louis Philippe (France)
1831	Faraday, electro-magnetic induction
1831	Darwin sails on HMS *Beagle*
	Delacroix, *Liberty Leading the People*
1831–1838	Revolutions in Italian States
1831–1834	Labor protests in Lyons, France
1832	First Reform Bill (Great Britain) Mazzini forms Young Italy Greek independence recognized Gauss and Weber, first electric telegraph (Göttingen) Goethe dies, *Faust* (Part II) Berlioz, *Symphonie fantastique*
1832–1833	Turko-Egyptian war, Russia supports Ottoman Empire
1833	Treaty of Unkiar-Skelessi (renewed 1841) Britain abolishes slavery in all its possessions
1836–1846	Boer "Great Trek" from Cape Colony
1834	New Poor Law (England) Prussian customs union (*Zollverein*) Slavery abolished in British possessions
1835–1848	Ferdinand I (Austria)
1837–1901	Queen Victoria (Great Britain)
1838	People's Charter (Great Britain) Dickens, *Oliver Twist*
1839	Second Turko-Egyptian War; Europe intervenes to save Ottoman Empire
1839	Exhibition of daguerreotypes Goodyear invents vulcanized rubber
1839–1842	First Opium War (Great Britain, China)
1840	Britain annexes New Zealand Proudhon, *What Is Property?* Cabet, *Voyage to Icaria*
1840–1861	Friedrich Wilhelm IV (Prussia)
1841	David Livingstone arrives in southeast Africa
1842	Chinese cede Hong Kong to Great Britain British recognize Boer Republics
1844	Silesian weavers' revolt Engels, *Condition of the Working Classes in England* Morse first electric telegraph system
1845–1849	Potato famine in Ireland

1846	European food crisis begins Repeal of Corn Laws (Great Britain)
1847	Economic crisis in Europe British train schedules coordinated to Greenwich Mean Time
1847–1848	Banquet campaign in France
1848	France abolishes slavery in its colonies Marx and Engels, *The Communist Manifesto* Mill, *Principles of Political Economy*
1848	Revolutions in Italy, France, Germany, the Habsburg monarchy, and elsewhere January, revolts in Sicily and Naples February, revolts in Paris, French Second Republic, universal male suffrage February, abdication of Louis Philippe (France) March, revolts in Munich, Vienna, Budapest, Venice, Krakow, Milan, Berlin March, Hungarian independence declared March, resignation of Metternich March, Piedmontese troops invade Lombardy April, abolition of serfdom in central Europe April, Chartist demonstrations in London May, Slav Congress, Prague May, Frankfurt parliament June, revolt in Prague defeated June, revolt in Paris defeated July–August, Austria reconquers northern Italy October, Vienna defeated, surrenders December, Ferdinand of Austria abdicates, Franz Josef ascends throne (Austria)
1849	March–April, Frankfurt Assembly votes German crown to Prussia, king rejects offer April, Kossuth deposes Habsburgs in Hungary May, Franz Josef invites Nicholas I to aid in suppressing revolts, agrees to aid Austria against Hungary July, French troops suppress Roman Republic August, Hungarian nationalists defeated Austria recaptures Venice
1848–1849	California Gold Rush
1848–1916	Franz Josef (Austria)
1848–1852	Louis-Napoleon elected president of Second Republic
1851	Singer, sewing machine The Great Exhibition, London
1852–1870	Louis-Napoleon proclaimed emperor Napoleon III
1853–1856	Crimean War (Russia, Turkey, Britain, France)

1854–1865	French expand in West Africa (Senegal)
1857–1858	Sepoy Rebellion in India; British East India Company dissolved, British government assumes direct rule in India
1857–1860	Second Opium War
1859	Austro-French-Piedmontese war; Austria loses Lombardy Darwin, *On the Origin of Species* Mill, *On Liberty*
1860	October Diploma Garibaldi and his "Thousand" sail for Sicily, invade mainland
1861	Kingdom of Italy declared, King Vittorio Emanue II Emancipation of Serfs (Russia) Britain annexes Lagos and Niger
1861–1888	Wilhelm I (king of Prussia, emperor of Germany)
1862	Bismarck appointed minister-president of Prussia Paris Opera House Hugo, *Les Misérables* Turgenev, *Fathers and Children*
1863	Revolt in Poland suppressed by Russia Salon des Refusés (France) Manet, *Le Déjeuner sur l'herbe* Chernyshevsky, *What Is to Be Done?*
1861–1874	Era of Great Reforms (Russia)
1864	War over Schleswig-Holstein (Prussia, Austria) Tolstoy, *War and Peace* Pius IX, *Syllabus of Errors* The First International
1865	Transatlantic telegraph cable completed
1865–1876	Russians expand in central Asia
1866	Austro-Prussian "Six Weeks" War Austria expelled from Germany Italy gains Venetia from Austria Nobel invents dynamite Dostoevsky, *Crime and Punishment*
1867	Compromise (*Ausgleich*) establishing Dual Monarchy: Austria becomes Austria-Hungary Discovery of diamonds in South Africa Second Reform Bill (Great Britain) Zola, *Thérèse Raquin* Marx, *Capital*, vol. 1
1868	February, Disraeli prime minister (First time) December, Gladstone prime minster (first time)
1869	Suez Canal opens Mill, *On the Subjection of Women*

1870–1871	Franco-Prussian War German Empire founded French Third Republic declared
1870–1914	Irish Home Rule movement
1871	Paris Commune: uprising, defeat, massacre
1871–1888	Wilhelm I (Germany)
1871–1872	Algerian revolt Eliot, *Middlemarch*
1871–1878	Kulturkampf
1872	Commercial oil extraction begins at Baku
1873	Financial crisis and beginning of Great Depression (–1890s) League of the Three Emperors (Germany, Austria-Hungary, Russia) First Impressionist exhibition
1874	H. J. Lawson's chain-driven bicycle
1875	Revolt in Bosnia-Herzegovina German Social Democratic party founded Britain acquires financial control of Suez Canal
1875–1885	French expeditions to Equatorial Africa
1876	Queen Victoria declared Empress of India Alexander Bell obtains patent for telephone Wagner, *The Ring of the Nibelungs* (first performance) Edison invents phonograph, filament lamp Renoir, *Le Moulin de la Galette*
1877–1878	Russo-Turkish War
1878	Congress of Berlin renegotiates peace settlement of Russo-Turkish war Austria occupies Bosnia-Herzegovina Antisocialist law (Germany) Degas, *Dancer on the Stage*
1879	Dual Alliance, Austria-Hungary and Germany
1880–1881	First Boer War; semi-independence
1881	Alexander II assassinated Irish Land Act
1881–1886	Welfare reforms in Germany
1881–1894	Alexander III (Russia)
1882	Triple Alliance (Germany, Austria, Italy) Italy expands in Ethiopia British occupy Egypt French begin conquest of western Sudan Daimler, petroleum engine Wagner, *Parsifal*
1883	Nietzsche, *Thus Spake Zarathustra*

1884	Maxim, machine gun Germany begins colonization in Africa
1884–1885	Berlin Conference, regulation of African partition
1884–1886	Germany expands in Cameroons, Togoland, Southwest Africa, Tanganyika
1884–1887	Russia completes conquest of central Asia
1885	Leopold II (Belgium) establishes Congo Free State General Gordon killed at Khartoum Daimler, internal combustion engine Discovery of gold in South Africa Cézanne, *Mont Sainte-Victoire*
1886	British East Africa Company occupies Kenya Britain annexes Burma
1887	Reinsurance Treaty (Germany, Russia) Boulanger crisis (France) Edison invents motion picture process and viewer Nietzsche, *On the Genealogy of Morals*
1888	Dunlop, pneumatic tire
1888–1918	Wilhelm II (Germany)
1889	Eiffel Tower opened The Second International
1890	Bismarck dismissed; Germany drops Reinsurance Treaty Frazer, *The Golden Bough* Ibsen, *Hedda Gabler*
1890–1891	British South Africa company occupies Rhodesia
1890–1898	Male suffrage Spain, Belgium, Netherlands, Norway
1891	Pop Leo XIII, *Rerum novarum*
1892	James Keir Hardie elected to Parliament (Great Britain)
1891–1892	Famine in Russia
1893	Munch, *The Scream*
1894	Franco-Russian alliance President Carnot assassinated (France) Italy invades Ethiopia Dreyfus condemned for treason Alexander III (Russia) dies
1894–1917	Nicholas II (Russia)
1895	Lumière brothers invent cinematograph portable motion picture camera, projector Marconi, wireless radio Röntgen discovers X-rays Oscar Wilde sentenced for sodomy

1895–1898	Russia gains control of Manchuria
1896	Ethiopia defeats Italy at Adowa Russian Social Democratic Labor party founded Freud invents psychoanalysis First modern Olympics, Athens
1897	Karl Lueger becomes mayor of Vienna Spanish prime minster assassinated Germany begin building fleet Russia adopts gold standard
1898	British defeat Mahdists at Omdurman, Sudan Fashoda crisis (Britain, France) Empress Elizabeth of Austria assassinated Marie and Pierre Curie discover polonium and radium Rodin, *Balzac*
1899–1902	Second Boer War
1899	Dreyfus pardoned
1900	British Labour party founded Freud, *The Interpretation of Dreams* King Umberto of Italy assassinated Pan-African Conference, London Russia occupies Manchuria Boxer Rebellion (China) Planck, discovery of quanta
1901	Weber, *The Protestant Ethic and the Spirit of Capitalism* U.S. President McKinley assassinated Oil discovered in Texas
1902	Hobson, *Imperialism: A Study* Lenin, *What Is to Be Done?* Conrad, *Heart of Darkness*
1903	King and queen of Serbia assassinated Russian Social Democrats split into Bolsheviks and Mensheviks First Tour de France bicycle race
1904	Entente Cordiale (Great Britain and France) Chekhov, *The Cherry Orchard* Russian banquet campaign Trans-Siberian railway completed (1904)
1904–1905	Russo-Japanese War
1905	First Moroccan crisis Einstein, *Theory of Relativity*
1905	Revolution (Russia) January, Bloody Sunday massacre of unarmed workers October, General strike; first soviets formed October, Tsar promises constitution and elected parliament December, armed uprising suppressed

1906	Constitution granted in Russia Launch of HMS *Dreadnought*
1907	Universal male suffrage in Austria Picasso, *Les Demoiselles d'Avignon*
1908	Austria annexes Bosnia-Herzegovina King and crown prince of Portugal assassinated Revolution of "Young Turks" in Ottoman Empire Oil discovered in Persia Matisse, *Harmony in Red*
1908–1914	Gandhi campaigns for Indian rights in South Africa
1909	Belgian government takes over Congo Free State Schoenberg, Opus 11, no. 1, for piano; first entirely atonal composition
1910	Union of South Africa formed
1911	Second Moroccan Crisis Prime Minister Stolypin of Russia assassinated Kandinsky, *On the Spiritual in Art*
1912	German Social Democrats become largest party in parliament
1912–1913	Balkan Wars
1913	Stravinsky and Nijinsky, *The Rite of Spring* Malevich, *Square on a White Ground* Proust, *Swann's Way* International Women's Suffrage Association conference, Budapest
1914	Irish Home Rule bill passes Joyce, *Dubliners*
1914	Outbreak of First World War June, Archduke Franz Ferdinand assassinated, Sarajevo July, Russia threatens war if Austria-Hungary attacks Serbia Austria-Hungary mobilizes against Serbia Russia begins mobilization August, Germany declares war on Russia Germany declares war on France, invades Belgium Britain declares war on Germany Austria-Hungary declares war on Russia

Suggested Readings

General Works on the Nineteenth Century

Bonnie Anderson and Judith Zinsser, *A History of Their Own: Women in Europe from Prehistory to the Present*, vol. 2. London, 1990.

M. S. Anderson, *The Ascendancy of Europe, 1815–1914*. 3rd ed. London, 2003.

C. A. Bayly, *The Birth of the Modern World, 1780–1914*. Oxford, 2004.

Michael Bentley, *Politics Without Democracy: Great Britain, 1815–1914*. Oxford, 1985.

Ivan T. Berend, *History Derailed: Central and Eastern Europe in the Long Nineteenth Century*. Berkeley, 2003.

David Blackbourn, *The Fontana History of Germany, 1780–1918: The Long Nineteenth Century*. London, 1987.

Gordon Craig, *Germany, 1866–1945*, New York, 1978.

Roy Foster, *Modern Ireland*. London, 1988.

Gregory Freeze, ed., *Russia: A History*. Oxford and New York, 1997.

Jason Goodwin, *Lords of the Horizons: A History of the Ottoman Empire*, New York, 1998.

William Hagen, *Germans, Poles and Jews: The Nationality Conflict in the Prussian East, 1772–1914*. Chicago, 1980.

Geoffrey Hosking, *Russia: People and Empire 1552–1917*. London, 1997.

Jerzy Jedlicki, *A Suburb of Europe: Nineteenth-century Polish Approaches to Western Civilization*. Budapest, 1999.

Barbara Jelavich, *History of the Balkans*. Cambridge, 1983.

R. A. Kann and Z. V. David, *The Peoples of the Eastern Habsburg Lands, 1526–1918*. Seattle, 1984.

David Kirby, *The Baltic World, 1772–1993*. London, 1995.

Mark Mazower, *The Balkans: A Short History*, London and New York, 2000.

William O. McCagg, *A History of Habsburg Jews*. Bloomington, IN, 1989.

John Merriman, *A History of Modern Europe: From the French Revolution to the Present*, New York and London, 1996.

Boris Mironov, *A Social History of Imperial Russia, 1700–1917*. Boulder, CO, 2000.

Karen Offen, *European Feminisms 1700–1950, a Political History*. Stanford, 2000.

Robin Okey, *Eastern Europe 1740–1980*. Minneapolis, 1982.

David Saunders, *Russia in the Age of Reaction and Reform, 1801–1881*. London, 1992.

Derek Sayer, *The Coasts of Bohemia*. Princeton, NJ, 1998.

James J. Sheehan, *German History, 1770–1866*. Oxford, 1987.

Alan Sked, *The Decline and Fall of the Habsburg Empire, 1815–1918*. London, 2001.

Bonnie Smith, *Changing Lives: Women in European History Since 1700*. New York, 1989.

Peter Sugar, ed., *A History of Hungary*. Bloomington, IN, 1990.

Victor Tapié, *The Rise and Fall of the Habsburg Monarchy*. New York, 1971.

Robert Tombs, *France, 1814–1914*. London, 1996.

Piotr Wandycz, *The Lands of Partitioned Poland, 1795–1918*. Seattle, 1984.

Theodore Zeldin, *France, 1848–1945*, 2 vols. Oxford, 1973–1977.

The Internet Modern History Sourcebook (offers primary sources on all the subjects discussed in this book):
http://www.fordham.edu/halsall/mod/modsbook.html
The Victorian Web:
http://www.victorianweb.org/

CHAPTER 1: Restoration and Revolution, 1815–1840

Louis Chevalier, *Labouring Classes and Dangerous Classes in Paris During the First Half of the Nineteenth Century,* Princeton, NJ, 1973.
Clive Church, *Europe in 1830: Revolution and Political Change.* London, 1983.
Linda Colley, *Britons: Forging the Nation, 1707–1837.* New Haven, CT, 1992.
Janet M. Hartley, *Alexander I.* Harlow, U.K., 1994.
Keith Hitchins, *The Rumanian National Movement in Transylvania, 1780–1849.* Cambridge, MA, 1969.
Eric J. Hobsbawm, *The Age of Revolution, 1789–1848.* London, 1962.
Charles Jelavich and Barbara Jelavich, *The Establishment of the Balkan National States, 1804–1920.* Seattle, 1977.
R. F. Leslie, *Polish Politics and the Revolution of 1830.* London, 1956.
Matthew Levinger, *Enlightened Nationalism: The Transformation of Prussian Political Culture, 1806–1848.* Oxford, 2000.
W. Bruce Lincoln, *Nicholas I: Emperor and Autocrat of All the Russias.* DeKalb, Il, 1989.
John M. Merriman, ed., *1830 in France.* New York, 1975.
Harold Nicholson, *The Congress of Vienna: A Study in Allied Unity, 1812–1822.* New York, 1946.
Mary Anne Perkins, *Nation and Word: 1770–1850: Religious and Metaphysical Language in European National Consciousness.* Aldershot, U.K., 1999.
Marc Raeff, *The Decembrist Movement.* New York, 1966.
Paul W. Schroeder, *The Transformation of European Politics, 1763–1848.* Oxford, 1994.
William Sewell, *Work and Revolution in France: The Language of Labor from the Old Regime to 1848.* Cambridge, 1980.
Dennis Mack Smith, *Mazzini.* New Haven, CT, 1996.
Dorothy Thompson, *The Chartists: Popular Politics in the Industrial Revolution.* New York, 1984.
Andrzej Walicki, *The Enlightenment and the Birth of Modern Nationhood: Polish Political Thought from Noble Republicanism to Tadeusz Kosciuszko.* Notre Dame, IN, 1989.

CHAPTER 2: Romanticism

Meyer Abrams, *The Mirror and the Lamp: Romantic Theory and the Critical Tradition.* New York, 1958.
Benedict Anderson, *Imagined Communities: Reflections on the Origin and Spread of Nationalism.* London, 1983.
Ivo Banac, *The National Question in Yugoslavia.* Ithaca, NY, 1984.
George Barany, *Stephen Szechenyi and the Awakening of Hungarian Nationalism, 1791–1841.* Princeton, NJ, 1968.
Betty Bennett and Stuart Curran, eds., *Shelley: Poet and Legislator of the World.* Baltimore and London, 1996.
T. J. Binyon, *Pushkin.* New York, 2003.
Peter Brooks, *The Melodramatic Imagination: Balzac, Henry James, Melodrama, and the Mode of Excess.* New Haven, CT, 1995.

Donald Fanger, *Dostoevsky and Romantic Realism: A Study of Dostoevsky in Relation in Balzac, Dickens, and Gogol*. Chicago, 1965.
Monika Greenleaf and Stephen Moeller-Sally, *Russian Subjects: Empire, Nation, and the Culture of the Golden Age*. Evanston, IL, 1998.
Andrew Hemingway, *Landscape Imagery and Urban Culture in Early Nineteenth-century Britain*. Cambridge, 1992.
Glyn T. Hughes, *Romantic German Literature*. London, 1979.
Lloyd Kramer, *Nationalism: Political Cultures in Europe and America. 1775–1865*. New York, 1998.
Lauren Leighton, *Russian Romanticism*. The Hague, 1975.
Ivo Lederer and Peter Sugar, *Nationalism in Eastern Europe*. Seattle, 1969.
Anne Mellor, *Romanticism and Gender*. New York and London, 1993.
———, *Mary Shelley: Her Life, Her Fiction, Her Monsters*. New York, 1988.
Alan Menhennet, *The Romantic Movement, 1795–1830*. Totowa, NJ, 1981. [Germany]
Paul Robinson, *Opera and Ideas: From Mozart to Strauss*. New York, 1985.
Edward Said, *Orientalism*. New York, 1978.
John Toews, *Hegelianism: The Path Toward Dialectical Humanism, 1805–1841*. Cambridge, 1980.
William Vaughn, *German Romantic Painting*. New Haven, CT, 1981.
Andrzej Walicki, *Philosophy and Romantic Nationalism*. Oxford, 1982.

Romanticism on the Net:
http://www.ron.umontreal.ca
The William Blake Archive:
http://www.blakearchive.org

CHAPTER 3: The Industrial Age Begins

Iván Berend and György Ránki, *The European Periphery and Industrialization, 1780–1914*. Cambridge, 1982.
William Blackwell, *The Beginnings of Russian Industrialization, 1800–1860*. Princeton, NJ, 1968.
Phyllis Deane, *The First Industrial Revolution*. 2nd ed. Cambridge, 1979.
——— and W. A. Cole, *British Economic Growth, 1688–1959*. Cambridge, 1967.
Paul R. Gregory, *Before Command: An Economic History of Russia from Emancipation to the First Five-year Plan*. Princeton, NJ., 1994.
W. O. Henderson, *The Rise of German Industrial Power*. Berkeley, 1975.
E. L. Jones, *Agriculture and the Industrial Revolution*. New York, 1974.
Tom Kemp, *Industrialization in Nineteenth-century Europe*. London, 1985.
D. S. Landes, *The Unbound Prometheus: Technological Change and Industrial Development in Western Europe from 1750 to the Present*. Cambridge, 1969.
Cormac Ó Gráda, *Black '47 and Beyond: The Great Irish Famine in History, Economy, and Memory*, Princeton, NJ, 1999.
Sidney Pollard, *Peaceful Conquest: The Industrialization of Europe, 1760–1970*. Oxford, 1981.
Kenneth Pomerantz, *The Great Divergence: Europe, China, and the Making of the Modern World Economy*. Princeton, NJ, 2000.
Roger Price, *The Economic Transformation of France*. London, 1975.
Wolfgang Schivelbusch, *The Railway Journey: The Industrialization of Time and Space in the 19th Century*. Leamington Spa, U.K., 1986.

Mikuláš Teich and Roy Porter, *The Industrial Revolution in National Context (Europe and United States)*. Cambridge, 1996.
Clive Trebilcock, *The Industrialization of the Continental Powers, 1780–1914*. London, 1981.
Han-Joachim Voth, *Time and Work in England, 1750–1830*. Oxford, 2000.

The Railway Museum:
http://www.nrm.org.uk/
Steve Taylor, *Views of the [Irish] Famine, 1845–1851:*
http://vassun.vassar.edu/~sttaylor/FAMINE/

CHAPTER 4: Social Change and Social Life

Asa Briggs, *An Age of Improvement, 1783–1867*. New York, 2000.
———, *Victorian Cities*. London, 1963.
———, *Victorian Things*. London, 1988.
Louis Chevalier, *Laboring Classes and Dangerous Classes in Paris During the First Half of the Nineteenth Century*. Princeton, NJ, 1973.
Anna Clark, *The Struggle for the Breeches: Gender and the Making of the British Working Class*. Berkeley, 1995.
Judith Coffin, *The Politics of Women's Work: The Paris Garment Trades, 1750–1915*. Princeton, NJ, 1996.
Alain Corbin, *The Foul and the Fragrant: Odor and the French Social Imagination*. Cambridge, MA, 1986.
H. J. Dyos and Michael Wolff, *The Victorian City: Images and Realities*. 2 vols. London, 1973.
Richard Evans, *Death in Hamburg: Society and Politics in the Cholera Years, 1830–1870*. Oxford, 1987.
Michel Foucault, *Discipline and Punish: The Birth of the Prison*. New York, 1977.
Laura Frader and Sonya Rose, eds., *Gender and Class in Modern Europe*. Ithaca, NY, 1996.
Peter Gay, *Schnitzler's Century: The Making of Middle-Class Culture, 1815–1914*. New York and London, 2002.
———, *The Bourgeois Experience: Victoria to Freud*. 5 vols. 1984–1998.
Gareth Stedman Jones, *Languages of Class: Studies in English Working Class History, 1832–1982*. Cambridge, 1983.
———, *Outcast London*. Oxford, 1971.
Jurgen Kocka and Allen Mitchell, eds. *Bourgeois Society in Nineteenth Century Europe*. Oxford, 1993.
Peter Kolchin, *Unfree Labor: American Slavery and Russian Serfdom*, Cambridge, MA, 1987.
Dominic Lieven, *The Aristocracy in Europe, 1815–1914*. London 1992.
Arno Mayer, *The Persistence of the Old Regime*. New York, 1981.
Mark Mazower, *The Balkans*. London, 2000.
Stephen Mennell, *All Manners of Food: Eating and Taste in England and France from the Middle Ages to the Present*. Oxford, 1985.
David Moon, *The Russian Peasantry 1600–1930: The World the Peasants Made*. Harlow, U.K., 1999.
Mary Neuburger, *The Orient Within: Muslim Minorities and the Negotiation of Nationhood in Modern Bulgaria*. Ithaca, NY, 2004.

Jacques Rancière, *The Nights of Labor: The Workers Dream in Nineteenth Century France.* Philadelphia, 1989.
William Sewell, *Work and Revolution in France: The Language of Labor from the Old Regime to 1848.* Cambridge, 1980.
David Sorkin, *The Transformation of German Jewry, 1780–1940.* Oxford, 1987.
Louise Tilly and Joan Scott, *Women, Work, and Family.* New York, 1978.
E. P. Thompson, *The Making of the English Working Class.* New York, 1966.
F. M. L. Thompson, *The Rise of Respectable Society: A Social History of Victorian Britain, 1830–1900.* Cambridge, MA, 1988.
Nikolay Todorov, *The Balkan City, 1400–1900.* Seattle, 1983.
Maria Todorova, *Imagining the Balkans.* New York, 1997.
Katherine Verdery, *Transylvanian Villagers.* Berkeley, 1983.
Dror Wahrman, *Imagining the Middle Class: The Political Representation of Class in Britain c. 1780–1840.* Cambridge, 1995.

Edwin Chadwick's Report on Sanitary Conditions:
http://www.victorianweb.org/history/chadwick2.html
Peter Higginbotham, *The Workhouse:*
http://www.workhouses.org.uk/

CHAPTER 5: Ideas and Ideologies

Paul Avrich, *Anarchist Portraits,* Princeton, NJ, 1988.
Jonathan Beecher, *Charles Fourier: The Visionary and His World.* Berkeley, 1986.
Isaiah Berlin, *Russian Thinkers.* New York, 1978.
John Brueilly, *Labor and Liberalism in Nineteenth-century Europe,* Manchester, U.K., 1992.
Gregory Claeys, *Machinery, Money and the Millennium: From Moral Economy to Socialism, 1815–1860.* Cambridge, 1987.
Maurice Cowling, *Mill and Liberalism.* 2nd ed. Cambridge, 1990.
Jurgen Habermas, *The Structural Transformation of the Public Sphere: An Inquiry into a Category of Bourgeois Society.* Cambridge, MA, 1989.
Leopold Haimson, *The Russian Marxists and the Origins of Bolshevism,* New York, 1955.
George Lichtheim, *Marxism: An Historical and Cultural Study.* London, 1964.
———, *A Short History of Socialism.* New York, 1970.
Martin Malia, *Alexander Herzen and the Birth of Russian Socialism, 1812–1855.* New York, 1971.
Guido de Ruggiero, *The History of European Liberalism.* London, 1927.
James Sheehan, *German Liberalism in the Nineteenth Century.* Chicago, 1978.
Paul Smart, *Mill and Marx: Individual Liberty and the Roads to Freedom.* Manchester, U.K., 1991.
Raymond Williams, *Culture and Society, 1750–1950,* Garden City, NY, 1958.

The Marx–Engels Internet Archive:
http://www.marx.org

CHAPTER 6: The Revolutions of 1848

Maurice Agulhon, *The Republican Experiment, 1848–1852.* Cambridge, 1983.
István Deák, *The Lawful Revolution: Louis Kossuth and the Hungarians 1848–49.* London, 1979.

Frank Eyck, *The Revolutions of 1848–49*. New York, 1972.
Alice Freifield, *Nationalism and the Crowd in Liberal Hungary, 1848–1914*. Washington DC, 2000.
Alexander Herzen, *The Memoirs of Alexander Herzen*. vol 2. London, 1968.
Karl Marx, *Class Struggles in France, 1848–1850*. New York, 1934.
John Merriman, *Agony of the Republic: The Repression of the Left in Revolutionary France, 1848–51*. New Haven, CT, 1978.
Stanley Pech, *The Czech Revolution of 1848*. Chapel Hill, NC, 1969.
Priscilla Robertson, *Revolutions of 1848: A Social History*. Princeton, NJ, 1952.
Peter Sahlins, *Forest Rites: The War of the Demoiselles in Nineteenth-century France*. Cambridge, MA, 1994.
Alan Sked, *The Survival of the Habsburg Empire: Radetzky, the Imperial Army, and the Class War, 1848*. London, 1979.
Jonathan Sperber, *The European Revolutions 1848–51*. Cambridge, 1994.
———, *Rhineland Radicals: The Democratic Movement and the Revolution of 1848–1849*. Princeton, N.J., 1991.
Peter N. Stearns, *1848: The Revolutionary Tide in Europe*. New York, 1974.
Charles Tilly and Louise Tilly, *The Rebellious Century, 1830–1930*. Cambridge, 1975.
Isser Woloch, ed., *Revolution and the Meanings of Freedom in the Nineteenth Century*. Stanford, 1996.

CHAPTER 7: The Modern Nation-State

Derek Beales, *The Risorgimento and the Unification of Italy*. London, 1982.
Eugenio Biagini, *Liberty, Retrenchment and Reform. Popular Liberalism in the Age of Gladstone, 1860–1880*, Cambridge, 1992.
Peter Brock and H. Gordon Skilling, eds., *The Czech Renaissance of the Nineteenth Century*. Toronto, 1976.
Geoff Eley, *Forging Democracy: The History of the Left in Europe, 1850–2000*. Oxford, 2002.
———, and Ronald Grigor Suny, eds., *Becoming National: A Reader*. Oxford, 1996.
Erich Eyck, *Bismarck and the German Empire*, New York, 1968.
John Gillis, *The Prussian Bureaucracy in Crisis, 1840–1860: Origins of an Administrative Ethos*. Stanford, 1971.
Gay Gullickson, *Unruly Women of Paris: Images of the Commune*. Ithaca, NY, 1996.
William Hagen, *Germans, Poles, Jews: The Nationality Conflict in the Prussian East, 1772–1914*. Chicago, 1980.
Keith Hitchens, *The Idea of a Nation: The Romanians of Transylvania, 1691–1849*. Bucharest, 1985.
Eric Hobsbawm, *The Age of Capital, 1848–1875*. London, 1975.
Miroslav Hroch, *Social Preconditions of National Revival in Europe*. Cambridge, 1985.
Patrick Joyce, *Visions of the People: Industrial England and the Question of Class 1848–1914*, Cambridge, 1991.
Robert Kann, *The Multinational Empire: Nationalism and National Reform in the Habsburg Monarchy, 1848–1918*. 2 vols. New York, 1950.
W. Bruce Lincoln, *The Great Reforms*. DeKalb, IL, 1990.
Wolfgang Mommsen, *Imperial Germany, 1867–1918*. London, 1995.
D. Moon, *The Abolition of Serfdom in Russia*. Harlow, U.K. 2001.
Emil Niederhauser, *The Rise of Nationality in Eastern Europe*. Budapest, 1982.
Philip G. Nord, *Paris Shopkeepers and the Politics of Resentment*. Princeton, NJ, 1986.

Otto Pfalnze, *Bismarck and the Development of Germany: The Period of Unification, 1815–1871.* Princeton, NJ, 1963.
David Pinkney, *Napoleon III and the Rebuilding of Paris.* Princeton, NJ, 1972.
James Sheehan, *German Liberalism in the Nineteenth Century.* Chicago, 1978.
Anthony D. Smith, *The Ethnic Origins of Nations.* Oxford, 1986.
Bonnie Smith, *Ladies of the Leisure Class: The Bourgeoises of Northern France in the Nineteenth Century.* Princeton, NJ, 1981.
Dennis Mack Smith, *The Making of Italy, 1796–1870.* New York, 1968.
Richard Stites, *The Women's Liberation Movement in Russia.* Princeton, NJ, 1991.
Gale Stokes, *Politics as Development: The Emergence of Political Parties in Nineteenth-century Serbia.* Durham, NC, 1990.
R. Sussex and J. E. Eade, eds., *Culture and Nationalism in Nineteenth-century Eastern Europe.* Columbus, OH, 1984.
A. J. P. Taylor, *The Struggle for Mastery in Europe, 1848–1914.* Oxford, 1954.
Vera Tolz, *Russia: Inventing the Nation.* London and New York, 2001.
Franco Venturi, *Roots of Revolution.* Chicago, 1983.
Andrzej Walicki, *Philosophy and Romantic Nationalism: The Case of Poland.* Oxford, 1982
Reginald E Zelnik, *Law and Disorder on the Narova River: The Kreenholm Strike of 1872.* Berkeley, 1995.

The Nationalism Project:
http://www.nationalismproject.org/
Literary, religious, and scientific texts on line:
http://www.victorianweb.org/books/victorian.html

CHAPTER 8: Realism, Rationality, Respectability

Patricia Anderson, *The Printed Image and the Transformation of Popular Culture.* Oxford 1991.
Jeffrey Auerbach, *The Great Exhibition of 1851: A Nation on Display.* New Haven, CT, 1999.
Christopher Breward, *The Hidden Consumer: Masculinities, Fashion and City Life, 1860–1914.* Manchester, U.K., 1999.
Lucy Brown, *Victorian News and Newspapers.* Oxford, 1985.
T. J. Clark, *The Painting of Modern Life: Paris in the Art of Manet and His Followers.* Princeton, NJ, 1984.
Michael Fried, *Manet's Modernism, or, The Face of Painting in the 1860s.* Chicago, 1996.
Michael Ghiselin, *The Triumph of the Darwinian Method.* Berkeley, 1969.
Sandra M. Gilbert and Susan Gubar. *The Madwoman in the Attic: The Woman Writer and the Nineteenth-century Literary Imagination.* New Haven, CT, 1979.
Rosalind Gray, *Russian Genre Painting in the Nineteenth Century.* Oxford, 2000.
Victoria de Grazia, *The Sex of Things.* Berkeley, 1996
Patricia Mainardi, *The End of the Salon: Art and the State in the Early Third Republic.* Cambridge, 1993.
Louise McReynolds, *The News Under Russia's Old Regime.* Princeton, NJ, 1991.
Linda Nochlin, *Realism.* Harmondsworth, U.K., 1971.
Thomas Richards, *The Commodity Culture of Victorian England: Advertising and Spectacle, 1851–1914.* Stanford, 1990.
Norman Russell, *The Novelist and Mammon: Literary Responses to the World of Commerce in the Nineteenth Century.* Oxford, 1986.

Aaron Scharf, *Art and Photography*. London, 1968.
Elizabeth Krid Valkenier, *Russian Realist Art: The Peredvizhniki and Their Tradition*. Ann Arbor, MI, 1977.
Whitney Walton, *France at the Crystal Palace*. Berkeley, 1992.

Dime novels and penny dreadfuls:
http://www-sul.stanford.edu/depts/dp/pennies/home.html
The Musée D'Orsay (Paris) collection highlights:
http://www.musee-orsay.fr:8081/ORSAY/ORSAYGB/HTML.NSF/By+File-name/mosimple+collect+index?OpenDocument

CHAPTER 9: The Age of Imperialism, 1870–1914

Michael Adas, *Machines as the Measure of Man: Science, Technology, and Ideologies of Western Dominance*. Ithaca, NY 1989.
Mark Bassin, *Imperial Visions: Nationalism and Geographical Imagination in the Russian Far East, 1840–1865*. Cambridge, 1999.
Winifred Baumgart, *Imperialism: The Idea and Reality of British and French Colonial Expansion, 1880–1914*. New York, 1982.
Gail Bederman, *Manliness and Civilization*. Chicago, 1995.
Daniel Brower and Edward Lazzerini, *Russia's Orient: Imperial Borderlands and Peoples, 1700–1917*. Bloomington, IN, 1997.
P. J. Cain and A. G. Hopkins, *British Imperialism: Innovation and Expansion 1688–1914*. London, 1993.
Alice Conklin, *A Mission to Civilize: The Republican Idea of Empire in France and West Africa, 1895–1930*. Stanford, 1997.
Frederick Cooper and Ann Stoler, eds., *Tensions of Empire: Colonial Cultures in a Bourgeois World*. Berkeley, 1997.
Michael Doyle, *Empires*. Ithaca, NY, 1986.
Dietrich Geyer, *Russian Imperialism: The Interaction of Domestic and Foreign Policy, 1860–1914*. New Haven, CT, 1987.
Ivan Hannaford, *Race: The History of an Idea in the West*. Washington, DC, and Baltimore, 1996.
Daniel Headrick, *The Tools of Empire: Technology and European Imperialism in the Nineteenth Century*. New York, 1981.
Eric Hobsbawm, *The Age of Empire, 1875–1914*. London, 1987.
Adam Hochschild, *King Leopold's Ghost: A Story of Greed, Terror, and Heroism in Colonial Africa*. New York, 1998.
Thomas C. Holt, *The Problem of Freedom: Race, Labor, and Politics in Jamaica and Britain, 1832–1938*. Baltimore, 1992.
Andreas Kappeler, *The Russian Empire: A Multiethnic History*. Harlow, U.K., 2001.
Andrew Porter, ed. William Roger Louis, gen. ed., *The Oxford History of the British Empire*. Oxford, 1999.
David Northrup, *Indentured Labor in an Age of Imperialism, 1834–1922*. Cambridge, 1995.
Anthony Pagden, *People and Empires*. London, 2001.
Thomas Pakenham, *The Scramble for Africa*. New York, 1991.
Mary Louise Pratt, *Imperial Eyes: Travel Writing & Transculturation*. London, 1992.
David Prochaska, *Making Algeria French*. Cambridge, 1990.
Jonathan Schneer, *London 1900: The Imperial Metropole*. New Haven, CT, 1999.

Julia Clancy-Smith and Frances Gouda, eds., *Domesticating the Empire: Race, Gender, and Family Life in French and Dutch Colonialism*. Charlottesville, VA, 1998.
Theodore Weeks, *Nation and State in Late Imperial Russia. Nationalism and Russification on the Western Frontier, 1863–1914* DeKalb, IL, 1996.

Stereoscopes of War and Empire: The Congo Free State and Belgian Congo:
http://www.boondocksnet.com/stereo/congo.html
The Empire That Was Russia: The Prokudin–Gorskii Photographic Record Recreated:
http://www.loc.gov/exhibits/empire/

CHAPTER 10: The Challenges of Modernity

Richard Abel, *The Cine Goes to Town. French Cinema, 1896–1914*. Berkeley, 1994.
Lenard Berlanstein *The Working People of Paris, 1871–1914*. Baltimore, 1984.
Renate Bridenthal et al., eds., *Becoming Visible: Women in European History*. 2nd ed. Boston, 1987.
Kathleen Canning, *Languages of Labor and Gender: Female Factory Work in Germany, 1850–1914*. Ithaca, NY, 1996.
Rose Glickman, *Russian Factory Women*, Berkeley, 1984.
Carol Dyhouse, *Feminism and the Family in England, 1880–1939*. Oxford, 1989.
Stephen Kern, *The Culture of Time and Space, 1880–1918*. Cambridge, MA, 1983.
Gareth Stedman Jones, *Outcast London*. Oxford, 1971.
Patrick Joyce, *Visions of the People: Industrial England and the Question of Class, 1848–1914*. New York, 1991.
John Lucas, *Budapest, 1900*. New York, 1988.
Vernon Lidke, *The Alternative Culture: Socialist Labor in Imperial Germany*. New York, 1985.
Tessie Liu, *The Weavers' Knot: The Contradictions of Class Struggle and Family Solidarity in Western France, 1750–1914*. Ithaca, NY, 1994.
Louise McReynolds, *Russia at Play*. Ithaca, NY, 2003.
Michael Miller, *The Bon Marché: Bourgeois Culture and the Department Store, 1869–1920*. Princeton, NJ, 1981.
Philip Nord, *The Republican Moment: The Struggle for Democracy in Nineteenth-century France*. Cambridge, MA, 1995.
Robert Nye, *Crime, Madness, and Politics in Modern France: The Medical Concept of National Decline*. Princeton, NJ, 1984.
Peter Paret, *German Encounters with Modernism, 1840–1945*. Cambridge, 2001.
Ellen Ross, *Love and Toil: Motherhood in Outcast London, 1870–1918*. New York, 1993.
Raphael Samuel, *Village Life and Labour*, London, 1975.
Carl Schorske, *Fin-de-Siècle Vienna: Politics and Culture*. New York, 1980.
Vanessa Schwartz, *Spectacular Realities: Early Mass Culture in Fin-de-Siècle Paris*. Berkeley, 1998.
Deborah Silverman, *Art Nouveau in Fin-de-Siècle France: Politics, Psychology and Style*. Berkeley, 1989.
Lisa Tickner, *The Spectacle of Women: Imagery of the Suffrage Campaign, 1907–14*. Chicago, 1988.
Judith Walkowitz, *Prostitution and Victorian Society: Women, Cities and the State*. Cambridge, 1980.
Eugen Weber, *Peasants into Frenchmen: The Modernization of Rural France*. Stanford, 1976.
———, *Fin-de-Siécle France*. Cambridge, MA, 1986.

Allan Wildman, *The Making of a Workers' Revolution: Russian Social Democracy, 1891–1903.* Chicago, 1967.
Rosalind Williams, *Dream Worlds: Mass Consumption in Late Nineteenth-century France.* Berkeley, 1982.
Robert Wohl, "Heart of Darkness: Modernism and Its Historians," *Journal of Modern History* 74 (September 2002), 573–621.
Charters Wynn, *Workers, Strikes and Pogroms: The Donbass–Dnepr Bend in Late Imperial Russia, 1870–1905.* Princeton, NJ, 1992.

Landmarks of Early Film, 1896–1913, (DVD) Chatsworth, CA, Image Entertainment, 1994.
Relativity explained:
http://www.astro.ucla.edu/~wright/relatvty.htm
The Paris Expositions:
http://www.photoart.plus.com/expos/index.htm
The Museum of Modern Art (New York) collection highlights:
http://www.moma.org/collection/depts/paint_sculpt/blowups/paint_sculpt_001.html
http://www.moma.org/collection/depts/prints_books/blowups/prints_books_001.html

CHAPTER 11: Political Polarization and Conflict

Abraham Ascher, *The Russian Revolution of 1905.* 2 vols. Stanford, 1988–1992.
———, *P. A. Stolypin: The Search for Stability in Late Imperial Russia.* Stanford, 2001.
Edward Berenson, *The Trial of Madame Caillaux.* Berkeley, 1992.
Jean-Denis Bredin, *The Affair: The Case of Alfred Dreyfus.* New York, 1986.
David Cannadine, *The Decline and Fall of the British Aristocracy,* New Haven, CT, 1990.
Gordon Craig, *Germany, 1866–1914.* Oxford, 1978.
Richard Evans, ed., *Society and Politics in Wilhelmine Germany.* London, 1978.
E. H. H. Green, *The Crisis of Conservatism: The Politics, Economics and Ideology of the British Conservative Party, 1880–1914.* London, 1994.
———, ed., *An Age of Transition: British Politics 1880–1914,* Edinburgh, 1997.
Alvin Jackson, *Home Rule: An Irish History 1800–2000.* London, 2003.
Andrew Janos, *The Politics of Backwardness in Hungary, 1825–1945.* Princeton, NJ, 1981.
James Joll, *Europe Since 1870: A International History.* London, 1973.
———, *The Origins of the First World War.* London, 1984.
Alfred Kelly, *The Descent of Darwin: The Popularisation of Darwin in Germany, 1860–1914.* Chapel Hill, NC, 1981.
Paul Kennedy, *The Rise of the Anglo-German Antagonism, 1860–1914.* New York, 1980.
Ian Machin, *The Rise of Democracy in Britain, 1830–1918.* Houndmills, Basingstoke, Hampshire, U.K., 2001.
Rohan McWilliam, *Popular Politics in Nineteenth-century England.* London, 1998.
Benjamin Nathans, *Beyond the Pale: The Jewish Encounter with Late Imperial Russia.* Berkeley, 2002.
Hans Rogger, *Russia in the Age of Modernization and Revolution.* London, 1983.
J. C. Rohl, *The Kaiser and His Court: Wilhelm II and the Government of Germany.* Cambridge, 1994.
Carl Schorske, *German Social Democracy, 1905–1917: The Development of the Great Schism.* New York, 1955.

Mark Steinberg, *The Fall of the Romanovs: Political Dreams and Personal Struggles in a Time of Revolution*. New Haven, CT, 1995.
Zara Steiner, *Britain and the Origins of the First World War*. New York, 1977.
Hans-Ulrich Wehler, *The German Empire, 1871–1918*. Leamington Spa, U.K., 1973.

Women and Parliament, 1884–1945:
http://www.parliament.uk/parliamentary_publications_and_archives/parliamentary_archives/archives_the_suffragettes.cfm

Index

CPSIA information can be obtained at www.ICGtesting.com
Printed in the USA
BVOW03s2219280915

419976BV00006BA/25/P

9 780195 156225